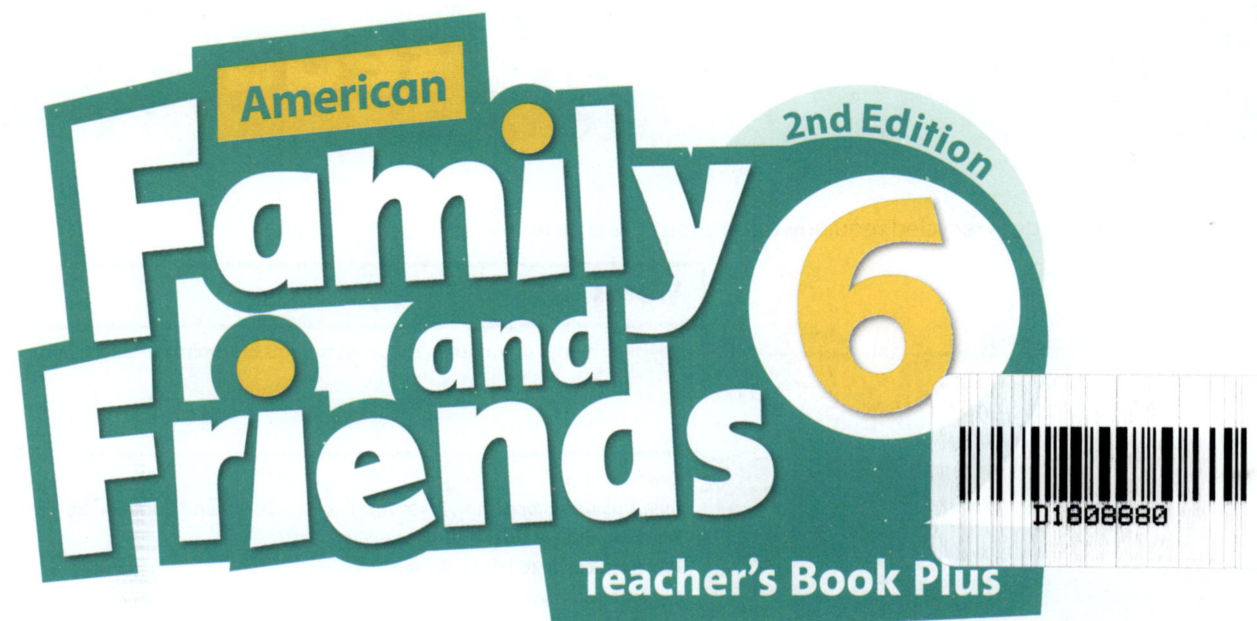

Julie Penn
Introduction by **Naomi Simmons and Barbara Mackay**

Scope and sequence

All core language is recycled regularly throughout the course.

Unit	Page	Words
Starter: Welcome back!	p31	Revision: names of countries, simple past forms of common irregular verbs
1 Art project!	p34	**Describing art** *mural, painting, landscape, portrait, art gallery, foreground, background, sculpture* **Working with words: Prefixes** ***un- / im-*** **Words in context: Island Adventure** Student Book: *stare, borrow, row, smoke, hit, splash, float (v), tie (v)* Workbook: *lightning, oars, grab, bank*
Fluency Time! 1	p42	**Detailed descriptions** *What's it made of? It's made of cotton. It feels like… It's looks like…*
2 Sports adventures!	p44	**Extreme sports** *ice skating, skiing, baseball, ice hockey, mountain biking, caving, paragliding, rock climbing* **Working with words: Prefixes** ***dis- / in-*** **Words in context: William Trubridge** Student Book: *diving, pearl, equipment, talented, freedom, environment, wildlife, snorkeling* Workbook: *provide, volunteer, skills, protect*
Health Time!	p52	**The Human Body**
3 It's festival time!	p54	**Festival adjectives** *original, awful, amazing, deserted, disgusting, traditional, bright, delicious* **Working with words: Suffix** *-ous* **Words in context: Top Food Festivals** Student Book: *last (v), celebrate, snack, brick, garlic, demonstration, spicy, sweet, harvest, fillings* Workbook: *hang, decorate, recipe, bunch*
4 Transportation of the future!	p62	**Forms of transportation** *hot-air balloon, submarine, bus, yacht, helicopter, motorcycle, truck, barge* **Working with words: Phrasal verbs** **Words in context: Transportation Around the World** Student Book: *ideal, loads, connect, local, private, balance, mud, log* Workbook: *package, 4 by 4 vehicle, railway, sand dunes*
Fluency Time! 2	p70	**Discussing future plans** *Are you doing anything special? We're … / No, not really. Why don't you…? I'd love to. / Sorry, I can't. / I'm not sure.*
5 The greatest inventions!	p72	**Inventions** *design, discover, invent, build, device, machine, inspiration, experiment* **Working with words: Suffix** ***-ment*** **Words in context: The History of the Pen** Student Book: *sharp, clay, hollow, nib, ink, reservoir, rotated, cartridge* Workbook: *underwater, rod, press, string*
Science Time!	p80	**Energy**
6 You've won a computer!	p82	**Computer verbs** *connect, disconnect, log on, log off, download, upload, surf, attach* **Working with words: Homonyms** **Words in context: Computers – Fun Facts** Student Book: *complication, create, experimental, huge, cursor, immediately, president, market* Workbook: *public, available, expect, ordinary*

Grammar	Skills	
Revision: simple present, present progressive, simple past, past progressive, irregular past forms	**Reading:** understanding a short story, identifying true or false sentences **Speaking:** using the past progressive and simple past to talk about actions	**Writing focus:** practicing the simple past forms of common irregular verbs
Going to and *will* *I'm going to visit an art gallery this afternoon.* *I'll come with you.* Present progressive with future meaning *We're meeting at ten o'clock.*	**Reading:** a story: *Island Adventure* (reading and understanding an extract from a story, understanding words from the context) (Cross-curricular link) **Listening:** listening for details about a painting **Speaking:** asking and answering questions about paintings	**Writing focus:** writing a story **Writing outcome:** completing a story (Workbook)
Craft: a knowledge game		
First conditional and first conditional questions *If the weather is good, we'll go paragliding.* *Will you come for a walk if the weather is good?* Second conditional and second conditional questions *If I had a camera, I'd take a picture.* *Would you play baseball if you lived in the U.S.A.?*	**Reading:** a sports profile: *William Trubridge* (reading and understanding a biographical article, understanding words from the context) **Listening:** listening for detail in a sports profile **Speaking:** asking and answering questions about sports	**Writing focus:** using a concept map to plan **Writing outcome:** completing a concept map and using it to write a brochure (Workbook)
Project: a pop-up book		
Present perfect: *for / since / already / just / yet / before* *I've been here since nine o'clock.* *The festival has been on for five days.* *The procession has already finished.* *I've just eaten some delicious pancakes.* *I haven't seen any fireworks yet.* *I've never eaten anything so delicious before.* Simple past and present perfect *I went to that festival last year.* *I've made my costume.*	**Reading:** a travel article: *Top Food Festivals* (reading and understanding a travel article, understanding words from the context) **Listening:** listening for detail in an interview **Speaking:** asking and answering questions about food festivals	**Writing focus:** letter writing conventions **Writing outcome:** writing a letter to a friend (Workbook)
Present perfect progressive 1 *Passengers have been waiting for five hours.* Time markers *for / since / all morning / all day / all week* Present perfect progressive 2 *I'm tired because I've been working on a new invention.* *What have you been doing?* *Have you been swimming?*	**Reading:** a book extract: *Transportation Around the World* (reading and understanding a book extract, understanding words from the context) **Listening:** listening for detail in an interview **Speaking:** asking and answering questions about different forms of transportation	**Writing focus:** using process diagrams **Writing outcome:** using a process diagram to explain how to ride a bike (Workbook)
Craft: a datebook		
The passive (simple present and simple past) *Many kinds of chewing gum are made.* *The gum wasn't advertised.* The passive (present progressive) *My computer is being repaired at the moment.*	**Reading:** a timeline: *The History of the Pen* (reading and understanding a text with a timeline, understanding words from the context) (Cross-curricular link) **Listening:** identifying opinions **Speaking:** asking and answering questions about inventions	**Writing focus:** writing a biography **Writing outcome:** writing a biography (Workbook)
Project: an interactive poster		
The passive (future) *You will be given ten new laptops.* The passive (present perfect) *These wires have been disconnected.*	**Reading:** a website article: *Computers – Fun Facts* (reading and understanding a webpage, understanding words from the context) (Cross-curricular link) **Listening:** listening for detail about why people use computers **Speaking:** asking and answering questions about computers	**Writing focus:** presenting a research report **Writing outcome:** writing a research report (Workbook)

<table>
<tr><td>Relative pronouns: who, which
There are many climbers who successfully climb Mount Everest.
They climb a mountain there which is the highest mountain in the world.
Reported pronouns: that
He met a man that was more than 120 years old.</td><td>Reading: an encyclopedia entry: Famous Shipwrecks (reading and understanding a factual text, understanding words from the context) (Cross-curricular link)
Listening: listening for detail in a tour guide
Speaking: asking and answering questions about being an explorer</td><td>Writing focus: writing a personalized text
Writing outcome: writing a personalized text (Workbook)</td></tr>
<tr><td colspan="3">Craft: an inventions poster</td></tr>
<tr><td>Past perfect
After they had climbed onto the ship, they saw there was no one there.
Past perfect questions and negative sentences
Had people invented trucks and trains before they built the Pyramids?
They hadn't invented trucks and trains before they built the Pyramids.</td><td>Reading: an interview: The Nazca Lines
(reading and understanding an interview, understanding words from the context)
(Cross-curricular link)
Listening: listening for detail in an advertisement
Speaking: asking and answering questions about mysteries</td><td>Writing focus: features of a tourist information brochure
Writing outcome: writing a tourist information brochure (Workbook)</td></tr>
<tr><td colspan="3">Project: a time capsule</td></tr>
<tr><td>Third conditional
If the machine had worked, he would have been happy.
Modal verbs: have to, must, should, and ought to
You have to bring a water bottle.
You mustn't leave the group.
You shouldn't bring valuable possessions.
You ought to bring a camera.</td><td>Reading: a story extract: Robinson Crusoe (reading and understanding a story extract, understanding words from the context)
Listening: listening and ordering events
Speaking: asking and answering questions about surviving on a desert island</td><td>Writing focus: features of an advice text
Writing outcome: writing an advice text (Workbook)</td></tr>
<tr><td>Reported speech (all tenses)
He said he wanted to visit many countries.
He said he was looking forward to the trip.
He said he had cycled around Africa.
He said he had had lessons in French and Arabic.
He said the trip would take about two years.
Reflexive pronouns: myself, yourself, itself, himself, herself, ourselves, yourselves, and themselves
The machine turned itself off.</td><td>Reading: a Question and Answer text: Languages of the World (reading and understanding a Question and Answer text, understanding words from the context) (Cross-curricular link)
Listening: listening and matching speakers to statements
Speaking: asking and answering questions about languages</td><td>Writing focus: writing an advertisement
Writing outcome: writing an advertisement (Workbook)</td></tr>
<tr><td colspan="3">Craft: a survival game</td></tr>
<tr><td>Reported speech: Wh- questions: Where, Why, What, Who, and When
He asked him where he was.
Reported speech: commands and requests told / asked
He told us to turn off our cell phones.
He asked them to leave quietly.</td><td>Reading: a poem: Dreaming in a Spaceship (reading and understanding a poem, understanding words from the context) (Cross-curricular link)
Listening: listening and identifying missing words in a poem
Speaking: asking and answering questions about space</td><td>Writing focus: writing a poem and using similes
Writing outcome: writing a poem using similes (Workbook)</td></tr>
<tr><td colspan="3">Project: a project board</td></tr>
<tr><td>wish
I wish I was taller.
I wish I could fly.
I wish it wasn't the last day of our vacation.
Question tags
There are lots of robots, aren't there?
You can swim, can't you?
You like ice cream, don't you?</td><td>Reading: a travel blog: My Year Around the World (reading and understanding an Internet travel blog, understanding words from the context) (Cross-curricular link)
Listening: listening for detail in an interview
Speaking: asking and answering questions about traveling</td><td>Writing focus: structuring an opinion essay
Writing outcome: writing an opinion essay (Workbook)</td></tr>
</table>

Introduction

American Family and Friends 2nd Edition is a complete six-level course of English for students in primary schools. It uses a clear grammar-based curriculum alongside parallel syllabi in skills and phonics. In this way, students develop the confidence and competence to communicate effectively in English, as well as understanding and processing information from a wide range of sources. The course combines the most effective literacy techniques used with native English speakers with proven techniques for teaching English as a foreign language to students.

Students have different learning styles. Some learn better by seeing (visual learners), some by listening (auditory learners), some by reading and writing, and some with movement (kinasthetic learners). *American Family and Friends 2nd Edition* uses all of these approaches to help every student realize his or her potential.

It also looks beyond the classroom and promotes the values of family and friendship: co-operation, sharing, helping, and appreciating those who help us.

This level of *American Family and Friends 2nd Edition* includes the following:

- Student Book
- Workbook with Online Practice
- Student website with Online Play
- Teacher's Book Plus containing:
  - Assessment and Resource CD-ROM
  - Assessment Audio CD
  - Fluency DVD
  - Online Practice
- iTools (Digital Class Resources)
- Class Audio CDs
- Alphabet Book
- Writing posters
- Readers

Also available as supplementary material, *Grammar Friends* is a six-level grammar reference and practice series that matches the syllabus of *American Family and Friends 2nd Edition*. The grammar is presented within everyday contexts familiar to pupils from the other materials they use in class. The course can be used as supplementary support and resource material providing practice and reinforcement in class or at home.

Methodology

Words and grammar

New words are introduced in relation to each unit's topic or theme. Students meet the first group of words passively in the story in Lesson 1. The words are presented formally in Lesson 2 through illustrations and recordings. The students can check meaning and develop their dictionary skills in the Dictionary pages.

A second group of words is presented in the *Working with words* section in lesson 2, giving further scope for practicing dictionary skills. The accompanying Workbook pages provide practice of building new words following the patterns in the *Working with words* section.

The third group of words is presented in Lesson 6. Students are encouraged to work out the meaning of these words from the text in Lesson 5, where they first appear. They then check the meaning of the words in the Dictionary pages. The Workbook provides further practice of determining meaning from context.

Skills

Each unit of *American Family and Friends 2nd Edition* contains three pages dedicated to the development of reading, listening, speaking, and writing skills. The four skills are all integrated.

The reading texts in this section expose students to a balance of both familiar and new language. With a range of different text types of increasing complexity, students develop the confidence to recognize and use the language they know in a wide range of situations. They develop the skills of reading for gist and detail, both of which are essential for complete communicative competence.

After every three units there are two pages of extra reading material in the form of non-fiction and fiction texts. These longer texts are to be used for extensive reading so students do not have to understand every word. These texts are optional activities to be done at the discretion of the teacher.

The listening tasks, which are linked to the core reading text in each unit, help students to practice listening for specific information and detail, as well as gist.

Speaking practice tasks are also integrated, so students will already have been exposed to key words to be used, which will give them the confidence when carrying out the task.

The writing skills section prepares students to write a certain type of text, e.g. a story, a poem, or a personal account. Before students begin the exercise in their Student Books, they look at a poster of the appropriate text type with their teacher. This helps them to visualize layout and draws their attention to key literacy points. Students then look at an annotated text in their Student Books. The annotations draw attention to conventions and techniques of structure and style that students should use in their own writing.

After students have answered the questions in their Student Books, they are ready to complete the writing tasks in their Workbooks.

Writing posters

There is a poster for each of the writing lessons. These should be used by the teacher as a visual aid when discussing how particular types of text should be laid out and what should be included in them. Full notes are given on how to use the posters at the start of Lesson 7.

The poster worksheets on the Assessment and Resource CD-ROM contain the text for each of the Writing posters. These should be photocopied for each student so they can follow the text as the teacher reads. Students should be asked to keep their poster text safe in their files as they will need it again for the Assessment and Resource CD-ROM Writing skills task.

Stories

Every unit contains a story which provides a fun and motivating context in which the new language appears. In Level 6, we rejoin Fin, Libby, Kate, and Ed for more adventures with their youth group, the *Do Something Different Club*. This happy extended family is joined by Tom, who is Libby and Fin's cousin from Canada.

The stories also provide ideal scenarios for practicing and reviewing language structures and key words in a cyclical manner.

Songs

Every unit in *American Family and Friends 2nd Edition* contains a song for students to practice the new target grammar structure.

Melody and rhythm are an essential aid to memory. By singing students are able to address fears and shyness, and practice the language in a joyful way together. Songs are also fun and motivating activities and are a good opportunity to add movement to the lessons.

Drama and Total Physical Response (TPR)

Students of any age, especially kinasthetic learners, benefit from associating language with movement and actions. In *American Family and Friends 2nd Edition* students are given the opportunity to act out the stories with simple drama activities. One of the main obstacles to language learning at any age is self-consciousness. Drama, by appealing to the imagination, is an excellent way for students to 'lose themselves' in the story, thereby increasing their communicative ability. Like other skills work, drama helps students to communicate and be understood. By developing performance skills, they practice and become fluent in expressing real-life situations, starting with the story in the classroom and then moving on to real-world contexts.

Classroom management

Students learn best when the atmosphere in the classroom is relaxed, happy, and well-ordered.

Success is a great motivator. Try to make every student feel successful and praise their attempts enthusiastically. Students should all be familiar with expressions such as, *Good work! Good job! Excellent try! You did that very well.*

Errors need to be corrected, but use positive and tactful feedback so that students are not afraid of making mistakes. If a student makes a mistake, say *Good try. Try again*, then model the correct answer for the student to repeat. Avoid using words such as *No* or *That's wrong*, as these can create negative associations to learning.

Establish a clear and consistent set of classroom rules and ensure that all the students know what to expect. Always praise good behavior so that bad behavior does not become a means of gaining attention.

Games

Games provide a natural context for language practice and are very popular with students. They promote the development of wider cognitive skills such as memory sequencing, motor skills, and deductive skills. If required, all the games in *American Family and Friends 2nd Edition* can take place at the students's desks with a minimum of classroom disruption.

Involving parents

Learning involves a co-operative relationship between home and school, and it is important to establish clear communication with parents to encourage home support. The following are suggestions about possible ways of doing this:

- Keep parents informed about what their students are learning and their progress. Parents might benefit from receiving newsletters listing what students are now able to do, and what words and phrases they are studying.
- Show parents the completed Values worksheets from the Assessment and Resource CD-ROM.
- Organize a concert or parents' afternoon where the students can perform the unit stories, plays and the songs they have learnt, along with their actions.

oxfordparents

Help your child with English

Oxford Parents is a website where your students' parents can find out how they can help their student with English. They can find lots of activities to do in the home or in everyday life. Even if the parent has little or no English, they can still find ways to help. We have lots of activities and videos to show parents how to do this.

Studies have shown that practicing English outside the classroom can help students become more confident using the language. If they speak English with their parents, they will see how English can be used in real-life situations and this can increase the students' motivation.

Parents can help by practicing stories, songs, and vocabulary that the students have already learned in the classroom. Tell your students' parents to visit www.oup.com/elt/oxfordparents and have fun helping their students with English!

Games

Lip reading

- Say the target word silently to the students, exaggerating the movements of your mouth. You may also like to give small miming or gestural clues.
- Ask students to guess the word.

Guess the word

- Write words from a vocabulary set students have just studied on the board, showing only the first two letters and the number of missing letters, e.g. *fr _ _ (frog).*
- Divide the class into two teams. A student from Team A tries to guess the correct answer. If s/he gets the correct answer, complete the word on the board and give the team a point. If the student guesses incorrectly, give the point to Team B.
- The winner of the game is the team with the most points.

Miming snap

- Choose a word from the vocabulary set that students are learning, or any other word that students know and you want to focus on. All the words must be things that can be clearly mimed.
- Say a word and mime the action. If the word matches the mime, students should *Snap!* If the word doesn't match the mime, students can be silent, or do an agreed action.
- Choose a student to mime another action. The student says a correct or incorrect word while s/he mimes the action.

Book race

- Use this activity in the last lesson of the unit to review the language in the unit.
- Tell students that they are going to do a book race. When you say words or phrases, the students have to find and point to a picture of that word or phrase in the unit, but they have to be fast!
- Call out a word or phrase students have just learned, e.g. food words or rules with *you must* and *you mustn't.*
- Students look quickly through the unit and find the pictures.
- Do an example with students, allowing them plenty of time to find the correct picture.
- Call out the first words or phrases slowly and gradually reduce the interval until it is a race to keep up.

Target words TPR

- This activity is particularly good with writing activities that focus on words like connectors and sequencers.
- Assign target words, e.g. *and* and *but* to students in the class by counting along the rows of students.
- Read out sentences containing the target words. Students must stand up or do another agreed action when they hear their word.
- Read out the sentences again, this time leaving a blank for the target word. Students who have been assigned that word stand up and say it.

Smiley face

- This game can be played as a whole-class activity or in teams and pairs.
- Think of a word and draw a short line for each letter on the board, one next to the other.
- Ask students to guess the letters that are in the secret word, one by one. If a student guesses a letter which is in the secret word, write the letter in the correct position.
- If a student guesses a letter which isn't in the word, write the letter on the board with a cross through it, and draw a large circle to represent a face. With each letter that is incorrect, add another feature to the face (two eyes, a nose, a smile, two ears, a neck, and hair).
- The game continues until either the word or the face is complete. If the word is completed, the class has won; if the face is completed, the teacher has won.
- The game can also be played with phrases and short sentences.

What's the picture?

- Invite a student to come to the front of the class. Whisper the name of an object s/he has to draw.
- The student draws the picture on the board for the rest of the class to guess.
- The first student who guesses correctly comes to the front of the class to draw the next picture. Repeat until all of the target vocabulary has been used.

A long sentence

- Say a sentence that ends with a word or phrase from the vocabulary set that you want to practice, e.g. *I'm going to the sports center.*
- Choose a student to continue the sentence, adding a new word to the end, e.g. *I'm going to the sports center and the movie theater.* This student then chooses another student, who says the sentence, adding another word to the end of it.

Bingo

- Ask students to draw a grid, three by three (or three by two) squares. In each of the squares they write a different word from the vocabulary set they are studying.
- Call out words from the vocabulary set in any order. Keep a record of the words as you say them so that you don't say the same word twice. Students cross off the words in their grids as they hear them. The first student to complete a line of three shouts *Bingo!* and is the winner.

Wrong word

- Write six to eight sentences on the board about a story, poem or factual text that students have recently read. One word in each sentence must be incorrect.
- Ask students to find the incorrect word in each sentence and then rewrite the sentences so they are correct.

True or false?

- Say a true or false statement about a topic or using a grammar point you want to practice, e.g. *I have two sisters.*
- If students think you are telling the truth, they call out *True!* If they don't, they call out *False!* Alternatively, students can do one or two agreed actions.
- Choose a student and then tell him or her if his/her answer is correct. Ask that student to say a true or false sentence for the class. Continue in this way around the class.

Whispers

- Organize students in groups of at least six. Show a flashcard to the first student in each group. This student whispers the word to the student next to him/her.
- Students continue whispering the word to the student next to them until the word reaches the final student.
- The final student says the word aloud, and the first student holds up the flashcard to see whether the word and the flashcard are the same.

Order the letters

- Choose a word. Write the jumbled-up letters of that word on the board, followed by the correct number of lines for the number of letters.
- Call students to come to the board to write one letter at a time to complete the word.

Time's up!

- Divide the class into two teams. Write the jumbled letters for a word from a vocabulary set on the board.
- Give students from the first team ten seconds to solve the anagram and say the word. If they don't guess the word correctly, call *Time's up!* And reveal the answer.
- Repeat the activity with a different word for the other team.
- Teams score one point for each word they guess correctly.

Definitions

- Describe a word from a vocabulary set that students have recently learned for the class to guess, e.g. *You can fly in it, but it isn't a plane. (Hot-air balloon).*
- Ask a student to stand up and describe another word from the vocabulary set.
- Continue with other words and different students.

Option: To make the game more challenging, give students slips of paper with words they are banned from saying written on them, e.g. for *hot-air balloon*: *balloon, air sky.*

Write one thing

- Write several themes relating to a reading or listening text that students have just covered on the board, e.g. *space, computers, extreme sports.*
- Ask students to write down one word for each category.
- Give each student a point if no other student in the class has the same word.

Talk!

- Ask a student to stand up. Choose a topic from the unit and write it on the board. Tell the student that s/he must talk about the topic for thirty seconds without pausing.
- If s/he fails, choose another student to talk on the same topic. If s/he succeeds, choose a different student and a different topic.

Twenty, twenty

- Choose a word from the vocabulary set or any other word that students know that you want to elicit or revise.
- Before playing the game, tell students the lexical group of the word they have to guess, e.g. *it's a job, it's a place.*
- Students take it in turns to ask yes/no questions. If they haven't been able to guess the word, give them clues until they guess it correctly.

Disappearing dialogue

- Choose one frame of the story dialogue and write it on the board. Read it with students, and then erase four words. The first worsts you erase should be words you particularly want students to remember.
- Ask students to read it again, saying the missing words.
- Erase four more words and repeat.
- Keep erasing the words until students are saying the text from memory. Leave only the character's names at the start of each line to help them.

Vanishing verse

- Play this game in the same way as Disappearing dialogue, but use a verse from a poem or song.
- Erase words until only the first word of each line remains.

Questions for answers

- Play this to check for comprehension of a text, or to practice grammar. Write a list of answers on the board, e.g.

  It sank when it hit an iceberg.

  It was sailing to New York.

  Over a thousand people drowned.

  I went to the festival yesterday.

  Yes, I have eaten Chinese food.
- Students must guess the question that fits each answer.

Fluency development

A sense of achievement and a sense of autonomy are essential ingredients in promoting fluency. The Fluency Time! lessons in *American Family and Friends 2nd Edition* give students the opportunity to personalise the language they learn and to practise speaking together in pairs and groups, to play games using the new language and to create their own dialogues, and to help boost their confidence and motivate them in the classroom.

It is important for language in the classroom to be meaningful and functional, so that learners can see how the language they are learning can be applied to everyday life. When learners are able to use the language they learn to communicate in a realistic situation, or to interact socially with others, they feel a sense of purpose in their learning.

Syllabus

The syllabus for the Everyday English phrases is based, in part, on the Cambridge English: Movers syllabus. Other useful phrases, which reflect daily life, have also been included. For learners who are preparing for the Cambridge exams, this will provide additional preparation and practice for the speaking parts of the exam, but for those not taking the exams, the Everyday English phrases will be equally useful and applicable to the situations they may face in the future.

In the Student Book and Workbook

The Fluency Time! lessons in *American Family and Friends 2nd Edition* provide learners with useful language for a variety of everyday situations.

Each of the four Fluency Time! lessons in *American Family and Friends 2nd Edition* consist of an Everyday English page followed by a craft page. The Everyday English pages teach phrases through mini stories in a meaningful context, and provide practice of the new language through a listening activity and a speaking activity, providing a gradual transition from receptive to productive skills. The craft pages give instructions for a craft project related to the context, and provide further, freer practice of the Everyday English phrases through a communicative game or speaking task, which involves acting out dialogues and using the craft object. In this way, learners can personalize and build on the key phrases, extending the language to incorporate recycled vocabulary and structures from the units they have covered so far.

The Workbook provides further written practice of the Everyday English language, including activities based on the Fluency Time! DVD.

In the Fluency DVD

The Everyday English dialogues are also presented in the new Fluency Time! DVD. The key Everyday English language is acted out by native speakers in various real-life locations. You can find suggestions on when to use the DVD in the Everyday English teaching notes.

21st Century Learning

The Four Cs

As our world becomes increasingly interconnected, today's young students must develop strong skills in creativity, collaboration, communication, and critical thinking.

Creativity

Creativity is an essential 21st Century Skill. Students who exercise and demonstrate creativity are better prepared to solve problems, make changes and express themselves clearly. Creativity can be fostered through project work and other arts-based hands-on experiences. However, creativity is also about thinking processes. Creative thinking can be encouraged through asking students interesting questions and having them ask their own questions. Using different techniques to approach problem solving also helps students to internalise meaning in a personal way. *American Family and Friends 2nd Edition* encourages creativity through the use of interesting texts which stimulate personal responses, craft activities which help students to understand the world around them and projects which require them to problem solve and express themselves.

Collaboration

Collaboration requires direct communication between students, which strengthens the skills of listening and speaking and the associated skills of turn-taking, clarifying, explaining and discussing. Students who work together often achieve better results, as they benefit from each other's strengths. But they also develop a sense of team spirit and pride throughout the process. *American Family and Friends 2nd Edition* offers opportunities for collaboration in every unit. Whether it is through project work, group games, or team discussions, students are sharing ideas, expressing personal opinions and developing important social skills.

Communication

Communication forms an important part of collaboration. Students need to learn the skills of listening, speaking, reading, and writing to effectively take part in an age of rapid change. As our world becomes increasingly interconnected, today's young students must develop skills that allow them to communicate in a variety of ways, including oral and written skills but also digital communication skills.

Critical Thinking

Students in the 21st century need to do more than acquire information. They need to be able to analyse the information by making sense of it critically. Critical thinking skills help students to determine facts, prioritize information, understand relationships, solve problems and deal with an ever changing world. *American Family and Friends 2nd Edition* encourages students to think about language, to focus on meaning and to react to the world of English in a personal way. Subject areas are introduced so that students can make connections between content and language, interesting facts are presented and students are invited to be curious and questioning.

Values

Values, which can also be called civic education, are a key strand in *American Family and Friends 2nd Edition*. Teaching values is important as it focuses on the whole student, not just language skills. It improves students's awareness of good behavior, and how their behavior and attitudes can impact on the people around them and their environment.

Areas for values teaching include helping students to understand about:

- Community, e.g. agreeing and following school rules, understanding the needs of people and other living things, understanding what improves and harms their environment, contributing to the life of the class and school.
- Health and hygiene, e.g. understanding the basics of healthy eating, maintaining personal hygiene, rules for keeping safe around the house and on the road.
- Interacting with others, e.g. listening to other people, playing and working co-operatively, sharing, identifying and respecting the differences and similarities between people, helping others in need.

Values are highlighted throughout the course in various places:

- In the four Values worksheets in the Assessment and Resource CD-ROM.
- In the exemplification of good behavior throughout the course, in particular in the two class plays in the Assessment and Resource CD-ROM, in the Student Book stories and their characters.
- In the co-operative learning activities throughout the course, which encourage students to work together and co-operate in order to complete activities.

CLIL

CLIL (Content and Language Integrated Learning) refers to teaching subjects (such as science, math, art, geography) through a foreign language. CLIL increases motivation by presenting language in natural, real-life contexts, which interests students and encourages them to communicate. *American Family and Friends 2nd Edition* provides four CLIL spreads to enable students to learn cross-curricular content and English simultaneously.

In the Student's Book and Workbook

All of the CLIL lessons in *American Family and Friends 2nd Edition* focus on a school subject. The content areas are carefully chosen to be interesting to students, while at the same time not overwhelming them with too much new information.

The CLIL pages in the Workbook provide further practice of the new language through reading, writing, listening, and speaking activities, ensuring that the students have plenty of practice of the new language and content in all four skills.

CLIL topic

Students are introduced to the subject topic and new vocabulary is pre-taught through a vocabulary presentation activity. The students read a text based on the lesson topic and complete a comprehension activity. A critical thinking activity is always included so that students can personalize the topic and the new language.

CLIL project

The vocabulary and skills focus is followed by a project related to the topic. This allows students to create something which demonstrates their understanding of the concepts and language from the subject lesson. It is followed by a stage where students present their projects to the class, increasing spoken confidence and general presentation skills.

Differentiation

Most classes contain students with mixed abilities. *American Family and Friends 2nd Edition* provides support for students who may be above or below the average level of the class. The Teacher's Book contains suggestions on how to make activities easier for students who require more support, or more challenging for students who need more independence. This ensures that all students remain confident and motivated throughout your lessons.

Classroom tips for mixed ability classes

- Think about where your students are sitting. Place less confident students closer to you, so that you can deal with any issues.
- Some more confident students may enjoy being "volunteer teaching assistants". This will allow confident students to revise new language while helping other students to learn it.
- Give simple, clear instructions so that students of all levels can understand you easily. Use hand gestures as well as words to explain the activities.
- Don't grade your language as much when talking to confident students. They will benefit from the extra natural language input and one-to-one interactions will encourage them to explore language further.
- Set goals for each lesson to help the students to focus. The goals can be different for each student, depending on their abilities, but reaching the goals will give the same sense of achievement to all students.

Support and extension material

There is a wealth of support and extension material available to *American Family and Friends 2nd Edition* students, offering additional practice in skills, vocabulary, and grammar. The Online Practice and eBooks, as well as the *Oxford Skills* series and *Grammar Friends*, provide plenty of reinforcement for less confident students and further practice for confident students.

American Family and Friends 2nd Edition includes a diagnostic test to be completed at the start of each year. This will enable you to assess your students' abilities and decide which material will be most useful. The progress tests after every three units will help you to check your students' progress and provide reinforcement where necessary.

Differentiation Map

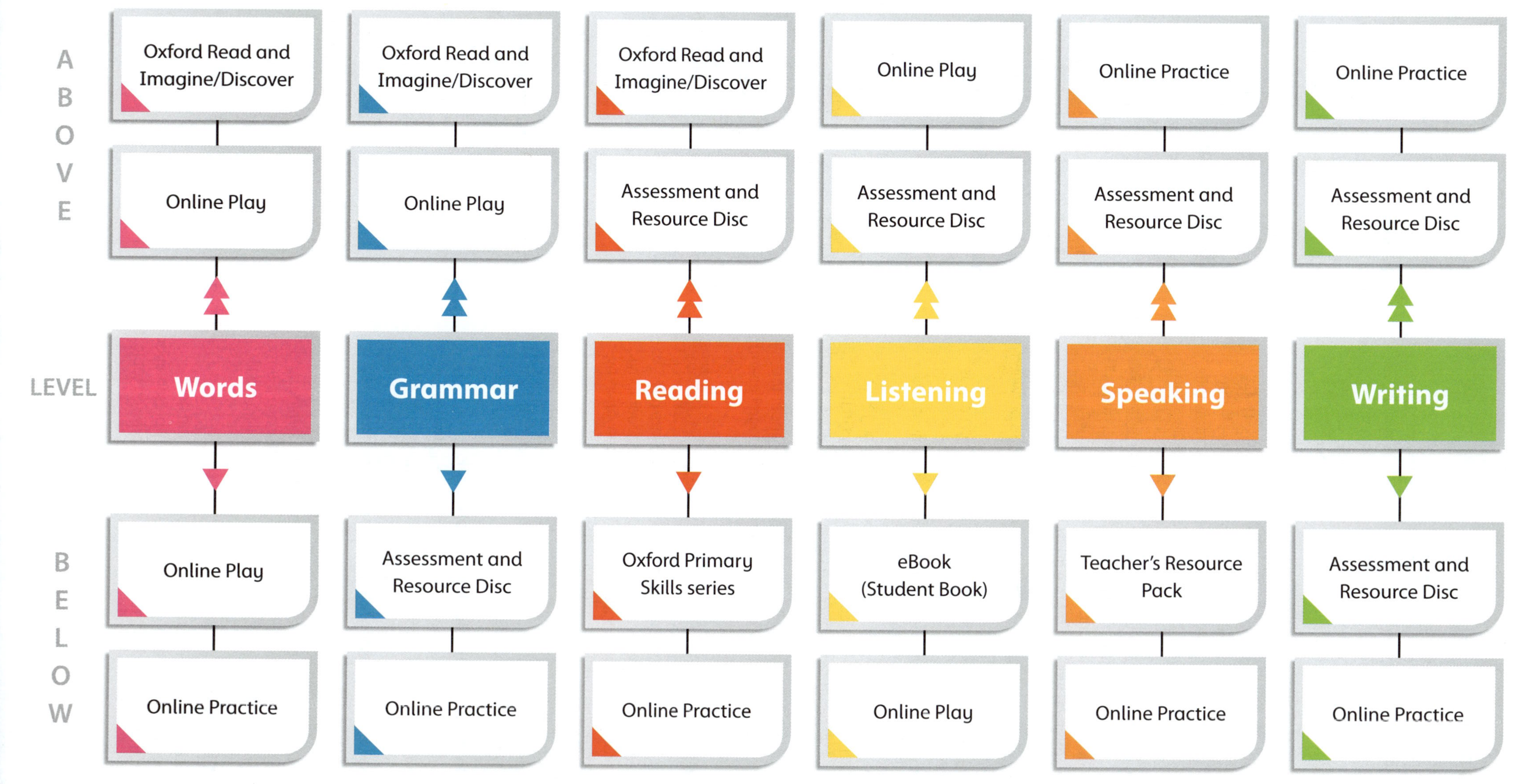

Drama in the classroom

How to present the stories

Each story has a receptive and a productive stage. In the receptive stage, students listen to the story and follow it in their Student Books. In the productive stage, students recall the story, listen to it again, and act it out.

Acting out the stories

There are various ways of acting out the stories, depending on the size and nature of your class.

Acting in groups

The following procedure is suggested in the teaching notes for each unit:

- Decide as a class on actions for each character at each stage of the story (students may suggest actions which are not shown in the pictures).
- Divide the class into groups so that there is one student to play each character. To keep disruption to a minimum, students could turn their chairs to work with those behind them and remain in their seats.
- Play the recording. Students practice the story in their groups, saying their character's lines (if they have any) and doing their actions. Props can be used if you wish, or you may prefer objects from the story to remain imaginary.
- At the end of the exercise, invite some of the groups to act out their story at the front of the class.

Acting as a class

As an alternative, you may wish to act out the story as a class:

- Decide together on actions for the story which students can do at their desks without standing up (e.g. they could 'walk' their fingers to show that the character is walking).
- Play the recording to practice reciting the lines. Students mime the actions for each character as they speak.
- Play the recording again for students to give their final performance.

Acting with a "lead group"

This is a combination of the two previous procedures:

- Decide on actions for the story as above.
- Divide the class into groups so that there is one student in each group to play each character. Students should all be facing the front of the class and not the other people in their groups. They won't need to leave their seats.
- Ask one of the groups to come to the front of the class.
- Play the recording. The group at the front demonstrate the actions to the class.
- Play the recording again for the rest of the students to join in with the actions.

Class plays

The Assessment and Resource CD-ROM contains two plays for the whole class to act out, one at the end of each semester.

Preparing the plays will take several lessons: discussing the play and allocating parts, deciding on and organizing props and costumes, and finally, rehearsing. If possible, arrange a performance of the plays for parents.

Assessment

Student's progress can be evaluated through ongoing assessment, self-assessment, and formal testing. *American Family and Friends 2nd Edition* offers a comprehensive range of course assessment and practice for external exams such as Cambridge English: Young Learners (YLE).

The Course Tests section in the Assessment and Resource CD-ROM offers:

- suggestions for ongoing classroom assessment
- an assessment sheet to keep a record of students's progress
- suggestions for encouraging students to self-assess
- 13 unit tests
- 4 progress tests (for use after every three units)
- 4 skills tests (for use after every three units)

The Cambridge English: YLE Practice section in the Assessment and Resource CD-ROM offers:

- Notes, tips, and vocabulary lists for the Flyers tests
- Preparation and practice tasks to help students become accustomed to the YLE task types
- The Preparation stage provides controlled practice of task types found in the Flyers tests, to help students gradually build up to the task. The Practice task then gives students a taster of a Cambridge style test before they attempt a complete YLE Practice Test
- Sample YLE Practice Tests for the Flyers Reading and Writing, Listening, and Speaking tests

Further information on testing and assessment (including the scoring system) can be found in the introduction sections of the Assessment and Resource CD-ROM.

Digital learning

The use of technology in language learning can allow the teacher to become a facilitator and a moderator, whilst the student is able to work more independently, connect to additional resources, and transfer knowledge both within and beyond the classroom. Immediate collaboration and feedback are also significant benefits of effective technology implementation, through the use of tablets, classroom presentation tools, and learning management systems.

eBooks

American Family and Friends 2nd Edition can be accessed in its print edition or in eBook form. eBooks are most commonly accessed on tablets, although they can also be used on laptop computers. Tablets provide a large amount of flexibility, not only because they allow students to store an enormous amount of text books and information on one, small device, but also because they contain innovative learning tools which can be used both inside and outside the classroom.

Learning Outcomes

Students can easily use tablets to help them search for vocabulary, translation, and pronunciation, as well as images, audio, and video. However, to ensure that the tablets are used effectively as a learning tool, teachers need to think about the following points:

- How will using the tablet help fulfil our learning outcomes?
- How will students be using the tablet?
- What is my role when the tablets are being used?

Fundamentally, tablets are just another useful tool to assist in language learning. Different learning outcomes will lead to varying amounts of tablet use. Just as with print textbooks, students need time to work together to complete exercises and activities, to check their work and to discuss ideas and work on projects. Spoken production should still be an important part of the lesson.

Classroom management

An eBook based lesson must be a controlled, well-planned lesson. Before starting, think about whether you want your students to work in groups or individually.

Independent work

- If each student has a set of headphones, they can work independently without disturbing others.
- Ask students to turn their devices face down until you tell them to start working in the eBooks. Tell students that they should complete interactive activities only when you give the go-ahead.
- Only upon your instruction should students press the 'check answers' button.

Group / paired work

- Put students into groups with one device per group. Students can take turns to answer a question within interactive activities.
- Groups can compete against each other for points.

Whole class work

- Designate one student to play audio on their device with the volume turned up for everyone to listen to as you work through the lessons.

Online Practice

For teachers

American Family and Friends 2nd Edition Online Practice is available using the access card in the Teacher's Book Plus. It allows teachers to:

- Create online classes for the course using the 'Manage Classes' feature.
- Assign work directly linked to the Student Book.
- Set practice activities dedicated to the course vocabulary, grammar and skills.
- Track student progress by viewing detailed class and student reports.
- Engage students in various forms of written English such as email and forum discussion.

For students

Online Practice is available to students using the access card in their Workbook (with Online Practice). Students will be able to:

- Complete specific language-focused activities that link directly to the course
- Have their work automatically scored and graded.
- Share their work with other students in the 'class' setup by the teacher.
- Send emails and take part in English discussions as their level increases.

Online Play

Online Play is a place for students to access the audio and video animations, downloadable activities, and to explore language further through fun vocabulary games and activities. Throughout the Teacher's Book lessons you will see Online Play icons, demonstrating how to integrate the audio and activities into lesson extensions.

Audio

Students need to listen to English again and again in order to improve their receptive skills. Online Play offers a place where students can access the songs, chants, and target language at home.

Stories

Watching the unit stories come to life provides consolidation of the target language from the first two lessons of each unit.

Downloadable activities

There are a number of fun craft and downloadable activities for students to complete at home. These can be done in conjunction with parents but are also simple enough for students to work with by themselves.

Language games

Students need to have fun with language. These games encourage students to work with target language at their own pace and without being graded. Many games have more than one level, providing support for less confident students and challenge and extension for more confident students.

Integrated Component Overview

Student Book

The Student Book contains 15 units. Each unit presents vocabulary and grammar with opportunity to practice both with a focus on all four skills. Fluency Time! pages provide Everyday English practice, and subject pages (such as Science Time!) bring content and language learning together.

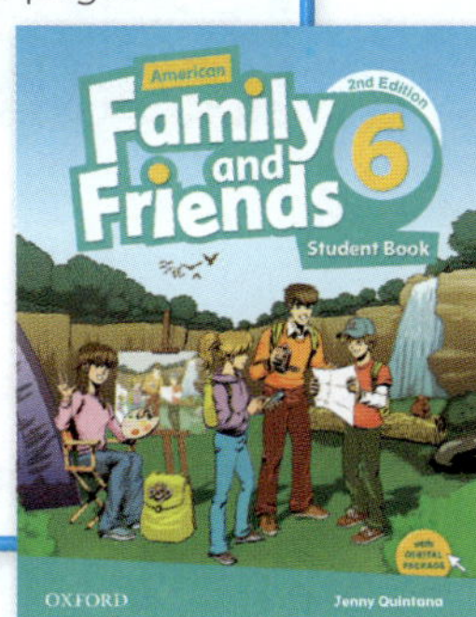

Workbook

The Workbook is designed to give students extra practice of the language and structures taught in class.

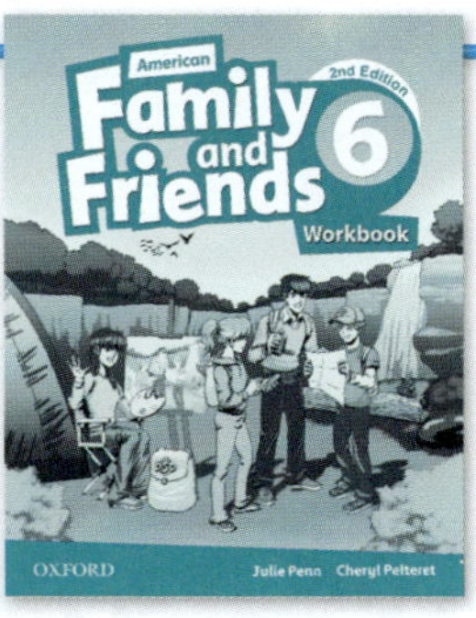

eBook

Both the Student Book and Workbook are available as eBooks. By accessing *American Family and Friends 2nd Edition* on a tablet or laptop, students can access extra interactivity types and control the audio and video features themselves.

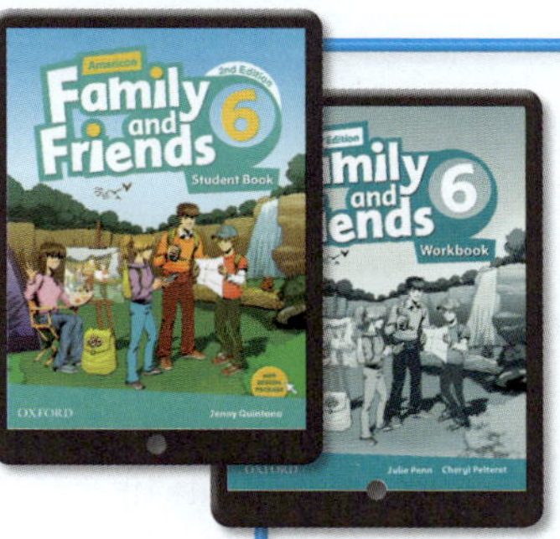

For the Student

Student Online Practice

Online Practice is a blended approach to learning where students can interact with activities to further practice the language and ideas taught in the Student Book.

Online Play

Online Play is the place for children to explore the language they are learning through fun games and activities. It includes the story animations, audio, games, and downloadable craft activities to do at home.

Recommended Readers

Family and Friends readers draw upon themes and language found in the Student Book. They provide extra exposure to the language in a new context.

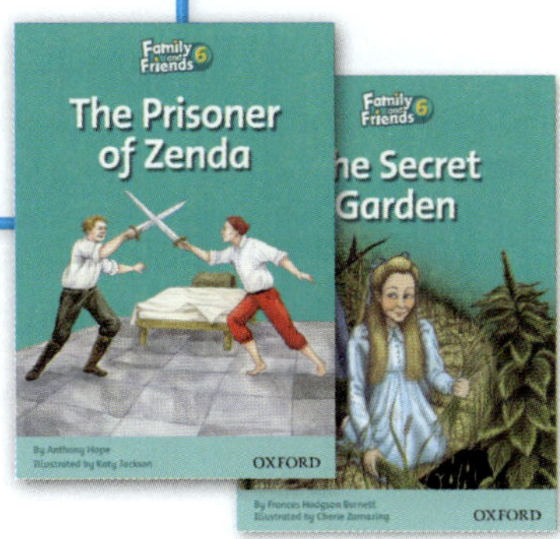

Recommended Dictionaries

Levels 1–4 *Oxford Basic American Dictionary*

Levels 5–6 *Oxford American Dictionary*

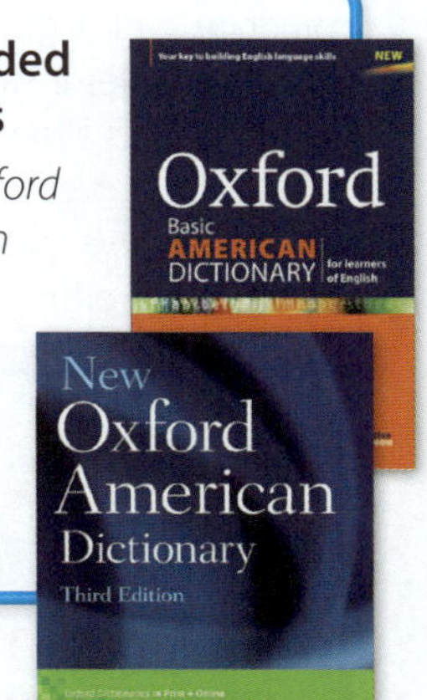

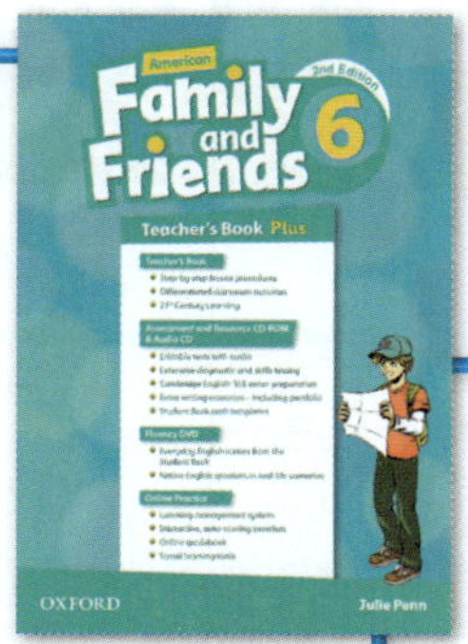

Teacher's Book Plus

The Teacher's Book is a clear guide for the teacher in all aspects of the course. It contains the Fluency Time! DVD, the Assessment and Resource CD-ROM and Assessment Audio CD, and the Online Practice Teacher Access Card.

Audio CD

The Class Audio CDs support teaching in class and contains recordings of all the listening texts, reading texts, songs, and speaking dialogues.

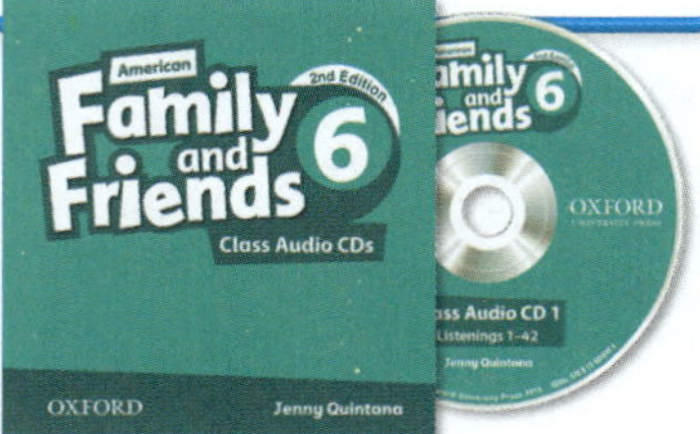

iTools

The *American Family and Friends 2nd Edition* iTools is a CD-ROM which contains digital class resources. All the iTools resources can be used either on an Interactive Whiteboard or on a projector.

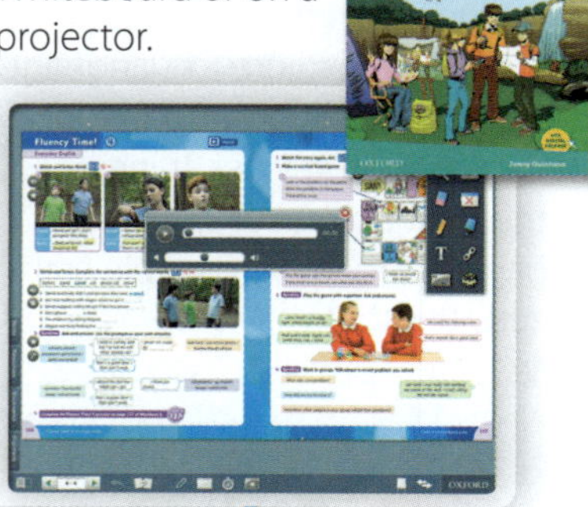

Teacher's Resource Pack

The Teacher's Resource Pack contains posters which depict the unit stories, flashcards, and phonics cards. All of these components act as visual learning aids, supporting language learning by providing extra practice outside the Student Book.

Online Practice

Teachers have complete access to students' online practice, with a grade book which enables instant marking. This allows teachers to see the scores in one place and to analyse their students' needs more effectively.

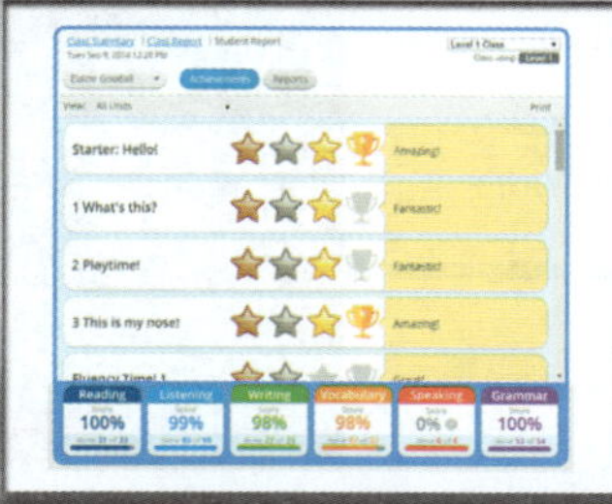

Fluency Time! DVD

This DVD contains native speakers in real-life scenarios and locations using the Everyday English taught in *American Family and Friends 2nd Edition* Fluency Time! This provides opportunities for students to combine core grammar structures with Everyday English and to model pronunciation and intonation on the examples provided by native speakers.

Assessment and Resource CD-ROM and Assessment Audio CD

The *American Family and Friends 2nd Edition* Assessment and Resource CD-ROM contains a wide range of editable and printable tests, as well as a variety of photocopiable resources to support and supplement the course. All of the audio for these tests is available both on the CD-ROM and the Assessment Audio CD, giving teachers a choice of how to access it, depending on classroom requirements. The CD-ROM contains:

Course Tests

- A diagnostic test so that students' level of ability going into this course is understood.
- Extensive testing for all four skills areas, including 5 Fluency Time! tests for use after every three units.
- Tests for each course unit and a progress test for use after every three units.

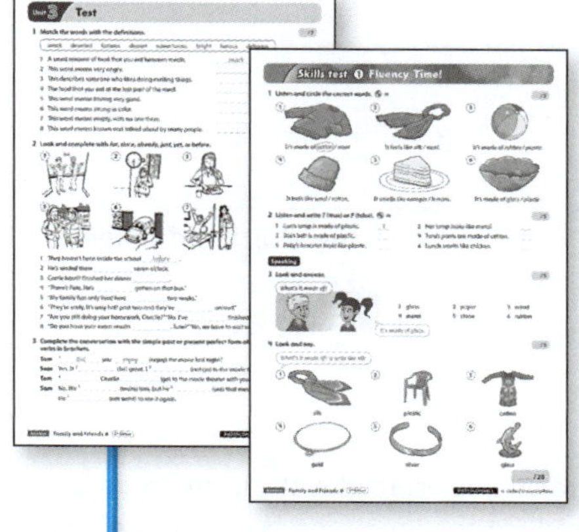

Cambridge English: YLE Practice

- Notes and tips for the Starters tests.
- Preparation and practice tasks to help children become accustomed to the YLE task types.
- Sample YLE Practice Tests for the Starters Reading and Writing, Listening, and Speaking tests.

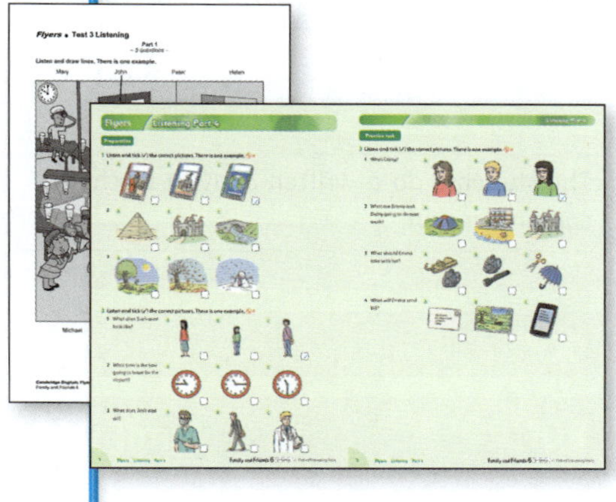

Course Resources

- Fluency Time! craft templates
- Writing Portfolio worksheets for freer and extended writing practice after every three units.
- Differentiated worksheets, Portfolio A and B, for mixed ability classes. Writing Portfolio A can be used with learners at or below level, while Portfolio B is aimed at providing activity extension for students above level.
- Extra Writing worksheets for further practice of each unit's writing objective
- Values worksheets for every course unit.
- Class play scripts for the end of each semester.

Differentiation Map

The Differentiation Map (see p.12 in this Teacher's Book) is an interactive navigation tool. It enables teachers to choose the appropriate content, within the Assessment and Resource CD-ROM, and other components to meet their students' individual needs.

Teacher's Website

The Teacher's Website provides additional materials for students and teachers to supplement all the other components available.

Parent Website

The Parent Website provides support and materials for parents of students studying with *American Family and Friends 2nd Edition*.

Tour of a unit

Lesson One Story

Lesson 1 presents the unit topic via a *Do Something Different Club* story. Students read and act out the story and are exposed to the language that they will be studying in Lesson 2.

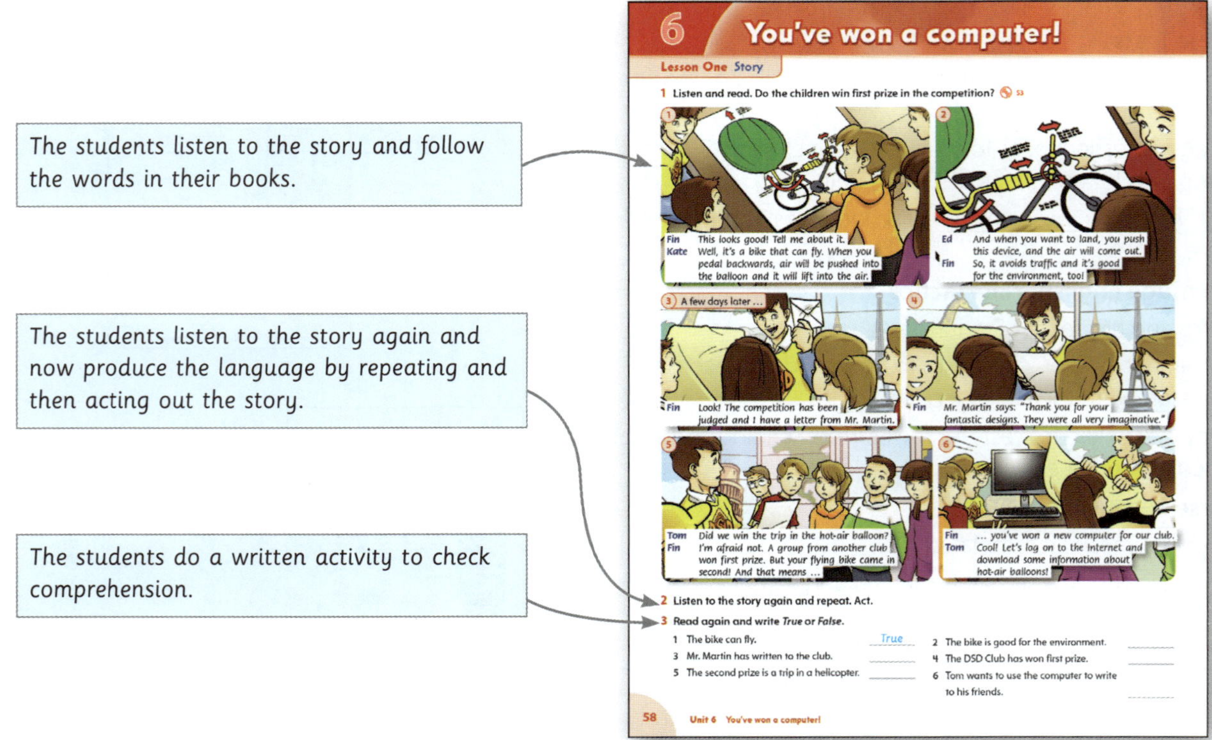

6 You've won a computer!

Lesson One Story

1 Listen and read. Do the children win first prize in the competition? 53

2 Listen to the story again and repeat. Act.

3 Read again and write *True* or *False*.

1 The bike can fly. True
2 The bike is good for the environment. ______
3 Mr. Martin has written to the club. ______
4 The DSD Club has won first prize. ______
5 The second prize is a trip in a helicopter. ______
6 Tom wants to use the computer to write to his friends. ______

58 Unit 6 You've won a computer!

Presenting the story and acting it out

- Focus students' attention on the pictures and the story. Ask simple prediction questions such as *Who's this? Where are they? What's this?*
- Play the recording the whole way through for students to listen and follow in their books. Then ask the gist question in Exercise 1.
- Play the recording a second time and ask more questions to check comprehension.
- Play the recording again. Pause after each line for students to repeat.
- Divide the class into groups, with each student having a different role in the story.
- As a class decide on actions for the story.
- Play the recording. Each student says the lines of his/her assigned character. Encourage students to perform actions as they speak.
- Repeat without the recording, encouraging students to remember the sentences.
- If you wish, move on to individual practice by calling groups to the front to act out the dialogues, with or without the recording.
- A final written activity consolidates comprehension of the main points of the story.

Workbook

The students do written activities to consolidate and extend their understanding of the story and its themes.

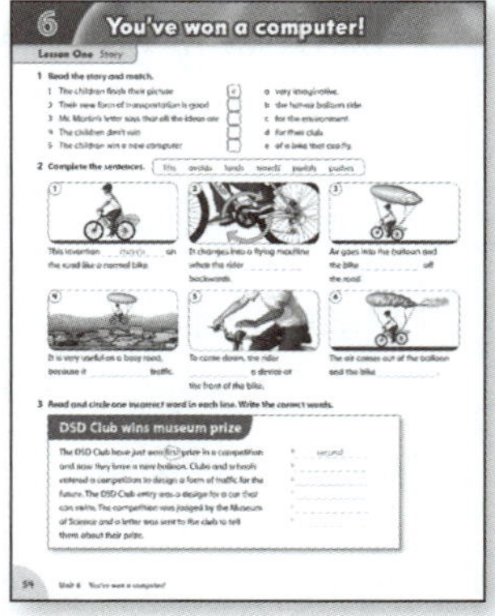

Online Practice allows the students to practice the language further.

Lesson Two Words

Lesson 2 teaches and practices the first new vocabulary set which the students have been exposed to in the Lesson 1 story. Students are also introduced to a *Working with words* vocabulary set and develop their dictionary skills.

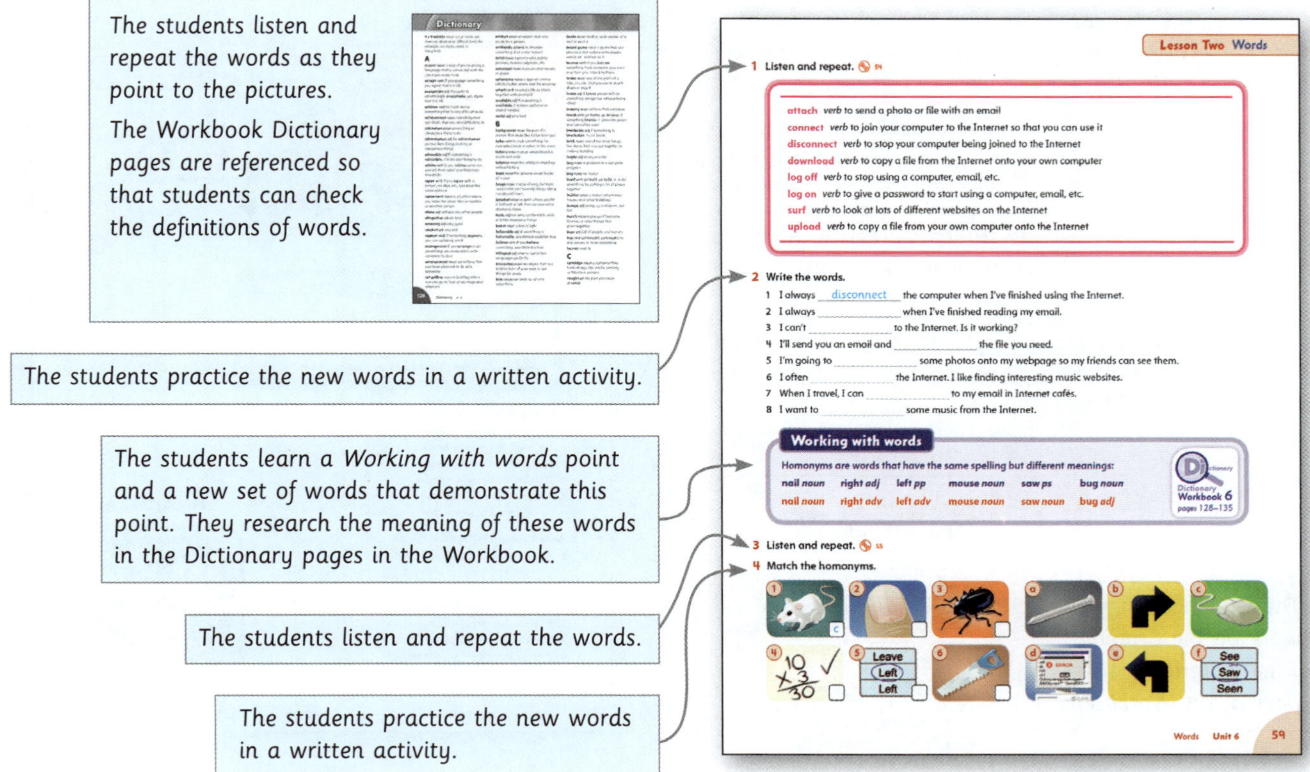

Teaching the words

Words

- Play the recording and ask students to repeat the words.
- In some units, definitions of words are given, and in others pictures illustrate their meanings. When pictures are given, the Workbook Dictionary pages are referenced so that students can also check the definitions of words.
- The students practice the words in a written activity.

Working with words

- Ask students to read *Working with words* box. Students research the meaning of the new words in the Dictionary pages.
- Play the recording and ask students to repeat words.
- The students practice the words in a written activity which can be done individually or in pairs.

Workbook

Students practice recognizing and writing the new words from the lesson. They also learn the new words that extend the *Working with words* set and practice writing the *Working with words* vocabulary.

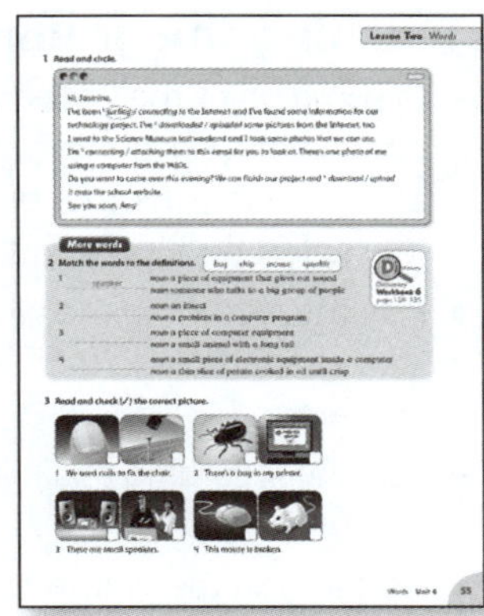

Online Practice allows students to practice the vocabulary further.

Lesson Three Grammar 1

Lesson 3 presents a grammar point in a variety of text types, including cartoon strips. Students learn and practice recognizing and producing this grammar point.

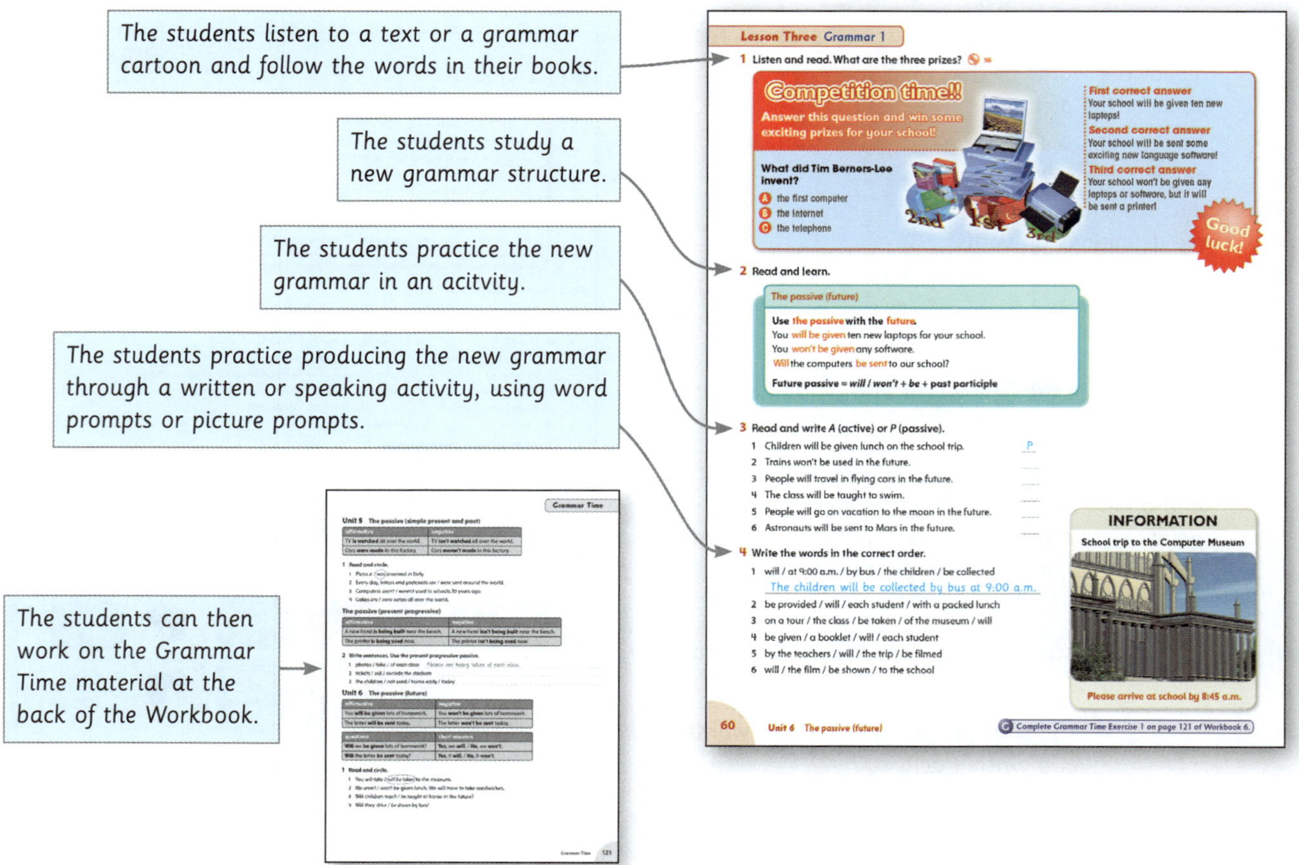

Teaching the grammar

- In some units, the new grammar is introduced in the context of a cartoon featuring *Professor* and his robot assistant *Chip*. In other units, the first grammar point is presented through a written text.
- Play the recording the whole way through for students to listen and follow in their books. Then ask the gist question in Exercise 1.
- Play the recording again and ask more questions to check comprehension.
- Go through the grammar rules with the class and check comprehension as suggested in the notes.
- The next activity is a written activity which practices and consolidates the grammar. A model is provided on the page. Students complete the activity independently.
- The final activity is a speaking or writing activity which gives students practice in manipulating the structure. Students work with their partner using the word or picture prompts.
- At this point students are encouraged to complete the relevant Grammar Time exercise at the back of their Workbooks.

Workbook

The students practice recognizing and writing the first grammar point from the lesson using the reference tables in the Grammar Time section at the back of the Workbook to help them.

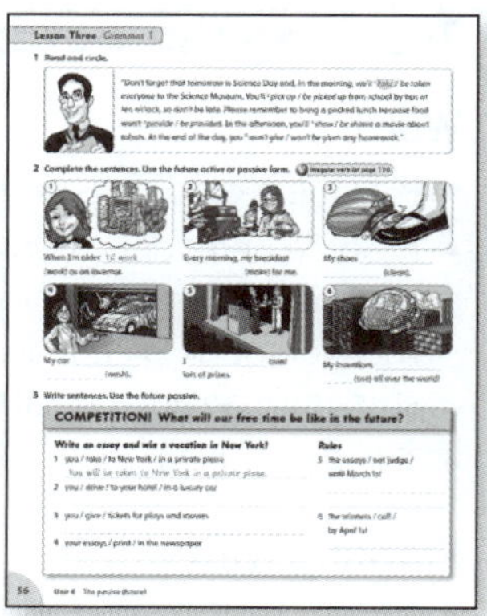

Online Practice allows students to practice the new grammar further.

Lesson Four Grammar 2

Lesson 4 presents a new grammar point in a variety of text types, sometimes via a short cartoon strip featuring fun and motivating characters *Professor* and his robot, *Chip*. Students learn and practice recognizing and producing this grammar point.

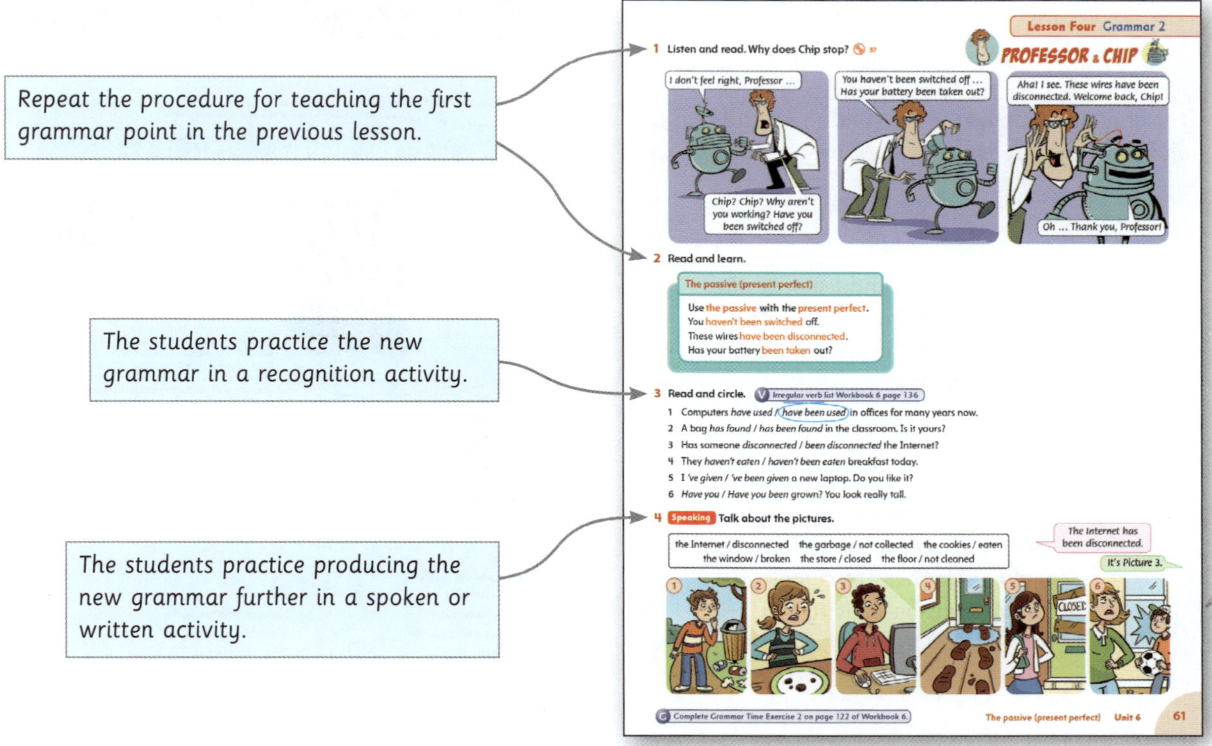

Repeat the procedure for teaching the first grammar point in the previous lesson.
The students practice the new grammar in a recognition activity.
The students practice producing the new grammar further in a spoken or written activity.

Lesson Four Grammar 2

PROFESSOR & CHIP

1 Listen and read. Why does Chip stop?

2 Read and learn.

The passive (present perfect)

Use the passive with the present perfect.
You haven't been switched off.
These wires have been disconnected.
Has your battery been taken out?

3 Read and circle. Irregular verb list Workbook 6 page 136

1 Computers have used / have been used in offices for many years now.
2 A bag has found / has been found in the classroom. Is it yours?
3 Has someone disconnected / been disconnected the Internet?
4 They haven't eaten / haven't been eaten breakfast today.
5 I've given / 've been given a new laptop. Do you like it?
6 Have you / Have you been grown? You look really tall.

4 Speaking Talk about the pictures.

the Internet / disconnected	the garbage / not collected	the cookies / eaten
the window / broken	the store / closed	the floor / not cleaned

Complete Grammar Time Exercise 2 on page 122 of Workbook 6.

The passive (present perfect) Unit 6 61

Teaching the grammar

- The grammar point is presented in a text or cartoon strip.
- Play the recording the whole way through for students to listen and follow in their books. Then ask the gist question in Exercise 1.
- The grammar rule activity is done in the same way as the first. If the two points are linked, elicit examples of the first grammar point and any 'rules' the students can remember.
- The next activity is a written activity which practices and consolidates the grammar. It can either be done in class or set for homework. A model is provided on the page.
- The final activity is a productive activity, either written or spoken. In this case, it is a spoken activity. Students practice manipulating and producing the structure.
- At this point students are encouraged to complete the relevant Grammar Time exercises at the back of the their Workbooks.

Workbook

The students practice recognizing and writing the second grammar point from the lesson using the reference tables in the Grammar Time section at the back of the Workbook to help them.

Assessment and Resource CD-ROM

There is extra written practice of the vocabulary and grammar from the unit in the Language practice worksheet. There is one Language practice worksheet for every unit.

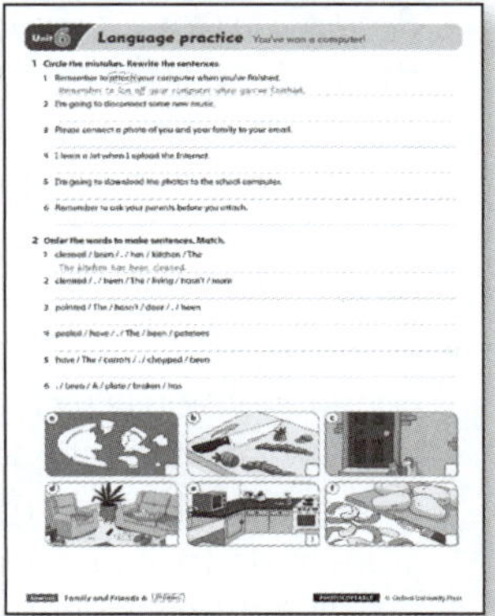

Online Practice allows students to practice the new grammar further.

Lesson Five Skills Time! Reading

Lesson 5, 6, and 7 provide a focused study of skills. Lesson 5 provides reading comprehension practice through a variety of reading texts.

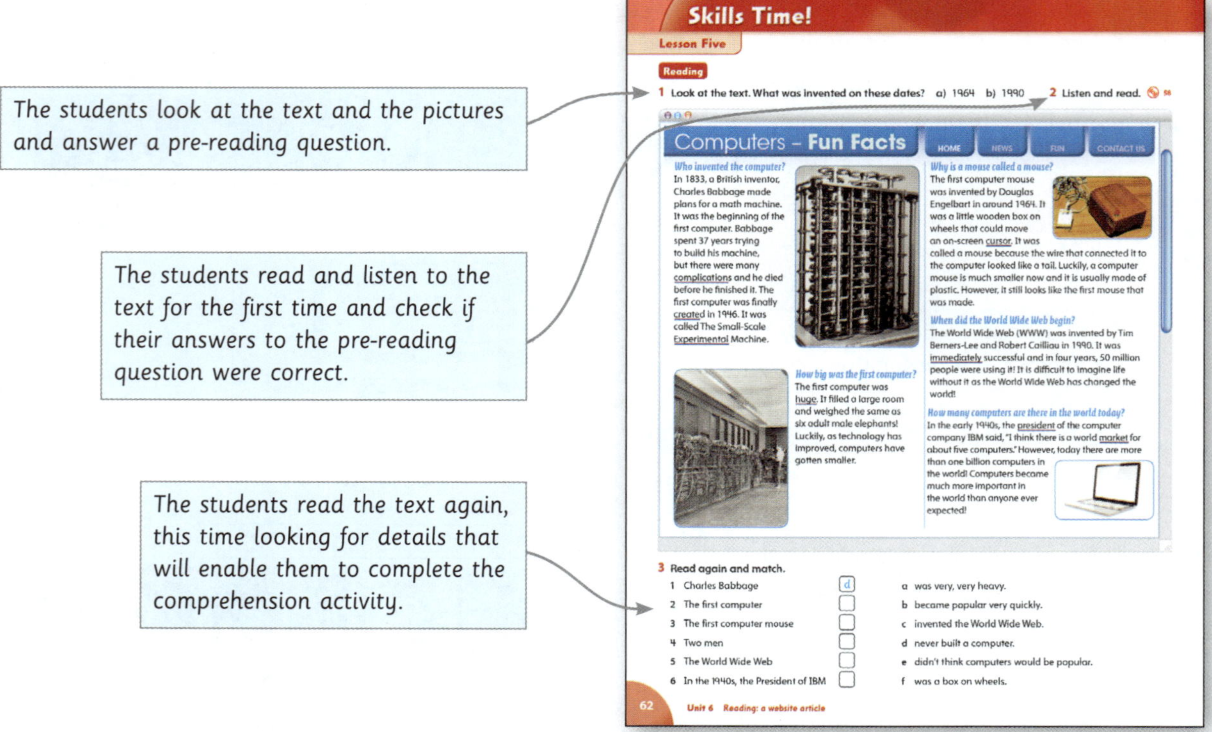

The students look at the text and the pictures and answer a pre-reading question.
The students read and listen to the text for the first time and check if their answers to the pre-reading question were correct.
The students read the text again, this time looking for details that will enable them to complete the comprehension activity.

Skills Time!

Lesson Five

Reading

1 Look at the text. What was invented on these dates? a) 1964 b) 1990

2 Listen and read. 58

Computers – Fun Facts

HOME NEWS FUN CONTACT US

Who invented the computer?
In 1833, a British inventor, Charles Babbage made plans for a math machine. It was the beginning of the first computer. Babbage spent 37 years trying to build his machine, but there were many complications and he died before he finished it. The first computer was finally created in 1946. It was called The Small-Scale Experimental Machine.

How big was the first computer?
The first computer was huge. It filled a large room and weighed the same as six adult male elephants! Luckily, as technology has improved, computers have gotten smaller.

Why is a mouse called a mouse?
The first computer mouse was invented by Douglas Engelbart in around 1964. It was a little wooden box on wheels that could move an on-screen cursor. It was called a mouse because the wire that connected it to the computer looked like a tail. Luckily, a computer mouse is much smaller now and it is usually made of plastic. However, it still looks like the first mouse that was made.

When did the World Wide Web begin?
The World Wide Web (WWW) was invented by Tim Berners-Lee and Robert Cailliau in 1990. It was immediately successful and in four years, 50 million people were using it! It is difficult to imagine life without it as the World Wide Web has changed the world!

How many computers are there in the world today?
In the early 1940s, the president of the computer company IBM said, "I think there is a world market for about five computers." However, today there are more than one billion computers in the world! Computers became much more important in the world than anyone ever expected!

3 Read again and match.

1 Charles Babbage [d]
2 The first computer [ ]
3 The first computer mouse [ ]
4 Two men [ ]
5 The World Wide Web [ ]
6 In the 1940s, the President of IBM [ ]

a was very, very heavy.
b became popular very quickly.
c invented the World Wide Web.
d never built a computer.
e didn't think computers would be popular.
f was a box on wheels.

62 Unit 6 Reading: a website article

Teaching reading

- Approach a new text in two stages. Explain to the students that they do not have to understand every word to understand a text. By focusing on the language they do understand, it is possible to guess or use logic to work out the meaning of the rest.
- *Pre-reading (Exercise 1):* This stage is about looking for clues to help the students piece together the meaning of the text. This includes looking at the picture and the text style to guess what type of text it is and what it is likely to be about. Point to the picture and ask students the pre-reading question.
- *Reading first for gist (Exercise 2):* Play the recording while the students follow the text in their books. They do not need to be able to read every word independently, but be able to read carefully enough to understand gist. Ask some simple comprehension questions to ensure they have understood the general point of the text.
- *Reading for detail (Exercise 3):* Go through the comprehension activity with the class so that students know what information to look for in the text. Give them time to read the text again to find the answers. Encourage students to try and work out the meaning of new words by using the surrounding words and the context to help them. Have a class feedback session.

Workbook

The students further practice reding for gist and detail in the Workbook. They read a new text of the same text type and complete a comprehension activity.

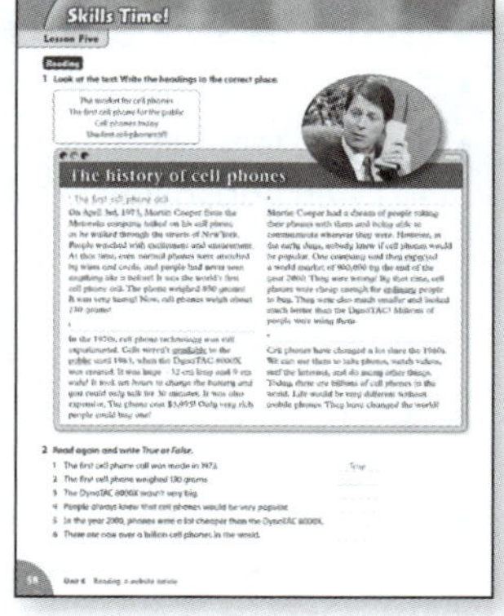

Skills Time!
Lesson Five
The history of cell phones

Online Practice allows students to practice reading further.

Lesson Six Skills Time! Listening and Speaking

Lesson 6 teaches the new vocabulary that students were exposed to in context in Lesson 5, and further develops dictionary skills. The lesson also focuses on listening comprehension and speaking skills.

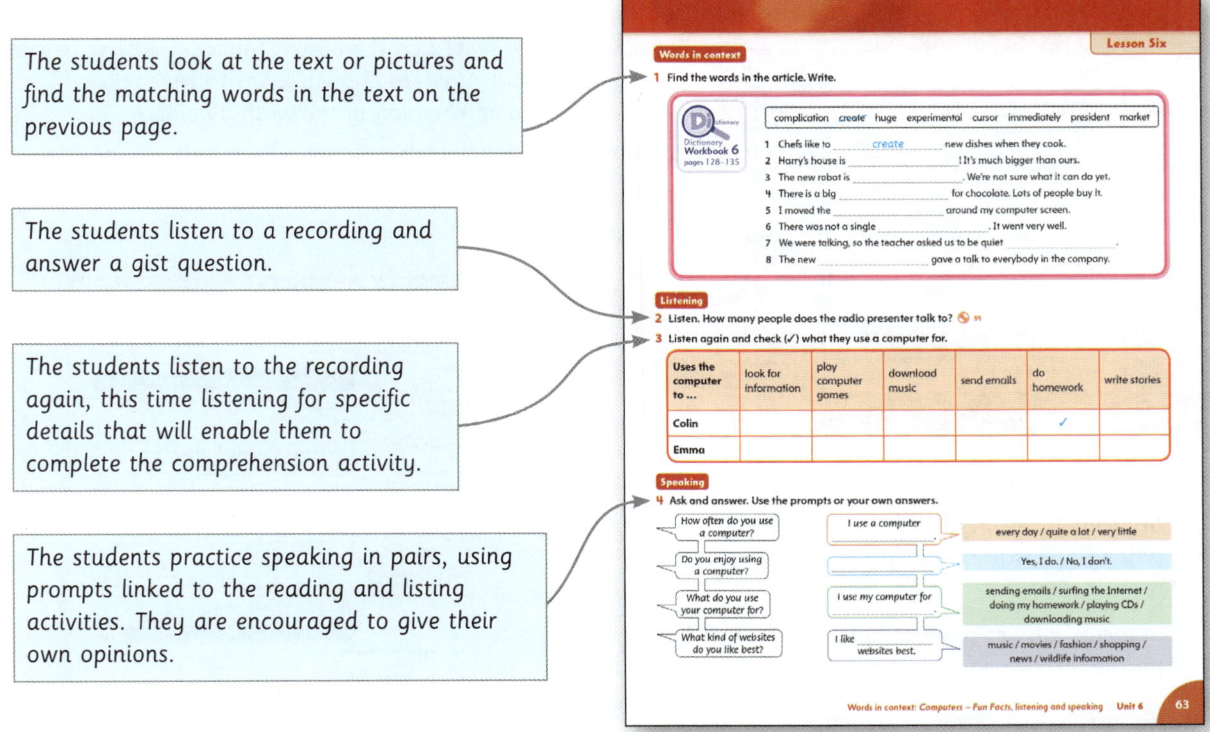

The students look at the text or pictures and find the matching words in the text on the previous page.

The students listen to a recording and answer a gist question.

The students listen to the recording again, this time listening for specific details that will enable them to complete the comprehension activity.

The students practice speaking in pairs, using prompts linked to the reading and listing activities. They are encouraged to give their own opinions.

Lesson Six

Words in context

1 Find the words in the article. Write.

Dictionary Workbook 6 pages 128–135

complication create huge experimental cursor immediately president market

1 Chefs like to create new dishes when they cook.
2 Harry's house is ______ ! It's much bigger than ours.
3 The new robot is ______. We're not sure what it can do yet.
4 There is a big ______ for chocolate. Lots of people buy it.
5 I moved the ______ around my computer screen.
6 There was not a single ______. It went very well.
7 We were talking, so the teacher asked us to be quiet ______.
8 The new ______ gave a talk to everybody in the company.

Listening

2 Listen. How many people does the radio presenter talk to?

3 Listen again and check (✓) what they use a computer for.

Uses the computer to ...	look for information	play computer games	download music	send emails	do homework	write stories
Colin					✓	
Emma						

Speaking

4 Ask and answer. Use the prompts or your own answers.

How often do you use a computer? — I use a computer ______. — every day / quite a lot / very little

Do you enjoy using a computer? — Yes, I do. / No, I don't.

What do you use your computer for? — I use my computer for ______. — sending emails / surfing the Internet / doing my homework / playing CDs / downloading music

What kind of websites do you like best? — I like ______ websites best. — music / movies / fashion / shopping / news / wildlife information

Words in context: Computers – Fun Facts, listening and speaking Unit 6 63

Teaching the words

Words in context

- Students look at the pictures or words and find the matching words in the text in Exercise 1 on the previous page.
- The students refer to their Dictionary pages to match words with their definitions.

Teaching listening and speaking

Listening

- To follow a listening text, the students should be aware that they do not need to understand every word. As students reading, they listen for the words they do know, and then use clues and logic to work out the rest.
- *Listening for gist (Exercise 2):* Play the recording the whole way through. The students listen and answer the gist question.
- *Listening for detail (Exercise 3):* Play the recording again, pausing for students to complete the activity.

Speaking

- The speaking task aims to develop speech that is clear and fluent. The students will also learn to speak expressively and confidently.
- Call two volunteers to come to the front and demonstrate how to ask and answer the questions using the dialogues in the speech bubbles. Explain that the prompts are only ideas and they can give different answers. Ask the volunteers to provide an alternative answer to one of the questions as an example.
- Ask the students to repeat chorally, emphasizing correct intonation in the questions and answers.
- The students then carry out the speaking activity in pairs.

Workbook

The students practice recognizing and writing the new words from the Student Book. They practice using their dictionary skills to check meaning of the words in the text on the previous page.

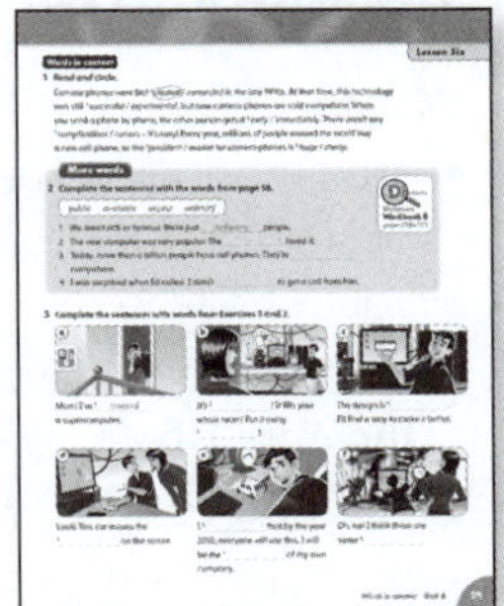

Assessment and Resource CD-ROM

For every unit there is a Speaking skills worksheet. This contains an extended information gap speaking task that students carry out in pairs.

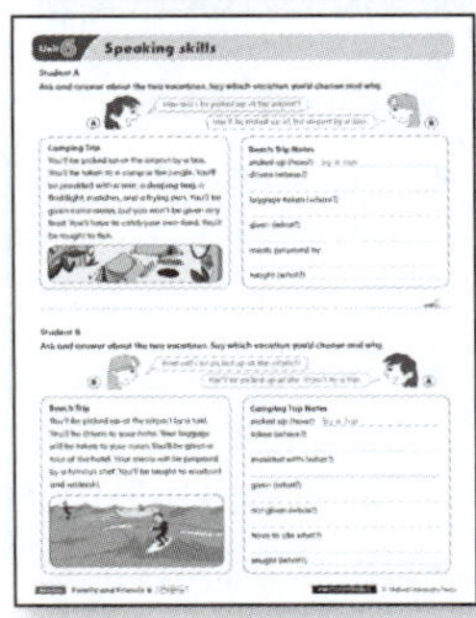

Online Practice allows students to practice the vocabulary further.

Lesson Seven Skills Time! Writing (Poster and Student Book)

In Lesson 7, the students learn key writing and literacy skills from the Poster and Student Book. Students' writing is then further developed in the Workbook.

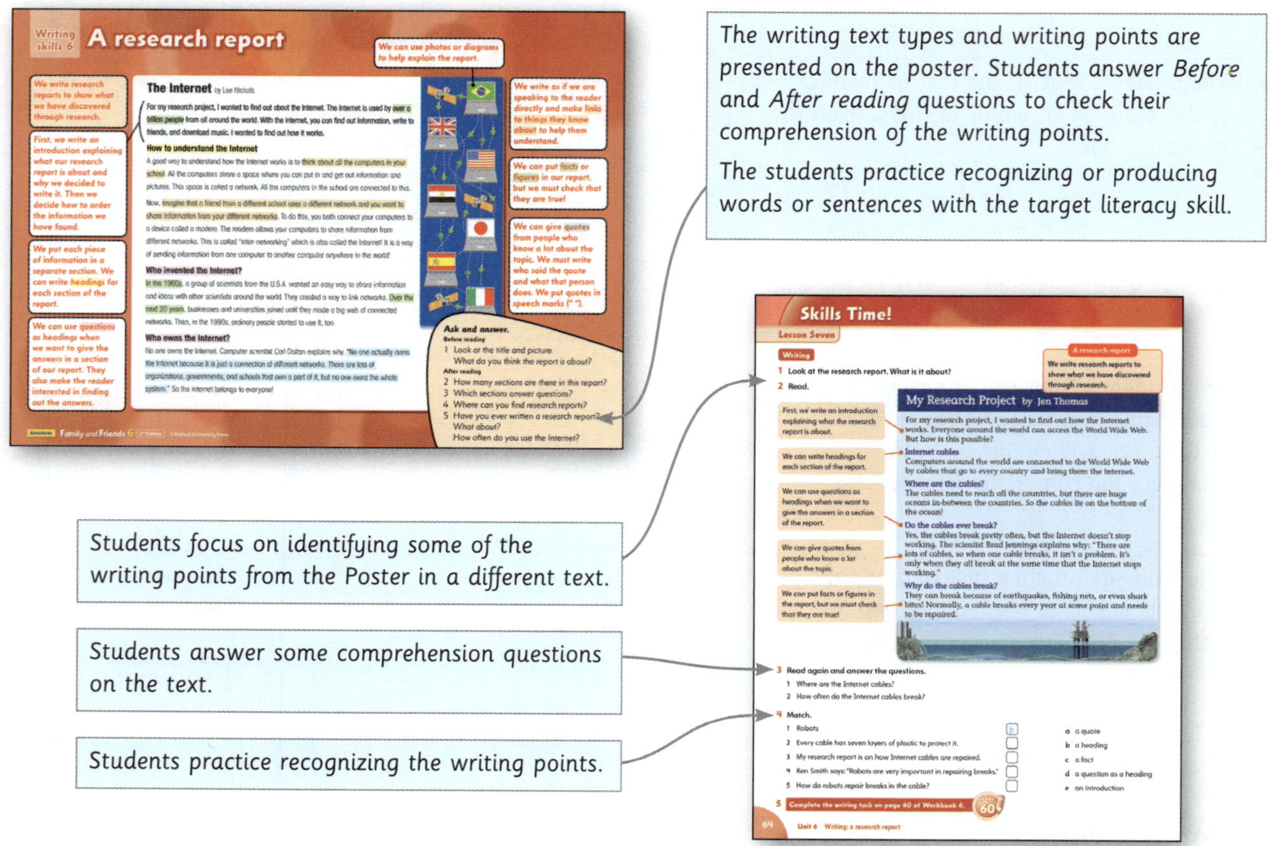

A research report
Skills Time!
The writing text types and writing points are presented on the poster. Students answer *Before* and *After reading* questions to check their comprehension of the writing points.
The students practice recognizing or producing words or sentences with the target literacy skill.
Students focus on identifying some of the writing points from the Poster in a different text.
Students answer some comprehension questions on the text.
Students practice recognizing the writing points.

Teaching writing

Poster

- Students look at the poster. They follow the text in the poster handout (Assessment and Resource CD-ROM) as you read it aloud.
- Discuss the text and the pointers in the text boxes with the class. Check comprehension.
- The students do the related exercises in their Student Books before moving on to the writing task in their Workbooks.

Student Book

- The students skim-read the text looking for key words rather than trying to understand every word. They then answer the gist question.
- The students read the text for the first time. Ask volunteers to read the text aloud to the class. Help with pronunciation of new words.
- The students read the text again silently and answer questions to check comprehension. Go through the answers with the class.
- The writing rule activity is done by students at their desks. They can take two or three minutes to silently read and learn the rules. Check comprehension by asking questions about the text and eliciting further examples.
- The final activity is a written activity which practices and consolidates the writing rule.

Assessment and Resource CD-ROM

Students follow their own copy of the Poster text on the Assessment and Resource CD-ROM handout.

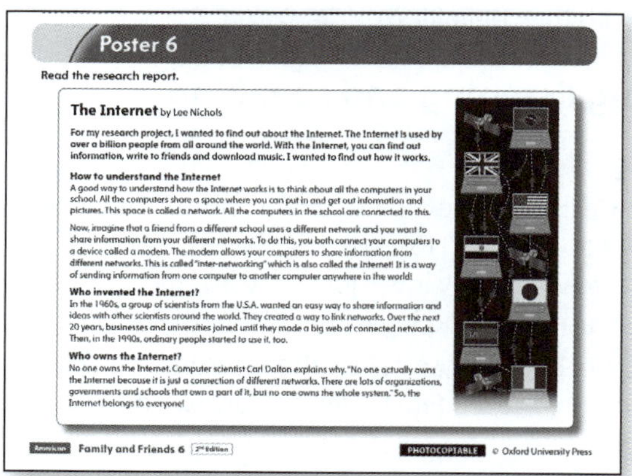

Online Practice allows students to practice the writing further.

Lesson Seven Skills Time! Writing (Workbook)

On the Workbook page, students do a further exercise to practice the writing point in the Student Book before going on to complete a free writing activity.

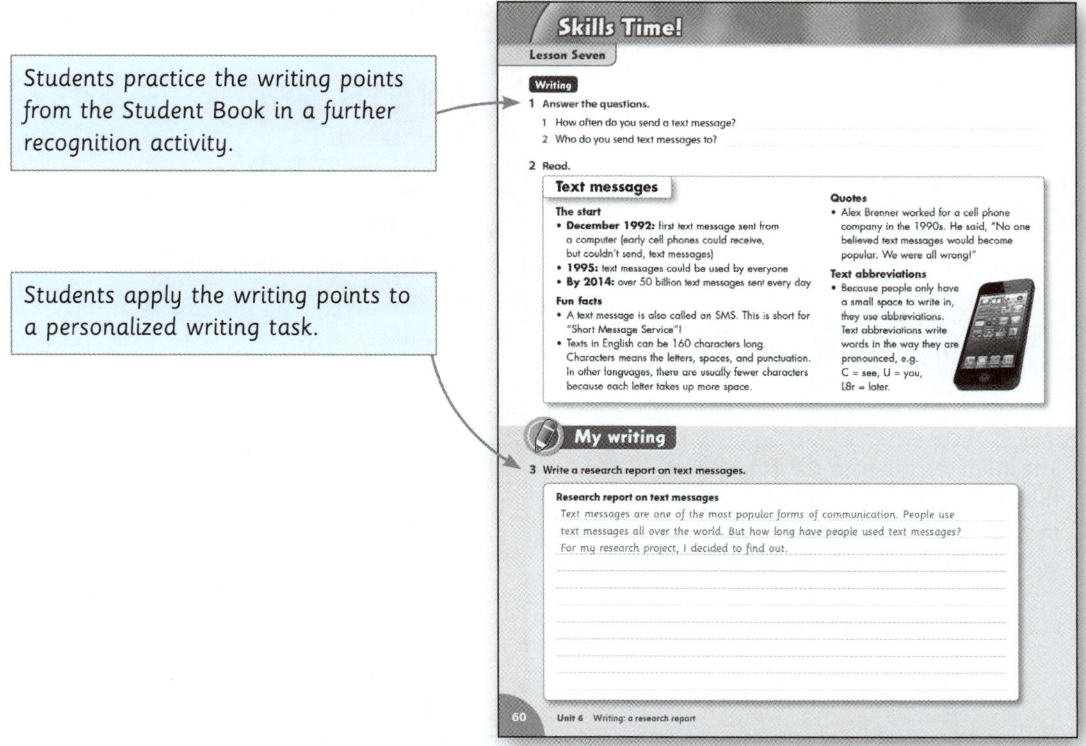
Students practice the writing points from the Student Book in a further recognition activity.
Students apply the writing points to a personalized writing task.

Skills Time!

Lesson Seven

Writing

1 Answer the questions.

1 How often do you send a text message?

2 Who do you send text messages to?

2 Read.

Text messages

The start

- **December 1992:** first text message sent from a computer (early cell phones could receive, but couldn't send, text messages)
- **1995:** text messages could be used by everyone
- **By 2014:** over 50 billion text messages sent every day

Fun facts

- A text message is also called an SMS. This is short for "Short Message Service"!
- Texts in English can be 160 characters long. Characters means the letters, spaces, and punctuation. In other languages, there are usually fewer characters because each letter takes up more space.

Quotes

- Alex Brenner worked for a cell phone company in the 1990s. He said, "No one believed text messages would become popular. We were all wrong!"

Text abbreviations

- Because people only have a small space to write in, they use abbreviations. Text abbreviations write words in the way they are pronounced, e.g. C = see, U = you, L8r = later.

My writing

3 Write a research report on text messages.

Research report on text messages

Text messages are one of the most popular forms of communication. People use text messages all over the world. But how long have people used text messages? For my research project, I decided to find out.

60 Unit 6 Writing: a research report

Workbook

Writing

- Students do the recognition activity alone or in pairs and then feed back to the class.
- This activity reinforces the writing points the students covered in the Poster and Student Book, and acts as preparation for the writing task they are about to complete.

My writing

- Students extend their writing skills through a personalized writing task. This is an opportunity for them to write an extended text following a model they have seen on the Student Book and Workbook pages.
- Where relevant, look at the visual prompts as a class. Ask students questions to check comprehension.
- Ensure that the students understand what type of sentences they need to produce in the writing task. Elicit examples and write them on the board.
- When they have finished, ask some students to read their texts to the class.

Assessment and Resource CD-ROM

For every unit there is a Writing skills worksheet on the Assessment and Resource CD-ROM. This allows students to combine the writing points they have learnt from the Poster and Student Book in a free writing task.

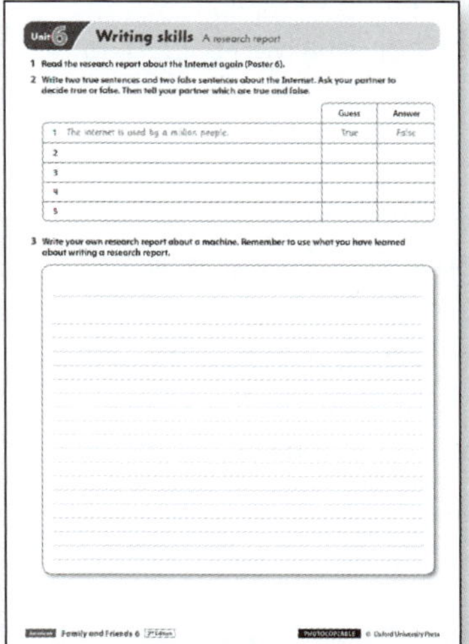

Unit 6 **Writing skills** A research report

1 Read the research report about the Internet again (Poster 6).

2 Write two true sentences and two false sentences about the Internet. Ask your partner to decide true or false. Then tell your partner which are true and false.

	Guess	Answer
1 *The internet is used by a million people.*	*True*	*False*
2		
3		
4		
5		

3 Write your own research report about a machine. Remember to use what you have learned about writing a research report.

Online Practice allows students to practice the writing further.

Lesson Eight Review

Lesson 8 reviews what the students have learnt in the unit. A quiz reviews the unit's story, language, and skills lessons, and a song allows the students to further practice their listening skills whilst reviewing the vocabulary and grammar they have learnt.

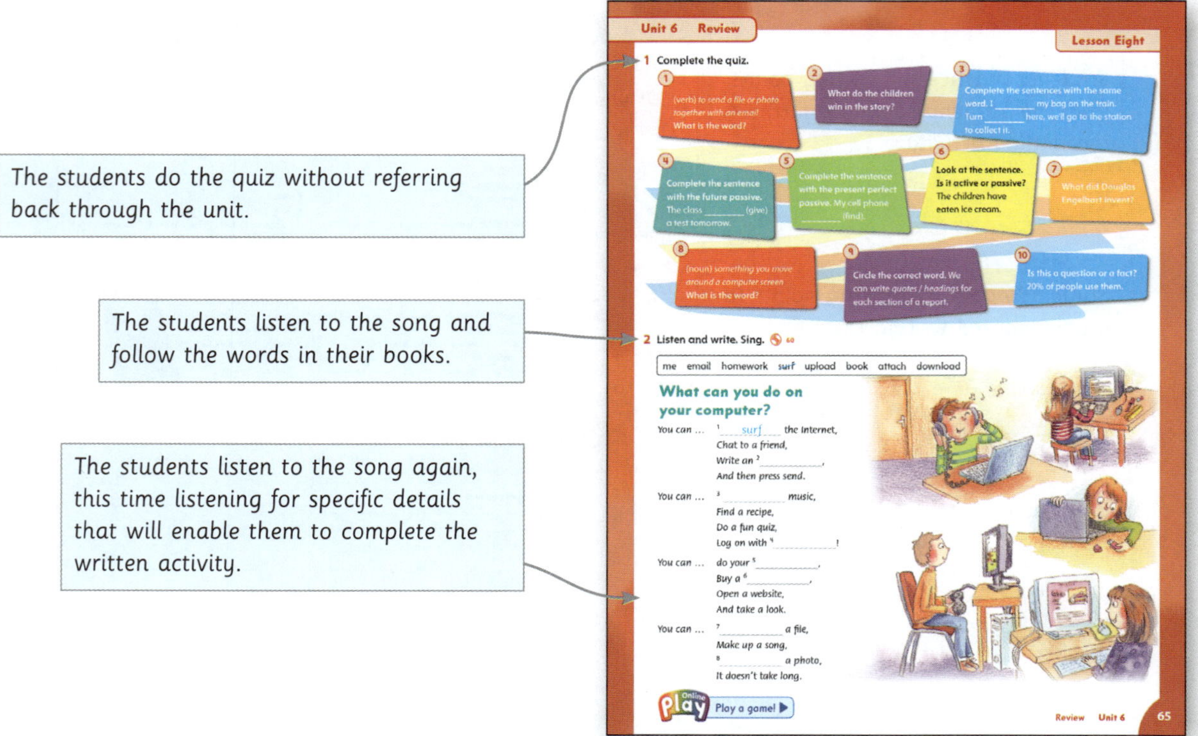

The students do the quiz without referring back through the unit.
The students listen to the song and follow the words in their books.
The students listen to the song again, this time listening for specific details that will enable them to complete the written activity.

Unit 6 Review

Lesson Eight

1 Complete the quiz.

1 (verb) to send a file or photo together with an email What is the word?

2 What do the children win in the story?

3 Complete the sentences with the same word. I ______ my bag on the train. Turn ______ here, we'll go to the station to collect it.

4 Complete the sentence with the future passive. The class ______ (give) a test tomorrow.

5 Complete the sentence with the present perfect passive. My cell phone ______ (find).

6 Look at the sentence. Is it active or passive? The children have eaten ice cream.

7 What did Douglas Engelbart invent?

8 (noun) something you move around a computer screen What is the word?

9 Circle the correct word. We can write quotes / headings for each section of a report.

10 Is this a question or a fact? 20% of people use them.

2 Listen and write. Sing. 60

me email homework surf upload book attach download

What can you do on your computer?

You can … [1] surf the Internet,
Chat to a friend,
Write an [2] ______,
And then press send.

You can … [3] ______ music,
Find a recipe,
Do a fun quiz,
Log on with [4] ______!

You can … do your [5] ______,
Buy a [6] ______,
Open a website,
And take a look.

You can … [7] ______ a file,
Make up a song,
[8] ______ a photo,
It doesn't take long.

Play Play a game!

Review Unit 6 65

Review Quiz

- The quiz provides a fun and motivating activity in which to revise the vocabulary and grammar structures which have been taught in the unit.
- Students work with books open but they are not allowed to refer to the unit when answering the questions.
- Students can do this activity individually, in pairs, or in teams.

Song

- Point to the pictures and ask questions.
- Play the song to the class once. Then play it again as students follow the words in their book.
- Recite the words of the song with the class, without the music. Say each line and ask the students to repeat.
- Now sing the song with the class a number of times with the recording.

Workbook

The students revise all the new structures from the unit in written activities.

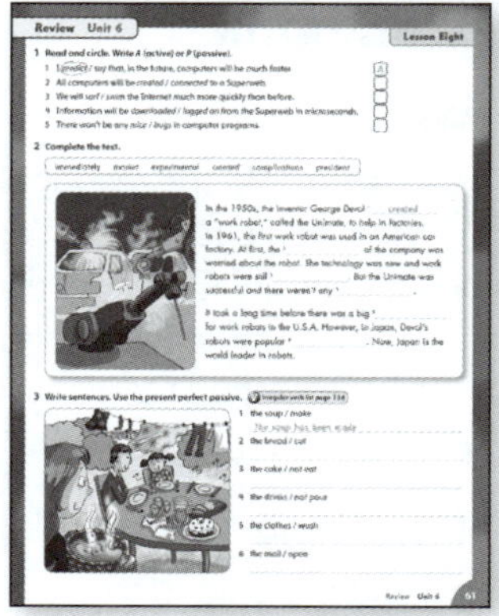

Progress certificate

After every unit and every three units, students self-assess their work by filling in the Progress certificate on the Assessment and Resource CD-ROM.

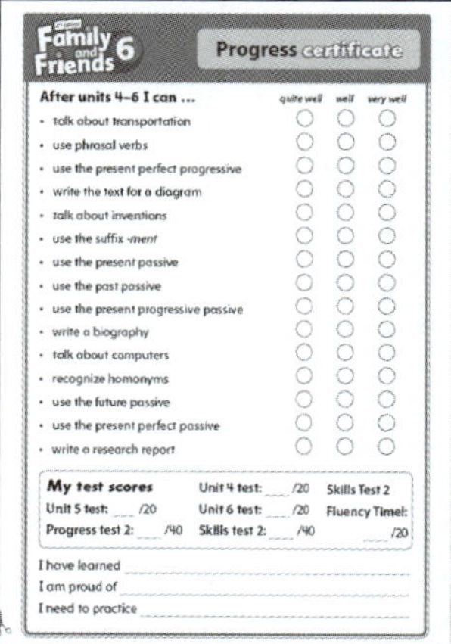

Family and Friends 6 Progress certificate

After units 4–6 I can …	quite well	well	very well
• talk about transportation	○	○	○
• use phrasal verbs	○	○	○
• use the present perfect progressive	○	○	○
• write the text for a diagram	○	○	○
• talk about inventions	○	○	○
• use the suffix *-ment*	○	○	○
• use the present passive	○	○	○
• use the past passive	○	○	○
• use the present progressive passive	○	○	○
• write a biography	○	○	○
• talk about computers	○	○	○
• recognize homonyms	○	○	○
• use the future passive	○	○	○
• use the present perfect passive	○	○	○
• write a research report	○	○	○

My test scores
Unit 4 test: ___ /20 Skills Test 2
Unit 5 test: ___ /20 Unit 6 test: ___ /20 Fluency Timel: ___ /20
Progress test 2: ___ /40 Skills test 2: ___ /40

I have learned ______
I am proud of ______
I need to practice ______

Online Practice allows students to practice the vocabulary further.

Fluency Time! Everyday English

The Fluency Time! lessons come after every three units and focus on developing fluency. The Everyday English lesson provides practice of new language used in functional situations through listening and speaking.

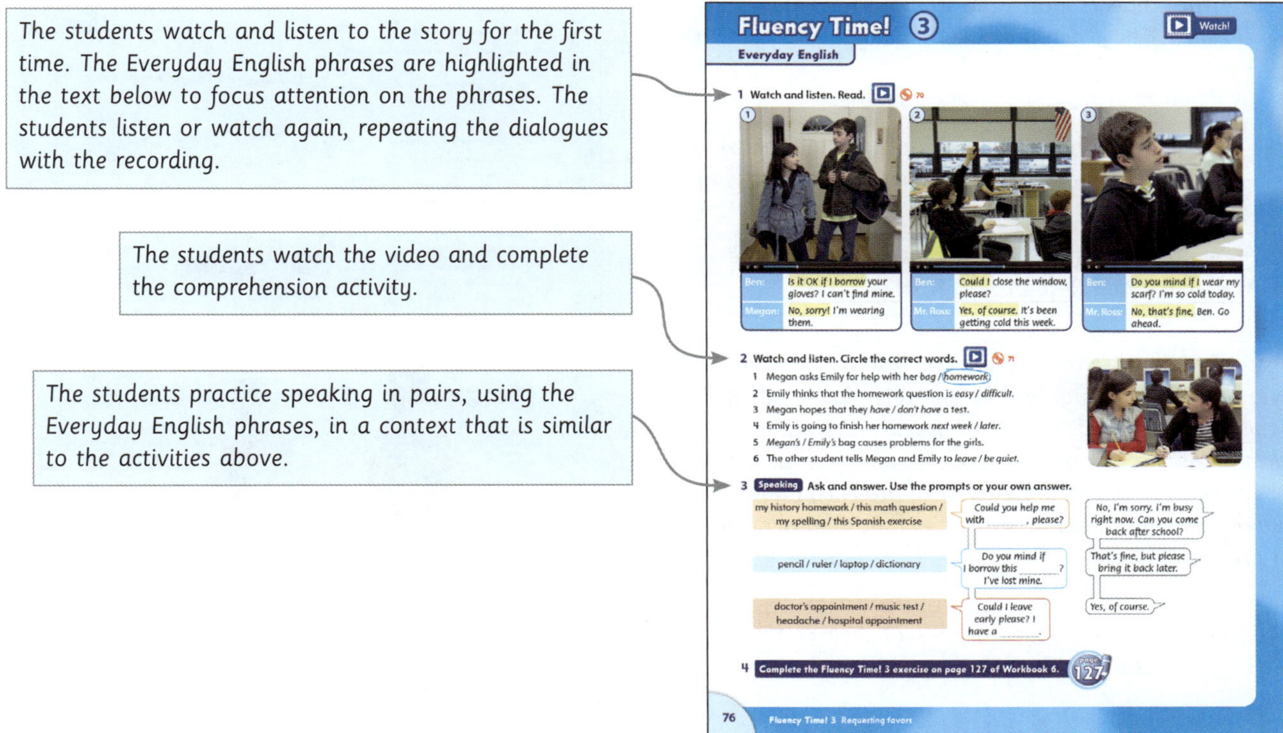

Teaching Everyday English

Story

- Focus on the pictures. Ask students who they can see in the pictures (*Ben and Megan*), where the characters are (*at school/in the classroom*) and what they are doing (*talking or listening in class*).
- Play the video or recording. Students watch, listen, and read. Encourage them to work out unknown words from the context. Answer any questions, then play the recording again, pausing for students to say the dialogue with the recording.
- Go through the highlighted phrases in the box with the class. Make sure they understand the meaning of each phrase and when we would use each phrase.
- Ask students to practice the dialogue in pairs, then invite pairs to act out the dialogue for the class.

Listening

- Focus on the exercise. Ask what they think is happening. Tell students they will watch the video and then complete the exercise.
- Play the recording all the way through, and then play it again, stopping after each question in the exercise is answered to give time for students to circle the correct answer.

Speaking

- Ask a volunteer to act out an example dialogue with you. Read the speech bubbles on the left and ask the volunteer to read out the speech bubbles on the right, choosing an answer for the first speech bubble and completing the gap in the second speech bubble with one of the prompts.
- In pairs, students act out dialogues with their partner.

Workbook

The children practice reading and writing the Everyday English phrases in a new context.

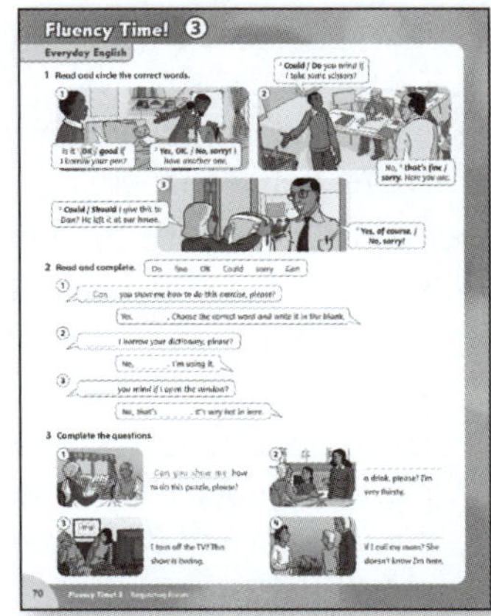

Students do exercises to practice the Everyday English phrases in the Online Practice Fluency section.

Fluency Time! Craft

The Craft lesson provides further and more extended speaking practice of the new language, by making and using a craft activity which is linked directly to the Fluency Time! topic.

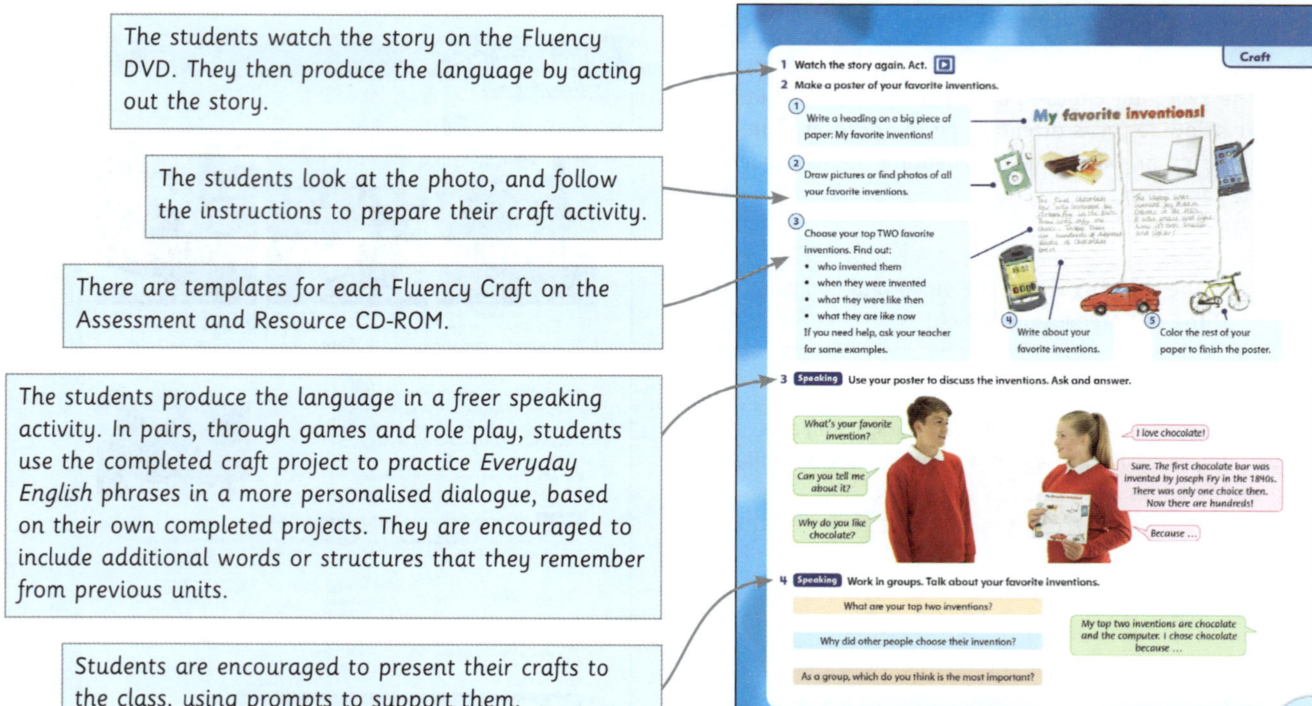

Teaching crafts

Acting out the Story

- Focus on the story in Exercise 1 on Student Book page 76. Ask students what they can remember about the story.
- Play Fluency DVD Fluency Time! 3. If you don't have time for the DVD, read the dialogue on Student Book page 76.
- Invite pairs of students to act out the dialogue. Encourage them to change details to make their own variations of the dialogue.

Craft

- Focus on the picture. Ask students what it shows (a poster of the student's favorite inventions) and what they can see on the poster.
- If you prefer, students can work in pairs to prepare one poster between them.
- Read out the instructions next to the poster in Activity 1.
- Show the class your own completed poster and ask questions about it, e.g. *What are my favorite inventions? Why do you think I chose them?*
- Move around the class as students work, asking questions, e.g. *Why did you choose these inventions? How do they change your life? What would you do without them??*

Speaking

- Focus on the photos. Tell students they are going to use their posters to act out dialogues with a friend. They will take turns to ask about their partner's chosen inventions, then express their opinions about them.
- Act out the example dialogue with a volunteer.
- Students then talk in pairs. Encourage them to compare and contrast different inventions and to express their opinions.
- Ask some pairs to act out dialogues for the class.
- Ask a volunteer to read out the example speech bubble, then invite students to tell the class about their wildlife poster. They can read the questions to help them, or you can ask the questions to prompt them.

Workbook

The students watch the Fluency DVD again and complete the comprehension activities on the DVD practice page.

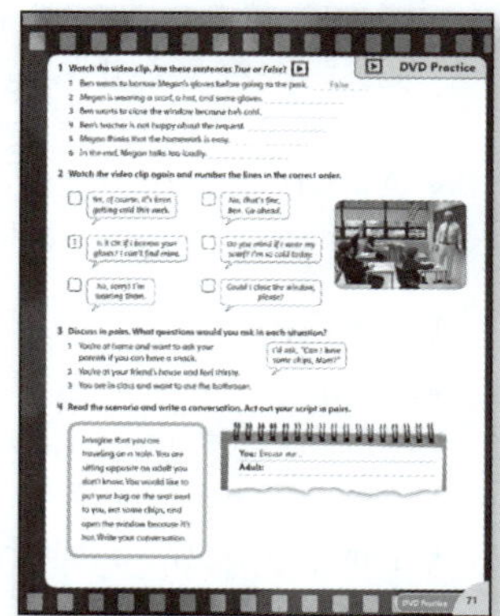

As their level increases, students can use Online Practice to write about their crafts.

History Time! Topic

The subject lessons come after every three units and focus on developing teaching content through English. The Topic lesson introduces new language related to the subject and provides reading and speaking practice.

Students look at the overall topic, including the pictures to understand the type of text they will read and to help them predict words and content about the topic.

Students read and listen to the text for the first time.

Students complete a comprehension task to check their understanding of the information in the text and to focus on the new vocabulary.

Students answer questions related to the topic. These questions invite them to personalize the information they have learnt in the text and to apply critical thinking skills to the topic.

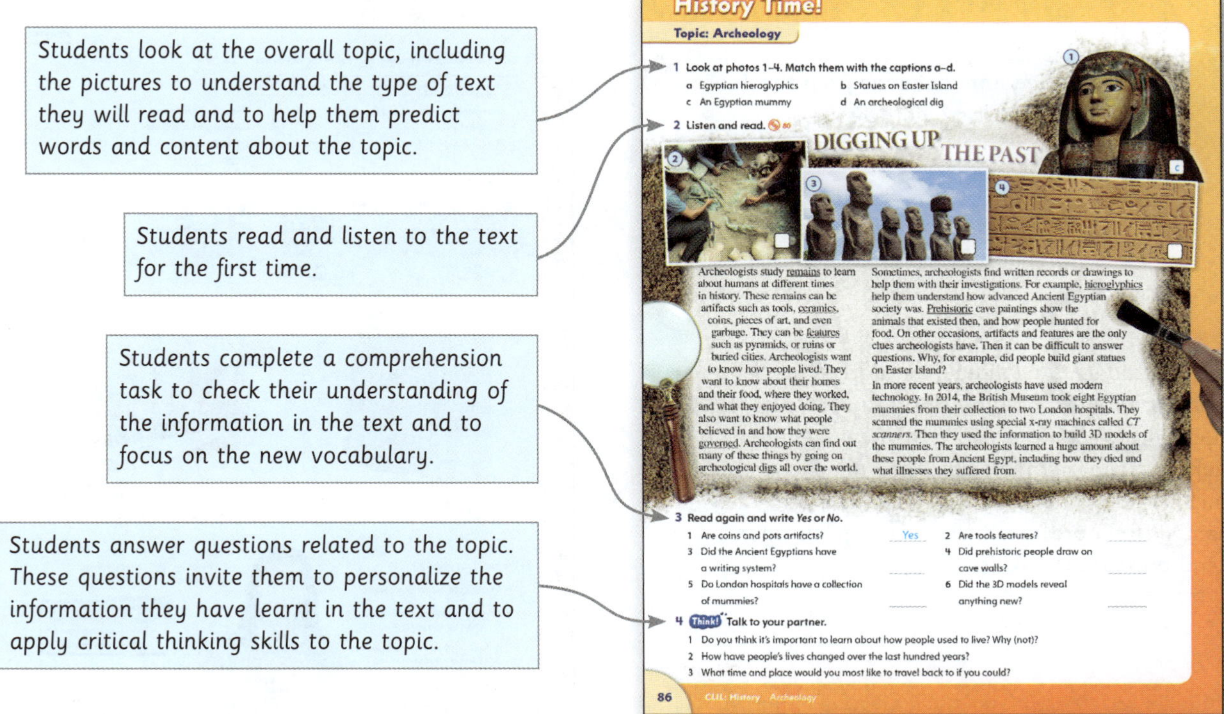

History Time!

Topic: Archeology

1 Look at photos 1–4. Match them with the captions a–d.

a Egyptian hieroglyphics b Statues on Easter Island
c An Egyptian mummy d An archeological dig

2 Listen and read. 80

DIGGING UP THE PAST

Archeologists study remains to learn about humans at different times in history. These remains can be artifacts such as tools, ceramics, coins, pieces of art, and even garbage. They can be features such as pyramids, or ruins or buried cities. Archeologists want to know how people lived. They want to know about their homes and their food, where they worked, and what they enjoyed doing. They also want to know what people believed in and how they were governed. Archeologists can find out many of these things by going on archeological digs all over the world.

Sometimes, archeologists find written records or drawings to help them with their investigations. For example, hieroglyphics help them understand how advanced Ancient Egyptian society was. Prehistoric cave paintings show the animals that existed then, and how people hunted for food. On other occasions, artifacts and features are the only clues archeologists have. Then it can be difficult to answer questions. Why, for example, did people build giant statues on Easter Island?

In more recent years, archeologists have used modern technology. In 2014, the British Museum took eight Egyptian mummies from their collection to two London hospitals. They scanned the mummies using special x-ray machines called *CT scanners*. Then they used the information to build 3D models of the mummies. The archeologists learned a huge amount about these people from Ancient Egypt, including how they died and what illnesses they suffered from.

3 Read again and write *Yes* or *No*.

1 Are coins and pots artifacts? Yes
2 Are tools features? ______
3 Did the Ancient Egyptians have a writing system? ______
4 Did prehistoric people draw on cave walls? ______
5 Do London hospitals have a collection of mummies? ______
6 Did the 3D models reveal anything new? ______

4 Think! Talk to your partner.

1 Do you think it's important to learn about how people used to live? Why (not)?
2 How have people's lives changed over the last hundred years?
3 What time and place would you most like to travel back to if you could?

86 CLIL: History Archeology

Teaching Topic lessons

Pre-reading

- Ask students to look at the pictures. Discuss the type of pictures in the text and how these pictures are related to the heading or title of the text.
- Ask students to match the photos with the captions. Check answers with the class.

Reading

- Use a variety of reading strategies in the different topic lessons. Have students read in pairs or read silently. Once students have read the text through for themselves, ask different students to each read a paragraph in the text aloud for the class.

Vocabulary/comprehension

- Before students complete the exercise ask them to find the words in the text.
- Encourage students to understand the meaning from the context. Tell them to look at the other words before and after the key word, and to read the entire sentence. In this way they can work out the part of speech and infer the general meaning.
- Have students complete the exercise and then check their answers in pairs before checking the answers with the class.

Speaking

- Explain the aim of the questions (to find out about the topic beyond the information given in the text).
- Have students write down the answers to the questions.
- Put students in pairs to discuss their answers, or in small groups for a wider discussion.
- Have pairs say their answers to the class.

Workbook

Students read another text about the same topic, and answer comprehension questions.

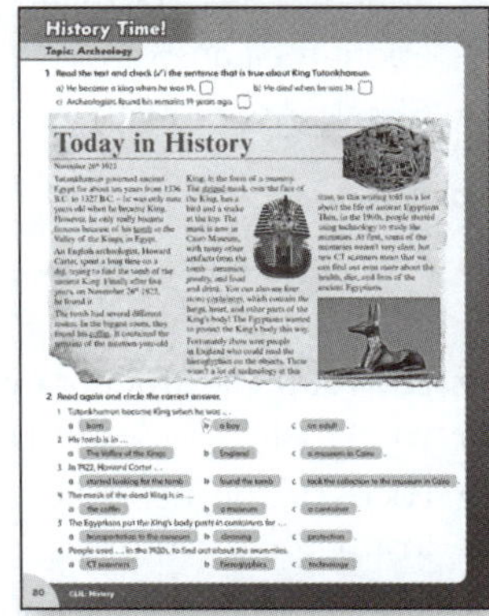

History Time!

Topic: Archeology

Today in History

Online Practice allows students to practice the vocabulary and explore the topic further.

History Time! Project

The Project lesson provides further and more extended speaking practice of the new language, by making and using a project which is linked directly to the topic.

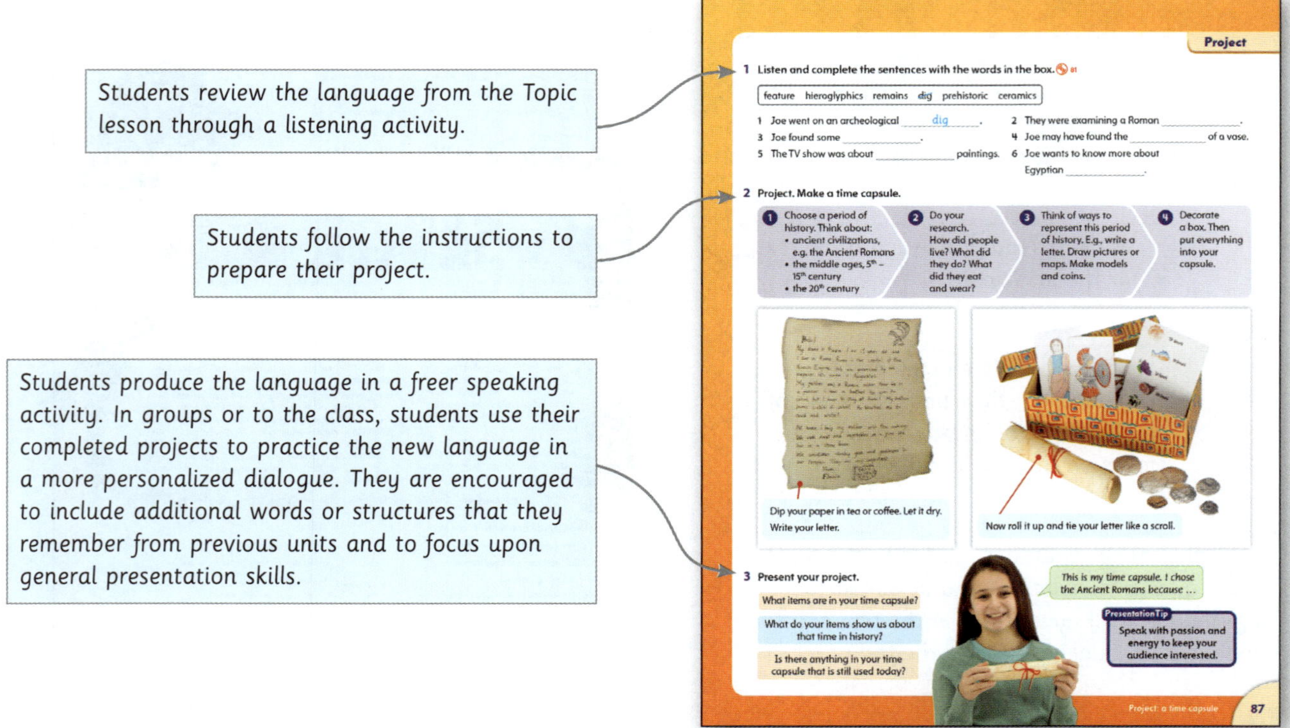

Teaching projects

Listening

- Explain that you are going to play a recording. Make sure students understand what they need to do while they are listening (check boxes, number pictures in the correct order, etc).
- Play the recording once through. Play again, pausing after each item so that students have time to think about their answer.
- Check answers with the class.

Project

- Explain the project to students and make sure they understand what they are going to make.
- Look at the instructions with the class and ask them what materials they will need to complete their project.
- Focus on the instructions. Ask a student to read out the instructions to the class.
- Divide the class into groups and hand out materials for the project. A list of materials for each project is provided in the main teaching notes.
- Move around the class as students work, making sure that they are on task and understand the processes they need to go through to complete their projects successfully.

NOTE: The Teacher's Book contains notes on how to adapt these activities for mixed ability classes.

Speaking

- Put students into pairs or groups. Tell them that they are now going to talk about their project with each other.
- Demonstrate by either holding up a completed project, or using the example in the Student Book. Hold up the project or book and talk about the project, as in the example, pointing to items as you mention them.
- Students work in groups to practice their presentation using the presentation prompts and tip from the Student Book. Encourage students to include language from previous units as they talk about their projects.
- Invite some students to stand up and present their projects to the whole class.

Workbook

Students practice the new vocabulary in a variety of exercises.

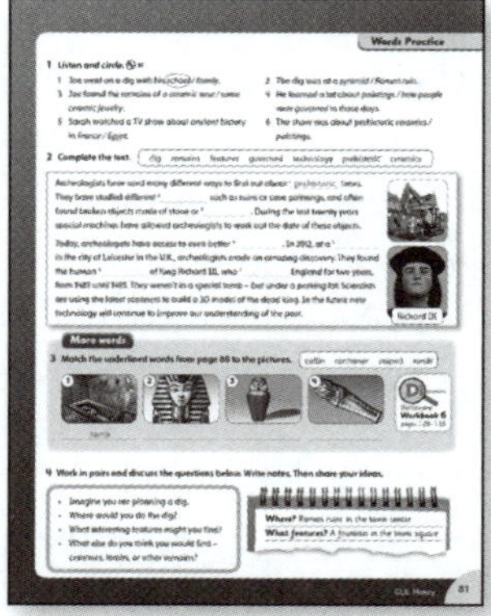

Students can use Online Practice to write about their projects.

Starter Welcome back!

Lesson One SB pages 4–5

Learning outcomes

To remember the characters and events from the DSD Club story

To read and understand a story

To act out a story

Language

Recycled: vocabulary and structures from *American Family and Friends 5*

Materials

CD 01

Oxford iTools Digital classroom • Starter Unit • Story

Warmer

- If this is a new class, ask students to tell you their names, ages, and what they do in their free time.
- Ask students what they remember about the DSD club from Level 5. Ask *Who is in the DSD Club? What does DSD mean? Can you remember what the children from club did together?*
- Ask students to look at the pictures before they read and listen to the story. Ask *What are the names of the children in the pictures? What do you think happens in this episode?*

1 Listen and read. Where does Tom come from?

01

- Play the recording for students to listen and follow along. Ask the gist question for the class to answer.
- Play the recording again. Ask comprehension questions, e.g. *Who are Tom's cousins? What do the children show Tom?*

ANSWER

Tom is from Canada.

2 Listen to the story again and repeat. Act.

- Play the recording again, pausing for students to repeat.
- Divide the class into groups of five to play Fin, Libby, Ed, Kate, and Tom.
- Let students practice acting out the story (see the suggested actions), then ask one or two groups to come to the front to act out the story.

Story actions

Frame 1: Libby enters and waves to Kate and Ed.
Frame 2: Fin extends his hand to introduce Tom.
Frame 3: Libby gestures towards Tom and Kate.
Frame 4: Kate and Libby point to the pictures.
Frames 5–8: The children point to other pictures.
Frame 9: Fin gives Tom his DSD Club T-shirt and cap.
Frame 10: The children cheer.

3 Read again and write *True* or *False*.

- Look at the example. Ask students to find the part of the story which says Ed and Kate went on vacation to Florida.
- Students read the sentences and write *True* or *False*.

Differentiation

Below level:

- Ask students to read the sentences aloud and then work together to find the answers in the story.
- Monitor and help as needed.

At level:

- Students complete the activity.

Above level:

- Students rewrite the false sentences to make them true.
- If time permits, students can come to the front and retell a short version of the story to the class.

ANSWERS

1. True 2. False 3. True 4. True 5. True 6. False

Further practice

Workbook pages 2–3

Online Practice • Starter • Lesson One

Lesson Two Grammar 1

PROFESSOR & CHIP

1 Listen and read. Where did Professor go? 02

2 Read and learn.

Simple present and present progressive	Simple past and past progressive
Use the simple present to talk about habits and routines. I go there every year. It's always great! Use the present progressive to talk about actions happening now. What are you doing? I'm looking for your present.	Use the simple past to talk about actions that interrupted other actions in the past. When I was sitting on the plane, it said hello to the man next to me! Use the past progressive to talk about actions that were interrupted. When I was walking around, I saw this.

3 Read and circle.

1 I go / *am going* swimming on Saturday mornings.
2 My brother *watches / is watching* TV right now.
3 My mom and dad *work / are working* every day.
4 We *have / are having* lunch now.
5 The boys *play / are playing* soccer in the park on Saturdays.
6 The children *work / are working* hard right now.

4 Speaking Ask and answer.

eat / ice cream play / soccer sit / on the grass

wait / for a bus go / into a café run / home

6 Starter Simple present, present progressive, simple past, and past progressive

Lesson Two SB page 6

Learning outcomes

- To use the simple present to talk about habits and routines
- To use the present progressive to talk about actions happening now
- To use the simple past to talk about actions that interrupted other actions in the past
- To use the past progressive to talk about actions that were interrupted
- Speaking: asking and answering questions about actions in the past

Language

Core: *I go there every year. It's always great. What are you doing? I'm looking for your present. When I was sitting on the plane, it said hello to the man next to me! When I was walking around, I saw this.*

Extra: *convention*

Materials

CD  02

Oxford iTools Digital classroom • Starter Unit • Grammar 1

Warmer

- Play *Twenty, twenty* (see page 9) with the word *robot*.
- Tell students they are going to read a story about the Professor and his robot, Chip. Ask what they remember about Professor and Chip from Level 5.

1 Listen and read. Where did Professor go? 02

- Ask students to look at the pictures. Point to each one and ask *What can you see?*
- Play the recording. Students listen and follow along. Ask *Where did Professor go?*
- Play it again. Ask comprehension questions, e.g. *How often does Professor go to the robot convention? What does Professor have for Chip?*

ANSWER

Professor went to the robot convention.

2 Read and learn.

- Ask about students' habits and routines, e.g. *When do you get up in the morning? How often do you go to the library?*
- Ask students to tell you what is happening right now in the classroom. Write some of their answers on the board as examples of present progressive sentences.
- Read the second box with the class.
- Write examples of sentences using the simple past and past progressive to show that one action has been interrupted by another: *While I was reading my book, Leyla phoned. When Mom was cooking dinner, Dad arrived home.*
- Read each sentence to the class. Ask *What was happening first? What interrupted the action?*

3 Read and circle.

- Before students look at the exercise in their books, copy the example onto the board. Ask students which form of the verb is needed and circle it.
- Students read the sentences and circle the correct form.

ANSWERS

1. go 2. is watching 3. work 4. are having
5. play 6. are working

4 Ask and answer.

- Ask students to look at the pictures. Explain that the first picture shows what the people were doing before the storm started, and the second shows what they did next.
- Students work in pairs. Student A chooses one of the people in the pictures. Student B asks the questions from the example. Student A uses the word prompts to answer the questions using the past progressive and the simple past. The partner then identifies the person.

Differentiation

Below level:

- Practice making sentences with the simple past and past progressive using the words in the boxes. Then have students look at number 1 on the left. Ask *What was he doing when the storm started?* Elicit the answer. Move on to number 1 on the right. Ask *What did he do next?* Elicit the answer. Put students in pairs to complete the activity.

At level:

- Students complete the activity.

Above level:

- Have students imagine there is one more picture. Students should ask *What did he do after that?* to extend the activity.

Further practice

Workbook page 4

Online Practice • Starter Unit • Lesson Two

Lesson Three Grammar 2

Irregular past forms

With some irregular verbs, the simple past and the past participle are the same.

	Verb	Past tense	Past participle
1	buy	bought	bought
2	hear		
3	make		
4	use		
5	keep		
6	have		
7	catch		
8	get		
9	find		

With other irregular verbs, the simple past and the past participle are different.

	Verb	Past tense	Past participle
1	speak	spoke	spoken
2	grow		
3	take		
4	wear		
5	write		
6	fly		
7	eat		
8	see		
9	go		

1 Complete the charts. V Irregular verb list Workbook 6 page 136

2 Listen and order the lines. Sing. 03

Welcome back!

1 You're back from your break in the sun.
__ And there's lots of work in store.
__ Now it's back to school once more
__ You're sad your vacation's done.

1 You had a good time by the sea
__ With your friends and your family.
__ But you can still have some fun,
__ Now your lessons have begun.

1 You visited people you knew,
__ So welcome back today.
__ You went on a picnic or two.
__ But you knew you couldn't stay,

Irregular past forms and song Starter 7

Lesson Three 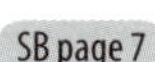 SB page 7

Learning outcomes

To write the simple past forms of common irregular verbs

To write the past participles of common irregular verbs

Language

Core: Simple past and past participles of: *buy, hear, make, use, keep, have, catch, get, find, speak, grow, take, wear, write, fly, eat, see, go*

Extra: funfair

Materials

CD 03

Oxford iTools Digital classroom • Starter Unit • Grammar 2

Warmer

- Ask students *What is a past participle? When do we use past participles?* Write the following verbs on the board: *eat, speak, make, use, have, go, wear, write.* Ask *What's the past participle?*

1 Complete the charts.

- Ask students to look at the charts in their books. Read the explanation and examples to the class. Tell students there is no rule for deciding which verbs have the same simple past and past participle forms, they have to be learned.
- Ask students to complete the charts with the past tenses and participles of each verb. Remind them to use the verb list on Workbook page 136.

Differentiation

Below level:

- Try eliciting the past tense from students by saying *Yesterday I …* and the past participle with *I have …* Help students to form the first three verbs in the left column. Ask them how to spell each and write them on the board. Do the same for the second column. Monitor and help as needed.

At level:

- Split the class into teams. Tell students you are going to say a verb and ask for the past tense or the past participle. If a child knows the answer, he or she has to stand up. Whoever stands up first and says the correct answer gets a point. The team with the most points wins.

Above level:

- Put students into pairs. Ask them to take out their Workbooks and turn to page 136. One child says the base form, and the other child recalls the other two forms. Then they switch for even practice. Monitor students' work.

ANSWERS

Verb	Past tense	Past part.	Verb	Past tense	Past part.
1 buy	bought	bought	1 speak	spoke	spoken
2 hear	heard	heard	2 grow	grew	grown
3 make	made	made	3 take	took	taken
4 use	used	used	4 wear	wore	worn
5 keep	kept	kept	5 write	wrote	written
6 have	had	had	6 fly	flew	flown
7 catch	caught	caught	7 eat	ate	eaten
8 get	got	got	8 see	saw	seen
9 find	found	found	9 go	went	gone

2 Listen and order the lines. Sing. 03

- Focus students' attention on the pictures. Point to each one and ask *What are the children doing?*
- Tell students that the words to the song are in their books but the lines are in the wrong order.
- Ask students to read through the words silently.
- Play the song. Students listen and point to each line as they hear it.
- Play the song again, pausing for students to number the lines.
- Play it a third time for students to check answers.
- Go through the answers. Ask a different student to read each line in the order that they heard it.
- Play the recording once more for students to sing along.

ANSWERS

Verse 1: 1, 4, 3, 2

Verse 2: 1, 2, 4, 3

Verse 3: 1, 3, 4, 2

Further practice

Workbook page 5

Starter test, Assessment and Resource CD-ROM

Online Practice • Starter Unit • Lesson Three

1 Art project!

1 Art project!

Lesson One Story

1 Listen and read. What is the theme for the mural? 04

2 Listen to the story again and repeat. Act.

3 Read again and write *True* or *False*.

1 The children are going to paint the walls. True
2 The theme is "Around the world." ______
3 Kate is good at drawing animals. ______
4 Ed wants to draw people. ______
5 Libby likes Kate's idea. ______
6 The children are going to meet the next day. ______

8 Unit 1 Art project!

Lesson One  SB page 8

Story

Learning outcomes

To read and understand a story

To act out a story

Language

Introducing core vocabulary (Lesson 2) through a story

Extra: *theme, impossible, flag*

Materials

CD 04

 Oxford iTools Digital classroom • Unit 1 • Story

Warmer

- Ask students to look at the story without reading. Discuss the characters together. Ask different students to choose one character and tell you all they can about him / her.
- Ask students to look again at the pictures in the story. What do they think the story is going to be about? Ask *Where are the children?*

1 Listen and read. What is the theme for the mural? 04

- Teach the word *mural*. Ask prediction questions for children to think about as they listen, e.g. *Where are the children going to paint the mural? Do the children know what to paint?*
- Play the recording. Students listen and follow along. Ask the gist question *What is the theme for the mural?* for the class to answer.

ANSWER

The theme for the mural is "Around the world."

- Play the recording a second time. Ask comprehension questions, e.g. *Why are the DSD Club going to paint murals? Do the children decide on what they are going to paint?*

2 Listen to the story again and repeat. Act.

- Play the recording again, pausing for students to repeat.
- Divide the class into groups of five to play Fin, Libby, Ed, Kate, and Tom.
- Students practice acting out the story.
- Ask one or two groups to act out the story for the class.

3 Read again and write *True* or *False*.

- Ask students to read the story again without the CD. Look at the example. Ask *Are the children going to paint the walls?* Establish that the statement is true.
- Students read the sentences and write *True* or *False*.

Differentiation

Below level:

- Ask students to read the sentences aloud and then work together to find the answers in the story. Monitor and help as needed.

At level:

- Students complete the activity.

Above level:

- Students rewrite the false sentences to make them true. If time permits, students can come to the front and retell a short version of the story to the class.

ANSWERS

1. True 2. True 3. False 4. True 5. False 6. True

Further practice

Workbook page 6

Online Practice • Unit 1 • Story

Lesson Two Words

1 Listen and repeat. 05

2 Write the words.

1 painting *noun* a picture that someone has painted
2 ______ *noun* a building where you can go to look at paintings and other art
3 ______ *noun* a picture of a person
4 ______ *noun* a picture of the countryside
5 ______ *noun* the part of a picture that looks like it's near you
6 ______ *noun* the part of a picture that looks like it's far from you
7 ______ *noun* an animal, a shape, or a person made from stone, wood, etc.
8 ______ *noun* a very big picture painted on a wall

Working with words

We add the prefixes *un-* or *im-* to some adjectives to make the meaning negative.

positive	popular	friendly	happy	patient	possible	polite
negative	unpopular	unfriendly	unhappy	impatient	impossible	impolite

Dictionary Workbook 6 pages 128–135

3 Listen and repeat. 06

4 Read and circle.

1 Tom is very *friendly / unfriendly*. He never speaks to anyone.
2 My sister is very *popular / unpopular*. Everyone likes her.
3 Jon is a very *polite / impolite* boy. He always says "please" and "thank you."
4 My little brother is very *patient / impatient*. He always waits calmly.
5 This math question is *possible / impossible*! I don't know the answer!

Words Unit 1 9

Lesson Two SB page 9

Words

Learning outcomes

To identify different words related to art

To use prefixes *un-* and *im-* to make words negative

Language

Words: *art gallery, mural, painting, portrait, landscape, background, foreground, sculpture*

Working with words: *popular / unpopular, friendly / unfriendly, happy / unhappy, patient / impatient, possible / impossible, polite / impolite* (Student Book); *lucky / unlucky, happy / unhappy, mature / immature, interesting / uninteresting* (Workbook)

Materials

CD 05–06 Dictionary Workbook pages 128–135; examples of different artwork taken from magazines or printed out from the Internet (optional)

Oxford iTools Digital classroom • Unit 1 • Words

Warmer

- Ask students to imagine they are going to visit an art gallery. Ask *What are you going to see?* Encourage students to make a lot of suggestions, to elicit art-related vocabulary. Write the words on the board.

1 Listen and repeat. 05

- Focus attention on the picture. Ask students if they see any of the things mentioned in the warm-up activity.
- Play the recording, pausing for students to repeat chorally.
- Play it a second time for students to repeat again.
- Ask individual students to say the words for the class.

NOTE: Remind students to consult the Dictionary pages in their Workbooks when completing Exercise 2.

2 Write the words.

- Ask students to read the definitions and write the correct words from Exercise 1 for each one.
- Check the answers and pronunciation with the class.

ANSWERS

1. painting 2. art gallery 3. portrait 4. landscape 5. foreground 6. background 7. sculpture 8. mural

3 Listen and repeat. 06

- Focus attention on the words in the box. Ask a student to read the explanation. Compare the words in the first and second rows. Ask *How do we make "popular" negative?*
- Make sure the students understand that adding the prefixes changes the adjectives to the negative. Establish that these prefixes don't work with all adjectives.
- Play the recording. Students repeat chorally.
- Play it a second time. Students listen and repeat again.
- Ask individual students to say the words. Ask questions, e.g. *What's the negative form of popular / patient / happy?*

4 Read and circle.

- Ask students to look at the instructions and say what they have to do. Look at the example to demonstrate how they should read the sentence and circle the correct word.
- Ask different students to read the sentences.

Differentiation

Below level:

- Ask students to read the second sentence of number 1 aloud. Ask students if this sounds like a friendly or unfriendly person. Elicit the answer. Students work in pairs to complete the activity. Encourage students to use the Dictionary in their Workbooks, if needed.

At level:

- Students complete the activity.

Above level:

- After students complete the activity, ask them to imagine that the opposite answer is true. Rewrite the second sentences to match, e.g. *Tom is very friendly. He speaks to everyone.*

ANSWERS

1. unfriendly 2. popular 3. polite 4. patient 5. impossible

NOTE: Students now do the tasks on Workbook page 7. Go through the exercises with them first if necessary. Remind students to consult the Workbook Dictionary pages.

Further practice

Workbook page 7

Online Practice • Unit 1 • Words

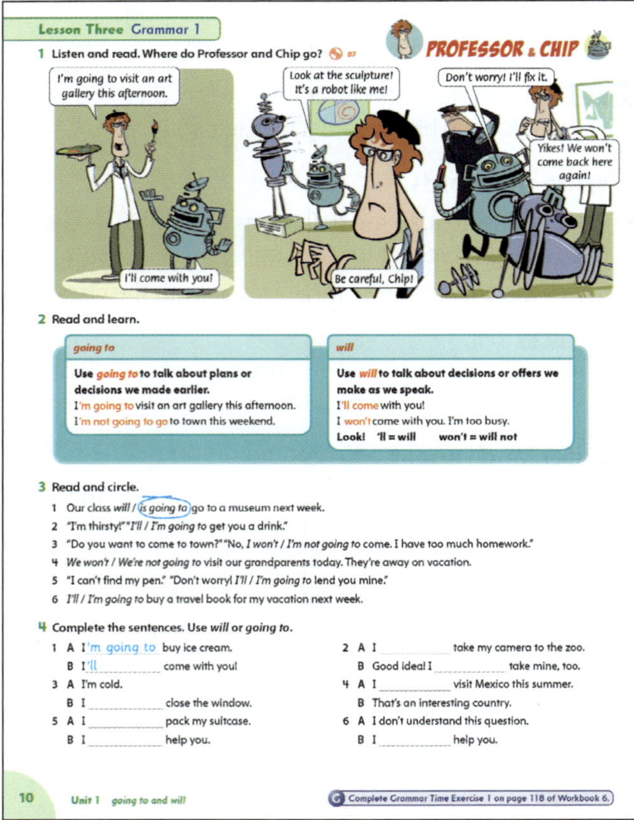
Lesson Three Grammar 1

1 Listen and read. Where do Professor and Chip go? 07

PROFESSOR & CHIP

2 Read and learn.

going to	*will*
Use *going to* to talk about plans or decisions we made earlier.	**Use *will* to talk about decisions or offers we make as we speak.**
I'm going to visit an art gallery this afternoon.	I'll come with you!
I'm not going to go to town this weekend.	I won't come with you. I'm too busy.
	Look! 'll = will won't = will not

3 Read and circle.

1 Our class *will* / *is going to* go to a museum next week.
2 "I'm thirsty!" "*I'll* / *I'm going to* get you a drink."
3 "Do you want to come to town?" "No, *I won't* / *I'm not going to* come. I have too much homework."
4 *We won't* / *We're not going to* visit our grandparents today. They're away on vacation.
5 "I can't find my pen." "Don't worry! *I'll* / *I'm going to* lend you mine."
6 *I'll* / *I'm going to* buy a travel book for my vacation next week.

4 Complete the sentences. Use *will* or *going to*.

1 A I'm going to buy ice cream.
B I'll come with you!
2 A I ______ take my camera to the zoo.
B Good idea! I ______ take mine, too.
3 A I'm cold.
B I ______ close the window.
4 A I ______ visit Mexico this summer.
B That's an interesting country.
5 A I ______ pack my suitcase.
B I ______ help you.
6 A I don't understand this question.
B I ______ help you.

10 Unit 1 *going to and will*

Complete Grammar Time Exercise 1 on page 118 of Workbook 6.

Lesson Three SB page 10

Grammar 1

Learning outcomes

To use *going to* to talk about plans and decisions made earlier

To use *will* to talk about decisions or offers made as we speak

Language

Core: *I'm going to visit an art gallery this afternoon. I'm not going to go to town this weekend. I'll come with you! I won't come with you. I'm too busy.*

Materials

CD 07

 Oxford iTools Digital classroom • Unit 1 • Grammar 1

Warmer

- Play *A long sentence* (see page 8) to energize the class and review vocabulary from the previous lesson. Begin with *I'm going to the art gallery to see some portraits.*
- Review future tenses with the class. Ask *Which tenses can we use to talk about the future?* Tell students that they are going to look at *going to* and *will*.

1 Listen and read. Where do Professor and Chip go? 07

- Ask students to look at the pictures. Ask *Who can you see?* Encourage students to tell you what they remember about Professor and Chip.
- Play the recording for students to follow in their books.
- Ask the class *Where do Professor and Chip go?*

ANSWER

Professor and Chip go to an art gallery.

- Play the recording again. Ask students to listen for examples of *going to* and *will*.

2 Read and learn.

- Focus on the grammar box. Ask one student to read out the rules for going to, and another to read out the rules for will.
- Ask students to look at the picture story in Exercise 1 again and point to examples of *going to* and *will*. Go through them together. Ask *Why do we use going to / will here?*

3 Read and circle.

- Read the instructions and ask students to say what they have to do. Look at the example together.
- Ask students to read the sentences and circle the answers.
- Review the answers together. Ask different students to read the sentences.

ANSWERS

1. is going to 2. I'll 3. I won't 4. We're not going to
5. I'll 6. I'm going to

4 Complete the sentences. Use *will* or *going to*.

- Focus on the example. Ask two children to read parts A and B of the dialogue.
- Ask students to read the rest of the dialogues and complete the sentences with the correct forms of going to or will.
- Go through the answers with the class, asking different students to read the completed dialogues.

Differentiation

Below level:

- Look at the example again. Ask if the decisions were made earlier or now. Elicit the answers.
- Then ask students to look at 2A and ask when the decision was made. Elicit *earlier*.
- Ask students if they should use *will* or *going to*. Elicit *going to*. Help students form the answer. Then they complete the activity. Monitor and help as needed.

At level:

- Students complete the activity.

Above level:

- Ask students if they have any plans this week, and have them write sentences with *going to* about them. Then students share their sentences with a partner. The partner should say *I'll / I won't come with you.*

ANSWERS

1. 'm going to; I'll 2. 'm going to; 'll 3. 'll
4. 'm going to 5. 'm going to, 'll 6. 'll

NOTE: Ask students to complete the first Grammar Time task on page 118 of the Workbook. See page 7 of the introduction for suggestions of how these tasks should be used.

Further practice

Grammar Time, Workbook page 118
Workbook page 8
Online Practice • Unit 1 • Grammar 1

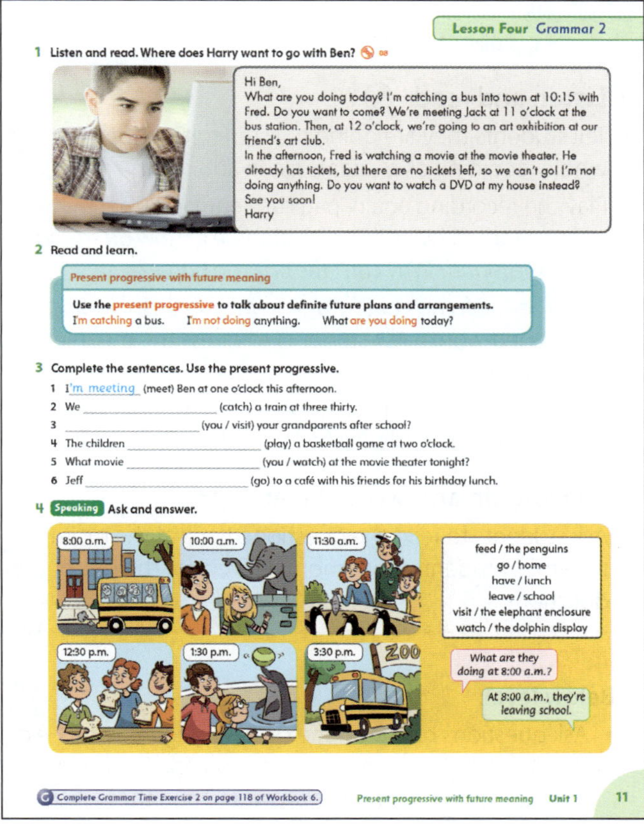

Lesson Four Grammar 2

1 Listen and read. Where does Harry want to go with Ben? 08

Hi Ben,
What are you doing today? I'm catching a bus into town at 10:15 with Fred. Do you want to come? We're meeting Jack at 11 o'clock at the bus station. Then, at 12 o'clock, we're going to an art exhibition at our friend's art club.
In the afternoon, Fred is watching a movie at the movie theater. He already has tickets, but there are no tickets left, so we can't go! I'm not doing anything. Do you want to watch a DVD at my house instead?
See you soon!
Harry

2 Read and learn.

Present progressive with future meaning

Use the present progressive to talk about definite future plans and arrangements.
I'm catching a bus. I'm not doing anything. What are you doing today?

3 Complete the sentences. Use the present progressive.

1 I'm meeting (meet) Ben at one o'clock this afternoon.
2 We ________ (catch) a train at three thirty.
3 ________ (you / visit) your grandparents after school?
4 The children ________ (play) a basketball game at two o'clock.
5 What movie ________ (you / watch) at the movie theater tonight?
6 Jeff ________ (go) to a café with his friends for his birthday lunch.

4 Speaking Ask and answer.

Complete Grammar Time Exercise 2 on page 118 of Workbook 6.

Present progressive with future meaning Unit 1 11

Lesson Four SB page 11

Grammar 2

Learning outcomes

To use the present progressive with future meaning

Speaking: asking and answering questions about what people are doing at specific times in the future

Language

Core: *We're meeting at ten o'clock. I'm not doing anything. What are they doing at 8.00 a.m.? At 8.00 a.m., they're leaving school.*

Extra: *art exhibition, display*

Materials

CD 08; a piece of paper for each group (optional)

Oxford iTools Digital classroom • Unit 1 • Grammar 2

Warmer

- Ask students to look at the photograph. Ask *What's the boy doing? Who do you think he's writing to?*
- Ask *Do you send a lot of emails? How many emails do you send a week? What do you email your friends about?*

1 Listen and read. Where does Harry want to go with Ben? 08

- Play the recording. The class follows along. Ask the gist question.

ANSWER

Harry wants to go into town with Ben.

- Play the recording again. Ask comprehension questions, e.g. *Who is Harry going into town with? Where are they meeting Jack?*

2 Read and learn.

- Focus on the grammar box. Ask a student to read the explanation and the examples.
- Ask *How do we form the present progressive? What do we put before the main verb? What do we add to the end of the main verb?*
- Ask students to look at Exercise 1 again and find examples of the present progressive. Write gapped sentences on the board, e.g. *I ________ (go) to the movies tomorrow. I ________ (meeting) my friend after school.*
- Invite different students to the front and complete the sentences using the present progressive form of the verb in brackets.

3 Complete the sentences. Use the present progressive.

- Ask a student to read the example for the class.
- Ask students to complete the rest of the sentences with the present progressive.

ANSWERS

1. 'm meeting 2. 're catching 3. Are you visiting
4. are playing 5. are you watching 6. is going

4 Ask and answer.

- Ask two students to read the example question and answer to the class.
- Students work in pairs. They take turns asking questions about what the children are doing at the different times.

Differentiation

Below level:

- Students first practice making sentences in pairs. Then they practice the example question and answer as a group. Switch the pairs and students complete the activity.

At level:

- Students complete the activity.

Above level:

- Ask students to draw more pictures, e.g. 7:00 a.m., 5:00 p.m. Switch partners. Students practice asking and answering again. Monitor and help as needed.

ANSWERS

What are they doing at …?

1. At 8:00 a.m., they're leaving school.
2. At 10:00 a.m., they're visiting the elephant enclosure.
3. At 11:30 a.m., they're feeding the penguins.
4. At 12:30 p.m., they're having lunch.
5. At 1:30 p.m., they're watching the dolphin display.
6. At 3:30 p.m., they're going home.

Further practice

Grammar Time, Workbook page 118

Workbook page 9

Unit 1 Language practice worksheet, Assessment and Resource CD-ROM

Online Practice • Unit 1 • Grammar 2

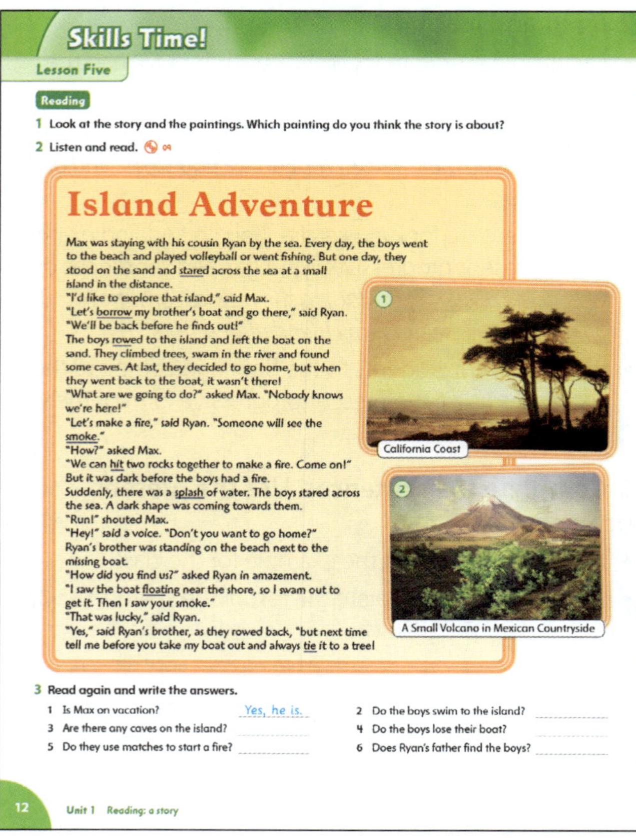

Skills Time!

Lesson Five

Reading

1 Look at the story and the paintings. Which painting do you think the story is about?

2 Listen and read. 09

Island Adventure

Max was staying with his cousin Ryan by the sea. Every day, the boys went to the beach and played volleyball or went fishing. But one day, they stood on the sand and stared across the sea at a small island in the distance.
"I'd like to explore that island," said Max.
"Let's borrow my brother's boat and go there," said Ryan. "We'll be back before he finds out!"
The boys rowed to the island and left the boat on the sand. They climbed trees, swam in the river and found some caves. At last, they decided to go home, but when they went back to the boat, it wasn't there!
"What are we going to do?" asked Max. "Nobody knows we're here!"
"Let's make a fire," said Ryan. "Someone will see the smoke."
"How?" asked Max.
"We can hit two rocks together to make a fire. Come on!"
But it was dark before the boys had a fire.
Suddenly, there was a splash of water. The boys stared across the sea. A dark shape was coming towards them.
"Run!" shouted Max.
"Hey!" said a voice. "Don't you want to go home?"
Ryan's brother was standing on the beach next to the missing boat.
"How did you find us?" asked Ryan in amazement.
"I saw the boat floating near the shore, so I swam out to get it. Then I saw your smoke."
"That was lucky," said Ryan.
"Yes," said Ryan's brother, as they rowed back, "but next time tell me before you take my boat out and always tie it to a tree!

1 California Coast

2 A Small Volcano in Mexican Countryside

3 Read again and write the answers.

1 Is Max on vacation? Yes, he is.
2 Do the boys swim to the island? ....
3 Are there any caves on the island? ....
4 Do the boys lose their boat? ....
5 Do they use matches to start a fire? ....
6 Does Ryan's father find the boys? ....

12 Unit 1 Reading: a story

Lesson Five SB page 12

Skills Time!

Skills development

Reading: read and understand an extract from a story
Reading: work out the meaning of new words from the context

Language

Recycled: vocabulary and structures seen previously

Extra: *stare, in the distance, borrow, row, smoke, hit, splash, missing, float (v), tie (v)*

Materials

CD 09; photocopies of landscape paintings by different artists (optional)

Oxford iTools Digital classroom • Unit 1 • Reading

Warmer

- Hold up a photocopy of a landscape painting so all the students can see it. Ask students *What can you see? Where do you think this place is? What do you think might happen here?*
- Ask students to look at the pictures. Ask questions about each one, e.g. *What can you see? Where is it?*

1 Look at the story and the paintings. Which painting do you think the story is about?

- Ask students to look at the pictures again. Tell them to skim the text to find out which painting the story is about. Tell them not to worry if they don't understand the meaning of all the words for now.

ANSWER

The story is about picture 1.

2 Listen and read. 09

- Tell students they are going to listen to the story. Play the whole recording as students listen and read.
- Play the recording again, pausing regularly. Check understanding by asking questions, e.g. *How do the boys get to the island? Why can't the boys go home?*
- Elicit the meanings of any unknown words, including the underlined words. Ask students to guess the meaning from context.
- Play the recording again. Focus on the pronunciation of the underlined words. Pause for students to repeat.

3 Read again and write the answers.

- Ask students to read the questions. Look at the example together. Students write short answers for the rest of the questions.

Differentiation

Below level:

- Ask questions based on the questions in Activity 3, e.g. *Where is Max? How do they get to the island?* Students look at the text to find the answers. Then they complete the activity independently.

At level:

- Ask students to re-read the text. Write these sentences on the board. Students say if they are true or false. *Max was staying with his cousin. (T) / The boys played on the beach every day. (T) / Lots of people lived on the island. (F) / The boat didn't belong to the boys. (T) / The boys left the boat in the water. (F) / The boys explored the island. (T) / The boys used matches to make a fire. (F) / Jeff's brother didn't see the smoke from the fire. (F)*

Above level:

- Let students complete the activity, then check answers. If the answer is *No*, encourage students to give the correct answer.
- Ask students to think about what kind of adventure Max and Ryan would have if the story were about picture 2. Put students into groups to write a short paragraph.

ANSWERS

1. Yes, he is.
2. No, they don't. (They row a boat to the island.)
3. Yes, there are.
4. Yes, they do.
5. No, they don't. (They hit two rocks together to make a fire.)
6. No, he doesn't. (Jeff's brother finds them.)

Further practice

Workbook page 10

Online Practice • Unit 1 • Reading

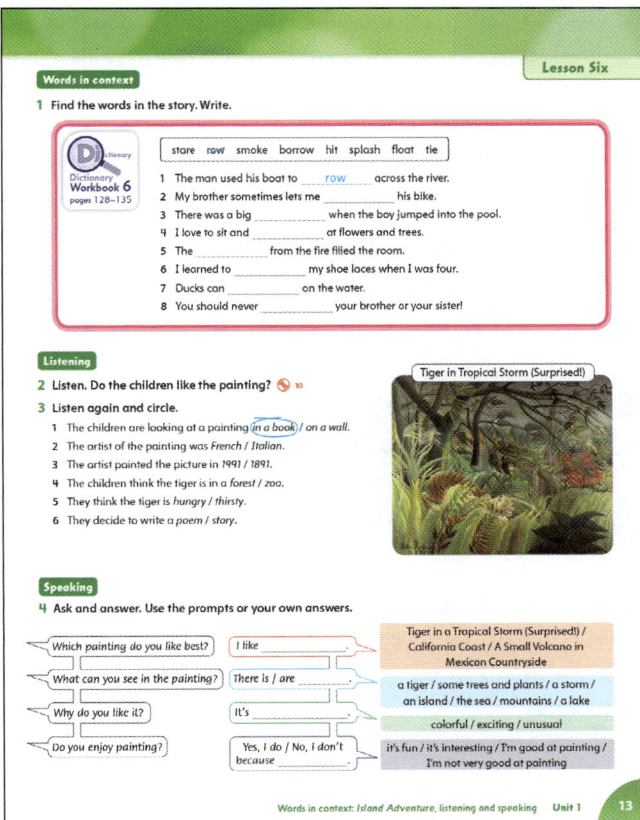

Lesson Six

Words in context

1 Find the words in the story. Write.

Dictionary Workbook 6 pages 128–135

stare row smoke borrow hit splash float tie

1 The man used his boat to row across the river.
2 My brother sometimes lets me ______ his bike.
3 There was a big ______ when the boy jumped into the pool.
4 I love to sit and ______ at flowers and trees.
5 The ______ from the fire filled the room.
6 I learned to ______ my shoe laces when I was four.
7 Ducks can ______ on the water.
8 You should never ______ your brother or your sister!

Listening

2 Listen. Do the children like the painting? 10

3 Listen again and circle.

1 The children are looking at a painting *in a book / on a wall.*
2 The artist of the painting was *French / Italian.*
3 The artist painted the picture in *1991 / 1891.*
4 The children think the tiger is in a *forest / zoo.*
5 They think the tiger is *hungry / thirsty.*
6 They decide to write a *poem / story.*

Tiger in Tropical Storm (Surprised!)

Speaking

4 Ask and answer. Use the prompts or your own answers.

Which painting do you like best? — I like ______. — Tiger in a Tropical Storm (Surprised!) / California Coast / A Small Volcano in Mexican Countryside
What can you see in the painting? — There is / are ______. — a tiger / some trees and plants / a storm / an island / the sea / mountains / a lake
Why do you like it? — It's ______. — colorful / exciting / unusual
Do you enjoy painting? — Yes, I do / No, I don't because ______. — it's fun / it's interesting / I'm good at painting / I'm not very good at painting

Words in context: *Island Adventure*, listening and speaking Unit 1 13

Lesson Six SB page 13

Skills Time!

Skills development
Dictionary: discover meaning of words in context
Listening: listen for specific information
Speaking: ask and answer questions about a painting

Language
Words in context: *stare, row, smoke, borrow, hit, splash, float, tie* (Student Book); *lightning, oars, grab, bank* (Workbook)
Extra: *French, Italian, tropical, coast, Mexican*

Materials
CD 10; Dictionary Workbook pages 128–135

Oxford iTools Digital classroom • Words, Listening, Speaking

Warmer
- Play *Smiley face* (see page 8) with the unit vocabulary.
- With books closed, ask questions about the story from the previous lesson, e.g. *Where was Max staying? What went wrong?*

NOTE: Remind students to consult the Dictionary pages in their Workbooks when completing Exercise 1.

1 Find the words in the story. Write.
- Ask the students to look at the words in the box. Explain that the words come from the story on page 12.
- Ask students to look at the story again and find all of the underlined words. They read the sentences with each word and try to determine the meaning from the context.
- Students read the sentences on page 13 and complete them with the correct words.
- Go through answers together. Ask individual students to read aloud.

ANSWERS
1. row 2. borrow 3. splash 4. stare 5. smoke
6. tie 7. float 8. hit

2 Listen. Do the children like the painting? 10
- Focus attention on the picture. Ask the class *What can you see in the painting? Do you like it? Why / Why not?*
- Tell students they are going to hear two children talking about the painting. They must listen and find out if the children like it.
- Play the whole recording.
- Ask the class *Do the children like the painting?*

ANSWER
Yes, the children like the painting.

3 Listen again and circle.
- Ask students to read the sentences silently before you play the recording again.
- Play the recording, pausing for students to circle the correct words. Play the recording again if necessary.
- Review the answers together.

ANSWERS
1. in a book 2. French 3. 1891 4. forest
5. hungry 6. story

4 Ask and answer. Use the prompts or your own answers.
- Tell students they are going to have a conversation about a painting they like. Ask two students to read the speech bubbles for the class, using the prompts or their own ideas to give answers.
- Ask students to work in pairs. They take turns asking and answering questions about their favorite painting.

Differentiation

Below level:
- Read the questions aloud to the students. Pause after each one, and ask them to circle their answer from the prompts.

At level:
- Students complete the activity.

Above level:
- After students finish, switch pairs. Ask students to ask and answer about the painting they like least.

NOTE: Students now do the task on Workbook page 11. Remind them to consult the Workbook Dictionary pages.

Further practice
Workbook page 11
Unit 1 Speaking skills worksheet, Assessment and Resource CD-ROM
Online Practice • Unit 1 • Words in context, Listening, and Speaking

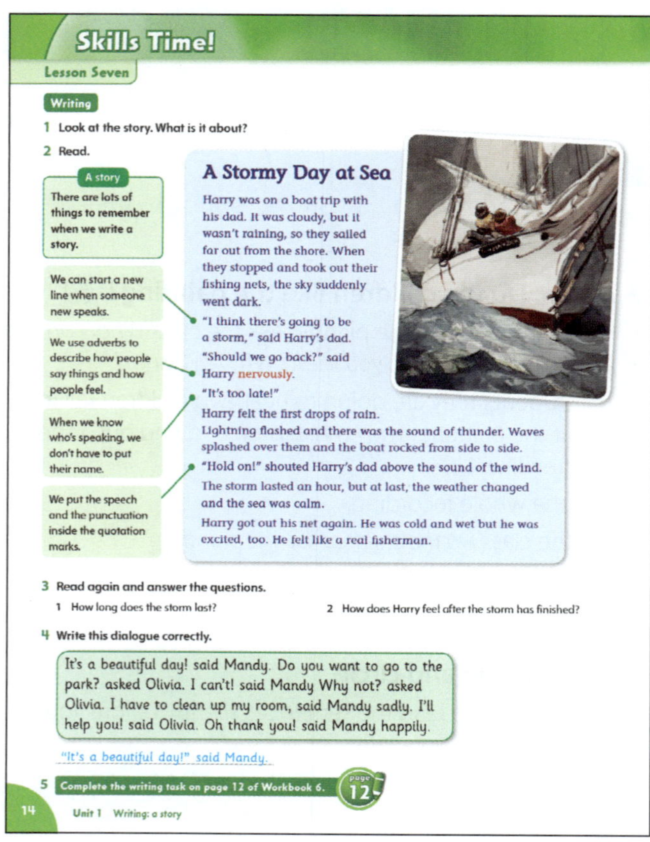

Skills Time!

Lesson Seven

Writing

1 Look at the story. What is it about?

2 Read.

A story

There are lots of things to remember when we write a story.

We can start a new line when someone new speaks.

We use adverbs to describe how people say things and how people feel.

When we know who's speaking, we don't have to put their name.

We put the speech and the punctuation inside the quotation marks.

A Stormy Day at Sea

Harry was on a boat trip with his dad. It was cloudy, but it wasn't raining, so they sailed far out from the shore. When they stopped and took out their fishing nets, the sky suddenly went dark.

"I think there's going to be a storm," said Harry's dad.

"Should we go back?" said Harry nervously.

"It's too late!"

Harry felt the first drops of rain.

Lightning flashed and there was the sound of thunder. Waves splashed over them and the boat rocked from side to side.

"Hold on!" shouted Harry's dad above the sound of the wind.

The storm lasted an hour, but at last, the weather changed and the sea was calm.

Harry got out his net again. He was cold and wet but he was excited, too. He felt like a real fisherman.

3 Read again and answer the questions.

1 How long does the storm last?

2 How does Harry feel after the storm has finished?

4 Write this dialogue correctly.

It's a beautiful day! said Mandy. Do you want to go to the park? asked Olivia. I can't! said Mandy Why not? asked Olivia. I have to clean up my room, said Mandy sadly. I'll help you! said Olivia. Oh thank you! said Mandy happily.

"It's a beautiful day!" said Mandy.

5 Complete the writing task on page 12 of Workbook 6. page 12

14 Unit 1 Writing: a story

Lesson Seven SB page 14

Skills Time!

Skills development

Writing focus: using speech in fictional writing

Writing outcome: write a story based on / inspired by a painting (Workbook)

Language

Recycled: vocabulary and structures seen previously

Extra: *quotation marks*

Materials

Writing poster 1; a copy of the text from poster 1, Assessment and Resource CD-ROM, for each student

Oxford iTools Digital classroom • Unit 1 • Writing

Warmer

- Play *Guess the word* (see page 8).

Poster 1: A story

- Hand out a photocopy of the poster text to each student.
- Ask the "Before reading" question in the bottom right-hand corner. Encourage students to discuss their ideas.
- Ask students to read the story silently. Ask comprehension questions, e.g. *Where did Toby and Rick go? What did they take with them?*
- Read the first two text boxes on the left-hand side to the class. Ask *What do we write in our story? What do we use to describe how people say things or how they feel?*
- Read the final text box on the left. Ask *How do we show dialogue in a story? What goes inside the quotation marks?*
- Read the first text box on the right. Ask *What do we use time markers for?* Find the time markers in the story.
- Read the rest of the text on the right. Ask *What can we use to make our writing more interesting?*
- Ask the "After reading" questions in the bottom right-hand corner. Discuss some answers with the class.

1 Look at the story. What is it about?

- Focus on the picture. Ask *What can you see?* Ask students to look at the title and glance quickly through the text, without reading it in detail. Ask *What is the story about?*

2 Read.

- Ask comprehension questions, e.g. *How does Harry's dad know there's going to be a storm?*
- After reading, discuss the story. Were their predictions correct?

3 Read again and answer the questions.

- Ask students to read the story again silently.
- Ask students to read and answer the questions.

ANSWERS

1. The storm lasts an hour.
2. After the storm, Harry feels excited.

4 Write this dialogue correctly.

- Ask students to look at the story again and focus on how the speech is shown. Ask *What do we put around the speech? Where does the punctuation go?*
- Tell students they are going to use this information to rewrite the dialogue in Exercise 4.
- Let students complete the activity, then check answers.

Differentiation

Below level:

- Ask students to underline the words said / asked in the activity. Ask students *What did (Mandy) say?* Have students draw in quotation marks.

At level:

- Students complete the activity.

Above level:

- Ask students to extend the dialogue by a few lines.

ANSWERS

"It's a beautiful day!" said Mandy. "Do you want to go to the park?" asked Olivia. "I can't!" said Mandy. "Why not?" asked Olivia. "I have to clean my room," said Mandy sadly. "I'll help you!" said Olivia. "Oh thank you!" said Mandy happily.

5 Complete the writing task on page 12 of Workbook 6.

- Students now do the writing task on Workbook page 12.

Further practice

Workbook page 12

Unit 1 Writing skills worksheet, Assessment and Resource CD-ROM

Online Practice • Unit 1 • Writing

Unit 1 Review

Lesson Eight

1 Complete the quiz.

1 (noun) *a picture of a person* What is the word?

2 What does Fin want the children to do in the story?

3 Make the word negative. possible

4 Correct the sentence. I will going to the beach today.

5 Correct the sentence. I'll to help you with your homework.

6 Correct the sentence. We catch a bus at 5:00 p.m.

7 How does Ryan's brother know the boys are on the island in "Island Adventure?"

8 (noun) *it's gray and it comes from fire* What is the word?

9 Correct the punctuation. "What's your name"? asked Jessica.

10 Correct the punctuation. "It looks like a storm, said the girl nervously."

2 Listen and write. Sing. 11

landscape blue clouds ~~painting~~ green colors black mural

Painting by colors

I'm going to paint a [1] painting
In [2] _____ *silver and* [3] _____,
Bright stars and oceans,
And maybe a dolphin or two.

I'm going to paint a [4] _____
In colors [5] _____ *and gray,*
Dark skies and dark [6] _____,
A cold and stormy day.

I'm going to paint a [7] _____
In colors yellow and [8] _____,
Sunshine and lemon trees,
A sunny country scene.

Review Unit 1 15

Lesson Eight SB page 15

Unit 1 Review

Learning outcomes

Review vocabulary and structures practiced previously

To use vocabulary and structures from the unit in the context of a song

Language

Recycled: vocabulary and structures seen previously

Materials

CD 11

Oxford iTools Digital classroom • Unit 1 • Review

Warmer

- Play *Book race* (see page 8) using the sentences below. Give students 15 seconds per sentence to find the answer.
  We won't come back here again! (Lesson 3)
  The artist of the painting was French. (Lesson 6)
  Do you want to watch a DVD at my house instead? (Lesson 4)
  I think there's going to be a storm. (Lesson 7)
  How did you find us? (Lesson 5)
  How about flags or maps? (Lesson 1)
  It's a robot like me! (Lesson 3)
  What will we paint? (Lesson 1)
- Review the answers together.

1 Complete the quiz.

- Tell students they are going to do a quiz based on the unit. Do this individually, in pairs, or in teams.
- Students work with books open to page 15, but they may not look up the answers.

ANSWERS

1. portrait
2. He wants them to paint a mural for the DSD Club wall.
3. impossible
4. I'm going to the beach today.
5. I'll help you with your homework.
6. We're catching a bus at 5 p.m.
7. He saw the boat near the shore.
8. smoke
9. "What's your name?" asked Jessica.
10. "It looks like a storm," said the girl nervously.

Differentiation

Below level:

- Play *Order the letters* (see page 9) using words from the unit.

At level:

- Play *Wrong word* (see page 8) with sentences about the unit. Divide the class into two teams and read the statements below to each team in turn.
  The DSD Club children have to paint a portrait. (mural) / Libby suggests going to the art gallery. (library) / Professor and Chip see a mural. (sculpture) / Harry writes Ben a letter. (email) / Max and Jeff went to a city. (island) / Max and Jeff lost their bike. (boat) / Henri Rousseau was a French chef. (artist) / Harry went on a boat trip with his mom. (dad)

Above level:

- Play the "at level" game, but ask students to think of some sentences of their own. Students read their statements to the other team.

2 Listen and write. Sing. 11

- Focus students' attention on the paintings. Point to each and ask *What can you see?* Ask what they think the song is about (*painting a picture*).
- Play the whole song for students to follow along.
- Play the song a second time, pausing for students to write the words in the blanks.
- Play the song a third time if necessary.
- Go through the answers together.
- Play the recording again. Students sing along.

ANSWERS

1. painting 2. colors 3. blue 4. mural 5. black 6. clouds 7. landscape 8. green

Further practice

Workbook page 13

Unit 1 test, Assessment and Resource CD-ROM

Progress certificate, Assessment and Resource CD-ROM

Online Practice • Unit 1 • Review

Fluency Time! 1

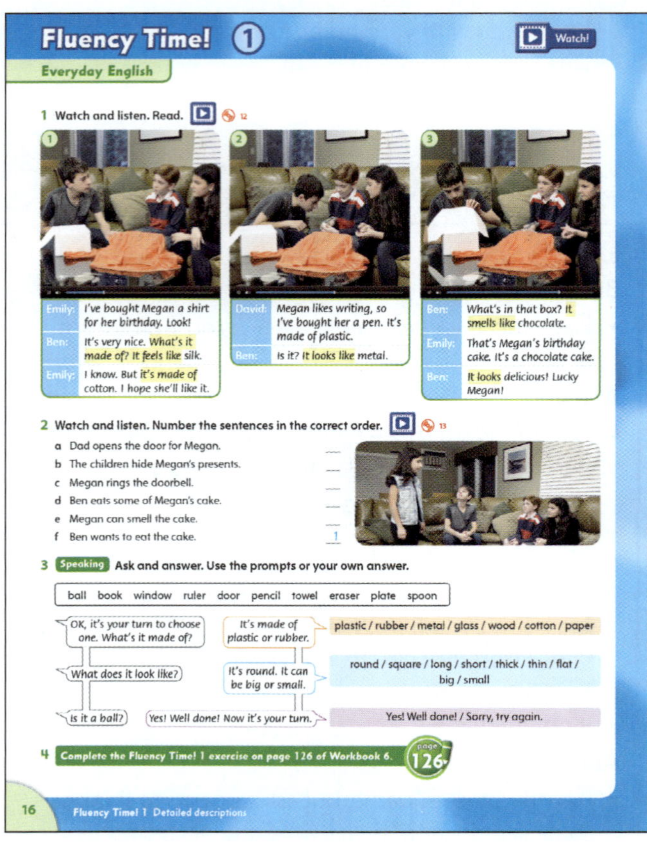

Fluency Time! 1

Watch!

Everyday English

1 Watch and listen. Read. 12

Emily:	I've bought Megan a shirt for her birthday. Look!
Ben:	It's very nice. What's it made of? It feels like silk.
Emily:	I know. But it's made of cotton. I hope she'll like it.

David:	Megan likes writing, so I've bought her a pen. It's made of plastic.
Ben:	Is it? It looks like metal.

Ben:	What's in that box? It smells like chocolate.
Emily:	That's Megan's birthday cake. It's a chocolate cake.
Ben:	It looks delicious! Lucky Megan!

2 Watch and listen. Number the sentences in the correct order. 13

a Dad opens the door for Megan. ___
b The children hide Megan's presents. ___
c Megan rings the doorbell. ___
d Ben eats some of Megan's cake. ___
e Megan can smell the cake. ___
f Ben wants to eat the cake. 1

3 Speaking Ask and answer. Use the prompts or your own answer.

ball book window ruler door pencil towel eraser plate spoon

OK, it's your turn to choose one. What's it made of?
It's made of plastic or rubber.
plastic / rubber / metal / glass / wood / cotton / paper
What does it look like?
It's round. It can be big or small.
round / square / long / short / thick / thin / flat / big / small
Is it a ball?
Yes! Well done! Now it's your turn.
Yes! Well done! / Sorry, try again.

4 Complete the Fluency Time! 1 exercise on page 126 of Workbook 6. page 126

16 Fluency Time! 1 Detailed descriptions

Everyday English SB page 16

Learning outcomes

To learn some useful language about making detailed descriptions

Language

What's this made of? It feels like silk. It's made of plastic. It looks like metal. It smells like chocolate. It looks delicious!

Materials

CD 12–13; Fluency DVD Fluency Time! 1

Oxford iTools Digital classroom Fluency Time! 1 • Everyday English

Warmer

- Tell the class they are going to learn some useful language for making detailed descriptions.
- Remind students of the verbs for the senses: *looks*, *smells*, *feels*, *tastes*, and *sounds*.
- Ask questions, e.g. *What does a lemon taste like? How does sandpaper feel?* Elicit responses.

1 Watch and listen. Read. 12

- Focus on the pictures. Ask students who they see in the pictures (*Emily, Ben, and David*), where they are (*in the living room*), and what they are doing (*waiting*).
- Children watch the DVD. Play the DVD again for students to listen and read. Answer any questions. Play the DVD again, pausing for students to say the dialogue.
- Go through the highlighted phrases in the box with the class. Make sure they understand each one.
- Ask students what senses are used in the dialogue.
- Ask students to practice the dialogue. Then invite pairs to act for the class.

2 Watch and listen. Number the sentences in the correct order. 13

- Ask students to read the sentences. Explain that they need to listen and number them in order.
- Play the first part of the recording and focus on the example. Then play the whole recording. Students listen and number.
- Ask different students to read the sentences in order. Play the recording again to check answers.

ANSWERS

a. 3 b. 4 c. 2 d. 6 e. 5 f. 1

3 Ask and answer. Use the prompts or your own answer.

- Ask a volunteer to act out a dialogue with you.
- Tell students to use the prompts, or their own answers, to act out dialogues with their partner.
- Invite some pairs to act for the class.

Differentiation

Below level:

- Break the dialogue up into three shorter exchanges. Have students practice the first question and answer a few times, then move on to the second and third ones.

At level:

- Play a guessing game. Invite a child to come up and mime an object from the box in Exercise 3. The class guesses the object, what it's made of, and what it looks like. Encourage students to make sentences, e.g. *It's a window. It made of glass. It's square.* The first child to guess correctly comes up and acts out another object.

Above level:

- Ask students to think of other objects to describe. Give them paper and colored pencils to draw two objects. Put students in pairs to describe each other's drawings. Monitor and help as needed.

Further practice

Workbook page 14
Everyday English phrase bank, Workbook page 126
Fluency Time! 1, Fluency DVD
Online Practice • Fluency Time! 1

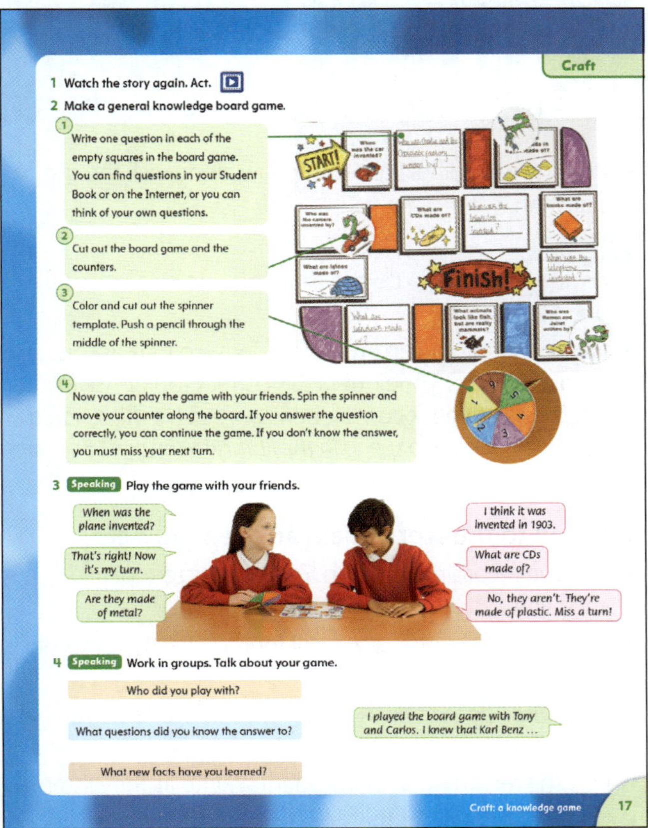

Craft

1 Watch the story again. Act.

2 Make a general knowledge board game.

1 Write one question in each of the empty squares in the board game. You can find questions in your Student Book or on the Internet, or you can think of your own questions.

2 Cut out the board game and the counters.

3 Color and cut out the spinner template. Push a pencil through the middle of the spinner.

4 Now you can play the game with your friends. Spin the spinner and move your counter along the board. If you answer the question correctly, you can continue the game. If you don't know the answer, you must miss your next turn.

3 Speaking Play the game with your friends.

4 Speaking Work in groups. Talk about your game.

Who did you play with?

What questions did you know the answer to?

What new facts have you learned?

Craft: a knowledge game 17

Craft SB page 17

Learning outcomes

To make a knowledge board game

To talk about your knowledge board game

Language

When was the plane invented? I think it was invented in 1903. What are CDs made of? Are they made of metal? No, they aren't. They're made of plastic.

Materials

Fluency DVD Fluency Time! 1; Fluency Craft 1 (Assessment and Resource CD-ROM) (one template for each student); completed board game; colored pencils, scissors, and glue for each group

Oxford iTools Digital classroom • Fluency Time! 1 • Craft

1 Watch the story again. Act.

- Focus on the story in Exercise 1 on Student Book page 16. Ask students what they remember about the story.
- Play Fluency Time! 1 Everyday English. If you don't have time for the DVD, read the dialogue on Student Book page 16.
- Ask groups of students to act out the dialogue. Encourage them to change details to make their own variations.

2 Make a general knowledge board game.

- Focus on the picture. Ask students to say what the picture shows (*a board game and spinner*) and what is in the board game squares, e.g. *a car, a CD, an igloo*.
- Hand out copies of the board game template and the spinner and counters template (see Fluency Craft 1, Assessment and Resource CD-ROM).
- Read the tips in Exercise 1. Show the class your completed board game and spinner. Demonstrate how to push a pencil through the middle of the spinner to make it spin. Make sure students understand how to complete the board game.
- Ask questions as students work, e.g. *When was this invented? What is this made of?*

3 Play the game with your friends.

- Focus on the photos. Tell students they are going to play their board games with a partner.
- The students place their counters on the *Start* arrow. They take turns to spin and move their counter the correct number of squares. They must answer the question on the square they land on. Their partner must say whether the answer is correct or not. The first child to reach the *Finish* square is the winner.

4 Work in groups. Talk about your game.

- Ask a volunteer to read the example speech bubble, then invite students to tell the class about their game. They can read the questions to help them, or you can ask the questions to prompt them.

Differentiation

Below level:

- Ask students to take out their notebooks and write one or two sentences about something new they learned, e.g. *I learned that…* Monitor and help as needed.

At level:

- Ask students to share their questions. Call students one at a time to the front to ask their classmates a question. Whoever answers correctly comes up and asks another question. Help and elicit as needed.

Above level:

- Switch the groups. Ask students to think of five more questions they could add to the board game. Have them write questions and answers. If time permits, they can ask their classmates.

Watch the DVD!

- You can now play Fluency Time! 1 Everday English again to review the language of the lesson.
- The children can now complete the DVD Practice page in the Workbook (page 15). Play each scene again for the children to complete the activities.

Further practice

Workbook page 15
Skills test 1 Fluency Time!, Assessment and Resource CD-ROM
Fluency Time! 1, Fluency DVD
Online Practice • Fluency Time! 1

2 Sports adventures!

2 Sports adventures!

Lesson One Story

1 Listen and read. Why doesn't Kate want to do the drawing? 14

2 Listen to the story again and repeat. Act.

3 Read again and write the names. Ed Kate Libby Tom

1 Ed finds a useful section in the library.
2 ________ finds a book about sports.
3 ________ asks who is free.
4 ________ is studying in the evening.
5 ________ and Tom are going ice skating.
6 ________ has time to do the drawing.

18 Unit 2 Sports adventures!

Lesson One  SB page 18

Story

Learning outcomes

To read and understand a story

To act out a story

Language

Introducing core vocabulary (Lesson 2) through a story

Extra: *section, ice hockey, ice skating, drawing*

Materials

CD 14

 Oxford iTools Digital classroom • Unit 2 • Story

Warmer

- Ask students what they remember about the last episode of the story. Ask questions, e.g. *Who was the new person at the club? What did Fin want the children to do?*
- Ask students to make predictions about this episode. Ask students to suggest possible topics for the mural and write their suggestions on the board.

1 Listen and read. Why doesn't Kate want to do the drawing? 14

- Focus on the pictures and the story. Ask prediction questions, e.g. *Where do the children go to get ideas? Is Kate happy at the end of the story?*
- Play the recording. Students follow along. Ask the gist question.

ANSWER

Kate doesn't want to do the drawing because she's terrible at art.

- Play the recording again. Ask students to look at the list of topics. Did anyone guess the correct topic? Ask further questions to check comprehension, e.g. *Do the children have a lot of time to spend in the library? Why can't Ed / Tom / Libby draw the pictures?*

2 Listen to the story again and repeat. Act.

- Play the recording, pausing for students to repeat each line.
- Divide the class into groups of four to play the parts of Libby, Ed, Tom, and Kate.
- If the class doesn't divide exactly, some students can have more than one role.
- Play the recording again. Students mime as they listen.
- Let students act out the story in their groups, then ask one or two groups to act out the story for the class.

3 Read again and write the names.

- Look at the example. Explain that students have to read the sentences and write the name of the character.
- Allow time for students to read and write, then go through answers with the class.

Differentiation

Below level:

- With books closed, ask students who said these lines of dialogue. Write on the board: *Where shall we start? (Libby) / Maybe we could draw sports that are popular in other countries. (Tom) / Great idea! (Ed) / I have too much homework. (Ed) / I'm going ice skating with my parents. (Tom) / I don't dislike art, but I'm terrible at it! (Kate)*
- Students say the names and check answers on page 18.

At level:

- Copy the dialogue from frame 4 onto the board and play *Disappearing dialogue* with the class (see page 9).

Above level:

- Extend the "at level" activity to include frames 3 and 4.

ANSWERS

1. Ed 2. Tom 3. Libby 4. Ed 5. Libby 6. Kate

Further practice

Workbook page 16

Online Practice • Unit 2 • Story

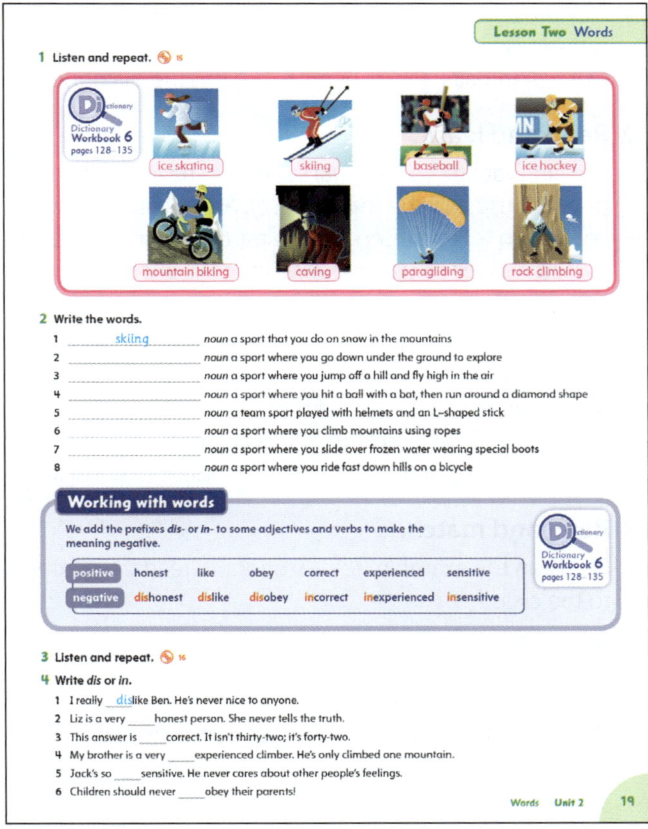

Lesson Two Words

1 Listen and repeat. 15

Dictionary Workbook 6 pages 128–135

ice skating · skiing · baseball · ice hockey · mountain biking · caving · paragliding · rock climbing

2 Write the words.

1 ___skiing___ *noun* a sport that you do on snow in the mountains
2 ______ *noun* a sport where you go down under the ground to explore
3 ______ *noun* a sport where you jump off a hill and fly high in the air
4 ______ *noun* a sport where you hit a ball with a bat, then run around a diamond shape
5 ______ *noun* a team sport played with helmets and an L-shaped stick
6 ______ *noun* a sport where you climb mountains using ropes
7 ______ *noun* a sport where you slide over frozen water wearing special boots
8 ______ *noun* a sport where you ride fast down hills on a bicycle

Working with words

We add the prefixes *dis-* or *in-* to some adjectives and verbs to make the meaning negative.

positive	honest	like	obey	correct	experienced	sensitive
negative	dishonest	dislike	disobey	incorrect	inexperienced	insensitive

Dictionary Workbook 6 pages 128–135

3 Listen and repeat. 16

4 Write *dis* or *in*.

1 I really __dis__like Ben. He's never nice to anyone.
2 Liz is a very ____honest person. She never tells the truth.
3 This answer is ____correct. It isn't thirty-two; it's forty-two.
4 My brother is a very ____experienced climber. He's only climbed one mountain.
5 Jack's so ____sensitive. He never cares about other people's feelings.
6 Children should never ____obey their parents!

Words Unit 2 19

Lesson Two SB page 19

Words

Learning outcomes

To identify different types of sports

To use prefixes *dis-* and *in-* to make some adjectives and verbs negative

Language

Words: *ice skating, skiing, baseball, ice hockey, mountain biking, caving, paragliding, rock climbing*

Working with words: *honest / dishonest, like / dislike, obey / disobey, correct / incorrect, experienced / inexperienced, sensitive / insensitive* (Student Book); *agree / disagree, complete / incomplete, appear / disappear, visible / invisible* (Workbook)

Materials

CD 15–16 Dictionary Workbook pages 128–135

Oxford iTools Digital classroom • Unit 2 • Words

Warmer

- With books closed, ask students what they remember about the story from Lesson 1. Ask questions, e.g. *Where did the children go? What did they choose to draw about?*
- Discuss sports with the class. Ask *Which sports do you like / not like? Which new sports would you like to try?* Write the names of the different sports on the board.

1 Listen and repeat. 15

- Ask students to open their books and look at the pictures and words. Play the recording. Students listen and repeat the words chorally.
- Play it again for students to listen and repeat.
- Ask individual students to say the words for the class.

NOTE: Students can refer to the Workbook Dictionary pages.

2 Write the words.

- Read the first definition with the class and draw attention to the answer.
- Ask students to read the other definitions and write a sport from Exercise 1 next to each one.
- Students complete the activity, then check answers.

ANSWERS

1. skiing 2. caving 3. paragliding 4. baseball 5. ice hockey 6. rock climbing 7. ice skating 8. mountain biking

3 Listen and repeat. 16

- Before doing the activity, focus students' attention on the *Working with words* section above.
- Tell students you are going to look at two more prefixes which can make certain verbs and nouns negative. Explain that these prefixes can't always be used. It is simply a case of learning them.
- Play the recording. Students listen and repeat the words.
- Play the recording a second time. Students listen and repeat. Repeat as often as necessary.
- Ask individual students to say the words for the class.

4 Write *dis* or *in*.

- Look at the example with the class. Ask students *What's the opposite of "like"?* to elicit *dislike*.
- Ask students to write the correct prefixes. They check their answers against the words in the box.

Differentiation

Below level:

- Write *dis-* and *in-* on the board in one column and the positive adjectives in a second column. Ask students to come to the board and draw a line from the prefix to the word to make it negative. Prefixes will be used more than once.

At level:

- Play a game with the prefixes *dis-* and *in-*. Students close their books. Divide the class into two teams. Read a positive adjective from Exercise 3 for the first team. One student gives the negative version. Correct answers get one point. Alternate between the teams until all the words have been used. The team with the most points wins.

Above level:

- Play the "at level" game but make sentences using the words instead.

ANSWERS

1. dis 2. dis 3. in 4. in 5. in 6. dis

Further practice

Workbook page 17

Online Practice • Unit 2 • Words

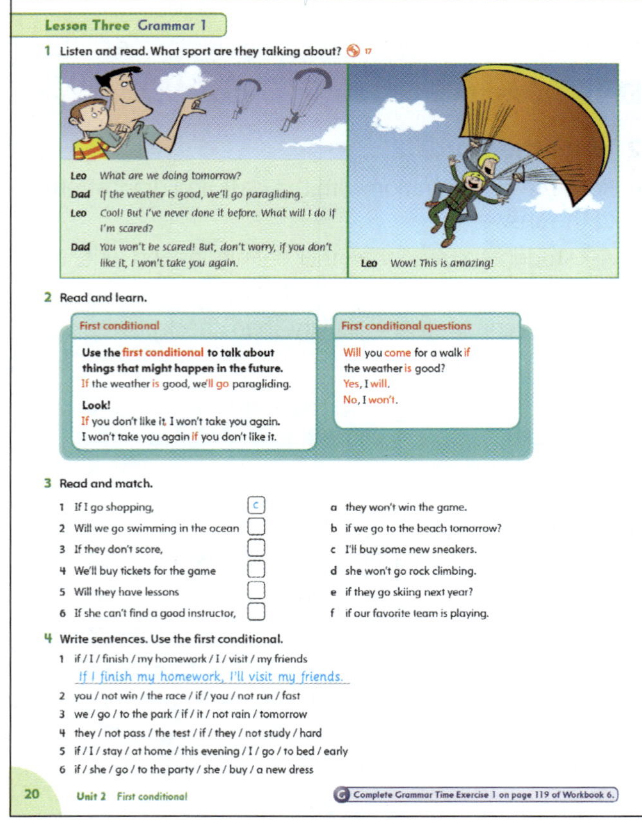

Lesson Three Grammar 1

1 Listen and read. What sport are they talking about? 17

2 Read and learn.

First conditional

Use the first conditional to talk about things that might happen in the future.
If the weather is good, we'll go paragliding.

Look!
If you don't like it, I won't take you again.
I won't take you again if you don't like it.

First conditional questions

Will you come for a walk if the weather is good?
Yes, I will.
No, I won't.

3 Read and match.

1 If I go shopping, c
2 Will we go swimming in the ocean
3 If they don't score,
4 We'll buy tickets for the game
5 Will they have lessons
6 If she can't find a good instructor,

a they won't win the game.
b if we go to the beach tomorrow?
c I'll buy some new sneakers.
d she won't go rock climbing.
e if they go skiing next year?
f if our favorite team is playing.

4 Write sentences. Use the first conditional.

1 if / I / finish / my homework / I / visit / my friends
If I finish my homework, I'll visit my friends.
2 you / not win / the race / if / you / not run / fast
3 we / go / to the park / if / it / not rain / tomorrow
4 they / not pass / the test / if / they / not study / hard
5 if / I / stay / at home / this evening / I / go / to bed / early
6 if / she / go / to the party / she / buy / a new dress

20 Unit 2 First conditional

Complete Grammar Time Exercise 1 on page 119 of Workbook 6.

Lesson Three SB page 20

Grammar 1

Learning outcomes

To use the first conditional to talk about things that might happen

To write first conditional sentences

Language

Core: *If the weather is good, we'll go paragliding. Will you come for a walk if the weather is good? Yes, I will. No, I won't.*

Extra: *instructor*

Materials

CD 17

Oxford iTools Digital classroom • Unit 2 • Grammar 1

Warmer

- Tell students they are going to plan an activity day for school next week. On one side of the board write *Good weather*. On the other, write *Bad weather*. Ask students to suggest different types of sports and activities they could do for each, e.g. *Good weather: baseball, tennis; Bad weather: indoor soccer, indoor volleyball.*

1 Listen and read. What sport are they talking about? 17

- Play the recording. Students follow along.
- Ask the gist question *What sport are they talking about?*

ANSWER

They are talking about paragliding.

- Play the recording a second time. Ask comprehension questions, e.g. *Is the boy excited about paragliding? Is he worried?* In pairs, ask students to act out the dialogue.

2 Read and learn.

- Explain that first conditional sentences have two parts (the *if* clause and the main clause). Ask students to tell you which tense is used in each part. (The simple present is used in the *if* clause and *will* future is used in the main clause.)
- Ask students to find the first conditional in the dialogue from Exercise 1.
- Ask students to look at the list of activities from the beginning of the lesson. Begin a sentence, e.g. *If the weather's good, we'll…* and invite a student to finish it.

3 Read and match.

- Focus on the example. Ask a student to read the sentence to the class.

ANSWERS

1. c 2. b 3. a 4. f 5. e 6. d

4 Write sentences. Use the first conditional.

- Write the example sentence on the board and ask a student to read it aloud. Underline the *if* clause in one color. Ask *Which tense do we use here?* Underline the main clause in another color. Ask *Which tense do we use here?*
- Remind students that the clauses can go the other way around, but that in this case we don't need a comma between them. Rewrite the example beginning with the main clause: *I'll visit my friends if I finish my homework.*
- Allow time for students to write the rest.

Differentiation

Below level:

- Look at the first conditional box in Activity 2 again. Ask students to underline all the verbs they see. Then write Activity 4, number 2 on the board without the slash marks. Ask students what the verbs should be. Work together to make the sentence. Then students complete the activity.

At level:

- Students complete the activity.

Above level:

- Have students switch the order of the clauses and rewrite the sentences, e.g. *I'll visit my friends if I finish my homework.*

ANSWERS

1. If I finish my homework, I'll visit my friends.
2. You won't win the race if you don't run fast.
3. We'll go to the park if it doesn't rain tomorrow.
4. They won't pass the test if they don't study hard.
5. If I stay at home this evening, I'll go to bed early.
6. If she goes to the party, she'll buy a new dress.

Further practice

Grammar Time, Workbook page 118

Workbook page 19

Online Practice • Unit 2 • Grammar 1

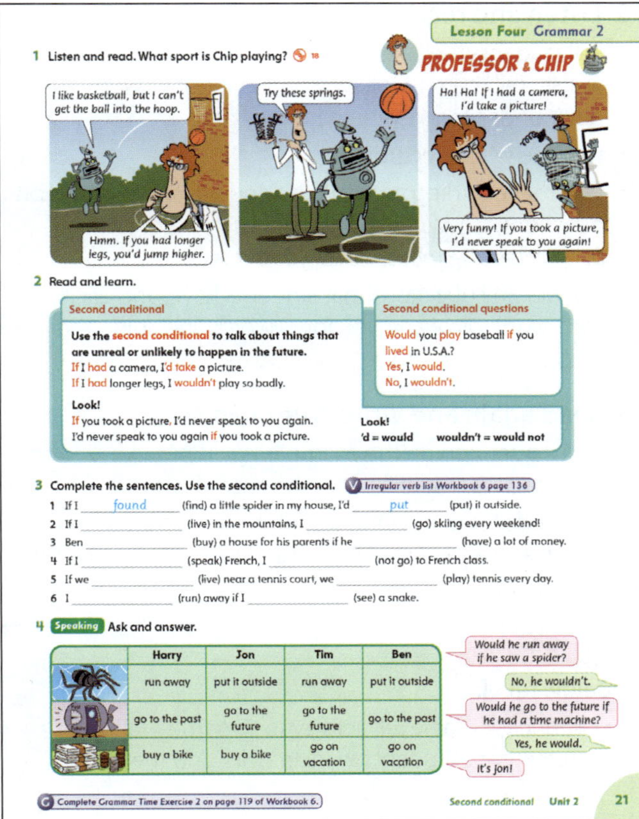
Lesson Four Grammar 2

1 Listen and read. What sport is Chip playing? 18

PROFESSOR & CHIP

2 Read and learn.

Second conditional

Use the second conditional to talk about things that are unreal or unlikely to happen in the future.
If I had a camera, I'd take a picture.
If I had longer legs, I wouldn't play so badly.

Look!
If you took a picture, I'd never speak to you again.
I'd never speak to you again if you took a picture.

Second conditional questions

Would you play baseball if you lived in U.S.A.?
Yes, I would.
No, I wouldn't.

Look!
'd = would   wouldn't = would not

3 Complete the sentences. Use the second conditional. Irregular verb list Workbook 6 page 136

1 If I ___found___ (find) a little spider in my house, I'd ___put___ (put) it outside.
2 If I ________ (live) in the mountains, I ________ (go) skiing every weekend!
3 Ben ________ (buy) a house for his parents if he ________ (have) a lot of money.
4 If I ________ (speak) French, I ________ (not go) to French class.
5 If we ________ (live) near a tennis court, we ________ (play) tennis every day.
6 I ________ (run) away if I ________ (see) a snake.

4 Speaking Ask and answer.

	Harry	Jon	Tim	Ben
	run away	put it outside	run away	put it outside
	go to the past	go to the future	go to the future	go to the past
	buy a bike	buy a bike	go on vacation	go on vacation

Complete Grammar Time Exercise 2 on page 119 of Workbook 6.

Second conditional Unit 2 21

Lesson Four SB page 21

Grammar 2

Learning outcomes

To use the second conditional to talk about unreal or unlikely situations

Speaking: asking and answering questions using the second conditional

Language

Core: *If I had a camera, I'd take a picture. Would you play baseball if you lived in the U.S.A.? Yes, I would. No, I wouldn't.*

Extra: *hoop, springs, spider*

Materials

CD 18

Oxford iTools Digital classroom • Unit 2 • Grammar 2

Warmer

- Play *True or false?* (see page 9) to review the first conditional using these sentences: *If it rains this afternoon, we'll go to the beach./ If you don't do your homework, I won't be happy. If you feel cold, I'll open all the windows. / If you listen to the teacher, you'll learn your grammar.*
- Focus on the pictures. Ask *Who can you see?*

1 Listen and read. What sport is Chip playing? 18

- Play the recording. Students follow the words in their books. Ask the gist question.

ANSWER

Chip is playing basketball.

- Play it again and explain any new words as necessary.
- Ask comprehension questions, e.g. *Why can't Chip get the ball into the hoop? What is Professor's idea?*

2 Read and learn.

- Focus on the rule and example sentences. Explain that the second conditional sentences have two parts (the *if* clause and the main clause).
- Copy the first example onto the board. Underline the *if* clause in one color. Ask *Which tense do we use here?* (Simple past). Underline the main clause. Ask *What do we use here?* (*would* + verb)
- Tell students that the clauses can appear either way around. Ask them to help you rewrite the sentence on the board so the main clause comes first.
- Ask students to find second conditional sentences in Exercise 1.

3 Complete the sentences. Use the second conditional.

- Ask a student to read the example for the class. Ask students to complete the rest using the second conditional.

ANSWERS

If I found a little spider in my house, I'd put it outside.
If I lived in the mountains, I'd go skiing every weekend!
Ben would buy a house for his parents if he had a lot of money.
If I spoke French, I wouldn't go to French class.
If we lived near a tennis court, we would play tennis every day.
I'd run away if I saw a snake.

4 Ask and answer.

- Ask students to look at the chart showing what Harry, Jon, Tim, and Ben would do in different situations.
- Explain that students are going to choose one of the boys from the chart and their partners are going to ask questions to find out who it is that they have chosen.
- Ask a pair of students to read out the example dialogue.
- Students take turns to choose a boy and answer questions.

Differentiation

Below level:

- Simplify the activity by having students focus on one question at a time. After they've answered this for each boy in the chart, move to the next row.

At level:

- Students complete the activity.

Above level:

- Extend the activity by asking students to make two columns in their notebooks for themselves and their partner. Fill in the chart. Then ask and answer.

Further practice

Grammar Time, Workbook page 118
Workbook page 19
Unit 2 Language practice worksheet, Assessment and Resource CD-ROM
Online Practice • Unit 2 • Grammar 2

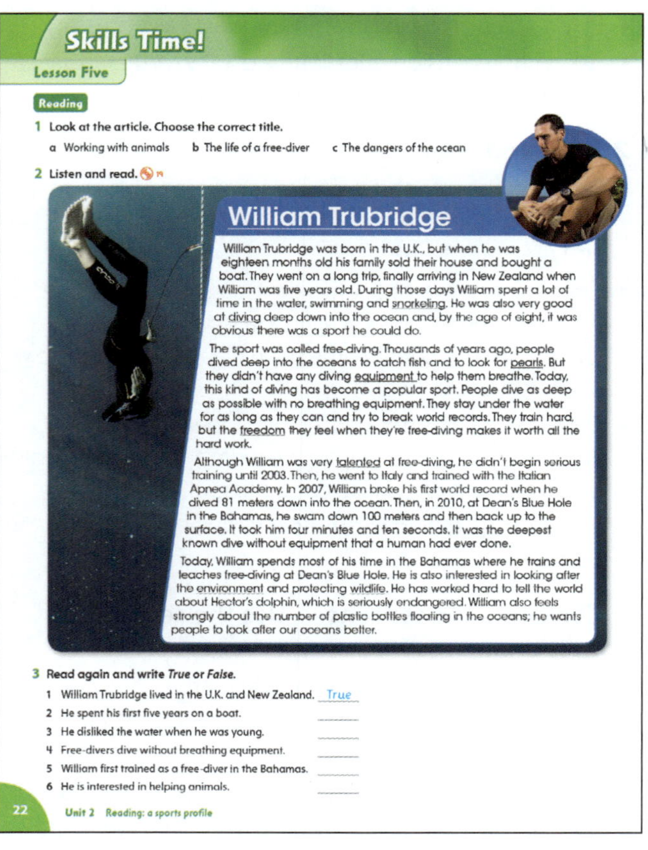

Skills Time!

Lesson Five

Reading

1 Look at the article. Choose the correct title.

a Working with animals b The life of a free-diver c The dangers of the ocean

2 Listen and read. 19

William Trubridge

William Trubridge was born in the U.K., but when he was eighteen months old his family sold their house and bought a boat. They went on a long trip, finally arriving in New Zealand when William was five years old. During those days William spent a lot of time in the water, swimming and snorkeling. He was also very good at diving deep down into the ocean and, by the age of eight, it was obvious there was a sport he could do.

The sport was called free-diving. Thousands of years ago, people dived deep into the oceans to catch fish and to look for pearls. But they didn't have any diving equipment to help them breathe. Today, this kind of diving has become a popular sport. People dive as deep as possible with no breathing equipment. They stay under the water for as long as they can and try to break world records. They train hard, but the freedom they feel when they're free-diving makes it worth all the hard work.

Although William was very talented at free-diving, he didn't begin serious training until 2003. Then, he went to Italy and trained with the Italian Apnea Academy. In 2007, William broke his first world record when he dived 81 meters down into the ocean. Then, in 2010, at Dean's Blue Hole in the Bahamas, he swam down 100 meters and then back up to the surface. It took him four minutes and ten seconds. It was the deepest known dive without equipment that a human had ever done.

Today, William spends most of his time in the Bahamas where he trains and teaches free-diving at Dean's Blue Hole. He is also interested in looking after the environment and protecting wildlife. He has worked hard to tell the world about Hector's dolphin, which is seriously endangered. William also feels strongly about the number of plastic bottles floating in the oceans; he wants people to look after our oceans better.

3 Read again and write *True* or *False*.

1 William Trubridge lived in the U.K. and New Zealand. True
2 He spent his first five years on a boat. ______
3 He disliked the water when he was young. ______
4 Free-divers dive without breathing equipment. ______
5 William first trained as a free-diver in the Bahamas. ______
6 He is interested in helping animals. ______

22 Unit 2 Reading: a sports profile

Lesson Five SB page 22

Skills Time!

Skills development

Reading: read a biographical article

Language

Recycled: vocabulary and structures seen previously

Extra: *free-diver, snorkeling, diving, free-diving, pearls, equipment, world record, talented, freedom, environment, wildlife*

Materials

CD 19

Oxford iTools Digital classroom • Unit 2 • Reading

Warmer

- Ask students to imagine their dream job. Discuss their ideas. Ask questions, e.g. *What would you do? Why would you like this job?*
- Ask students to look at the pictures. Ask students to suggest what William is doing in the photograph. Ask *Where does William Trubridge work? Does he enjoy his job?*

1 Look at the article. Choose the correct title.

- Ask students to skim the article to find out what happens. Explain that they should not read it in detail. Ask them to choose the best title.

ANSWER

The correct title is b.

2 Listen and read. 19

- Tell students they are going to listen to a recording of the article. Tell them to follow along, but not to worry if they don't understand every word they hear.
- Play the whole recording.
- Play the recording again. Pause and ask comprehension questions, e.g. *When did William start diving? Why did people free dive thousands of years ago?*
- Answer any questions that students have, and elicit the meanings of any unknown words, including the underlined ones, from the context.

3 Read again and write *True* or *False*.

- Focus attention on the example. Ask *Where did William Trubridge live?* Establish that the example is true.
- Ask students to read the rest of the sentences and then read the article to check whether they are true or false.
- Review answers with the class.

Differentiation

Below level:

- Reduce the "at level" activity to two true / false statements. Students work in pairs, and then swap papers with a neighbor.

At level:

- Ask students to write down four of their own true / false statements about William. Students swap sentences with their partners, who read them and mark them true or false.

Above level:

- Ask students to work in pairs to do a TV interview. One student is William Trubridge and the other is a reporter. Students re-read the article and write five questions to ask William. The student playing the reporter asks the questions. The student playing William answers them using information from the text and further details from his / her own imagination. Ask some pairs to act out their interviews for the class.

ANSWERS

1. True 2. False 3. False 4. True 5. False 6. True

Further practice

Workbook page 20

Online Practice • Unit 2 • Reading

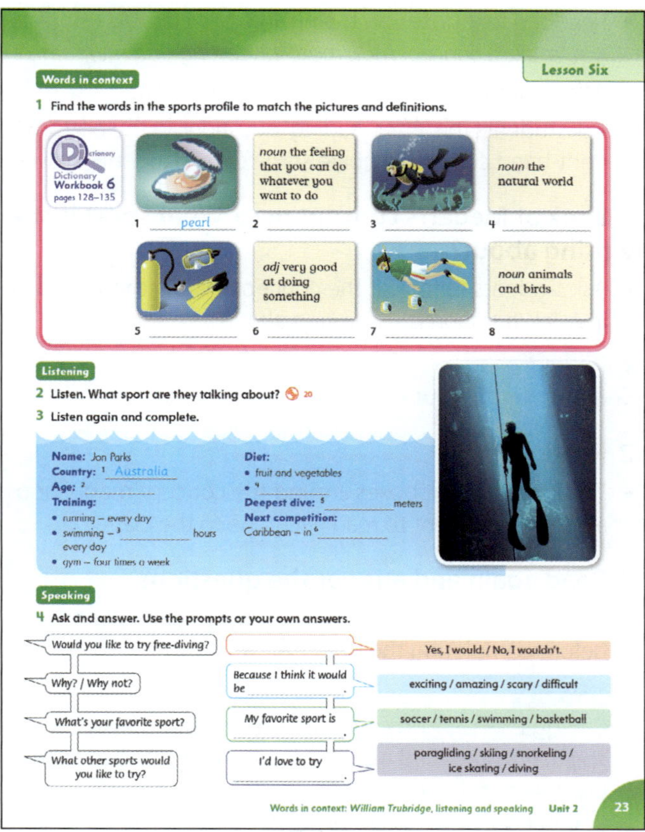

Lesson Six

Words in context

1 Find the words in the sports profile to match the pictures and definitions.

Dictionary Workbook 6 pages 128–135

1 pearl
2 *noun* the feeling that you can do whatever you want to do
3
4 *noun* the natural world
5
6 *adj* very good at doing something
7
8 *noun* animals and birds

Listening

2 Listen. What sport are they talking about? 20

3 Listen again and complete.

Name: Jon Parks
Country: [1] Australia
Age: [2] ______
Training:
- running – every day
- swimming – [3] ______ hours every day
- gym – four times a week

Diet:
- fruit and vegetables
- [4] ______

Deepest dive: [5] ______ meters
Next competition: Caribbean – in [6] ______

Speaking

4 Ask and answer. Use the prompts or your own answers.

Would you like to try free-diving? — ______ — Yes, I would. / No, I wouldn't.
Why? / Why not? — Because I think it would be ______. — exciting / amazing / scary / difficult
What's your favorite sport? — My favorite sport is ______. — soccer / tennis / swimming / basketball
What other sports would you like to try? — I'd love to try ______. — paragliding / skiing / snorkeling / ice skating / diving

Words in context: *William Trubridge*, listening and speaking Unit 2 23

Lesson Six SB page 23

Skills Time!

Skills development

Dictionary: discover meaning of words in context
Listening: listen for specific detail

Speaking: ask and answer questions about your favorite sport

Language

Words in context: *diving, pearl, equipment, talented, freedom, environment, wildlife* (Student Book); *provide, volunteer, skills, protect* (Workbook)

Materials

CD 20; Dictionary Workbook pages 128–135

Oxford iTools Digital classroom • Unit 2 • Words, Listening, Speaking

Warmer

- With books closed, ask students what they remember about the article from the previous lesson.
- Ask questions if necessary, e.g. *Where did William grow up? How does he train?*
- Write key vocabulary from the discussion on the board.

NOTE: Remind students to consult the Dictionary pages in their Workbooks when completing Exercise 1.

1 Find the words in the sports profile to match the pictures and definitions.

- Ask the students to open their Student Books and look at the pictures and definitions in Exercise 1.
- Look at the example together. Explain that *pearl* is one of the underlined words from the article on page 22.
- Tell students that they have to find the underlined words from the article that match the rest of the pictures and definitions. Go through the answers with the class.

ANSWERS

1. pearl 2. freedom 3. diving 4. environment
5. equipment 6. talented 7. snorkeling 8. wildlife

NOTE: Ask students to check the words in the Dictionary pages in their Workbooks.

Differentiation

Below level:

- Ask students to close their Student Books, take out their Workbooks, and turn to page 128. Divide students into teams. Say a vocabulary word, and students have to find it in the Dictionary. Whoever finds it first, gets a point. The team with the most points wins.

At level:

- Ask students to close their books. Play *Definitions* (see page 9) with the class to practice the new vocabulary.

Above level:

- Ask students to write a sentence for each of the new words. If time permits, students share with the class.

2 Listen. What sport are they talking about? 20

- Tell students they are going to hear an interview. Explain that they have to listen and identify the sport they are talking about.
- Play the whole recording, then elicit the answer from the class.

ANSWER

They are talking about free-diving.

3 Listen again and complete.

- Focus attention on the factfile. Tell students they are going to hear the recording again and must complete the missing information. Allow students time to read.
- Play the recording again, pausing for students to write the missing information.

ANSWERS

1. Australia 2. twenty-two 3. three 4. fish
5. 110 6. April

4 Ask and answer. Use the prompts or your own answers.

- Ask students to look at the example. Choose a strong student and ask him / her the questions.
- Ask students to work in pairs. Tell them they are going to take turns asking questions. Their partner must answer using the prompts or his / her own ideas.

Further practice

Workbook page 21

Unit 2 Speaking skills worksheet, Assessment and Resource CD-ROM

Online Practice • Unit 2 • Words in context, Listening, and Speaking

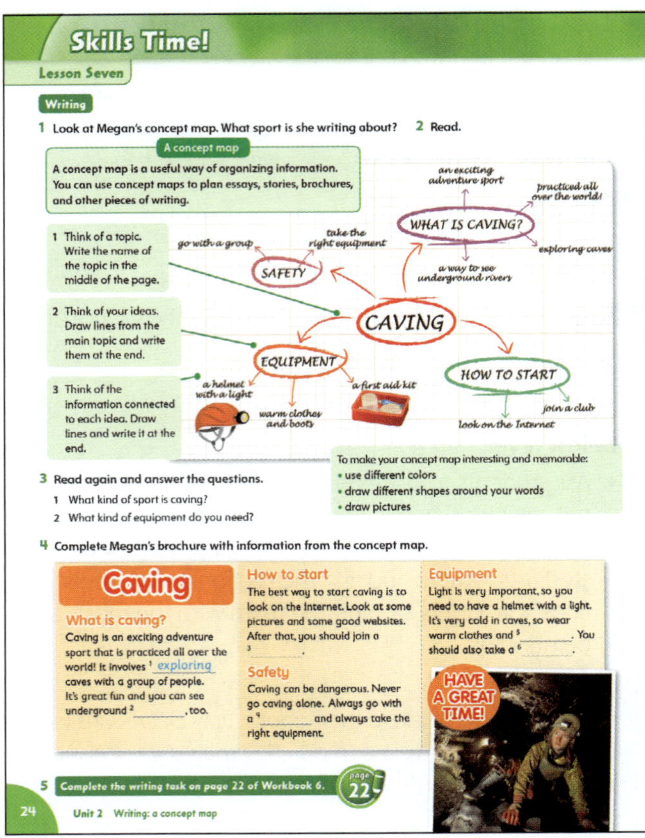

Skills Time!

Lesson Seven

Writing

1 Look at Megan's concept map. What sport is she writing about? 2 Read.

A concept map

A concept map is a useful way of organizing information. You can use concept maps to plan essays, stories, brochures, and other pieces of writing.

1 Think of a topic. Write the name of the topic in the middle of the page.

2 Think of your ideas. Draw lines from the main topic and write them at the end.

3 Think of the information connected to each idea. Draw lines and write it at the end.

To make your concept map interesting and memorable:
- use different colors
- draw different shapes around your words
- draw pictures

3 Read again and answer the questions.

1 What kind of sport is caving?
2 What kind of equipment do you need?

4 Complete Megan's brochure with information from the concept map.

Caving

What is caving?
Caving is an exciting adventure sport that is practiced all over the world! It involves [1] exploring caves with a group of people. It's great fun and you can see underground [2] ________, too.

How to start
The best way to start caving is to look on the Internet. Look at some pictures and some good websites. After that, you should join a [3] ________.

Safety
Caving can be dangerous. Never go caving alone. Always go with a [4] ________ and always take the right equipment.

Equipment
Light is very important, so you need to have a helmet with a light. It's very cold in caves, so wear warm clothes and [5] ________. You should also take a [6] ________.

HAVE A GREAT TIME!

5 Complete the writing task on page 22 of Workbook 6. page 22

24 Unit 2 Writing: a concept map

Lesson Seven 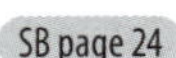

SB page 24

Skills Time!

Skills development

Writing focus: find and reproduce information from a concept map

Writing outcome: complete a concept map; write about sailing (Workbook)

Language

Recycled: vocabulary and structures seen previously

Extra: *adventure sport, helmet, concept map, memorable, brochure, underground*

Materials

Writing poster 2; a copy of the text from poster 2, Assessment and Resource CD-ROM, for each student

Oxford iTools Digital classroom • Unit 2 • Writing

Warmer

- Play *Order the letters* (see page 9) with the class to review the vocabulary from the previous lesson.

Poster 2: A concept map

- Ask the "Before reading" question in the bottom right-hand corner. Encourage students to discuss their ideas.
- Ask students to read the concept map. Read the first text box on the left of the map to the class. Ask *What can you use a concept map for?*
- Read the second text box on the left to the class. Ask *Where do you write the name of the topic? How do you connect your ideas?*
- Read the text boxes on the right to the class. Ask *How do you make a concept map more interesting and memorable?*
- Ask students to read the text on windsurfing.
- Ask students the "After reading" questions in the bottom right-hand corner. Compare some of the students' answers.

1 Look at Megan's concept map. What sport is she writing about?

- Ask students to look at the concept map without reading it. Ask *What sport is she writing about?*

ANSWER

She is writing about caving.

2 Read.

- Focus on the text boxes around the concept map. Choose a different student to read each one to the class.

3 Read again and answer the questions.

- Ask students to read the concept map again silently before completing the exercise.

ANSWERS

1. Caving is exploring caves. It's an exciting adventure sport. It's practiced all over the world. It's a way to see underground rivers.
2. You need a helmet with a light, warm clothes and boots, and a first aid kit.

4 Complete Megan's brochure with information from the concept map.

- Focus attention on the brochure. Tell students that Megan has used information from the concept map to write it.
- Look at the example together. Ask students to find the missing word, "exploring" on the concept map.
- Students find the rest of the missing words.

Differentiation

Below level:

- Ask students to match the headings in the brochure to those in the concept map. Students underline pieces of the brochure with information from the map.

At level:

- Put students in small groups. Ask groups to think of a topic, e.g. a sport or a hobby. Students work together to make a concept map.

Above level:

- Do the "at level" activity, then make a poster using their map. Students should use full sentences and pictures.

ANSWERS

1. exploring 2. rivers 3. club 4. group 5. boots 6. first aid kit

5 Complete the writing task on page 22 of Workbook 6.

- Refer students to the Workbook to complete the writing task. Go through the activity with them first.

Further practice
Workbook page 22
Unit 2 Writing skills worksheet, Assessment and Resource CD-ROM
Online Practice • Unit 2 • Writing

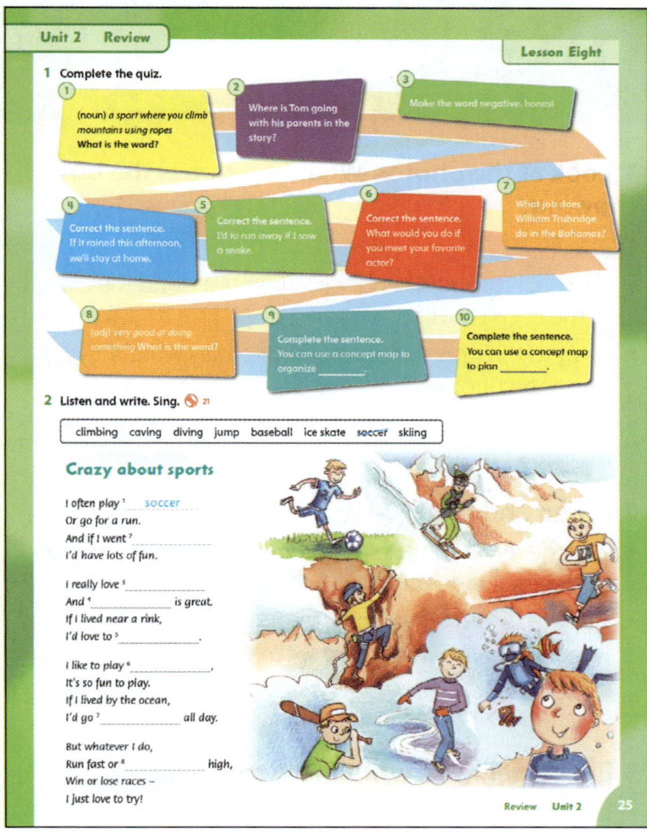
Unit 2 Review

Lesson Eight

1 Complete the quiz.

1. (noun) *a sport where you climb mountains using ropes* What is the word?
2. Where is Tom going with his parents in the story?
3. Make the word negative. honest
4. Correct the sentence. If it rained this afternoon, we'll stay at home.
5. Correct the sentence. I'd to run away if I saw a snake.
6. Correct the sentence. What would you do if you meet your favorite actor?
7. What job does William Trubridge do in the Bahamas?
8. (adj) *very good at doing something* What is the word?
9. Complete the sentence. You can use a concept map to organize ______.
10. Complete the sentence. You can use a concept map to plan ______.

2 Listen and write. Sing. 21

climbing caving diving jump baseball ice skate ~~soccer~~ skiing

Crazy about sports

I often play [1] soccer
Or go for a run.
And if I went [2] ______
I'd have lots of fun.

I really love [3] ______
And [4] ______ *is great.*
If I lived near a rink,
I'd love to [5] ______.

I like to play [6] ______,
It's so fun to play.
If I lived by the ocean,
I'd go [7] ______ *all day.*

But whatever I do,
Run fast or [8] ______ *high,*
Win or lose races –
I just love to try!

Review Unit 2 25

Lesson Eight SB page 25

Unit 2 Review

Learning outcomes
To review vocabulary and structures practiced previously

Language
Recycled: vocabulary and structures seen previously

Materials
CD 21

Oxford iTools Digital classroom • Unit 2 • Review

Warmer

- Play *Book race* (see page 8) to review the unit.
- Read the sentences below. Give students 20 seconds to find each one.
- *If the weather is good, we'll go paragliding. (Lesson 3)*
  A concept map is a useful way of organizing information. (Lesson 7)
  I don't dislike art, but I'm terrible at it! (Lesson 1)
  If you took a picture, I'd never speak to you again! (Lesson 4)
  Would you like to try free-diving? (Lesson 6)
  During those days William spent a lot of time in the water, swimming and snorkelling. (Lesson 5)
  Caving can be dangerous. (Lesson 7)
  Try these springs. (Lesson 4)

1 Complete the quiz.

- Tell students they are going to do a quiz based on this unit. They can work individually, in pairs, or in teams.
- Students work with books open to page 25, but they may not look up the answers.

ANSWERS
1. rock climbing 2. ice skating 3. dishonest
4. If it rains this afternoon, we'll stay at home.
5. I'd run away if I saw a snake.
6. What would you do if you met your favorite actor?
7. He's a free-diving teacher. 8. talented
9. You can use a concept map to organize information.
10. You can use a concept map to plan essays, stories, brochures, and other pieces of writing.

2 Listen and write. Sing. 21

- Focus students' attention on the pictures. Ask *Which sports can you see? Which sports does the boy do? Which sports would the boy like to do?*
- Play the whole song as students follow along. Ask *Which sports does the boy do? Which sports would the boy like to do?*
- Play the song a second time, pausing for students to write the missing words.
- Play the recording a third time if necessary.
- Review the answers. Ask students to read each line aloud, saying the missing word.
- Play the recording once more for students to sing along

Differentiation

Below level:
- Discuss different sports with the class. Ask students *Which sports do you like? How often do you go swimming / play soccer? etc.* Elicit and help as needed.

At level:
- Ask students to imagine they lived in a different place and talk about it. For example, ask *Which sports would you play if you lived by the ocean / in the mountains?*

Above level:
- Ask different students to say second conditional sentences about sports they would do in different circumstances, e.g. *I would go skiing if I lived in the mountains.*

ANSWERS
1. soccer 2. skiing 3. climbing 4. caving
5. ice skate 6. baseball 7. diving 8. jump

Further practice
Workbook page 23
Unit 2 test, Assessment and Resource CD-ROM
Progress certificate, Assessment and Resource CD-ROM
Online Practice • Unit 2 • Review

Health Time!

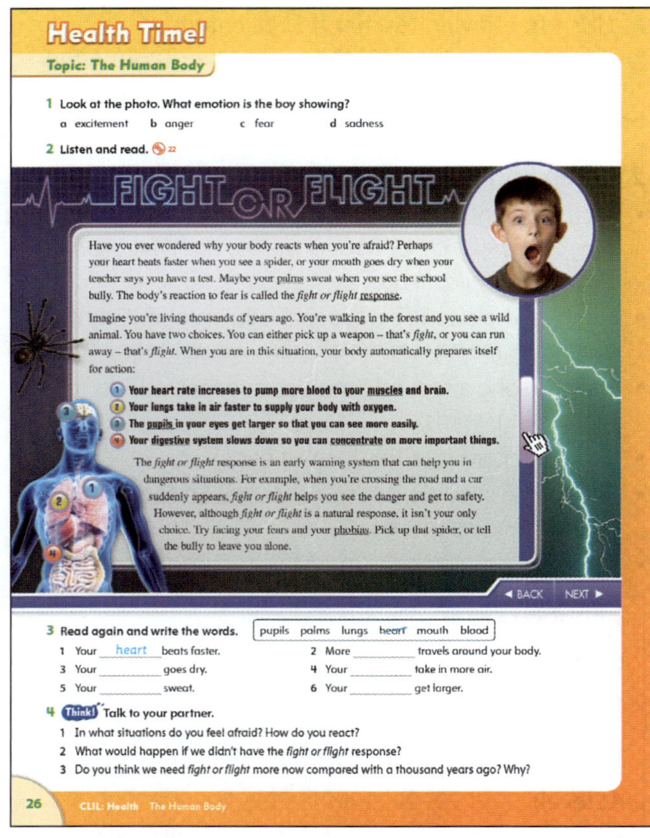

Health Time!

Topic: The Human Body

1 Look at the photo. What emotion is the boy showing?

a excitement b anger c fear d sadness

2 Listen and read. 22

FIGHT OR FLIGHT

Have you ever wondered why your body reacts when you're afraid? Perhaps your heart beats faster when you see a spider, or your mouth goes dry when your teacher says you have a test. Maybe your palms sweat when you see the school bully. The body's reaction to fear is called the *fight or flight* response.

Imagine you're living thousands of years ago. You're walking in the forest and you see a wild animal. You have two choices. You can either pick up a weapon – that's *fight*, or you can run away – that's *flight*. When you are in this situation, your body automatically prepares itself for action:

1. **Your heart rate increases to pump more blood to your muscles and brain.**
2. **Your lungs take in air faster to supply your body with oxygen.**
3. **The pupils in your eyes get larger so that you can see more easily.**
4. **Your digestive system slows down so you can concentrate on more important things.**

The *fight or flight* response is an early warning system that can help you in dangerous situations. For example, when you're crossing the road and a car suddenly appears, *fight or flight* helps you see the danger and get to safety. However, although *fight or flight* is a natural response, it isn't your only choice. Try facing your fears and your phobias. Pick up that spider, or tell the bully to leave you alone.

◀ BACK NEXT ▶

3 Read again and write the words. pupils palms lungs ~~heart~~ mouth blood

1 Your heart beats faster. 2 More ______ travels around your body.
3 Your ______ goes dry. 4 Your ______ take in more air.
5 Your ______ sweat. 6 Your ______ get larger.

4 Think! Talk to your partner.

1 In what situations do you feel afraid? How do you react?
2 What would happen if we didn't have the *fight or flight* response?
3 Do you think we need *fight or flight* more now compared with a thousand years ago? Why?

26 CLIL: Health The Human Body

Topic: The Human Body SB page 26

Learning outcomes

To learn some useful content and language about the human body

Language

Core: *palms, response, muscles, pupils, digestive, concentrate, phobia*

Extra: *fight, flight, rate, response, react, reaction, sweat, fear, weapons, brain, lungs, heart, mouth, blood*

Materials

CD 22

Oxford iTools Digital classroom • Health Time! • The Human Body

Warmer

Critical Thinking

- Ask students what things make them feel scared and why.

Lead-in

- Tell students that they are going to learn about the human body. Ask them to say how their body feels when they are scared.

1 Look at the photos. What emotion is the boy showing?

Critical Thinking

- Read out the words and ask students around the class to mime each emotion.
- Point to the photos . Ask students to say what they can see in the photos.
- Focus on the photo of the boy. Ask students how they think the boy feels.

2 Listen and read. 22

- Play the recording for students to listen and follow the text in their Student Books.
- Play the recording again. Ask comprehension questions, e.g. *What does your heart do when you are scared? How does the fight or flight response help you? Why do the pupils in your eyes get bigger when you are scared?*

3 Read again and write the words.

- Explain that students need to find information in the text to complete the sentences with the words in the box. Read out the first sentence and allow students time to look at the text and find the answer.
- Students complete the rest of the activity individually.

ANSWERS

1. heart 2. blood 3. mouth 4. lungs 5. palms 6. pupils

4 Think. Talk to your partner.

Critical Thinking

- Read out the questions and elicit suggestions from students around the class.

Collaboration

- Put students in pairs to discuss their answers.
- Have pairs report back to the class.

Differentiation

Below level:

- Divide the class into three groups. Assign one question to each group. Students talk together to decide on the best answer to their question.
- Invite students from each group to report their answer to the class.

At level:

- Students complete the activity.

Above level:

- When students have finished discussing the questions and have reported back to the class, ask them to work in pairs to make a list of things they are afraid of, then discuss how they could face those fears.

Further practice

Workbook page 24

Online Practice • Health Time!

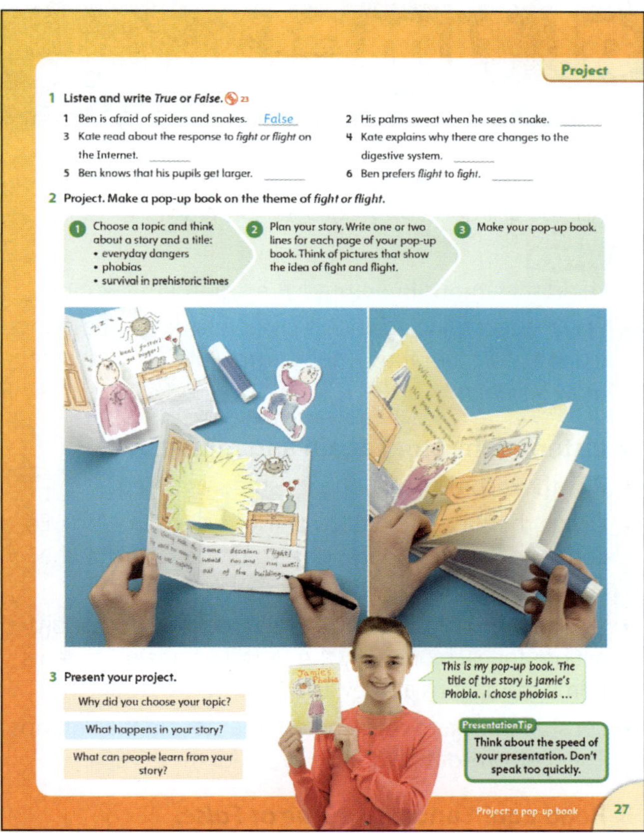

Project

1 Listen and write *True* or *False*. 23

1 Ben is afraid of spiders and snakes. False
2 His palms sweat when he sees a snake. ____
3 Kate read about the response to *fight or flight* on the Internet. ____
4 Kate explains why there are changes to the digestive system. ____
5 Ben knows that his pupils get larger. ____
6 Ben prefers *flight* to *fight*. ____

2 Project. Make a pop-up book on the theme of *fight or flight*.

1 Choose a topic and think about a story and a title:
• everyday dangers
• phobias
• survival in prehistoric times

2 Plan your story. Write one or two lines for each page of your pop-up book. Think of pictures that show the idea of fight and flight.

3 Make your pop-up book.

3 Present your project.

Why did you choose your topic?

What happens in your story?

What can people learn from your story?

PresentationTip
Think about the speed of your presentation. Don't speak too quickly.

Project: a pop-up book 27

Project SB page 27

Learning outcomes

To listen and mark sentences *True* or *False*

To make a pop-up book on the theme of *fight or flight*

Language

This is my pop-up book. The title of the story is Jamie's Phobia. I chose phobias…

Materials

CD 23; paper, colored pencils, scissors, glue

Oxford iTools Digital classroom • Health Time! • Project

Warmer

- Ask students what they can remember about the text on Student Book p26. Ask them to say what your heart, mouth, lungs, pupils, and palms do when you are scared.

1 Listen and write *True* or *False*. 23

- Play the recording. Students need to listen and decide whether each sentence is true or false.
- Play the recording once through. Play again, pausing after each answer is mentioned so that students have time to think about their answers.

ANSWERS

1. False 2. True 3. True 4. True 5. False 6. True

2 Project. Make a pop-up book on the theme of *fight or flight*.

Creativity

- Explain that students are going to make a pop-up book on the theme of fight of flight. Their story needs to be about fear and the response to that fear. Ask *What do you need to make this project?* Elicit *paper, colored pens* or *pencils, scissors, glue*.
- Focus on the instructions. Ask a student to read out the instructions to the class.
- Students choose a topic for their story and decide what their story is going to be about.
- Hand out paper, scissors, coloured pencils, and glue. Show students how to fold the paper to make the pages of their books.
- With the page folded, show students how to make two small cuts into the folded edge (about 2cm long). When they open the book, they can push the strip through so that it "pops up" on the inside (see photos).
- Have students write a couple of lines of their story and draw pictures on each page of their book.
- Show students how to glue a picture of a person or thing to the "pop-up" strip on each page.

Differentiation

Below level:

- Write the topics on the board and encourage students around the class to suggest everyday dangers, phobias, and the dangers people faced in prehistoric times. Write their suggestions on the board, under the correct topics.
- Choose one suggestion from the board and start a story about it, e.g. *Sam woke up late yesterday morning. He was in a hurry to get to school. He got dressed and ate his breakfast very quickly. Then he ran out of the house.* Encourage a student to continue the story with a sentence, then ask another student to add another sentence. Repeat until you have a short story. Ask questions to prompt students, e.g. *What do you think he saw? How do you think he felt? What do you think he did?*
- Students choose a story and work in pairs to produce their pop-up books.

At level:

- Students complete the activity.

Above level:

- When students have completed their pop-up books, ask them to write three questions about their story, then swap stories with a partner. When they have finished reading each other's stories, they can ask and answer the questions.

3 Present your project.

Communication

- Put students into groups of three or four. Tell them that they are now going to talk about their projects with each other.
- Demonstrate by either holding up a completed pop-up book, or using the example in the Student Book. Talk about the pop-up book, as in the example.
- Students talk in groups.
- Invite individual students to stand up and present their projects to the class.

Further practice
Workbook page 25
Online Practice • Health Time!

3 It's festival time!

3 It's festival time!

Lesson One Story

1 Listen and read. What does Kate draw? 24

2 Listen to the story again and repeat. Act.

3 Read again and write *True* or *False*.

1 Kate arrives early at the club. False
2 Kate has told Ed about the pictures. ______
3 Kate has changed their idea. ______
4 Kate tells the club about their pictures. ______
5 Fin makes the food for the celebration. ______
6 The wall doesn't look good. ______

28 Unit 3 It's festival time!

Lesson One SB page 28

Story

Learning outcomes

To read and understand a story

To act out a story

Language

Introducing core vocabulary (Lesson 2) through a story

Extra: *towers*

Materials

CD 24; a plain piece of paper for each student

Oxford iTools Digital classroom • Unit 3 • Story

Warmer

- Ask students to tell you what they remember about the last episode. If necessary, ask questions, e.g. *What topic did the children choose for their mural? Why wasn't Kate happy?*
- Ask students to make predictions about what might happen in this episode. Ask *Do you think Kate's pictures will be good? Why / Why not?*

1 Listen and read. What does Kate draw? 24

- Focus students' attention on the pictures and the story. Discuss with the class whether their responses to the warm-up questions were correct.
- Play the recording. Students listen and follow along.
- Ask the gist question *What does Kate draw?*

ANSWER

Kate draws famous buildings from around the world.

- Play the recording again. Ask comprehension questions, e.g. *What did the group want Kate to draw? Why did Kate draw buildings?*

2 Listen to the story again and repeat. Act.

- Play the recording, pausing for students to repeat.
- Divide the class into groups of five to play Fin, Libby, Ed, Tom, and Kate. If the class doesn't divide evenly, some students can have multiple roles.
- Ask children to look at the story frames and decide on actions for each one. Play the recording again. Students mime the actions as they listen.
- Let students practice acting out the story in their groups. Then ask one or two groups to act for the class.

3 Read again and write *True* or *False*.

- Look at the example together. Ask *Does Kate arrive early at the club?* Establish that the example is false.
- Ask students to read the rest of the sentences and write *True* or *False*.

Differentiation

Below level:

- Ask students to read the sentences aloud. Then work together to find the answers in the story. Monitor and help as needed.

At level:

- Students complete the activity.

Above level:

- Students rewrite the false sentences to make them true. If time permits, students can come to the front and retell a short version of the story to the class.

ANSWERS

1. False 2. False 3. True 4. True 5. False 6. False

Further practice

Workbook page 26

Online Practice • Unit 3 • Story

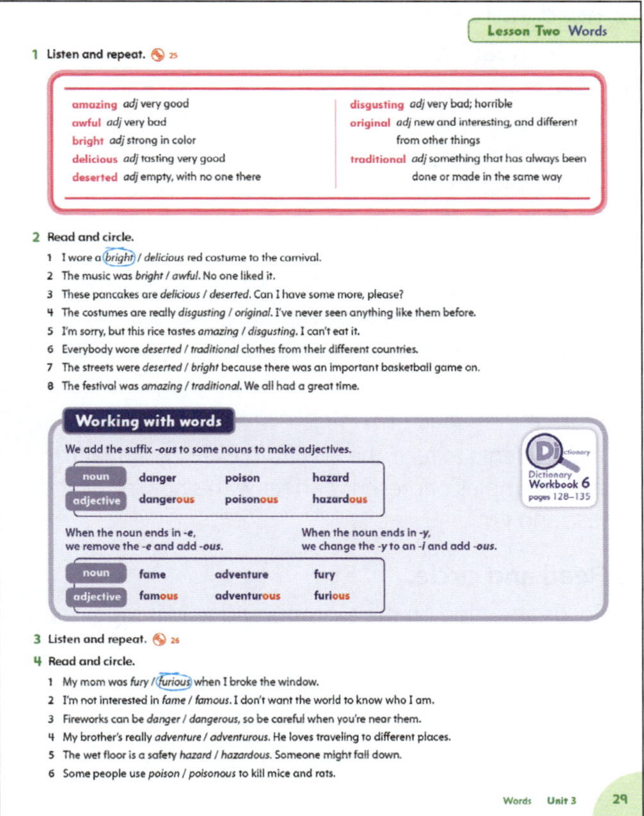

Lesson Two Words

1 Listen and repeat. 25

amazing *adj* very good
awful *adj* very bad
bright *adj* strong in color
delicious *adj* tasting very good
deserted *adj* empty, with no one there
disgusting *adj* very bad; horrible
original *adj* new and interesting, and different from other things
traditional *adj* something that has always been done or made in the same way

2 Read and circle.

1 I wore a *bright* / *delicious* red costume to the carnival.
2 The music was *bright* / *awful*. No one liked it.
3 These pancakes are *delicious* / *deserted*. Can I have some more, please?
4 The costumes are really *disgusting* / *original*. I've never seen anything like them before.
5 I'm sorry, but this rice tastes *amazing* / *disgusting*. I can't eat it.
6 Everybody wore *deserted* / *traditional* clothes from their different countries.
7 The streets were *deserted* / *bright* because there was an important basketball game on.
8 The festival was *amazing* / *traditional*. We all had a great time.

Working with words

We add the suffix *-ous* to some nouns to make adjectives.

noun	danger	poison	hazard
adjective	dangerous	poisonous	hazardous

When the noun ends in *-e*, we remove the *-e* and add *-ous*.

When the noun ends in *-y*, we change the *-y* to an *-i* and add *-ous*.

noun	fame	adventure	fury
adjective	famous	adventurous	furious

Dictionary Workbook 6 pages 128–135

3 Listen and repeat. 26

4 Read and circle.

1 My mom was *fury* / *furious* when I broke the window.
2 I'm not interested in *fame* / *famous*. I don't want the world to know who I am.
3 Fireworks can be *danger* / *dangerous*, so be careful when you're near them.
4 My brother's really *adventure* / *adventurous*. He loves traveling to different places.
5 The wet floor is a safety *hazard* / *hazardous*. Someone might fall down.
6 Some people use *poison* / *poisonous* to kill mice and rats.

Words Unit 3 29

Lesson Two SB page 29

Words

Learning outcomes

To identify different adjectives

To use the suffix *-ous* to make adjectives from certain nouns.

Language

Words: *original, awful, amazing, deserted, disgusting, traditional, bright, delicious*

Working with words: *danger / dangerous, poison / poisonous, hazard / hazardous, fame / famous, adventure / adventurous, fury / furious* (Student Book); *luxury / luxurious, mountain / mountainous, mystery / mysterious* (Workbook)

Extra: pancake, fireworks

Materials

CD 25–26 Dictionary Workbook pages 128–135

Oxford iTools Digital classroom • Unit 3 • Words

Warmer

- Write the nouns food, clothes, and places in overlapping circles on the board (in a Venn diagram). Point to the first word. Ask students to think of different adjectives to describe food. If the word can be used to describe other nouns, write it in the appropriate overlapping section.
- Do the same with the other nouns. These may not generate as many words, as they may have already been suggested.
- Ask students to use some of the adjectives to describe food / clothes / places that they like or dislike, e.g. *I hate cabbage. It's disgusting!*

1 Listen and repeat. 25

- Play the recording, pausing for students to repeat.
- Play a second time. Students listen and repeat.
- Ask individual students to say the words for the class.

2 Read and circle.

- Draw attention to the example. Ask students *Does "delicious" describe clothes? What does it describe?* Establish that *delicious* is used to describe food, not clothes, so *bright* must be the correct answer.
- Ask students to read the sentences and circle the correct adjectives.
- Ask different students to read the sentences aloud.

ANSWERS

1. bright 2. awful 3. delicious 4. original
5. disgusting 6. traditional 7. deserted 8. amazing

3 Listen and repeat. 26

- Before doing the activity, focus students' attention on the *Working with words* section.
- Tell students you are going to look at a suffix used to make certain nouns into adjectives. Ask *Does a suffix come at the beginning or the end of a word?*
- Read the rules and examples with the class. Ask comprehension questions, e.g. *What is the rule for adding -ous when the noun ends in "e"? What is the rule when the noun ends in "y"?*
- Play the recording. Students listen and repeat.
- Play the recording a second time. Students listen and repeat. Repeat as often as necessary.

4 Read and circle.

- Look at the example together. Ask *Do we need an adjective or a noun to complete this sentence?* Establish that we need an adjective so the correct word must be *furious*. Ask students to read the rest of the sentences and circle the correct words.
- Ask individual students to read the sentences aloud.

Differentiation

Below level:

- Have students read number 1. Ask *How did Mom feel?* Elicit *furious*. Look at number 2. *Ask What isn't she interested in?* Elicit *fame*. Point out that if they are looking for the answer to *how*, use an adjective. For the answer to *what*, use a noun. Students complete the activity.

At level:

- Students complete the activity.

Above level:

- After students complete the activity, ask them to write sentences using the uncircled words from the exercise, e.g. *The soccer player ran with fury toward the goal.*

ANSWERS

1. furious 2. fame 3. dangerous 4. adventurous
5. hazard 6. poison

Further practice

Workbook page 27

Online Practice • Unit 3 • Words

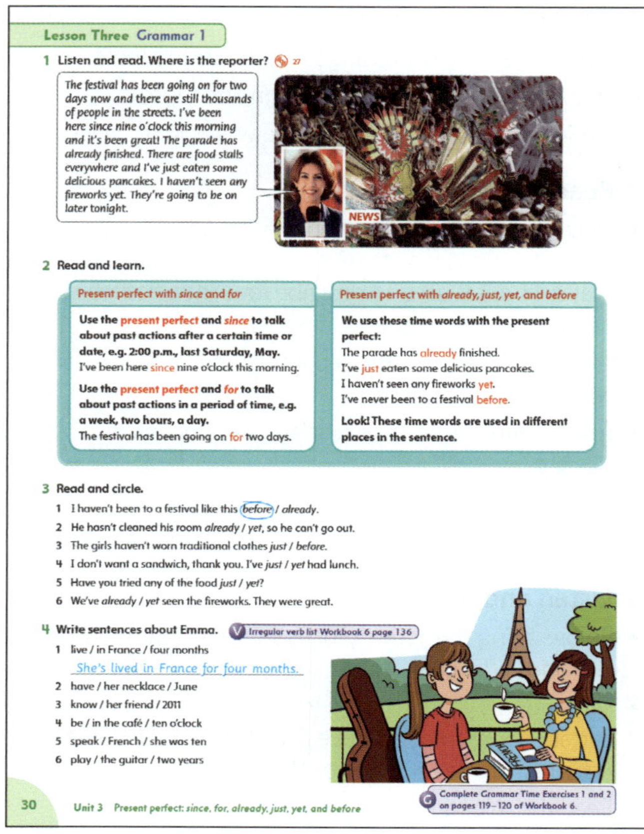

Lesson Three Grammar 1

1 Listen and read. Where is the reporter? 27

The festival has been going on for two days now and there are still thousands of people in the streets. I've been here since nine o'clock this morning and it's been great! The parade has already finished. There are food stalls everywhere and I've just eaten some delicious pancakes. I haven't seen any fireworks yet. They're going to be on later tonight.

2 Read and learn.

Present perfect with *since* and *for*

Use the present perfect and *since* to talk about past actions after a certain time or date, e.g. 2:00 p.m., last Saturday, May.
I've been here since nine o'clock this morning.

Use the present perfect and *for* to talk about past actions in a period of time, e.g. a week, two hours, a day.
The festival has been going on for two days.

Present perfect with *already, just, yet,* and *before*

We use these time words with the present perfect:
The parade has already finished.
I've just eaten some delicious pancakes.
I haven't seen any fireworks yet.
I've never been to a festival before.

Look! These time words are used in different places in the sentence.

3 Read and circle.

1 I haven't been to a festival like this *before* / *already*.
2 He hasn't cleaned his room *already* / *yet*, so he can't go out.
3 The girls haven't worn traditional clothes *just* / *before*.
4 I don't want a sandwich, thank you. I've *just* / *yet* had lunch.
5 Have you tried any of the food *just* / *yet*?
6 We've *already* / *yet* seen the fireworks. They were great.

4 Write sentences about Emma. Irregular verb list Workbook 6 page 136

1 live / in France / four months
She's lived in France for four months.
2 have / her necklace / June
3 know / her friend / 2011
4 be / in the café / ten o'clock
5 speak / French / she was ten
6 play / the guitar / two years

30 Unit 3 Present perfect: *since, for, already, just, yet,* and *before*

Complete Grammar Time Exercises 1 and 2 on pages 119–120 of Workbook 6.

Lesson Three SB page 30

Grammar 1

Learning outcomes

To use the present perfect with *since* and *for*

To use the present perfect with *already*, *just*, *yet*, and *before*

Language

Core: *I've been here since nine o'clock this morning. The festival has been going on for two days. The parade has already finished. I've just eaten some delicious pancakes. I haven't seen any fireworks yet. I've never been to a festival before.*

Extra: *parade, necklace*

Materials

CD 27

Oxford iTools Digital classroom • Unit 3 • Grammar 1

Warmer

- Discuss festivals with the class. Ask *What is your favorite festival? What do people eat during this festival? Do you know any festivals from other countries?*

1 Listen and read. Where is the reporter? 27

- Focus attention on the photograph. Ask *What can you see?*
- Play the recording. Students follow along. Ask the gist question *Where is the reporter?*

ANSWER

The reporter is at a festival.

- Play the recording again. Ask comprehension questions, e.g. *How long has the festival been going on?*

2 Read and learn.

- Read the rules and examples in the first box together.
- Write the following sentences on the board and invite students to write *for* or *since*.
  I've been here _______ 20 minutes.
  They've been at the park _________ 11 o'clock.
  I've had this book ________ I was eight.
  We've been friends _________ five years.
- Read the second box together. Ask *Which word do we use… to say that something has happened very recently? (just) / in negative sentences and questions? (yet) / to talk about things we have or haven't done in the past? (before) / to show that something happened earlier? (already)*
- Ask students to read the text from Exercise 1 again and find examples of present perfect with *since, for, already, just*, and *yet*.

3 Read and circle.

- Focus attention on the example and read it together.
- Ask students to read the sentences and circle the correct words. Ask different students to read the sentences aloud.

ANSWERS

1. before 2. yet 3. before 4. just 5. yet
6. already

4 Write sentences about Emma.

- Ask students to look at the picture. Ask *Where does Emma live? Where is she? What instrument can she play?*
- Have students write sentences using the word prompts and *for* or *since*.
- Read the example with the class, then let students write the rest of the sentences from the word prompts.

Differentiation

Below level:

- Have students look at Workbook page 136 to review the past participle. Elicit the past participles for the verbs in the activity. Write some time phrases on the board, e.g. *July, 4:00 p.m., three weeks*. Ask children to write *since* or *for* next to each. Then students complete the activity.

At level:

- Students complete the activity.

Above level:

- Ask students to write sentences about themselves using the present perfect. Use Exercise 4 as a model.

ANSWERS

1. She's lived in France for four months.
2. She's had her necklace since June.
3. She's known her friend since 2011.
4. She's been in the café since ten o'clock.
5. She's spoken French since she was ten.
6. She's played the guitar for two years.

Further practice

Grammar Time, Workbook pages 119–120
Workbook page 28
Online Practice • Unit 3 • Grammar 1

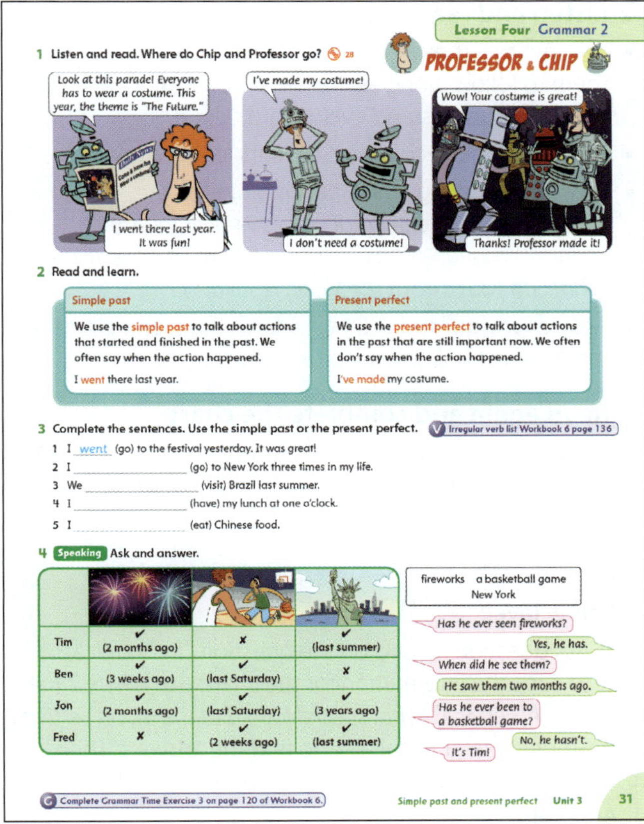

Lesson Four Grammar 2

1 Listen and read. Where do Chip and Professor go? 28

PROFESSOR & CHIP

2 Read and learn.

Simple past

We use the simple past to talk about actions that started and finished in the past. We often say when the action happened.

I went there last year.

Present perfect

We use the present perfect to talk about actions in the past that are still important now. We often don't say when the action happened.

I've made my costume.

3 Complete the sentences. Use the simple past or the present perfect. Irregular verb list Workbook 6 page 136

1 I went (go) to the festival yesterday. It was great!
2 I ______ (go) to New York three times in my life.
3 We ______ (visit) Brazil last summer.
4 I ______ (have) my lunch at one o'clock.
5 I ______ (eat) Chinese food.

4 Speaking Ask and answer.

	fireworks	a basketball game	New York
Tim	✔ (2 months ago)	✘	✔ (last summer)
Ben	✔ (3 weeks ago)	✔ (last Saturday)	✘
Jon	✔ (2 months ago)	✔ (last Saturday)	✔ (3 years ago)
Fred	✘	✔ (2 weeks ago)	✔ (last summer)

fireworks a basketball game New York

Complete Grammar Time Exercise 3 on page 120 of Workbook 6.

Simple past and present perfect Unit 3 31

Lesson Four SB page 31

Grammar 2

Learning outcomes

To use the simple past to talk about actions that started and finished in the past

To use the present perfect to talk about actions that started in the past and are still important now

Speaking: asking and answering questions about things that people have done

Language

Core: *I went to that festival last year. I've made my costume. Has he ever been to a festival? Yes, he has. Has he ever been to a soccer match? No, he hasn't.*

Extra: *Chinese*

Materials

CD 28

Oxford iTools Digital classroom • Unit 3 • Grammar 2

Warmer

- Discuss festivals with the class. Ask *Have you ever been to a festival? Where was it? What did you do there?* Encourage students to use the present perfect. Write any useful vocabulary on the board.

1 Listen and read. Where do Chip and Professor go? 28

- Play the recording. Students follow the words in their books. Ask the gist question.

ANSWER

Professor and Chip go to a festival.

- Play the recording again. Students read the text again. Ask comprehension questions, e.g. *What is the theme of the festival? Does Professor wear a costume?*
- Check that students understand the joke. Ask *Why does Chip say Professor made his costume?*

2 Read and learn.

- Focus on the rule and example in the first box. Elicit further examples of simple past sentences. Write them on one side of the board.
- Read the second box with the students. Elicit similar present perfect sentences from the class and write these on the other side of the board.
- Ask students to re-read the story and find further examples of simple past and present perfect sentences.

3 Complete the sentences. Use the simple past or the present perfect.

- Focus on the example and ask a student to read it to the class. Ask *Why do we use the simple past here?*
- Students read the rest of the sentences and complete them using the simple past or the present perfect.

ANSWERS

1. went 2. 've been 3. visited 4. had 5. 've eaten

4 Ask and answer.

- Ask students to look at the chart about Tim, Ben, Jon, and Fred's life experiences. Explain that students are going to choose one boy from the chart. Their partner is going to ask questions to find out who it is.
- Ask a pair of students to read the example dialogue.
- Students work in pairs. They take turns to choose a boy and answer their partner's questions about him.

Differentiation

Below level:

- Have students focus on one question at a time, e.g. *Has (Tim) ever seen fireworks?* After they've answered this for each boy in the chart, move on to the next column.

At level:

- Students complete the activity.

Above level:

- Extend the activity by asking students to make two columns in their notebooks for themselves and their partner. Fill in the chart. Then ask and answer.

Further practice

Grammar Time, Workbook page 119–120

Workbook page 29

Unit 3 Language practice worksheet, Assessment and Resource CD-ROM

Online Practice • Unit 3 • Grammar 2

Skills Time!

Lesson Five

Reading

1 Look at the travel article. Which countries are the festivals in?

2 Listen and read. 29

Top Food Festivals

Going to festivals is always fun, but going to festivals that have delicious food is even better! Here are some of our favorite festivals around the world.

1 If you like food, you'll love the Kimchi Festival. This festival takes place in October every year in Gwangju in Korea. It lasts for five days but what does it celebrate? Kimchi, of course! Kimchi is a traditional dish made with onions, garlic, peppers, and other vegetables. It is very spicy, but it can be sweet, too. It is also very good for you! At the festival, visitors can taste different kinds of kimchi. There are also kimchi-making competitions.

2 The Gilroy Garlic Festival is one of the largest food festivals in the U.S.A. The festival takes place every year in Gilroy, California. It happens on the last weekend in July and it's one of the best garlic festivals in the world. So what do people do during the festival? Well, they eat lots of things made with garlic including garlic ice cream and garlic fries. There are also garlic cooking demonstrations, music, and dancing.

3 People celebrate the Moon Festival in different parts of Asia including China. The festival takes place every year in September or October. It lasts for three days and people celebrate the end of the summer harvest. So, what do people eat? The traditional food is moon cakes. These are round, sweet cakes and they are very popular. The cakes have different fillings. You can have ice cream, chocolate, or traditional red-bean paste. People also carry lanterns at the festival and watch traditional dancing.

3 Read again and complete the chart.

Name?	The Kimchi Festival	The Gilroy Garlic Festival	The Moon Festival
Country?	Korea	1 ______	China
When?	2 ______	July	September / October
How long?	3 ______	A weekend	4 ______
Special food?	Kimchi	5 ______	6 ______

32 Unit 3 Reading: a travel article

Lesson Five SB page 32

Skills Time!

Skills development

Reading: read a magazine travel article

Language

Recycled: vocabulary and structures seen previously

Extra: *last (v), celebrate, garlic, spicy, sweet, demonstration, harvest, fillings*

Materials

CD 29; a piece of paper and colored pencils for each pair of students (optional)

Oxford iTools Digital classroom • Unit 3 • Reading

Warmer

- Tell students they are going to read about some interesting food festivals from different countries. Invite predictions about what kinds of food they might read about. Write students' suggestions on the board.

1 Look at the travel article. Which countries are the festivals in?

- Ask students to look at the photographs. Point to each. Ask students to tell you which country it is in. Ask students to skim the article to find out. They should not read in detail.
- Ask students if any of the foods mentioned in the warmer appeared in the article.

ANSWER

The festivals are in: Korea (picture 1) the U.S.A. (picture 2) China (picture 3)

2 Listen and read. 29

- Tell students they are going to listen to the article. Tell them to follow along as they listen, but not to worry if they don't understand every word.
- Play the whole recording. Students follow along.
- Play the recording again, pausing to check comprehension, e.g. *What can you see at the Kimchi Festival? What do people do at the Gilroy Garlic Festival? What can you taste at the Moon Festival?*
- Answer any questions that students have, and elicit the meanings of unknown words from context.

3 Read again and complete the chart.

- Focus attention on the chart. Ask questions such as *When is the Kimchi Festival? How long does the Moon Festival last? Where is the Gilroy Garlic Festival?*

Differentiation

Below level:

- Ask questions based on the questions in Exercise 3 to elicit the information for the chart, e.g. *Where is the Kimchi Festival? What special food is at the Moon Festival?* Students refer to the text to find the answers. Then students complete the activity independently.

At level:

- Put students in pairs. Give out paper and colored pencils. Tell students they are going to write a brochure about one of the festivals, using information from the text. They can make up further details if they wish. Monitor the activity and help where necessary.

Above level:

- Put students in groups. Ask students to think about what kind of food festival they would have. Ask students to write a brochure about it. If time permits, students can share with the class.

- Ask students to read the article again and complete the missing information.
- Review answers together.

ANSWERS

Name?	The Kimchi Festival	The Gilroy Garlic Festival	The Moon Festival
Country?	Korea	The U.S.A.	China
When?	October	July	September / October
How long?	Five days	A weekend	Three days
Special Food?	Kimchi	Garlic	Moon cakes

Further practice

Workbook page 30

Online Practice • Unit 3 • Reading

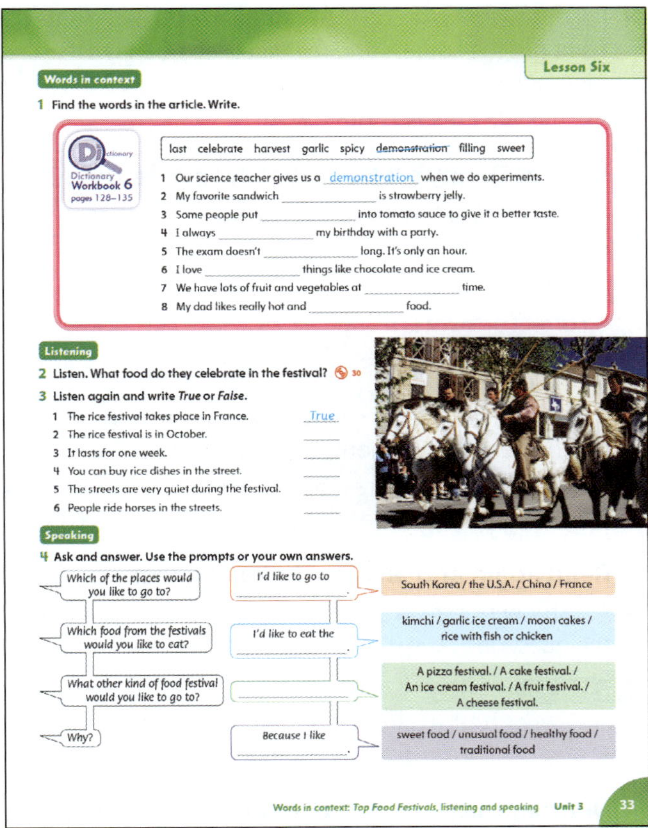

Lesson Six

Words in context

1 Find the words in the article. Write.

Dictionary Workbook 6 pages 128–135

last celebrate harvest garlic spicy ~~demonstration~~ filling sweet

1 Our science teacher gives us a demonstration when we do experiments.
2 My favorite sandwich __________ is strawberry jelly.
3 Some people put __________ into tomato sauce to give it a better taste.
4 I always __________ my birthday with a party.
5 The exam doesn't __________ long. It's only an hour.
6 I love __________ things like chocolate and ice cream.
7 We have lots of fruit and vegetables at __________ time.
8 My dad likes really hot and __________ food.

Listening

2 Listen. What food do they celebrate in the festival? 30

3 Listen again and write *True* or *False*.

1 The rice festival takes place in France. True
2 The rice festival is in October. ______
3 It lasts for one week. ______
4 You can buy rice dishes in the street. ______
5 The streets are very quiet during the festival. ______
6 People ride horses in the streets. ______

Speaking

4 Ask and answer. Use the prompts or your own answers.

Which of the places would you like to go to?
I'd like to go to __________.
South Korea / the U.S.A. / China / France

Which food from the festivals would you like to eat?
I'd like to eat the __________.
kimchi / garlic ice cream / moon cakes / rice with fish or chicken

What other kind of food festival would you like to go to?
____
A pizza festival. / A cake festival. / An ice cream festival. / A fruit festival. / A cheese festival.

Why?
Because I like __________.
sweet food / unusual food / healthy food / traditional food

Words in context: *Top Food Festivals*, listening and speaking Unit 3 33

Lesson Six SB page 33

Skills Time!

Skills development

Dictionary: discover meaning of words in context

Listening: listen for specific detail

Speaking: ask and answer questions about your food festivals

Language

Words in context: *last (v), celebrate, harvest, garlic, spicy, demonstration, filling, sweet* (Student Book); *hang, decorate, recipe, bunch* (Workbook)

Materials

CD 30; Dictionary Workbook pages 128–135; paper and colored pencils (optional)

Oxford iTools Digital classroom • Unit 3 • Words, Listening, Speaking

Warmer

- With books closed, ask students what they remember about the article from the previous lesson.
- Ask questions if necessary, e.g. *Which festivals did you read about? Where were they?*

1 Find the words in the article. Write.

- Ask the students to look at the words in the box. Explain that all of the words come from the article on page 32.
- Ask students to look at the article again and find all the underlined words. They try to determine the meaning of the words from the context.
- Students read the sentences on page 33 and complete them with the correct words.
- Review answers with the class.

Differentiation

Below level:

- Ask each student to look up one word in the Dictionary in their Workbooks. Give out paper and colored pencils. Tell children to write the definition on one side and draw a picture on the other. When students are finished, have each child hold up the picture for others to guess the word.

At level:

- Write the sentences from the activity on slips of paper. Ask students to close their books. Then play *Whispers* (see page 9).

Above level:

- Ask students to choose four of the new words and write true / false statements with them, e.g. *The Kimchi festival lasts five weeks. Ice cream is spicy.* Students swap sentences with their partners and mark them *True* or *False*.

ANSWERS

1. demonstration 2. filling 3. garlic 4. celebrate
5. last 6. sweet 7. harvest 8. spicy

2 Listen. What food do they celebrate in the festival? 30

- Tell students they are going to hear a radio interview about a food festival.
- Explain that they have to listen and identify which food is celebrated in the festival.
- Play the recording once. Then elicit the answer.

ANSWER

They celebrate rice in this food festival.

3 Listen again and write *True* or *False*.

- Look at the example together. Does anyone know where in France the festival is held? Tell students they are going to hear the recording again and to write *True* or *False*.
- Allow students time to read the sentences before you play the recording.
- Play the recording, pausing for students to write *True* or *False*.

ANSWERS

1. True 2. False 3. False 4. True 5. False 6. True

4 Ask and answer. Use the prompts or your own answers.

- Ask students to look at the example. Choose a strong student and ask him / her the questions.
- Ask students to work in pairs. Tell them to take turns asking their partner the questions. Their partner must answer using the prompts or his / her own ideas.
- If you wish, ask some of the pairs to ask and answer in front of the class.

Further practice

Workbook page 31

Unit 3 Speaking skills worksheet, Assessment and Resource CD-ROM

Online Practice • Unit 3 • Words in context, Listening, and Speaking

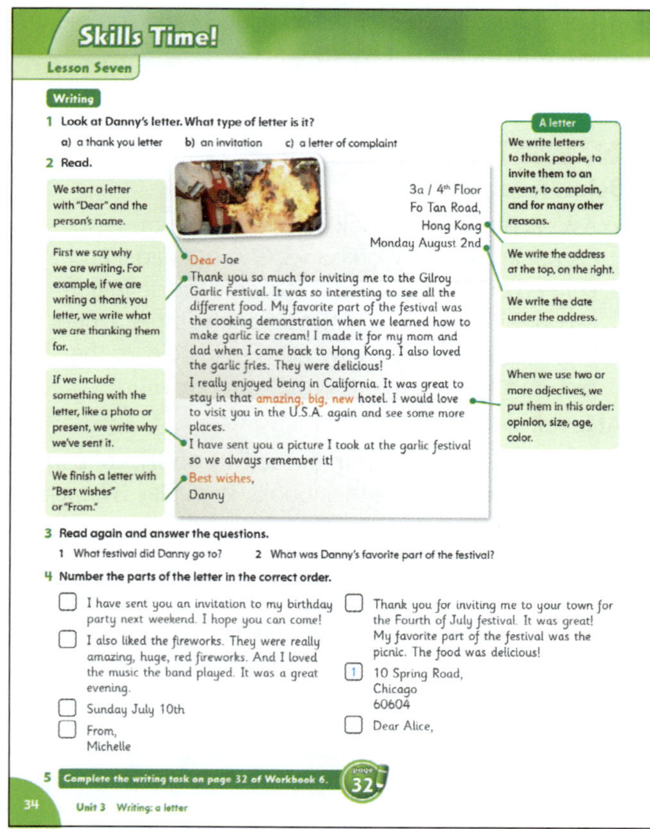

Skills Time!
Lesson Seven

Writing

1 Look at Danny's letter. What type of letter is it?

a) a thank you letter b) an invitation c) a letter of complaint

2 Read.

We start a letter with "Dear" and the person's name.

First we say why we are writing. For example, if we are writing a thank you letter, we write what we are thanking them for.

If we include something with the letter, like a photo or present, we write why we've sent it.

We finish a letter with "Best wishes" or "From."

3a / 4th Floor
Fo Tan Road,
Hong Kong
Monday August 2nd

Dear Joe

Thank you so much for inviting me to the Gilroy Garlic Festival. It was so interesting to see all the different food. My favorite part of the festival was the cooking demonstration when we learned how to make garlic ice cream! I made it for my mom and dad when I came back to Hong Kong. I also loved the garlic fries. They were delicious!

I really enjoyed being in California. It was great to stay in that amazing, big, new hotel. I would love to visit you in the U.S.A. again and see some more places.

I have sent you a picture I took at the garlic festival so we always remember it!

Best wishes,
Danny

A letter
We write letters to thank people, to invite them to an event, to complain, and for many other reasons.

We write the address at the top, on the right.

We write the date under the address.

When we use two or more adjectives, we put them in this order: opinion, size, age, color.

3 Read again and answer the questions.

1 What festival did Danny go to? 2 What was Danny's favorite part of the festival?

4 Number the parts of the letter in the correct order.

☐ I have sent you an invitation to my birthday party next weekend. I hope you can come!

☐ I also liked the fireworks. They were really amazing, huge, red fireworks. And I loved the music the band played. It was a great evening.

☐ Sunday July 10th

☐ From,
Michelle

☐ Thank you for inviting me to your town for the Fourth of July festival. It was great! My favorite part of the festival was the picnic. The food was delicious!

1 10 Spring Road,
Chicago
60604

☐ Dear Alice,

5 Complete the writing task on page 32 of Workbook 6. page 32

34 Unit 3 Writing: a letter

Lesson Seven SB page 34

Skills Time!

Skills development

Writing focus: lay out a personal letter correctly

Writing outcome: write a letter to a friend (Workbook)

Language

Recycled: vocabulary and structures seen previously

Extra: *complain, reason*

Materials

Writing poster 3; a copy of the text from poster 3, Assessment and Resource CD-ROM, for each student

Oxford iTools Digital classroom • Unit 3 • Writing

Warmer

- Play *Smiley face* (see page 8) with the class to review the vocabulary from the previous lesson.

Poster 3: A letter

- Hand out a photocopy of the poster text to each student. Encourage students to predict what the letter is about.
- Ask students the "Before reading" question in the bottom right-hand corner of the poster.
- Ask students to read the letter to themselves. Ask comprehension questions, e.g. *Who is the letter from?*
- Read the first text box on the left-hand side of the letter to the class. Ask *Why do you think Danny has written the letter?* Read the rest of the text boxes on the left. Read a little of each paragraph to show how the text of the letter relates to the instructions in the box.
- Read the text boxes on the right-hand side of the letter. Point out the address and the date. Read Danny's reasons for sending the picture in the third paragraph.
- Ask the "After reading" questions.

1 Look at Danny's letter. What type of letter is it?

- Give students a few seconds to skim the letter. Ask the gist question to the class.

ANSWER

The correct answer is *a*.

2 Read.

- Ask students to read the letter again silently. Ask comprehension questions, e.g. *Where does Joe live?*
- Draw attention to the text boxes around the letter. Choose a different student to read each text box to the class.

3 Read again and answer the questions.

- Ask students to read the letter again silently and answer the questions.

ANSWERS

Danny went to the Gilroy Garlic Festival. Danny's favorite part was the cooking demonstration.

4 Number the parts of the letter in the correct order.

- Hold up your book and point to the numbered example. Ask *What part of the letter is this? Where does it go?*
- Ask students to read the other parts of the letter and number them in the correct order.

Differentiation

Below level:

- Write a simple model letter on the board. Draw lines to various parts. Ask students to come up and label the parts of the letter, e.g. address, reason for writing.

At level:

- Ask students to suggest reasons you might write a letter to a friend. Choose one of the reasons and together, write a paragraph plan for the letter on the board, e.g. *1: Say thank you for a party invitation / 2: Say what your favorite part of the party was / 3: Say what else you enjoyed about the party / 4: Invite your friend to a food festival.* Ask students to copy the plan into their notebooks.

Above level:

- Extend the "at level" activity by using the plan to write a whole letter.

ANSWERS

1. 10 Spring Road, 2. Sunday July 10th 3. Dear Alice,
4. Thank you … 5. I also liked … 6. I have sent you …
7. From, Michelle

5 Complete the writing task on page 32 of Workbook 6.

- Refer students to the Workbook to complete the writing task. Go through the activity with them first.

Further practice

Workbook page 32

Unit 3 Writing skills worksheet, Assessment and Resource CD-ROM

Online Practice • Unit 3 • Writing

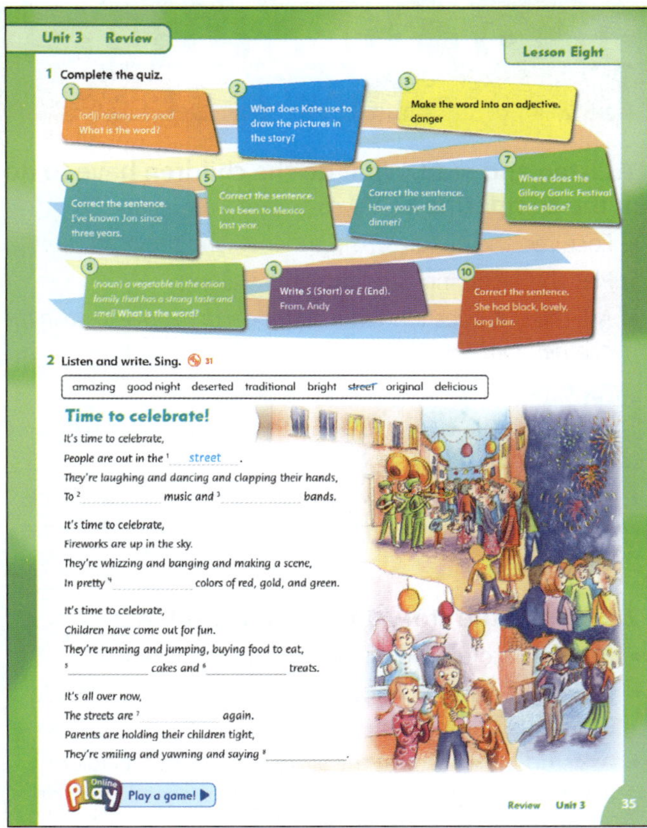
Unit 3 Review

Lesson Eight

1 Complete the quiz.

1 (adj) tasting very good What is the word?

2 What does Kate use to draw the pictures in the story?

3 Make the word into an adjective. danger

4 Correct the sentence. I've known Jon since three years.

5 Correct the sentence. I've been to Mexico last year.

6 Correct the sentence. Have you yet had dinner?

7 Where does the Gilroy Garlic Festival take place?

8 (noun) a vegetable in the onion family that has a strong taste and smell What is the word?

9 Write *S* (Start) or *E* (End). From, Andy

10 Correct the sentence. She had black, lovely, long hair.

2 Listen and write. Sing. 31

amazing good night deserted traditional bright ~~street~~ original delicious

Time to celebrate!

It's time to celebrate,
People are out in the [1] street .
They're laughing and dancing and clapping their hands,
To [2] ______ *music and* [3] ______ *bands.*

It's time to celebrate,
Fireworks are up in the sky.
They're whizzing and banging and making a scene,
In pretty [4] ______ *colors of red, gold, and green.*

It's time to celebrate,
Children have come out for fun.
They're running and jumping, buying food to eat,
[5] ______ *cakes and* [6] ______ *treats.*

It's all over now,
The streets are [7] ______ *again.*
Parents are holding their children tight,
They're smiling and yawning and saying [8] ______.

Review Unit 3 35

Lesson Eight SB page 35

Unit 3 Review

Learning outcomes

To review vocabulary and structures practiced previously

To use vocabulary and structures from the unit in the context of a song

Language

Recycled: vocabulary and structures seen previously

Extra: *whizz, bang*

Materials

CD 31

Oxford iTools Digital classroom • Unit 3 • Review

Warmer

- Play *Book race* (see page 8) to review words and structures from the unit. Read the sentences below and give students 20 seconds to find each one:
  I haven't seen any fireworks yet. (Lesson 3)
  It is very spicy, but it can be sweet, too. (Lesson 5)
  Our wall looks amazing! (Lesson 1)
  I really enjoyed being in California. (Lesson 7)
  The cakes have different fillings. (Lesson 5)
  Please bring some traditional food from around the world! (Lesson 1)
  Thank you so much for inviting me to the Gilroy Garlic Festival! (Lesson 7)
  Your costume is great! (Lesson 4)
- Review answers together.

1 Complete the quiz.

- Tell students they are going to do a quiz based on this unit. They can work individually, in pairs, or in teams.
- Students work with books open to page 35, but they may not look up the answers.

ANSWERS

1. delicious
2. a ruler
3. dangerous
4. I've known Jon for three years.
5. I went to Mexico last year.
6. Have you had dinner yet?
7. It takes place in the U.S.A. (California).
8. garlic
9. E
10. She had lovely, long, black hair.

2 Listen and write. Sing. 31

- Focus students' attention on the pictures. Ask *What can you see? What are the people doing?*
- Play the whole song as students follow along.
- Play the song again, pausing for students to write the missing words.
- Play the recording a third time if necessary.
- Review the answers. Ask students to read each line aloud, saying the missing word.
- Play the recording again. Students sing along.

Differentiation

Below level:

- Play *Vanishing verse* (see page 9).

At level:

- Ask students to work in pairs to write their own verse for the song.
- Together, brainstorm ideas about what to include. Write suggestions on the board.
- Tell students that they must begin their verse with the line *It's festival time again*, as in the book.
- Students write the remaining three lines. If time permits, students share with the class. Encourage them to sing.

Above level:

- Extend the "at level" activity by divide students into groups. Ask each group to write at least two verses to make a new song. Students practice their songs. If time permits, ask the groups to perform them.

ANSWERS

1. street 2. original 3. traditional 4. bright
5. Amazing 6. delicious 7. deserted 8. good night

Further practice

Workbook page 33
Unit 3 test, Assessment and Resource CD-ROM
Progress test 1, Assessment and Resource CD-ROM
Skills test 1, Assessment and Resource CD-ROM
Values 1 worksheet, Units 1–3, Assessment and Resource CD-ROM
Writing portfolio 1 worksheet, Assessment and Resource CD-ROM
Progress certificate, Assessment and Resource CD-ROM
Online Practice • Unit 3 • Review

4 Transportation of the future!

4 Transportation of the future!

Lesson One Story

1 Listen and read. What do the children have to do in the competition? 33

2 Listen to the story again and repeat. Act.

3 Read again and write the answers.

1 Is Mr. Martin from a museum? Yes, he is.
2 Is he talking about a visit to the museum?
3 Do the children have to draw a form of transportation?
4 Do they have two weeks to complete their work?
5 Is the first prize a ride in an airplane?
6 Do the children decide to go to the library?

38 Unit 4 Transportation of the future!

Lesson One SB page 38

Story

Learning outcomes

To read and understand a story

To act out a story

Language

Introducing core vocabulary (Lesson 2) through a story

Extra: *form, gas*

Materials

CD 33

Oxford iTools Digital classroom • Unit 4 • Story

Warmer

- Ask students what they remember about the last episode. If necessary, ask questions such as, *What did Kate draw pictures of? Did the children like Kate's drawings? What did Fin ask them to bring to the celebration?*
- Tell students this is the first episode of a new story about the DSD Club. Tell them the unit topic is *Transportation of the future!* Invite suggestions about what might happen in the story.

1 Listen and read. What do the children have to do in the competition? 33

- Focus on the pictures. Ask students who they can see.
- Play the recording. Students follow along.
- Ask the gist question *What do the children have to do in the competition?*

ANSWER

The children have to do a drawing of a future form of transportation.

- Play the recording again. Ask further questions to check comprehension, e.g. *Where is Mr. Martin from? What's the first prize?*

2 Listen to the story again and repeat. Act.

- Play the recording, pausing for students to repeat.
- Divide the class into groups of six to play Fin, Mr. Martin, Libby, Ed, Tom, and Kate.
- Ask students to look at the story frames and decide on actions for each one. Play the recording again. Students mime the actions as they listen.

Differentiation

Below level:

- Ask students to underline words in the story they don't know. Have them first guess the meaning with context clues. Then look the words up in a dictionary. Have students write the definitions in their own words in their notebooks.

At level:

- Write the dialogue from frame 4 on the board and read it with the students. Then play *Disappearing dialogue* (see page 9).

Above level:

- Extend the "at level" activity to include frames 3 and 4.

3 Read again and write the answers.

- Look at the example together. Elicit that the question has been given a short answer.
- Students read the questions and write short answers.

ANSWERS

1. Yes, he is. 2. No, he isn't. 3. Yes, they do.
4. Yes, they do. 5. No, it isn't. 6. No, they don't.

Further practice
Workbook page 34
Online Practice • Unit 4 • Story

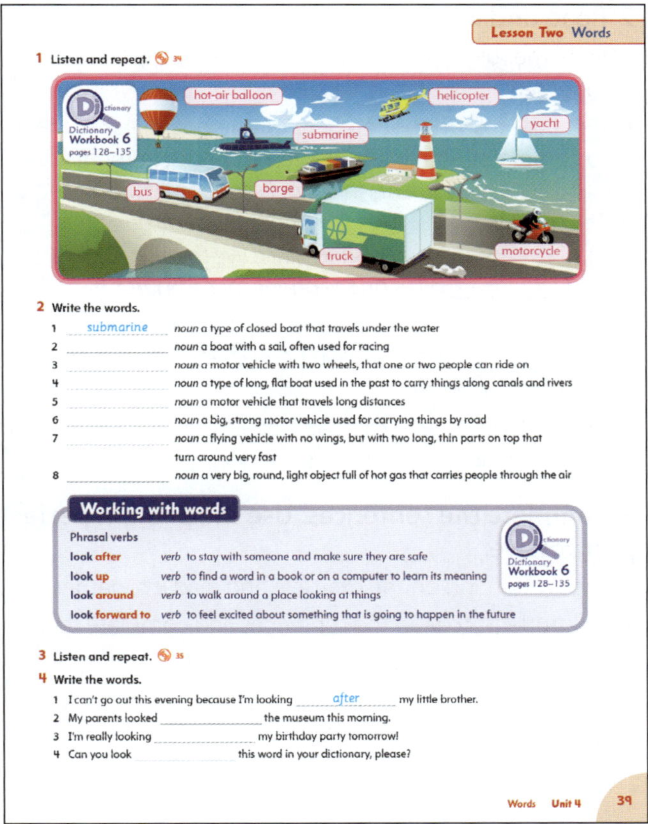
Lesson Two Words

1 Listen and repeat. 34

2 Write the words.

1 submarine *noun* a type of closed boat that travels under the water
2 ______ *noun* a boat with a sail, often used for racing
3 ______ *noun* a motor vehicle with two wheels, that one or two people can ride on
4 ______ *noun* a type of long, flat boat used in the past to carry things along canals and rivers
5 ______ *noun* a motor vehicle that travels long distances
6 ______ *noun* a big, strong motor vehicle used for carrying things by road
7 ______ *noun* a flying vehicle with no wings, but with two long, thin parts on top that turn around very fast
8 ______ *noun* a very big, round, light object full of hot gas that carries people through the air

Working with words

Phrasal verbs
look after *verb* to stay with someone and make sure they are safe
look up *verb* to find a word in a book or on a computer to learn its meaning
look around *verb* to walk around a place looking at things
look forward to *verb* to feel excited about something that is going to happen in the future

Dictionary Workbook 6 pages 128–135

3 Listen and repeat. 35

4 Write the words.

1 I can't go out this evening because I'm looking after my little brother.
2 My parents looked ______ the museum this morning.
3 I'm really looking ______ my birthday party tomorrow!
4 Can you look ______ this word in your dictionary, please?

Words Unit 4 39

Lesson Two SB page 39

Words

Learning outcomes

To identify different forms of transportation

To understand the meanings of different phrasal verbs with *look*

Language

Words: *hot-air balloon, submarine, bus, yacht, helicopter, motorcycle, truck, barge*

Working with words: *look after, look up, look around, look forward to* (Student Book); *look into, look for, look ahead, look up to* (Workbook)

Extra: canal, vehicle, gas

Materials

CD 34–35 Dictionary Workbook pages 128–135

Oxford iTools Digital classroom • Unit 4 • Words

Warmer

- Ask *How do you travel to school? Which types of transportation do you use to travel to different towns and cities? What's the most unusual type of transportation you have used?*

1 Listen and repeat. 34

- Ask students to look at the picture and the words. Play the recording, pausing for students to repeat.
- Play it again. Students listen and repeat.
- Ask individual students to say the words for the class.

2 Write the words.

- Draw attention to the example answer. Ask students to find the submarine in the picture from Exercise 1.
- Ask students to read the descriptions and write the correct form of transportation, using the Exercise 1 picture.

ANSWERS

1. submarine 2. yacht 3. motorcycle 4. barge 5. bus 6. truck 7. helicopter 8. hot-air balloon

3 Listen and repeat. 35

- Focus on the *Working with words* section first.
- Ask students *What is the root verb in all of the phrasal verbs?* Explain that sometimes we can work out the meaning of a phrasal verb but often we just have to learn them.
- Ask students to read the list of phrasal verbs and their meanings.
- Play the recording. Students listen and repeat.
- Play it again. Students listen and repeat.
- Ask individual students to say the words for the class.

4 Write the words.

- Look at the example together. Ask *What does "look after" mean?* Establish that this is the only correct answer.
- Ask students to read the rest of the sentences and complete them with the correct words.

Differentiation

Below level:

- Write *after*, *up*, *around*, and *forward to* on the board in one column. Ask children to say or mime what each one means. Then write *look* in front of each preposition. Explain that the meanings have changed. Write these fill-in-the-blank sentences on the board: *Can you (look after) my cat while I'm on vacation? / Please (look up) the new words in the dictionary. / I'm going to (look around) the store. / We're (looking forward to) visiting Grandma.* Ask students to write the answers. Then students complete the activity independently.

At level:

- Students complete the activity. Then check answers with a partner.

Above level:

- After students finish, ask them to write sentences of their own using the phrasal verbs. Monitor and help as needed.

ANSWERS

1. after 2. around 3. forward to 4. up

Further practice
Workbook page 35
Online Practice • Unit 4 • Words

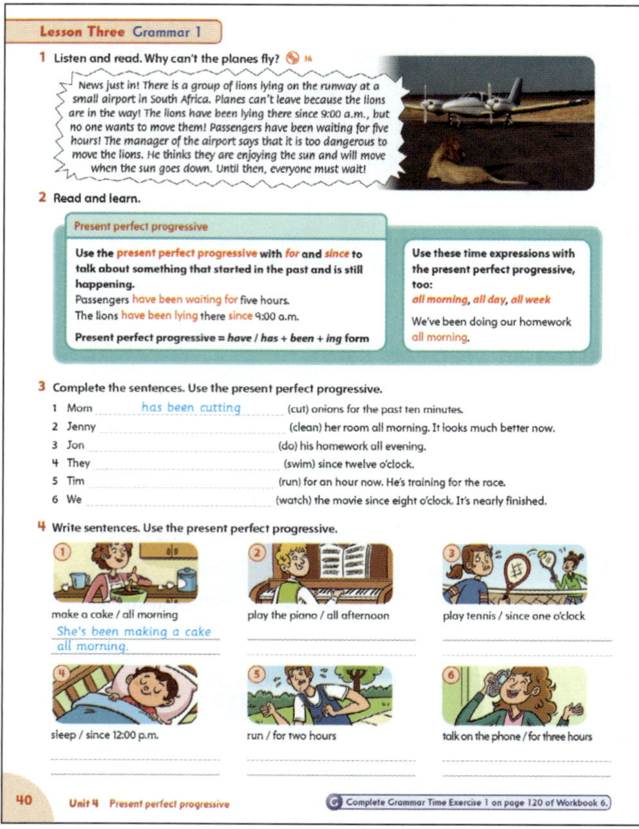

Lesson Three Grammar 1

1 Listen and read. Why can't the planes fly? 36

News just in! There is a group of lions lying on the runway at a small airport in South Africa. Planes can't leave because the lions are in the way! The lions have been lying there since 9:00 a.m., but no one wants to move them! Passengers have been waiting for five hours! The manager of the airport says that it is too dangerous to move the lions. He thinks they are enjoying the sun and will move when the sun goes down. Until then, everyone must wait!

2 Read and learn.

Present perfect progressive

Use the present perfect progressive with *for* and *since* to talk about something that started in the past and is still happening.
Passengers have been waiting for five hours.
The lions have been lying there since 9:00 a.m.

Present perfect progressive = *have* / *has* + *been* + *ing* form

Use these time expressions with the present perfect progressive, too:
all morning, *all day*, *all week*

We've been doing our homework all morning.

3 Complete the sentences. Use the present perfect progressive.

1 Mom has been cutting (cut) onions for the past ten minutes.
2 Jenny ______ (clean) her room all morning. It looks much better now.
3 Jon ______ (do) his homework all evening.
4 They ______ (swim) since twelve o'clock.
5 Tim ______ (run) for an hour now. He's training for the race.
6 We ______ (watch) the movie since eight o'clock. It's nearly finished.

4 Write sentences. Use the present perfect progressive.

1 make a cake / all morning
She's been making a cake all morning.
2 play the piano / all afternoon
3 play tennis / since one o'clock
4 sleep / since 12:00 p.m.
5 run / for two hours
6 talk on the phone / for three hours

40 Unit 4 Present perfect progressive

Complete Grammar Time Exercise 1 on page 120 of Workbook 6.

Lesson Three SB page 40

Grammar 1

Learning outcomes

To use the present perfect progressive to talk about something that started in the past and is still happening

To use the present perfect progressive with *all morning*, *all day*, and *all week*

Language

Core: *The lions have been lying there since 9:00 a.m. Passengers have been waiting for five hours. We've been doing our homework all morning.*

Extra: *runway, South Africa, manager, go down*

Materials

CD 36

Oxford iTools Digital classroom • Unit 4 • Grammar 1

Warmer

- Discuss plane travel together. Ask *Have you ever flown a plane? Which part of the plane's journey is most exciting / scary / boring?*

1 Listen and read. Why can't the planes fly? 36

- Focus attention on the photograph. Ask *What can you see?*
- Play the recording. Students follow along. Ask the gist question *Why can't the planes fly?*

ANSWER

The planes can't fly because there are lions on the runway!

- Play the recording again. Ask questions, e.g. *Where is the airport? How long have the lions been there?*

2 Read and learn.

- Read the rules and example sentences in the first box together.
- Write the following sentences on the board. Ask students to complete them with the present perfect progressive.
  The ________ students their books for 15 minutes.
  The children ____________ TV since seven o'clock.
  I ______________ the dinner since five thirty.
  Fred ______________ on the phone for an hour!
- Read the second box together. Ask for suggestions of things that students have been doing all day / all morning / all week.
- Ask students to read Exercise 1 again and find examples of present perfect progressive sentences.

3 Complete the sentences. Use the present perfect progressive.

- Focus attention on the example and read it together.
- Ask students to read the sentences and complete them with the present perfect progressive form of the verb in brackets.

ANSWERS

1. has been cutting 2. has been cleaning
3. has been doing 4. have been swimming
5. has been running 6. have been watching

4 Write sentences. Use the present perfect progressive.

- Read the instruction and review the example together. Ensure that students know to look at the pictures and make sentences in the present perfect progressive using the word prompts. Allow time for students to write the sentences.

Differentiation

Below level:

- Look at the present perfect progressive box in Exercise 2 again. Write the examples with singular subjects, e.g. *A passenger, A lion* on the board. Ask students what else needs to change (*have* changes to *has*). Build number 2 together. Then students complete the activity.

At level:

- Students complete the activity.

Above level:

- Have students invent their own sentences about things they have been doing. They can swap these with a partner.

ANSWERS

1. She's been making a cake all morning.
2. He's been playing the piano all afternoon.
3. They've been playing tennis since one o'clock.
4. He's been sleeping since 12:00 p.m.
5. He's been running for two hours.
6. She's been talking on the phone for three hours.

Further practice
Grammar Time, Workbook page 120
Workbook page 36
Online Practice • Unit 4 • Grammar 1

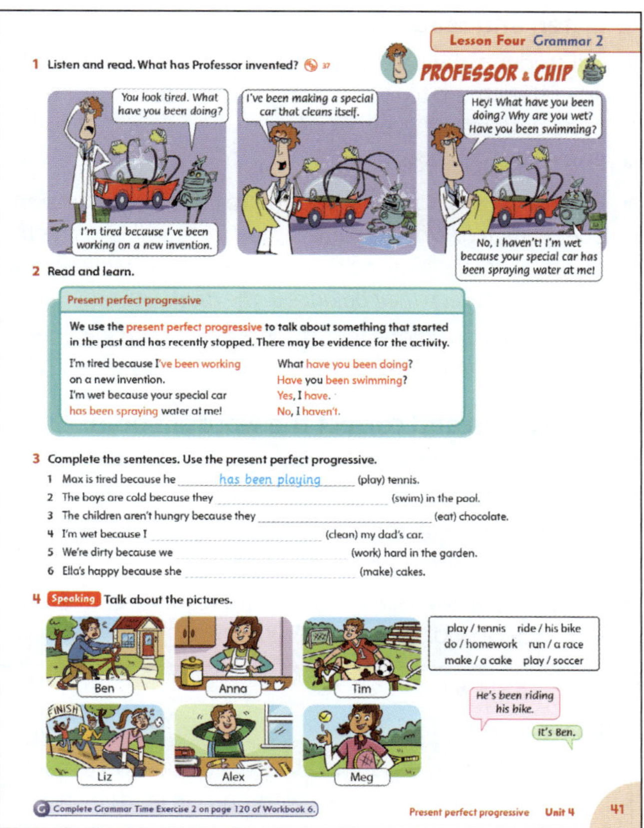

Lesson Four Grammar 2

1 Listen and read. What has Professor invented? 37

PROFESSOR & CHIP

2 Read and learn.

Present perfect progressive

We use the present perfect progressive to talk about something that started in the past and has recently stopped. There may be evidence for the activity.

I'm tired because I've been working on a new invention.
I'm wet because your special car has been spraying water at me!

What have you been doing?
Have you been swimming?
Yes, I have.
No, I haven't.

3 Complete the sentences. Use the present perfect progressive.

1 Max is tired because he has been playing (play) tennis.
2 The boys are cold because they ______ (swim) in the pool.
3 The children aren't hungry because they ______ (eat) chocolate.
4 I'm wet because I ______ (clean) my dad's car.
5 We're dirty because we ______ (work) hard in the garden.
6 Ella's happy because she ______ (make) cakes.

4 Speaking Talk about the pictures.

Complete Grammar Time Exercise 2 on page 120 of Workbook 6.

Present perfect progressive Unit 4 41

Lesson Four SB page 41

Grammar 2

Learning outcomes

To use the present perfect progressive to talk about something that started in the past and has recently stopped

Speaking: asking and answering about what different people have been doing

Language

Core: *I'm tired because I've been working on a new invention. I'm wet because your special car has been spraying water at me. What have you been doing? Have you been swimming? Yes, I have. No, I haven't.*

Extra: *spray*

Materials

CD 37

Oxford iTools Digital classroom • Unit 4 • Grammar 2

Warmer

- Tell students that you are feeling very tired. Write the reason on a piece of paper without showing the class, e.g. *I've been playing tennis.* Ask the class to make suggestions about why. Ask *What have I been doing?*
- If students haven't guessed correctly, ask a student to read what is on the paper for the answer.

1 Listen and read. What has Professor invented? 37

- Play the recording. Students follow the words in their books. Ask the gist question *What has Professor invented?*

ANSWER

Professor has invented a car that cleans itself.

- Play the recording again. Students re-read the text. Ask comprehension questions, e.g. *Why is Professor tired? Has Chip been swimming?*

2 Read and learn.

- Read the rule and example in the box together. Write some sentence openers on the board and ask for suggestions of how to finish them, e.g. *I'm tired because … (I've been studying). / I'm wet because … (I've been walking in the rain.)*
- Ask students to re-read the story about Professor and Chip and find more examples of the present perfect progressive.

3 Complete the sentences. Use the present perfect progressive.

- Read the example together. Ask students to complete the rest of the sentences with the present perfect progressive form of the verb in brackets.
- Ask individual students to read the complete sentences.

ANSWERS

1. has been playing 2. have been swimming
3. have been eating 4. have been cleaning
5. have been working 6. has been making

4 Talk about the pictures.

- Ask students to look at the pictures. Tell the class you are thinking of a child and they have to guess who it is. Say *He's been doing his homework.* The class says *It's Alex.*
- Ask students to work in pairs. They take turns looking at the pictures and making sentences about them. Their partner guesses.

Differentiation

Below level:

- Draw a clock on the board. Set the time to 8:00. Ask a student to mime riding a bike and getting very tired. Change the time to 11:00. Ask the student to stop miming. Ask the other students *What has (Joe) been doing all morning? (He's been riding his bike.)* Then ask *Is (he) (riding it) now? (No.)* Continue with a few other actions. Then students complete the activity in pairs.

At level:

- Students complete the activity.

Above level:

- Play *Miming snap* (see page 8). Use sentences from the lesson or make up your own.

Further practice

Grammar Time, Workbook page 120
Workbook page 37
Unit 4 Language practice worksheet, Assessment and Resource CD-ROM
Online Practice • Unit 4 • Grammar 2

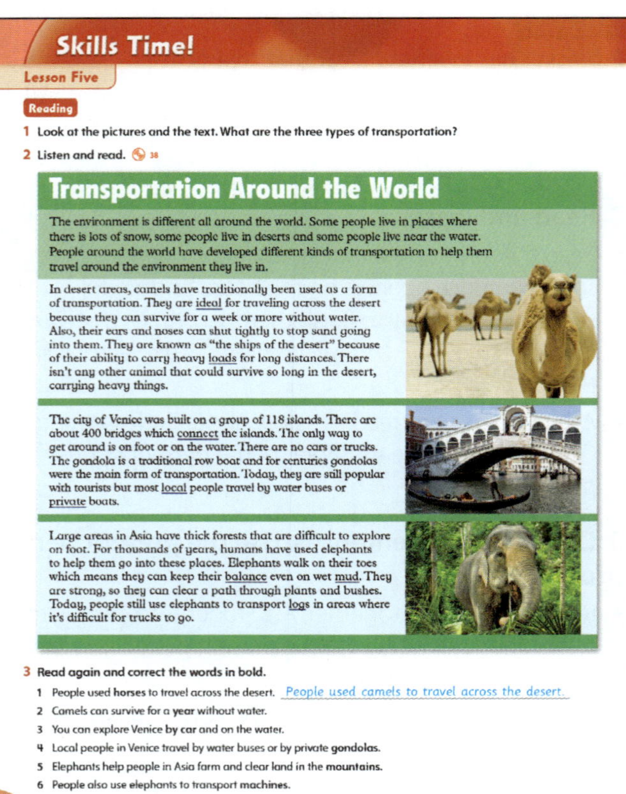

Skills Time!

Lesson Five

Reading

1 Look at the pictures and the text. What are the three types of transportation?

2 Listen and read. 38

Transportation Around the World

The environment is different all around the world. Some people live in places where there is lots of snow, some people live in deserts and some people live near the water. People around the world have developed different kinds of transportation to help them travel around the environment they live in.

In desert areas, camels have traditionally been used as a form of transportation. They are ideal for traveling across the desert because they can survive for a week or more without water. Also, their ears and noses can shut tightly to stop sand going into them. They are known as "the ships of the desert" because of their ability to carry heavy loads for long distances. There isn't any other animal that could survive so long in the desert, carrying heavy things.

The city of Venice was built on a group of 118 islands. There are about 400 bridges which connect the islands. The only way to get around is on foot or on the water. There are no cars or trucks. The gondola is a traditional row boat and for centuries gondolas were the main form of transportation. Today, they are still popular with tourists but most local people travel by water buses or private boats.

Large areas in Asia have thick forests that are difficult to explore on foot. For thousands of years, humans have used elephants to help them go into these places. Elephants walk on their toes which means they can keep their balance even on wet mud. They are strong, so they can clear a path through plants and bushes. Today, people still use elephants to transport logs in areas where it's difficult for trucks to go.

3 Read again and correct the words in bold.

1 People used **horses** to travel across the desert. People used camels to travel across the desert.
2 Camels can survive for a **year** without water.
3 You can explore Venice **by car** and on the water.
4 Local people in Venice travel by water buses or by private **gondolas**.
5 Elephants help people in Asia farm and clear land in the **mountains**.
6 People also use elephants to transport **machines**.

42 Unit 4 Reading: a book extract

Lesson Five 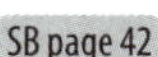 SB page 42

Skills Time!

Skills development

Reading: read a magazine article

Language

Recycled: vocabulary and structures seen previously

Extra: *develop, ideal, ability, loads, connect, gondola, Venice, row boat, local, private, clear (v), balance, mud, bush, log*

Materials

CD 38

Oxford iTools Digital classroom • Unit 4 • Reading

Warmer

- Write *deserts, islands*, and *forests* on the board. Ask students to make suggestions about the types of transportation people might use in and around these places. Ask questions such as *What type of animal is good at walking on sand? What can you use to travel across water?*
- Write students' suggestions on the board.

1 Look at the pictures and the text. What are the three types of transportation?

- Ask students to look at the photographs. Ask the gist question *What are the three types of transportation?* Compare students' answers with the suggestions on the board. How many types of transportation did students name?

ANSWER

The types of transportation are: a camel, a gondola, and an elephant.

2 Listen and read. 38

- Tell students they are going to listen to a recording of the article. Tell them to follow along, but not to worry if they don't understand every word.
- Play the whole recording.
- Play the recording again, pausing to ask comprehension questions, e.g. *Why are camels good for traveling across the desert? What ways are do people travel around Venice? How do elephants keep their balance in the mud?*
- Answer any questions that students have, and elicit the meanings of any unknown words from context.

3 Read again and correct the words in bold.

- Ask students to look at the example. Ask *Which is the wrong word?* Read the corrected sentence for the class.
- Ask students to read the sentences and rewrite them correctly, changing the words in bold.
- Review the answers. Ask students to read the corrected sentences aloud.

Differentiation

Below level:

- Put students in pairs, and assign one question to each. Have students find the answers and circle them in the text.

At level:

- Write the following questions on the board. Ask students to re-read the text to find the answers: *How can camels stop the sand from going into their ears and noses? / Why are camels called "the ship of the desert"? / How many bridges connect the islands of Venice? / What is a gondola? / Why do people use elephants for transportation in Asia? / What do people use elephants to transportat today?* Monitor and check answers.

Above level:

- Put students into groups. Assign camels, gondolas, or elephants to each group. Ask students to re-read their paragraph and make a simple concept map (see Student Book page 24) from the information.

ANSWERS

People used camels to travel across the desert.
Camels can survive for a week or more without water.
You can explore Venice on foot and on the water.
Local people in Venice travel by water buses or by private boats.
Elephants help people in Asia farm and clear the land in the forests.
People also use elephants to transport logs.

Further practice

Workbook page 38

Online Practice • Unit 4 • Reading

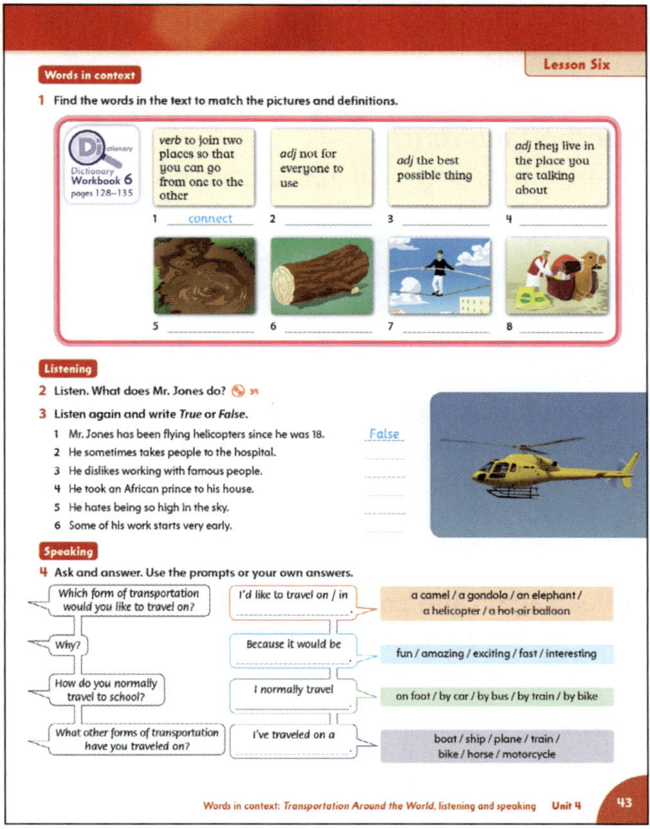

Lesson Six

Words in context

1 Find the words in the text to match the pictures and definitions.

Dictionary Workbook 6 pages 128–135

verb to join two places so that you can go from one to the other — 1 connect

adj not for everyone to use — 2

adj the best possible thing — 3

adj they live in the place you are talking about — 4

5 ______ 6 ______ 7 ______ 8 ______

Listening

2 Listen. What does Mr. Jones do? 39

3 Listen again and write *True* or *False*.

1 Mr. Jones has been flying helicopters since he was 18. False
2 He sometimes takes people to the hospital.
3 He dislikes working with famous people.
4 He took an African prince to his house.
5 He hates being so high in the sky.
6 Some of his work starts very early.

Speaking

4 Ask and answer. Use the prompts or your own answers.

Which form of transportation would you like to travel on? — I'd like to travel on / in ______. — a camel / a gondola / an elephant / a helicopter / a hot-air balloon

Why? — Because it would be ______. — fun / amazing / exciting / fast / interesting

How do you normally travel to school? — I normally travel ______. — on foot / by car / by bus / by train / by bike

What other forms of transportation have you traveled on? — I've traveled on a ______. — boat / ship / plane / train / bike / horse / motorcycle

Words in context: *Transportation Around the World*, listening and speaking Unit 4 43

Lesson Six SB page 43

Skills Time!

Skills development

Dictionary: discover meaning of words in context

Listening: listen for specific detail

Speaking: ask and answer questions about transportation

Language

Words in context: *ideal, loads, connect, local, private, balance, mud, log* (Student Book); *package, 4 x 4 vehicle, railroad, sand dunes* (Workbook)

Materials

CD 39; Dictionary Workbook pages 128–135

Oxford iTools Digital classroom • Unit 4 • Words, Listening, Speaking

Warmer

- With books closed, ask students what they remember about the article from the previous lesson.
- Ask questions if necessary, e.g. *What kind of transportation is good for travel in deserts / forests?*
- Write key vocabulary from the discussion on the board.

NOTE: Remind students to consult the Dictionary pages in their Workbooks for Exercise 1.

1 Find the words in the text to match the pictures and definitions.

- Ask students to look at the definitions and pictures. Explain that the words students need are underlined in the text on page 42.
- Ask students to look at the article again and find all the underlined words. Try to determine the meanings from context. Then write the correct words below each definition and picture on page 43.

Differentiation

Below level:

- Ask students to close their Student Books, take out their Workbooks, and turn to page 128. Divide students into teams. Tell them you are going to say a word, and they have to find it in the dictionary. Whoever finds it first, gets a point. Say each of the vocabulary words. The team with the most points wins.

At level:

- Play a game of *Whispers* (see page 9) with one, or both, of the sentences below:
  An elephant can balance well in mud. / The local people travel by boat.

Above level:

- Ask students to write a sentence for each new word. If time permits, students share with the class.

ANSWERS

1. connect 2. private 3. ideal 4. local
5. mud 6. log 7. balance 8. loads

2 Listen. What does Mr. Jones do? 39

- Tell students they are going to hear a man talking about his job. Explain that they have to listen and find out Mr. Jones's job.
- Play the whole recording. Elicit the answer from the class.

ANSWER

Mr. Jones is a helicopter pilot.

3 Listen again and write *True* or *False*.

- Read the instructions and look at the example together. Tell students to listen to the recording again and write *True* or *False*.
- Allow students time to read the sentences before playing the recording.
- Play the recording, pausing when appropriate.

ANSWERS

1. False 2. True 3. False 4. False 5. False 6. True

4 Ask and answer. Use the prompts or your own answers.

- Ask students to look at the example. Choose a strong student and ask him / her the questions.
- Ask students to work in pairs. Tell them to take turns asking their partner the questions. Their partner must answer using the prompts or his / her own ideas.

Further practice

Workbook page 39

Unit 4 Speaking skills worksheet, Assessment and Resource CD-ROM

Online Practice • Unit 4 • Words in context, Listening, and Speaking

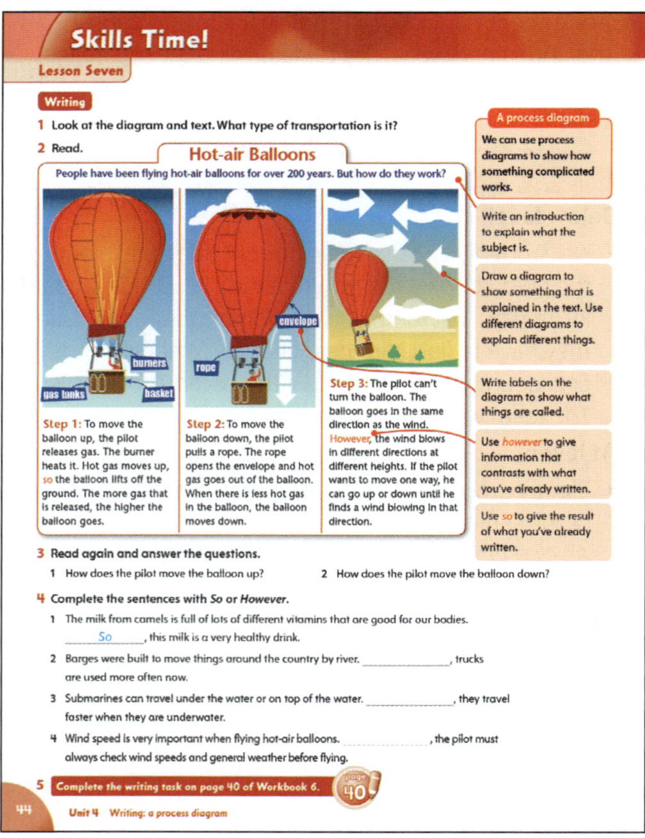

Skills Time!

Lesson Seven

Writing

1 Look at the diagram and text. What type of transportation is it?

2 Read.

Hot-air Balloons

People have been flying hot-air balloons for over 200 years. But how do they work?

Step 1: To move the balloon up, the pilot releases gas. The burner heats it. Hot gas moves up, so the balloon lifts off the ground. The more gas that is released, the higher the balloon goes.

Step 2: To move the balloon down, the pilot pulls a rope. The rope opens the envelope and hot gas goes out of the balloon. When there is less hot gas in the balloon, the balloon moves down.

Step 3: The pilot can't turn the balloon. The balloon goes in the same direction as the wind. However, the wind blows in different directions at different heights. If the pilot wants to move one way, he can go up or down until he finds a wind blowing in that direction.

A process diagram

We can use process diagrams to show how something complicated works.

Write an introduction to explain what the subject is.

Draw a diagram to show something that is explained in the text. Use different diagrams to explain different things.

Write labels on the diagram to show what things are called.

Use *however* to give information that contrasts with what you've already written.

Use *so* to give the result of what you've already written.

3 Read again and answer the questions.

1 How does the pilot move the balloon up? 2 How does the pilot move the balloon down?

4 Complete the sentences with *So* or *However*.

1 The milk from camels is full of lots of different vitamins that are good for our bodies. ___So___, this milk is a very healthy drink.

2 Barges were built to move things around the country by river. ________, trucks are used more often now.

3 Submarines can travel under the water or on top of the water. ________, they travel faster when they are underwater.

4 Wind speed is very important when flying hot-air balloons. ________, the pilot must always check wind speeds and general weather before flying.

5 Complete the writing task on page 40 of Workbook 6. page 40

44 Unit 4 Writing: a process diagram

Lesson Seven SB page 44

Skills Time!

Skills development

Writing focus: follow instructions with diagrams

Writing outcome: write instructions for riding a bike

Language

Recycled: vocabulary and structures seen previously

Extra: *diagram, complicated, gas, burner, heat (v), rise, envelope, height*

Materials

Writing poster 4; a copy of the text from poster 4, Assessment and Resource CD-ROM, for each student

Oxford iTools Digital classroom • Unit 4 • Writing

Warmer

- Play *Miming snap* (see page 8) together to review the vocabulary from the previous lesson.

Poster 4: A process diagram

- Hand out a photocopy of the poster text to each student.
- Ask students the "Before reading" question in the corner of the poster.
- Ask students to read silently. Ask comprehension questions, e.g. *Why does the plane lift up in the air?*
- Read the text boxes on the left to the class. Ask comprehension questions, e.g. *What can we use diagrams for? Why do we write an introduction?*
- Read the text boxes on the right-hand side of the poster. Ask comprehension questions, e.g. *What sort of sentences should we write? What tense should we use?*
- Ask students the "After reading" questions in the corner of the poster. Compare some of the students' answers.

1 Look at the diagram and text. What type of transportation is it?

- Ask students to look at the pictures and glance through the text without reading it. Ask the gist question *What type of transportation is it?*

ANSWER

It's a hot-air balloon.

2 Read.

- Ask a different student to read each paragraph of the text aloud. Ask comprehension questions, e.g. *What heats the gas? Why does the balloon lift off the ground?*
- Draw attention to the text boxes around the main text. Choose different students to read each text box to the class.

3 Read again and answer the questions.

- Ask students to read the text again silently to themselves.
- They read and answer the questions.

ANSWERS

The pilot moves the balloon up by releasing the gas.
The pilot moves the balloon down by pulling the rope to let hot gas out of the balloon.

Differentiation

Below level:

- Write these sentences on the board in random order: *To move the balloon up, the pilot releases gas. / When there is less hot gas in the balloon, it moves down. / The balloon goes in the same direction as the wind.* Ask students to number the sentences.

At level:

- Ask students to re-read the text, then close their books. Hold up your book to show the diagrams. Point to each diagram for students to explain what happens.

Above level:

- Put students in groups and ask them to think of something they can explain in three steps. Have them draw a poster with instructions. Encourage them to use *so* and *however*.

4 Complete the sentences with *So* or *However*.

- Ask students to look at the example. Make sure they understand the difference between *So* and *However*.
- Tell students to use the words *So* or *However* to complete the sentences. Ask students to read the sentences aloud.

ANSWERS

1. So 2. However 3. However 4. So

5 Complete the writing task on page 40 of Workbook 6.

- Refer students to the Workbook to complete the writing task. Go through the activity with them first.

Further practice

Workbook page 40

Unit 4 Writing skills worksheet, Assessment and Resource CD-ROM

Online Practice • Unit 4 • Writing

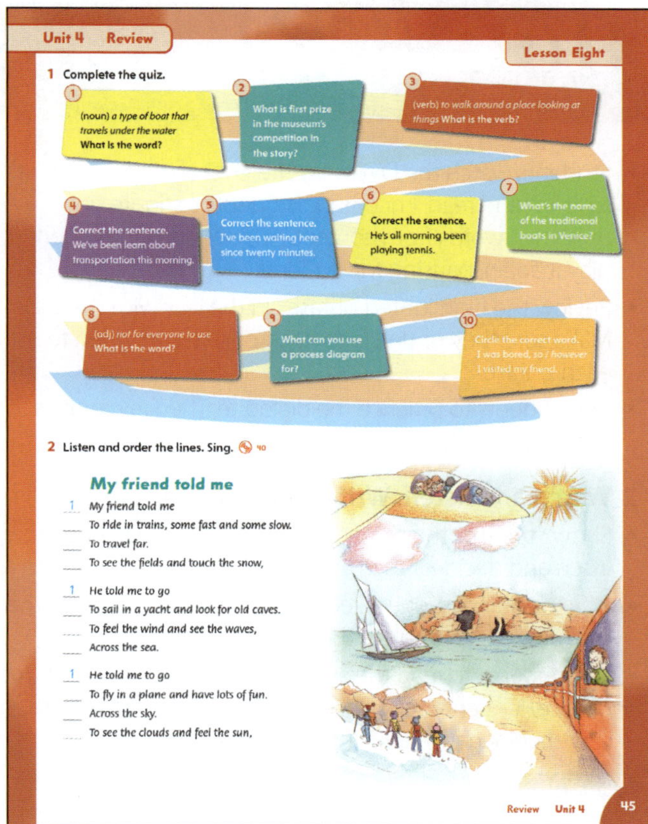

Unit 4 Review

Lesson Eight

1 Complete the quiz.

1. (noun) *a type of boat that travels under the water* What is the word?
2. What is first prize in the museum's competition in the story?
3. (verb) *to walk around a place looking at things* What is the verb?
4. Correct the sentence. We've been learn about transportation this morning.
5. Correct the sentence. I've been waiting here since twenty minutes.
6. Correct the sentence. He's all morning been playing tennis.
7. What's the name of the traditional boats in Venice?
8. (adj) *not for everyone to use* What is the word?
9. What can you use a process diagram for?
10. Circle the correct word. I was bored, so / *however* I visited my friend.

2 Listen and order the lines. Sing. 40

My friend told me

1 *My friend told me*
___ *To ride in trains, some fast and some slow.*
___ *To travel far.*
___ *To see the fields and touch the snow,*

1 *He told me to go*
___ *To sail in a yacht and look for old caves.*
___ *To feel the wind and see the waves,*
___ *Across the sea.*

1 *He told me to go*
___ *To fly in a plane and have lots of fun.*
___ *Across the sky.*
___ *To see the clouds and feel the sun,*

Review Unit 4 45

Lesson Eight SB page 45

Unit 4 Review

Learning outcomes

To review vocabulary and structures practiced previously

To use vocabulary and structures from the unit in the context of a song

Language

Recycled: vocabulary and structures seen previously

Materials

CD 40

Oxford iTools Digital classroom • Unit 4 • Review

Warmer

- Play *Book race* (see page 8) to review words and structures from this unit. Read these sentences and give students 20 seconds to find each one:
  The city of Venice was built on a group of 118 islands. (Lesson 5)
  I've been making a special car that cleans itself. (Lesson 4)
  What's the first prize? (Lesson 1)
  A pilot can't turn the balloon. (7)
  Planes can't leave because the lions are in the way! (Lesson 3)
  Have you been swimming? (Lesson 4)
  Our competition is about transportation. (Lesson 1)
  Passengers have been waiting for five hours! (Lesson 3)

1 Complete the quiz.

- Tell students they are going to do a quiz based on this unit. They can work individually, in pairs, or in teams.
- Students work with books open to page 45, but they may not look up the answers.

ANSWERS

1. submarine
2. a trip in a hot-air balloon
3. look around
4. We've been learning about transportation this morning.
5. I've been waiting here for twenty minutes.
6. He's been playing tennis all morning.
7. gondola
8. private
9. to show and explain how something complicated works
10. So

2 Listen and order the lines. Sing. 40

- Focus students' attention on the pictures. Ask *What can you see? What are the people doing?*
- Tell students the words to the song are in their books, but the lines are in the wrong order.
- Ask students to read silently.
- Play the song. Students listen and point to each line as they hear it.
- Play the song again, pausing for students to number the lines. Play the recording a third time. Students complete their answers.
- Review answers. Ask a different student to read each line in the order that they heard it.
- Play the recording once more. Students sing along.

Differentiation

Below level:

- Put students into groups. Assign each group a phrase, e.g. *ride in trains, feel the wind*. Students decide on actions for their phrases. Then play the song. Students should stand and do their action when they hear their phrase.

At level:

- Write each verse on pieces of paper, leaving blanks for key words. Divide the class into three groups to play a memory game. Ask students to close their books and work together to fill in the missing words.

Above level:

- Divide the class into three groups, one for each verse. Students work together to recall the words of their verse. They write the words on a large piece of paper. Students open their books to check answers.

ANSWERS

Verse 1: 1, 4, 2, 3
Verse 2: 1, 4, 3, 2
Verse 3: 1, 4, 2, 3

Further practice
Workbook page 41
Unit 4 test, Assessment and Resource CD-ROM
Progress certificate, Assessment and Resource CD-ROM
Online Practice • Unit 4 • Review

Fluency Time! ②

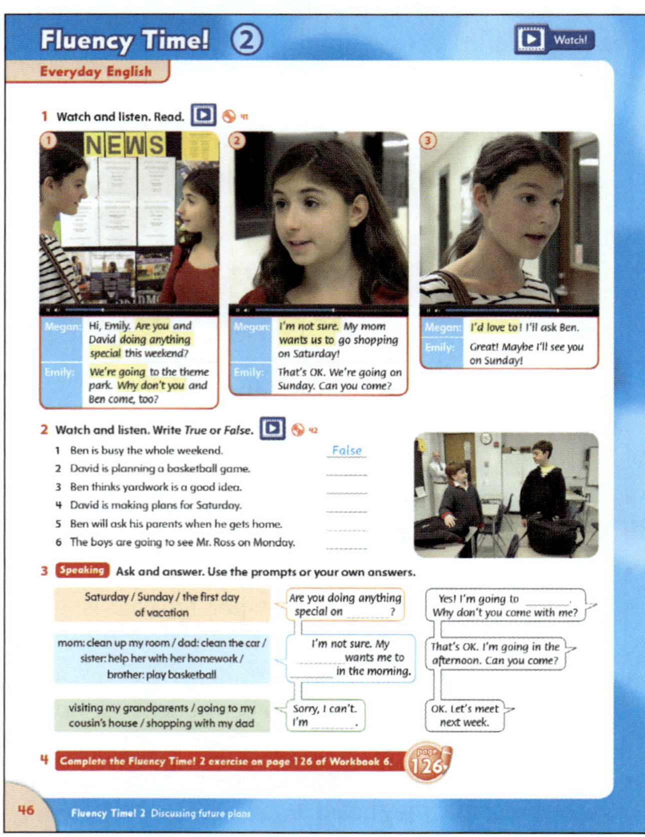

Fluency Time! ②

Watch!

Everyday English

1 Watch and listen. Read. 41

2 Watch and listen. Write *True* or *False*. 42

1 Ben is busy the whole weekend. False
2 David is planning a basketball game. ______
3 Ben thinks yardwork is a good idea. ______
4 David is making plans for Saturday. ______
5 Ben will ask his parents when he gets home. ______
6 The boys are going to see Mr. Ross on Monday. ______

3 Speaking Ask and answer. Use the prompts or your own answers.

4 Complete the Fluency Time! 2 exercise on page 126 of Workbook 6. page 126

46 Fluency Time! 2 Discussing future plans

Everyday English SB page 46

Learning outcomes

To learn some useful language for discussing future plans

Language

Are you and David doing anything special this weekend? We're going to the theme park. / No, not really. Why don't you and Ben come, too? I'd love to. / Sorry, I can't. I'm not sure. Mom wants us to go shopping on Saturday.

Materials

CD 41–42; Fluency DVD Fluency Time! 2

Oxford iTools Digital classroom • Fluency Time! 2 • Everyday English

Warmer

- Tell students they are going to learn some useful language for discussing future plans. Ask what structures we use to discuss future plans (*going to / present progressive*).
- Ask students *What are you doing on (Saturday)? Are you going anywhere nice this weekend? Are you doing anything special this weekend?*

1 Watch and listen. Read. 41

- Focus on the pictures. Ask students where the people are (in a classroom) and what they are doing (chatting). Reintroduce Megan, Emily, Ben, and David, using the pictures in Exercises 1 and 2. Remind students that Megan and Ben are brother and sister, and so are Emily and David. If the students used Level 5, ask if they remember any stories.
- Students watch the DVD. Play the DVD again for students to listen and read. Encourage students to figure out unknown words from context. Answer questions, then play it again, pausing for students to say the dialogue.
- Review the highlighted phrases in the box with the class. Make sure they understand each phrase and when to use each phrase.
- Ask students to practice the dialogue. Then invite pairs to act for the class.

2 Watch and listen. Write *True* or *False*. 42

- Show students the sentences. Explain that they need to listen and decide if they are true or false.
- Play the first part of the recording as an example. Play the rest. Students complete the activity.
- Ask students to read the sentences and say if they are true or false. If a sentence is false, ask students to make the sentence negative and correct it.

ANSWERS

1 True 2 True 3 False 4 False 5 True 6 False

3 Ask and answer. Use the prompts or your own answer.

- Ask a volunteer to act out a dialogue with you. You read the speech bubbles on the right, completing the blanks with the prompts. The volunteer reads the speech bubbles on the left, completing the first one with their own idea.
- In pairs, students use the prompts, or their own answers, to act out dialogues with their partner.

Differentiation

Below level:

- Break the dialogue up into three shorter exchanges. Have students practice the first question and answer a few times, then move on to the second and third ones. Make sure students switch roles for even practice.

At level:

- Play a guessing game. Ask students to write one of their plans for this weekend. Tell them to write the day, where they are going, and what they are going to do. Invite a student to come to the front. The rest of the class tries to guess his / her plans. They need to find out the day, where he / she is going, and what he / she is going to do, e.g. *You're playing soccer at the park on Sunday!*

Above level:

- Put students into pairs and ask them to write their own dialogue, like the one in Exercise 3. Students practice. If time permits, they can role-play for the class.

Further practice

Workbook page 42
Everyday English phrase bank, Workbook page 126
Fluency Time! 2, Fluency DVD
Online Practice • Fluency Time! 2

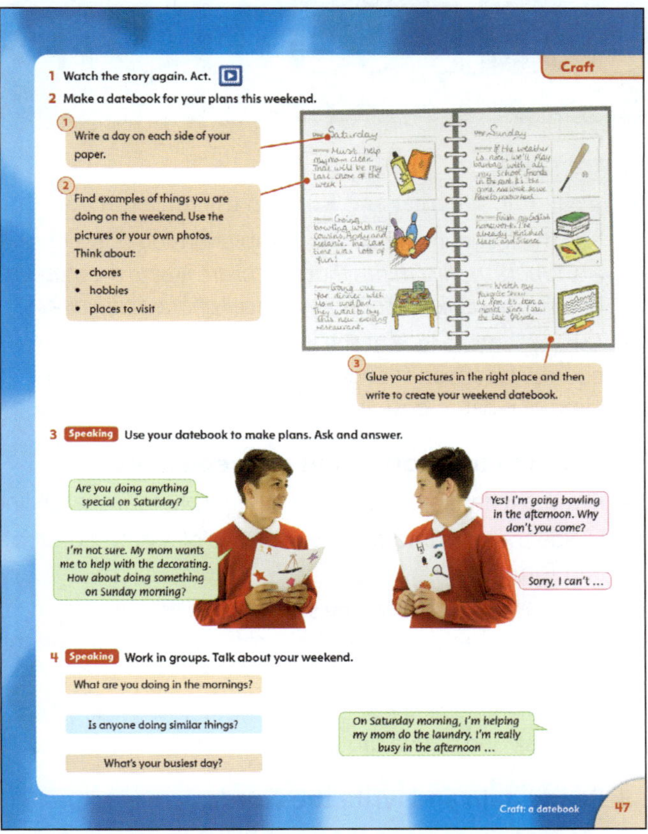

Craft SB page 47

Learning outcomes

To make a datebook for your plans this weekend

To practice talking about future plans

Language

Are you doing anything special on Saturday? I'm not sure. My mom wants me to …, How about doing something on Sunday morning? Yes! I'm going bowling in the afternoon. Why don't you come? Sorry, I can't …

Materials

Fluency DVD Fluency Time! 2; Fluency Craft 2 (see Assessment and Resource CD-ROM) (one set of templates for each child); completed datebook; colored pencils, scissors, and glue for each group

Oxford iTools Digital classroom • Fluency Time! 2 • Craft

1 Watch the story again. Act.

- Focus on the story in Exercise 1 on Student Book page 46. Ask students what they remember.
- Play Fluency Time! 2 Everyday English again. If you don't have enough time, read the dialogue from Student Book page 46.
- Invite two students to act out the dialogue. Encourage them to change details to make their own variations.
- Play Fluency Time! 2 Everyday English again for students to watch and listen.

2 Make a datebook for your plans this weekend.

- Focus on the picture. Ask students what the picture shows (a datebook) and what activities they see (dusting, bowling, going out for a meal, playing baseball, doing homework, watching TV).
- Hand out copies of the datebook and activity templates (see Fluency Craft 2, Assessment and Resource CD-ROM).
- Read the tips in Exercise 1. Show the class your completed datebook and ask if the activities are chores, hobbies, or places to visit.
- Ask questions as students work, e.g. *What are you doing on Saturday? Are you going bowling this weekend?*

NOTE: If you do not have time to use photocopies, ask students to make their datebooks on paper.

3 Use your datebook to make plans. Ask and answer.

- Focus on the photos. Tell students they are going to use their datebooks to act out making plans with a friend. They take turns asking their friend about their plans and try to arrange to get together.
- Act out the dialogue with a volunteer, then act out a similar one using the details in the datebook in Exercise 1, or your example datebook, to replace the activities.
- Students talk in pairs. Encourage them to add more language, e.g. *That sounds fun. / Yes, I'd love to. / I'm busy on Saturday. / That's a shame.*

4 Work in groups. Talk about your weekend.

- Ask a volunteer to read the speech bubble. Then invite students to tell the class about their datebooks. They can read the questions for help.

Differentiation

Below level:

- Put students in groups of three. Ask them to switch datebooks. One at a time, students take turns making one sentence about their classmate's weekend, e.g. *Kate is going to swimming practice on Saturday morning.* Monitor and help as needed.

At level:

- Play a memory game with the datebooks. Students work in pairs. They take turns looking at their partner's book for one minute. Then their partner takes it back and holds it so that the first child can't see it. The child holding the datebook should ask the other child five questions, e.g. *When am I going to the park? Who am I going to visit on Sunday? What am I going to watch on TV?* They should keep track of correct answers. Students swap roles and play again.

Above level:

- Do the "at level" activity. Then play *Talk!* (see page 9) to have students report back about their partner's weekend plans.

Further practice

Workbook page 43

Skills test 2 Fluency Time!, Assessment and Resource CD-ROM

Fluency Time! 2, Fluency DVD

Online Practice • Fluency time! 2

5 The greatest inventions!

5 The greatest inventions!

Lesson One Story

1 Listen and read. What kinds of transportation do the children see in the museum? 43

2 Listen to the story again and repeat. Act.

3 Read again and write the words. a brick a bike a hot-air balloon telephones front 1880s

1 Telephones were invented in 1876.
2 The first cell phones were as big as ______.
3 Bikes in the 1870s had big ______ wheels.
4 The car was made in the ______.
5 Tom suggests designing ______.
6 Their bike will be attached to ______.

48 Unit 5 The greatest inventions!

Lesson One SB page 48

Story

Learning outcomes

To read and understand a story

To act out a story

Language

Introducing vocabulary through a story

Extra: *come up with, traffic, attach, device, fill up, achievement, suggest, brick*

Materials

CD 43

Oxford iTools Digital classroom • Unit 5 • Story

Warmer

- Ask students what they remember about the story, e.g. *What did Mr. Martin tell the children about? What do the children have to do for the competition?*
- Ask students to predict what the children will decide to design for the competition. Write suggestions on the board.

1 Listen and read. What kinds of transportation do the children see in the museum? 43

- Focus attention on the pictures and the story. Ask *Where are the children?*
- Play the recording. Students follow along. Ask the gist question *What kinds of transportation do the children see in the museum?*

ANSWER

The children see a car and a bike in the museum.

- Play the recording again. Ask comprehension questions, e.g. *What's the first things that the children see in the museum? What do the children say about the cell phone / car / bike?*
- Ask students to look at the list of suggestions on the board. Was anyone's suggestion close to the children's ideas of what to design?

2 Listen to the story again and repeat. Act.

- Play the recording, pausing for students to repeat each line.
- Divide the class into groups of four to play Kate, Ed, Libby, and Tom.
- Ask students to look at the story frames and decide on actions for each one. Play the recording again for students to mime as they listen.
- Let students practice acting out the story in their groups. Then ask one or two groups to act for the class.

3 Read again and write the words.

- Focus on the words in the box. Ask *What was invented in 1876?* Then read the example together.
- Students read and complete the rest of the sentences.

Differentiation

Below level:

- Ask students to read the sentences aloud and then work together to find the answers in the story. Monitor and help as needed.

At level:

- Students complete the activity.

Above level:

- Give students paper and colored pencils. Ask them to draw the characters' idea for the hot-air balloon ride based on the text. If time permits, students talk about their drawings.

ANSWERS

1. telephones 2. a brick 3. front 4. 1880s
5. a bike 6. a hot-air balloon

Culture notes: Transportation inventions

- The car in frame 2 is a motorized tricycle created by Karl Benz in 1885. At the time, it was called a 'horseless carriage'. It was seen to be the world's first motor car, though some people dispute this, because it had three wheels. In 1893, Benz added a fourth wheel to his design.
- The vehicle in frame 3 is a high-wheeled bicycle, known as a "penny farthing". It was invented by Frenchman Eugene Meyer in 1869 and further developed by British engineer, James Starley. Early bikes did not have gears, so the large front wheel allowed the bike to travel further and faster as the pedals turned.

Further practice

Workbook page 44

Online Practice • Unit 5 • Story

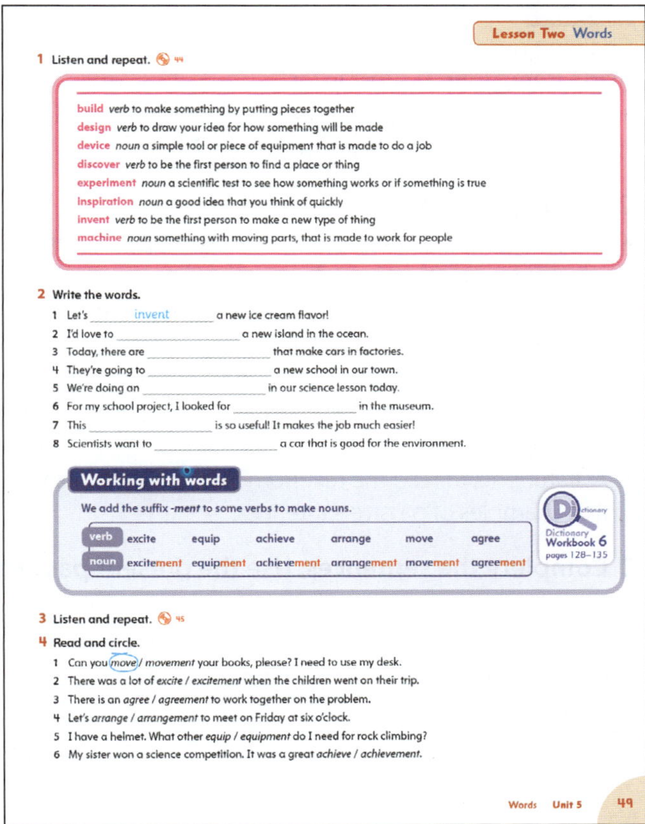
Lesson Two Words

1 Listen and repeat. 49

build *verb* to make something by putting pieces together
design *verb* to draw your idea for how something will be made
device *noun* a simple tool or piece of equipment that is made to do a job
discover *verb* to be the first person to find a place or thing
experiment *noun* a scientific test to see how something works or if something is true
inspiration *noun* a good idea that you think of quickly
invent *verb* to be the first person to make a new type of thing
machine *noun* something with moving parts, that is made to work for people

2 Write the words.

1 Let's ___invent___ a new ice cream flavor!
2 I'd love to ______ a new island in the ocean.
3 Today, there are ______ that make cars in factories.
4 They're going to ______ a new school in our town.
5 We're doing an ______ in our science lesson today.
6 For my school project, I looked for ______ in the museum.
7 This ______ is so useful! It makes the job much easier!
8 Scientists want to ______ a car that is good for the environment.

Working with words

We add the suffix *-ment* to some verbs to make nouns.

verb	excite	equip	achieve	arrange	move	agree
noun	excitement	equipment	achievement	arrangement	movement	agreement

Dictionary Workbook 6 pages 128–135

3 Listen and repeat. 45

4 Read and circle.

1 Can you *move* / *movement* your books, please? I need to use my desk.
2 There was a lot of *excite* / *excitement* when the children went on their trip.
3 There is an *agree* / *agreement* to work together on the problem.
4 Let's *arrange* / *arrangement* to meet on Friday at six o'clock.
5 I have a helmet. What other *equip* / *equipment* do I need for rock climbing?
6 My sister won a science competition. It was a great *achieve* / *achievement*.

Words Unit 5 49

Lesson Two SB page 49

Words

Learning outcomes

To identify and use words related to invention

To use the suffix *-ment* to make nouns from verbs

Language

Words: *build, design, device, discover, experiment, inspiration, invent, machine*

Working with words: *excite / excitement, equip / equipment, achieve / achievement, arrange / arrangement, move / movement, agree / agreement* (Student Book); *enjoy / enjoyment, pay / payment, develop / development, entertain / entertainment* (Workbook)

Materials

CD 44–45; Dictionary Workbook pages 128–135

Oxford iTools Digital classroom • Unit 5 • Words

Warmer

- Ask students to think of important inventions. Compile a list on the board.
- Ask different students to tell you about the inventions they think are the most important, e.g. *I think the most important invention is the Internet. We can use the Internet to find information about anything.*

1 Listen and repeat. 44

- Ask students to look at the words and their definitions. Ask students to read the definitions silently.
- Tell them to listen and repeat as you play the recording.
- Play the recording, pausing for students to repeat.
- Play the recording again. Repeat as often as necessary.

2 Write the words.

- Ask students *What is the verb when you are the first person to make a new type of thing?* Elicit the word *invent*.
- Focus on the example and read it together.
- Ask students to read the sentences and complete them with the correct words.

ANSWERS

1. invent 2. discover 3. machines 4. build
5. experiment 6. inspiration 7. device 8. design

3 Listen and repeat. 45

- Before doing the activity, focus students' attention on the *Working with words* section above.
- Ask students *What can the suffix -ment do to certain verbs?* Ask students to read the list of verbs and nouns.
- Play the recording. Students listen and repeat.
- Ask individual students to say the words for the class.

4 Read and circle.

- Look at the example together. Ask *Do we need a verb or a noun in this sentence?* Establish that you need a verb, so *move* is circled.
- Students read the sentences and circle the correct words.

Differentiation

Below level:

- Tell students you are going to read some short sentences. When they hear a verb from the lesson, they should wave their arms. For nouns ending in *-ment*, they should sit still. Read these: *I agree with you. / There's a lot of excitement. / You can achieve your dreams. / Do you like the arrangement of the desks? / Now get up and move around!* Then students complete the activity.

At level:

- Students complete the activity.

Above level:

- After students complete the activity, ask them to write sentences using the uncircled words, e.g. *The ant's movements are very fast.*

ANSWERS

1. move 2. excitement 3. agreement 4. arrange
5. equipment 6. achievement

Further practice

Workbook page 45

Online Practice • Unit 5 • Words

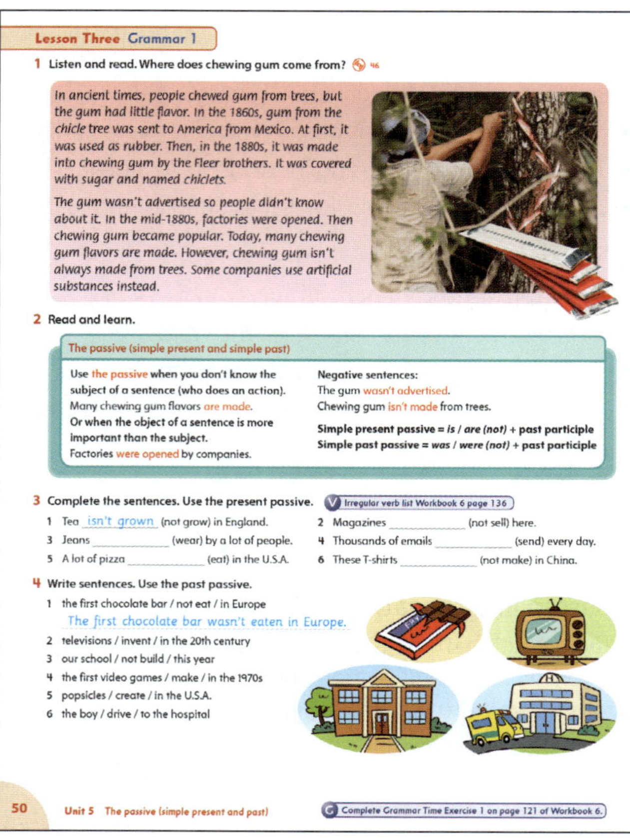

Lesson Three Grammar 1

1 Listen and read. Where does chewing gum come from? 46

In ancient times, people chewed gum from trees, but the gum had little flavor. In the 1860s, gum from the chicle tree was sent to America from Mexico. At first, it was used as rubber. Then, in the 1880s, it was made into chewing gum by the Fleer brothers. It was covered with sugar and named chiclets.

The gum wasn't advertised so people didn't know about it. In the mid-1880s, factories were opened. Then chewing gum became popular. Today, many chewing gum flavors are made. However, chewing gum isn't always made from trees. Some companies use artificial substances instead.

2 Read and learn.

The passive (simple present and simple past)

Use the passive when you don't know the subject of a sentence (who does an action).
Many chewing gum flavors are made.
Or when the object of a sentence is more important than the subject.
Factories were opened by companies.

Negative sentences:
The gum wasn't advertised.
Chewing gum isn't made from trees.

Simple present passive = *is / are (not)* + past participle
Simple past passive = *was / were (not)* + past participle

3 Complete the sentences. Use the present passive. Irregular verb list Workbook 6 page 136

1 Tea isn't grown (not grow) in England.
2 Magazines ________ (not sell) here.
3 Jeans ________ (wear) by a lot of people.
4 Thousands of emails ________ (send) every day.
5 A lot of pizza ________ (eat) in the U.S.A.
6 These T-shirts ________ (not make) in China.

4 Write sentences. Use the past passive.

1 the first chocolate bar / not eat / in Europe
The first chocolate bar wasn't eaten in Europe.
2 televisions / invent / in the 20th century
3 our school / not build / this year
4 the first video games / make / in the 1970s
5 popsicles / create / in the U.S.A.
6 the boy / drive / to the hospital

50 Unit 5 The passive (simple present and past)

Complete Grammar Time Exercise 1 on page 121 of Workbook 6.

Lesson Three SB page 50

Grammar 1

Learning outcomes

To use the passive when the subject of a sentence is unknown or unimportant

To use the passive in simple present and simple past sentences

To make negative passive sentences

Language

Core: *Many kinds of chewing gum flavors are made. Factories were opened by companies. The gum wasn't advertised. Chewing gum isn't made from trees.*

Extra: *chewing gum, culture, experiment, gum, advertise, company, artificial, substance, instead*

Materials

CD 46

Oxford iTools Digital classroom • Unit 5 • Grammar 1

Warmer

- Tell students they are going to read about another invention. They will play a game to find out what it is. Play *Twenty, twenty* (see page 9) with the word *chewing gum*.

1 Listen and read. Where does chewing gum come from? 46

- Focus attention on the photograph. Ask *What can you see? What do you think the person is taking from the tree?* Play the recording. Students follow along. Ask the gist question.

ANSWER

Chewing gum can be made from trees, but today it is also made from artificial substances.

- Play the recording again. Ask comprehension questions, e.g. *Who invented the first flavored gum?*

2 Read and learn.

- Read the rules and examples in the box together. Ask *When do we use the passive?*
- Write these sentences on the board. Ask students to help you complete them using the passive. *English is ________ (teach) in this room. / This bike was ________ (make) in France. / I wasn't ________ (invite) to the meeting.*
- Ask students to read the text from Exercise 1 again and find examples of passive sentences.

3 Complete the sentences. Use the present passive.

- Focus attention on the example and read it together.
- Ask students to read the rest of the sentences and complete them with the present passive form of the verb.

ANSWERS

1. isn't grown 2. aren't sold 3. are worn 4. are sent 5. is eaten 6. aren't made

Differentiation

Below level:

- Elicit the past participles for the verbs in the activity. Then students complete the activity. As you check answers, review the receivers and doers in each sentence, e.g. *What (isn't) (grown)? Who is (growing the tea)?*

At level:

- Write the passive statements below for students to read and write *True* or *False*: *Spanish is spoken in the U.S.A./ Cell phones are used all over the world. / Pasta was invented in Russia./ Cars aren't made by machines. / Chewing gum wasn't sold until the mid-1880s./ Cars were invented more than 100 years ago.* When students finish, ask them to rewrite the false sentences to make them true.

Above level:

- Ask students to write sentences about themselves using the present perfect.

4 Write the sentences. Use the past passive.

- Read the instruction and review the example together. Ensure that students know to look at the pictures and make sentences in the past passive using the word prompts.

ANSWERS

The first chocolate bar wasn't eaten in Europe.
Televisions were invented in the 20th century.
Our school wasn't built this year.
The first video games were made in the 1970s.
Popsicles were created in the U.S.A.
The boy was driven to the hospital.

Further practice

Grammar Time, Workbook page 121
Workbook page 46
Online Practice • Unit 5 • Grammar 1

Lesson Four Grammar 2

PROFESSOR & CHIP

1 Listen and read. Why can't Chip work? 47

2 Read and learn.

The passive (present progressive)

Use the passive with the present progressive.
My computer is being repaired.
The floor isn't being cleaned.

Present progressive passive =
***is / are (not) + being* + past participle**

3 Read and circle.

1 My jeans *are washing* / *are being washed* right now.
2 The boys *are cleaning* / *being cleaned* the car.
3 The boat *isn't being sailed* / *is sailing* right now.
4 A new train station *is building* / *is being built* in our town.
5 Tom *is using* / *being used* the computer now.
6 The class *is teaching* / *is being taught* the passive tense.

4 Speaking Talk about the pictures. Irregular verb list Workbook 6 page 136

a hospital / build
a motorcycle / fix
a rocket / launch
some jeans / wash
a house / paint
a car / wash

A hospital is being built.
It's Picture 3.

Complete Grammar Time Exercise 2 on page 121 of Workbook 6.

The passive (present progressive) Unit 5 51

Lesson Four SB page 51

Grammar 2

Learning outcomes

To use the passive with the present progressive to describe what is happening now

Speaking: talking about what is happening now

Language

Core: *My computer is being repaired. The floor isn't being cleaned.*

Extra: *lab, mechanical, launch (v)*

Materials

CD 47

Oxford iTools Digital classroom • Unit 5 • Grammar 2

Warmer

- Ask students to think about the Professor and Chip stories that they have read. Ask students to tell you as many of the Professor's inventions as they can.
- Ask *What happens when Professor's inventions go wrong?*

1 Listen and read. Why can't Chip work? 47

- Play the recording. Students listen and follow along. Ask the gist question *Why can't Chip work?*

ANSWER

Chip can't work because the mechanical mop isn't working.

- Play it again for students to re-read the text. Ask comprehension questions, e.g. *Why isn't Professor inventing anything today? What has happened to the mop?*

2 Read and learn.

- Read the rule and examples in the box together. Write the following sentences on the board. Ask students to help you complete them using the passive with the present progressive forms of the verb in brackets: *Lunch ______ (cook) in the kitchen. / The grass ______ (cut) outside. / Music ______ (not play) in the classroom. / The window______ (not clean).*
- Ask students to re-read the story and find more examples of the passive with the present progressive.

3 Read and circle.

- Look at the example sentence. Ask students *Is the sentence passive?* Establish that the sentence is passive so we need the passive form of the present progressive here.
- Ask students to read the rest of the sentences and circle the correct words.

ANSWERS

1. are being washed 2. are cleaning 3. isn't being sailed 4. is being built 5. is using 6. is being taught

4 Talk about the pictures.

- Ask students to look at the pictures. Ask the class to read the text in the speech bubbles aloud.
- Tell the class you are going to describe what's happening in one of the pictures and they have to say which one it is. Say *A rocket is being launched.* The class should respond *It's Picture 1.*
- Ask students to work in pairs. They take turns looking at the pictures and making sentences using the prompts. Their partner finds the picture and says which one it is. Remind students to use the irregular verb list.

Differentiation

Below level:

- Write this model sentence on the board: ___ *is / are being* ___. Call students to the board to make sentences using the words in the box. Then put students in pairs to complete the activity. Monitor and elicit as needed.

At level:

- Students complete the activity.

Above level:

- Ask students to think about who is doing the action in each picture. Point out that in the active, the receiver is at the end, but in the passive, it's at the beginning. Put students in pairs and have them write sentences in the active, e.g. *The astronauts launched the rocket.*

Further practice

Grammar Time, Workbook page 121
Workbook page 47
Unit 5 Language practice worksheet, Assessment and Resource CD-ROM
Online Practice • Unit 5 • Grammar 2

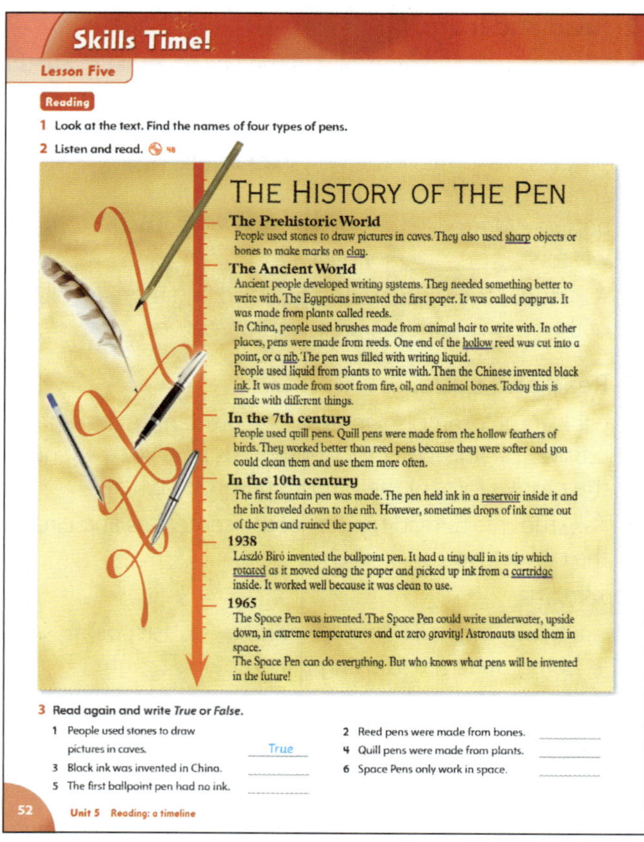

Skills Time!

Lesson Five

Reading

1 Look at the text. Find the names of four types of pens.

2 Listen and read. 48

THE HISTORY OF THE PEN

The Prehistoric World

People used stones to draw pictures in caves. They also used sharp objects or bones to make marks on clay.

The Ancient World

Ancient people developed writing systems. They needed something better to write with. The Egyptians invented the first paper. It was called papyrus. It was made from plants called reeds.

In China, people used brushes made from animal hair to write with. In other places, pens were made from reeds. One end of the hollow reed was cut into a point, or a nib. The pen was filled with writing liquid.

People used liquid from plants to write with. Then the Chinese invented black ink. It was made from soot from fire, oil, and animal bones. Today this is made with different things.

In the 7th century

People used quill pens. Quill pens were made from the hollow feathers of birds. They worked better than reed pens because they were softer and you could clean them and use them more often.

In the 10th century

The first fountain pen was made. The pen held ink in a reservoir inside it and the ink traveled down to the nib. However, sometimes drops of ink came out of the pen and ruined the paper.

1938

László Biró invented the ballpoint pen. It had a tiny ball in its tip which rotated as it moved along the paper and picked up ink from a cartridge inside. It worked well because it was clean to use.

1965

The Space Pen was invented. The Space Pen could write underwater, upside down, in extreme temperatures and at zero gravity! Astronauts used them in space.

The Space Pen can do everything. But who knows what pens will be invented in the future!

3 Read again and write *True* or *False*.

1 People used stones to draw pictures in caves. True

2 Reed pens were made from bones. ______

3 Black ink was invented in China. ______

4 Quill pens were made from plants. ______

5 The first ballpoint pen had no ink. ______

6 Space Pens only work in space. ______

52 Unit 5 Reading: a timeline

Lesson Five SB page 52

Skills Time!

Skills development

Reading: read a text with a timeline

Language

Recycled: vocabulary and structures seen previously

Extra: *sharp, object, mark (n), clay, Egyptian, hollow, nib, ink, dip, squeeze, quill pen, fountain pen, reservoir, ruin (v), ballpoint pen, tiny, rotate, pick up, cartridge, extreme, zero gravity*

Materials

CD 48

Oxford iTools Digital classroom • Unit 5 • Reading

Warmer

- With books closed, tell students they are going to read about an invention that was invented 7,000 years ago but we still use it every day. Ask *What is it?* Encourage suggestions and write them on the board.
- Ask students to open their books and look at the photographs. Ask *What can you see? What do you think the invention is?*
- Draw attention to the list on the board. Did anyone guess correctly?

1 Look at the text. Find the names of four types of pens.

- Ask students to skim the article briefly, without reading in detail, to find four types of pens.
- Check the answer together.

ANSWER

Five types of pen are mentioned: the reed pen, the quill pen, the fountain pen, the ballpoint pen, and the Space Pen

2 Listen and read. 48

- Tell students they are going to listen to the article. Tell them to follow along, but not to worry if they don't understand every word. Play the whole recording.
- Play the recording again, pausing to ask comprehension questions, e.g. *Who invented the first pens? How did reed pens work?*
- Answer any questions students have, and elicit the meanings of unknown words from context.

3 Read again and write *True* or *False*.

- Ask students to look at the example. Read the sentence together. Then ask students to find the part that tells them whether it is true or false.
- Ask students to read the article again and then mark the rest of the sentences *True* or *False*.
- Go through the answers. Ask students to correct the false sentences and read them aloud.

Differentiation

Below level:

- Ask information questions based on the questions in Exercise 3, e.g. *What did people use to draw in caves? What were reed pens made from?* Students refer back to the text to find the answers. Then students complete the activity independently.

At level:

- Students complete the activity.

Above level:

- After students finish, ask them to imagine the pen of the future. Give students paper and colored pencils to draw their idea and write a few sentences about it. If time permits, they can share with the class.

ANSWERS

1. True 2. False 3. True 4. False 5. False 6. False

Further practice

Workbook page 48

Online Practice • Unit 5 • Reading

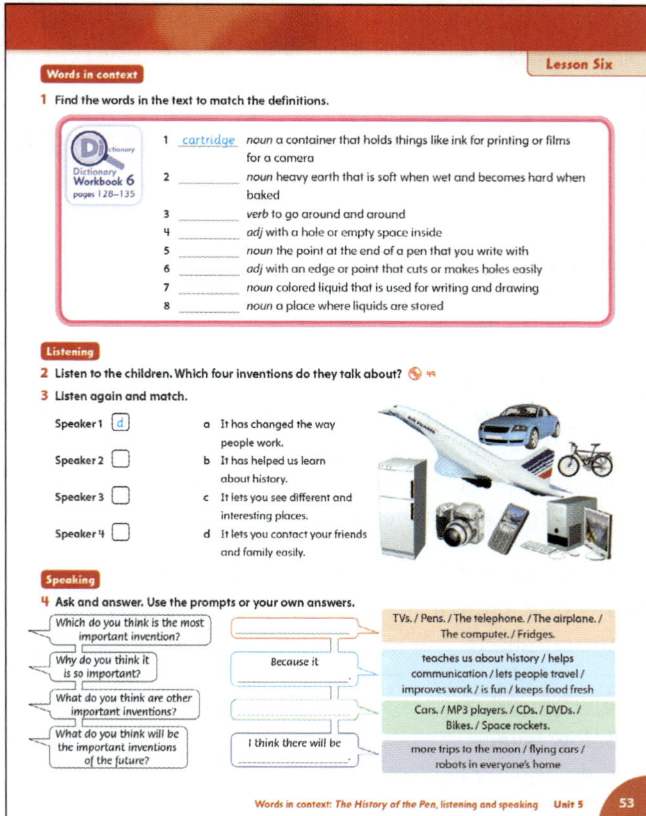

Lesson Six

Words in context

1 Find the words in the text to match the definitions.

Dictionary Workbook 6 pages 128–135

1 cartridge *noun* a container that holds things like ink for printing or films for a camera
2 ________ *noun* heavy earth that is soft when wet and becomes hard when baked
3 ________ *verb* to go around and around
4 ________ *adj* with a hole or empty space inside
5 ________ *noun* the point at the end of a pen that you write with
6 ________ *adj* with an edge or point that cuts or makes holes easily
7 ________ *noun* colored liquid that is used for writing and drawing
8 ________ *noun* a place where liquids are stored

Listening

2 Listen to the children. Which four inventions do they talk about? 49

3 Listen again and match.

Speaker 1 d
Speaker 2 ☐
Speaker 3 ☐
Speaker 4 ☐

a It has changed the way people work.
b It has helped us learn about history.
c It lets you see different and interesting places.
d It lets you contact your friends and family easily.

Speaking

4 Ask and answer. Use the prompts or your own answers.

Which do you think is the most important invention?
________ — TVs. / Pens. / The telephone. / The airplane. / The computer. / Fridges.

Why do you think it is so important?
Because it ________. — teaches us about history / helps communication / lets people travel / improves work / is fun / keeps food fresh

What do you think are other important inventions?
________ — Cars. / MP3 players. / CDs. / DVDs. / Bikes. / Space rockets.

What do you think will be the important inventions of the future?
I think there will be ________. — more trips to the moon / flying cars / robots in everyone's home

Words in context: *The History of the Pen*, listening and speaking Unit 5 53

Lesson Six SB page 53

Skills Time!

Skills development

Dictionary: discover meanings of words in context

Listening: listen for specific detail

Speaking: ask and answer questions about inventions

Language

Words in context: *cartridge, clay, hollow, ink, nib, reservoir, rotate, sharp* (Student Book); *underwater, rod, press, string* (Workbook)

Extra: *container, edge, store (v), contact (v), communication*

Materials

CD 49; Dictionary Workbook pages 128–135; paper and colored pencils (optional)

Oxford iTools Digital classroom • Unit 5 • Words, Listening, Speaking

Warmer

- With books closed, ask students what they remember from the previous lesson. Ask questions, e.g. *What were the different types of pens? Who invented the reed / fountain / ballpoint pen?*
- Write key vocabulary from the discussion on the board.

NOTE: Remind students to consult the Dictionary pages in their Workbooks.

1 Find the words in the text to match the definitions.

- Ask students to look at the definitions. Explain that the words are underlined in the text on page 52.
- Ask students to look at the text again and find the underlined words. They read the sentences and try to determine the meaning from the context.
- Students write the correct words for each definition.

Differentiation

Below level:

- Ask each student to look up one word in the Dictionary in their Workbooks. Give out paper and colored pencils. Tell children to write the definition on one side and draw a picture on the other. When students are finished, have each child hold up the picture for others to guess the word.

At level:

- Write the sentences from the activity on slips of paper. Ask students to close their books. Then play *Whispers* (see page 9).

Above level:

- Play a game of *Talk!* (see page 9) on the topic of pens. Monitor students' answers.

ANSWERS

1. cartridge 2. clay 3. rotate 4. hollow 5. nib 6. sharp 7. ink 8. reservoir

2 Listen to the children. Which four inventions do they talk about? 49

- Tell students they are going to hear four children talking about the invention they think is the most important. They listen to find out which inventions they talk about.
- Play the whole recording. Then elicit the answer.

ANSWER

The children talk about the telephone, the airplane, paper, and the computer.

3 Listen again and match.

- Tell students they are going to listen to the recording again. They must match the sentences with the speakers.
- Allow time for students to read the sentences before playing the recording.
- Play the recording, pausing after each section for students to match.
- Play the recording again. Students complete their answers.
- Review answers together.

ANSWERS

Speaker 1 = d; Speaker 2 = c; Speaker 3 = b; Speaker 4 = a

4 Ask and answer. Use the prompts or your own answers.

- Ask students to look at the example. Choose a strong student and ask him / her the questions.
- Put students in pairs. Tell them to take turns asking their partner questions. Their partner must answer using the prompts or his / her own ideas.

Further practice

Workbook page 49

Unit 5 Speaking skills worksheet, Assessment and Resource CD-ROM

Online Practice • Unit 5 • Words in context, Listening, and Speaking

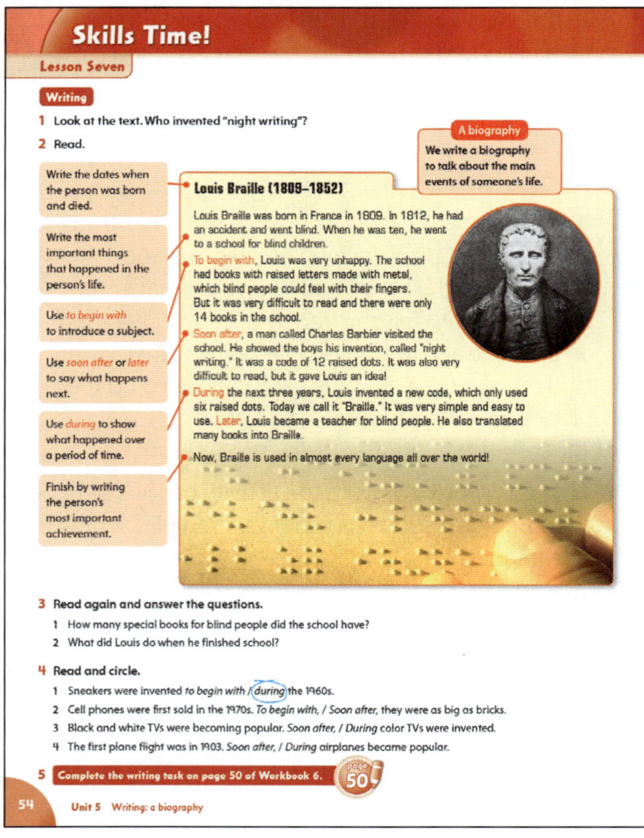

Skills Time!

Lesson Seven

Writing

1 Look at the text. Who invented "night writing"?

2 Read.

A biography

We write a biography to talk about the main events of someone's life.

Write the dates when the person was born and died.

Write the most important things that happened in the person's life.

Use *to begin with* to introduce a subject.

Use *soon after* or *later* to say what happens next.

Use *during* to show what happened over a period of time.

Finish by writing the person's most important achievement.

Louis Braille (1809–1852)

Louis Braille was born in France in 1809. In 1812, he had an accident and went blind. When he was ten, he went to a school for blind children.

To begin with, Louis was very unhappy. The school had books with raised letters made with metal, which blind people could feel with their fingers. But it was very difficult to read and there were only 14 books in the school.

Soon after, a man called Charles Barbier visited the school. He showed the boys his invention, called "night writing." It was a code of 12 raised dots. It was also very difficult to read, but it gave Louis an idea!

During the next three years, Louis invented a new code, which only used six raised dots. Today we call it "Braille." It was very simple and easy to use. Later, Louis became a teacher for blind people. He also translated many books into Braille.

Now, Braille is used in almost every language all over the world!

3 Read again and answer the questions.

1 How many special books for blind people did the school have?
2 What did Louis do when he finished school?

4 Read and circle.

1 Sneakers were invented *to begin with* / *during* the 1960s.
2 Cell phones were first sold in the 1970s. *To begin with,* / *Soon after,* they were as big as bricks.
3 Black and white TVs were becoming popular. *Soon after,* / *During* color TVs were invented.
4 The first plane flight was in 1903. *Soon after,* / *During* airplanes became popular.

5 Complete the writing task on page 50 of Workbook 6. page 50

54 Unit 5 Writing: a biography

Lesson Seven SB page 54

Skills Time!

Skills development

Writing focus: lay out a biography correctly

Writing outcome: write a biography

Language

Recycled: vocabulary and structures seen previously

Extra: *biography, to be born, blind, raised, code, dot, translate*

Materials

Writing poster 5; a copy of the text from poster 5, Assessment and Resource CD-ROM, for each student

Oxford **iTools** Digital classroom • Unit 5 • Writing

Warmer

- Tell students they are going to read an inventor's biography. Ask *What is a biography? What information does it give us?*

Poster 5: A biography

- Hand out the photocopy of the poster text to each student. Ask *What type of text is this?* Ask students the "Before reading" question in the corner of the poster.
- Ask students to read the text silently. Ask comprehension questions, e.g. *When was Thomas Edison born? What did Edison do on October 22nd 1879?*
- Read the text at the top of the page, then the text on the left. Ask *What do we write at the top of a biography? Why do we write biographies? What do we include?*
- Read the text on the right. Ask students to look through their copy and underline the sequencing words.
- Ask students the "After reading" questions.

1 Look at the text. Who invented "night writing"?

- Ask students to look at the pictures and skim the text. Ask the gist question *Who invented "night writing"?*

ANSWER

Charles Barbier invented "night writing."

2 Read.

- Ask a different student to read each paragraph. Ask comprehension questions, e.g. *What happened to Louis in 1812? What was "night writing"?*
- Look at the text boxes around the main text. Choose a different student to read each one to the class.

3 Read again and answer the questions.

- Ask students to read the text again silently and answer the questions.

Differentiation

Below level:

- Play *Guess the word* (see page 8) with words from the text, e.g. *biography, blind, metal.*

At level:

- Students complete the activity.

Above level:

- Ask children who they would like to write a biography about. Have them write three things they already know about the person and three questions they want to find out.

ANSWERS

1. It had fourteen books. 2. He became a teacher for blind people and also translated many books into Braille.

4 Read and circle.

- Ask students to find the linking words at the start of the second, third, and fourth paragraphs. Ask *Which word do we use to show what happened over a period of time? Which phrase do we use to introduce a subject? Which word do we use to show what happens next?*
- Ask students to look at the example in Exercise 4. Ask *Why do we use "during" here?*
- Students read the sentences and circle the correct words.

ANSWERS

1. during 2. To begin with, 3. Soon after,
4. Soon after,

5 Complete the writing task on page 50 of Workbook 6.

- Refer students to the Workbook to complete the writing task. Go through the activity with them first.

Further practice

Workbook page 50

Unit 5 Writing skills worksheet, Assessment and Resource CD-ROM

Online Practice • Unit 5 • Writing

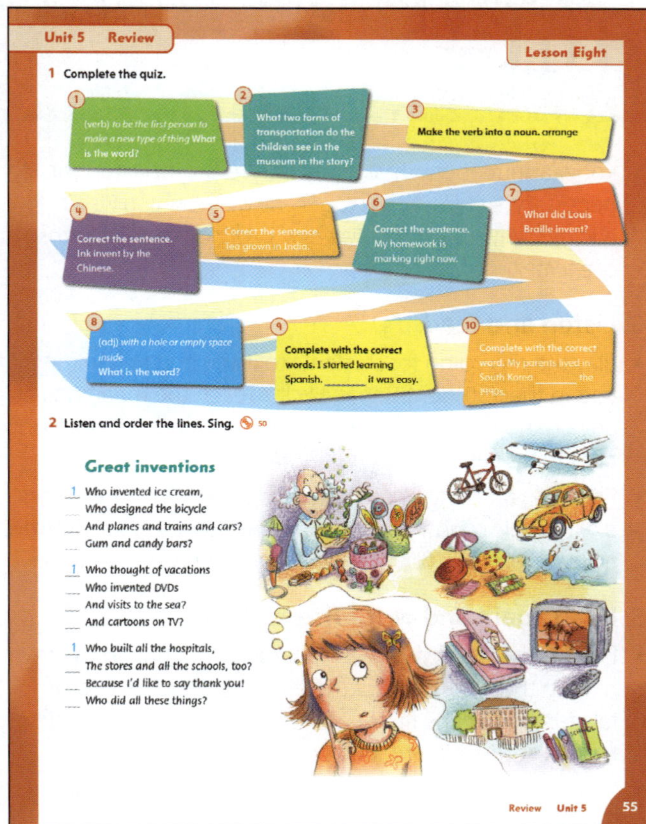

Unit 5 Review

Lesson Eight

1 Complete the quiz.

1. (verb) *to be the first person to make a new type of thing* What is the word?
2. What two forms of transportation do the children see in the museum in the story?
3. Make the verb into a noun. arrange
4. Correct the sentence. Ink invent by the Chinese.
5. Correct the sentence. Tea grown in India.
6. Correct the sentence. My homework is marking right now.
7. What did Louis Braille invent?
8. (adj) *with a hole or empty space inside* What is the word?
9. Complete with the correct words. I started learning Spanish. ______ it was easy.
10. Complete with the correct word. My parents lived in South Korea ______ the 1990s.

2 Listen and order the lines. Sing. 50

Great inventions

1 Who invented ice cream,
__ Who designed the bicycle
__ And planes and trains and cars?
__ Gum and candy bars?

1 Who thought of vacations
__ Who invented DVDs
__ And visits to the sea?
__ And cartoons on TV?

1 Who built all the hospitals,
__ The stores and all the schools, too?
__ Because I'd like to say thank you!
__ Who did all these things?

Review Unit 5 55

Lesson Eight SB page 55

Unit 5 Review

Learning outcomes

To review vocabulary and structures practiced previously

To use vocabulary and structures from the unit in the context of a song

Language

Recycled: vocabulary and structures seen previously

Materials

CD 50

Oxford iTools Digital classroom • Unit 5 • Review

Warmer

- Play *Book race* (see page 8) to review words and structures from this unit. Read these and give students 20 seconds to find each one:
  Quill pens were made from the hollow feathers of birds. (Lesson 5)
  What's happening in the kitchen? (Lesson 4)
  Think of that hot-air balloon ride! (Lesson 1)
  It was a code of 12 raised dots. (Lesson 7)
  My popcorn is being eaten! (Lesson 4)
  The Space Pen was invented. (Lesson 5)
  It looks like a brick! (Lesson 1)
  Some companies use artificial substances instead. (Lesson 3)

1 Complete the quiz.

- Tell students they are going to do a quiz based on this unit. They can work individually, in pairs, or in teams.
- Students work with books open to page 55. They may not refer back to the other lessons in the unit.

Differentiation

Below level:

- Use the words from pages 49 and 53 to play *Order the letters* (see page 9).

At level:

- Write the following topics on the board: *Braille, quill pens, transportation of the past, Space Pen, chewing gum, Charles Barbier, The Fleer brothers.* Divide the class into groups of four and ask students to play *Talk!* (see page 9).

Above level:

- Make the "at level" activity harder by increasing the time to 45 or 60 seconds. Monitor students' progress.

ANSWERS

1. inventor 2. a car and a bike 3. arrangement
4. Ink was invented by the Chinese.
5. Tea is grown in India.
6. My homework is being marked right now.
7. He invented a code of raised dots called Braille.
8. hollow 9. To begin with, 10. during

2 Listen and order the lines. Sing. 50

- Focus students' attention on the pictures. Ask *What is the girl thinking about?*
- Play the song. Students listen and point to each line as they hear it.
- Play it again, pausing for students to number the lines in order.
- Play the recording a third time. Students complete their answers.
- Play the recording once more. Students sing along.

ANSWERS

Verse 1: 1, 3, 2, 4
Verse 2: 1, 3, 2, 4
Verse 3: 1, 2, 4, 3

Further practice

Workbook page 51
Unit 5 test, Assessment and Resource CD-ROM
Progress certificate, Assessment and Resource CD-ROM
Online Practice • Unit 5 • Review

Science Time!

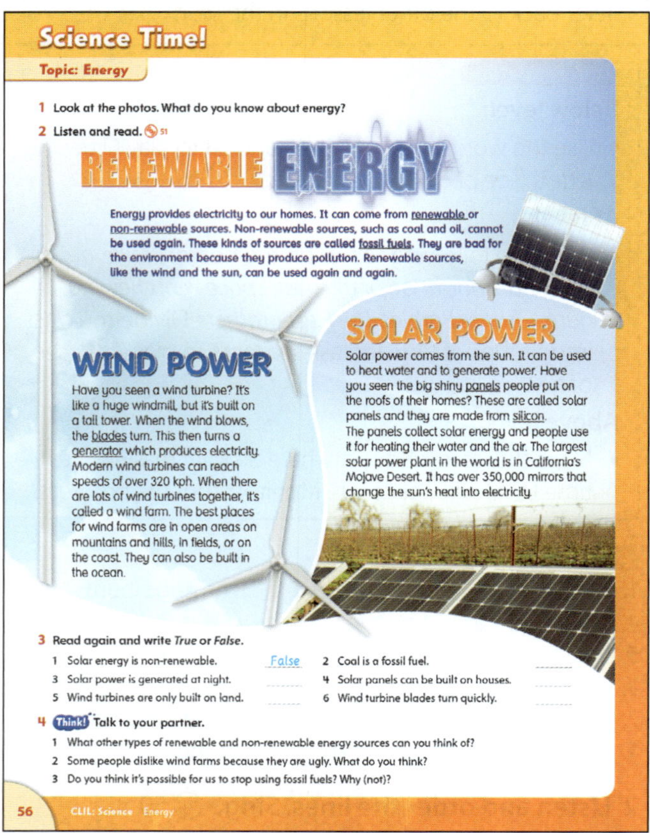

Science Time!

Topic: Energy

1 Look at the photos. What do you know about energy?

2 Listen and read. 51

RENEWABLE ENERGY

Energy provides electricity to our homes. It can come from renewable or non-renewable sources. Non-renewable sources, such as coal and oil, cannot be used again. These kinds of sources are called fossil fuels. They are bad for the environment because they produce pollution. Renewable sources, like the wind and the sun, can be used again and again.

WIND POWER

Have you seen a wind turbine? It's like a huge windmill, but it's built on a tall tower. When the wind blows, the blades turn. This then turns a generator which produces electricity. Modern wind turbines can reach speeds of over 320 kph. When there are lots of wind turbines together, it's called a wind farm. The best places for wind farms are in open areas on mountains and hills, in fields, or on the coast. They can also be built in the ocean.

SOLAR POWER

Solar power comes from the sun. It can be used to heat water and to generate power. Have you seen the big shiny panels people put on the roofs of their homes? These are called solar panels and they are made from silicon.
The panels collect solar energy and people use it for heating their water and the air. The largest solar power plant in the world is in California's Mojave Desert. It has over 350,000 mirrors that change the sun's heat into electricity.

3 Read again and write *True* or *False*.

1 Solar energy is non-renewable. False
2 Coal is a fossil fuel. ....
3 Solar power is generated at night. ....
4 Solar panels can be built on houses. ....
5 Wind turbines are only built on land. ....
6 Wind turbine blades turn quickly. ....

4 Think! Talk to your partner.

1 What other types of renewable and non-renewable energy sources can you think of?
2 Some people dislike wind farms because they are ugly. What do you think?
3 Do you think it's possible for us to stop using fossil fuels? Why (not)?

56 CLIL: Science Energy

Topic: Energy SB page 56

Learning outcomes

To learn some useful content and language about energy

Language

Core: *renewable, non-renewable, fossil fuels, blades, generator, panels, silicon*

Extra: *source, coal, oil, generate, approximately*

Materials

CD 51

Digital classroom • Science Time! • Energy

Warmer

Critical Thinking

- Ask students what things in our homes need energy to work, and how each of these things gets energy (*electricity*, *batteries*, *gas*, *solar power*, etc).

Lead-in

- Tell students they are going to learn about energy. Ask them to say what gives people / cars / fridges / cell phones energy.

1 Look at the photos. What do you know about energy?

Critical Thinking

- Ask students to look at the pictures. Read out the question and invite children around the class to tell you what they know about energy. Ask questions to prompt students if necessary, e.g. *How can we get energy? How can we save energy? Why are wind power and solar power good forms of energy?*

2 Listen and read. 51

- Play the recording for students to listen and follow the text in their Student Books. Elicit / Teach the meanings of any unknown words, or ask students to find the words in their dictionaries.
- Play the recording again. Ask comprehension questions, e.g. *Why are coal and oil called non-renewable sources? How do wind turbines work? What are solar panels made from?*

3 Read again and write *True* or *False*.

- Explain that students need to find information in the text to help them decide whether each sentence is true or false. Read out the first sentence and allow students time to look at the text and find the answer.
- Students complete the rest of the activity individually.

ANSWERS

1. False 2. True 3. False 4. True 5. False 6. True

4 Think! Talk to your partner.

Critical Thinking

- Read out the questions and elicit suggestions from students around the class.

Collaboration

- Put students in pairs to discuss their answers.
- Have pairs report back to the class.

Differentiation

Below level:

- Go through the questions one at a time, checking that students understand the meaning of each question.
- Elicit one or two answers or ideas and write them on the board for students to refer to when they discuss the questions in more detail with their groups.
- Divide the class into three groups. Assign one question to each group. Students talk together to decide on the best answer to their question.
- Invite students from each group to report their answer to the class.

At level:

- Complete the activity as suggested.

Above level:

- When students have finished discussing the questions and have reported back to the class, ask them to work in pairs to make a list of ways to save energy.
- Invite pairs to share their ideas with the class, and encourage other students in the class to say which of these things they do to save energy.

Further practice

Workbook page 52

Online Practice • Science Time!

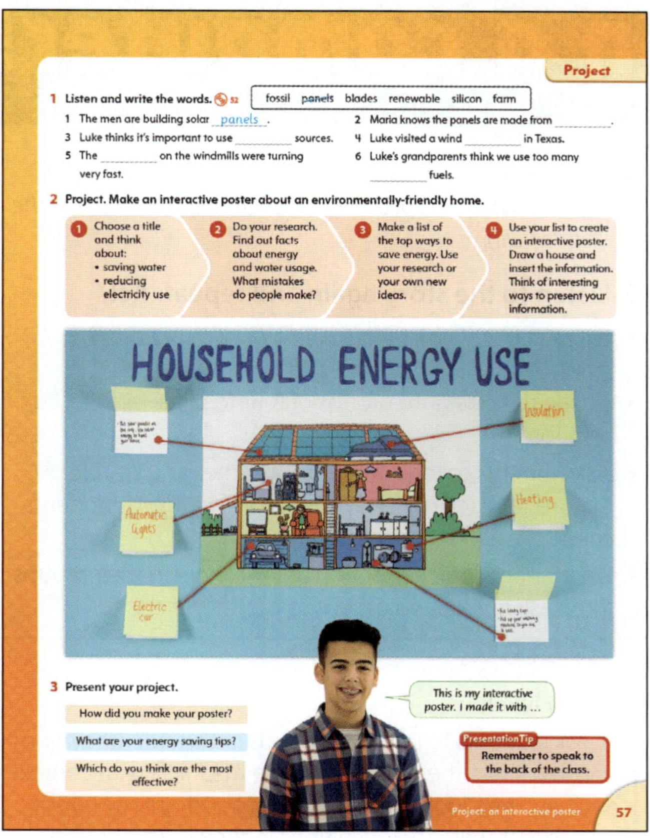

Project

1 Listen and write the words. 52

fossil panels blades renewable silicon farm

1 The men are building solar panels.
2 Maria knows the panels are made from ______.
3 Luke thinks it's important to use ______ sources.
4 Luke visited a wind ______ in Texas.
5 The ______ on the windmills were turning very fast.
6 Luke's grandparents think we use too many ______ fuels.

2 Project. Make an interactive poster about an environmentally-friendly home.

1 Choose a title and think about:
- saving water
- reducing electricity use

2 Do your research. Find out facts about energy and water usage. What mistakes do people make?

3 Make a list of the top ways to save energy. Use your research or your own new ideas.

4 Use your list to create an interactive poster. Draw a house and insert the information. Think of interesting ways to present your information.

3 Present your project.

How did you make your poster?

What are your energy saving tips?

Which do you think are the most effective?

Presentation Tip
Remember to speak to the back of the class.

Project: an interactive poster 57

Project SB page 57

Learning outcomes

To listen and complete sentences with missing words

To make an interactive poster about an environmentally-friendly home

Language

This is my interactive poster. I made it with…

Materials

CD 52; card/ paper, colored pens or pencils, scissors, glue, sticky notes, drawing pins, string

Oxford iTools Digital classroom • Science Time! • Project

Warmer

- Ask students what they can remember about the text on Student Book page 56. Ask them what different ways there are of making energy, and how they get energy for their homes.

1 Listen and write the words. 52

- Play the recording. Students need to listen and complete the sentences with the words in the box.
- Play the recording once through. Play again, pausing after each answer is mentioned so that students have time to think about their answers.
- Check answers with the class.

ANSWERS

1. panels 2. silicon 3. renewable 4. farm
5. blades 6. fossil

2 Project. Make an interactive poster about an environmentally-friendly home.

Creativity

- Explain that students are going to make an interactive poster about an environmentally-friendly home. Ask *What do you need to make this project?* Elicit *card/paper, coloured pens / pencils, scissors, glue, post-its, drawing pins, string.*
- Students work in pairs to choose a title for their poster and research on the Internet to find out the information they need. If you like, you can have students discuss their ideas in groups before they make their posters.
- Hand out card/paper, scissors, glue, sticky notes, drawing pins, and string to each pair. Before students begin to make their posters, discuss ideas with the class about how they can present the information in their posters, e.g. by writing captions in pictures of lightbulbs around the house / sticking coloured arrows onto their poster with energy-saving tips written on them / making small booklets full of tips and gluing them to the poster with string leading from parts of the house to each set of notes.
- Have students work in pairs to make their posters.

Differentiation

Below level:

- Find pictures of different environmentally-friendly homes and ask *How is this home environmentally-friendly?* Point to different things in the home to help students formulate their ideas. Write their ideas on the board.
- Students work in pairs or small groups, using the Internet or science books to find out more ways to save water / electricity.
- Write their new suggestions on the board.
- Have students work in pairs or small groups to complete their posters.

At level:

- Students complete the activity.

Above level:

- Encourage students to write reasons and explanations for each of their tips, e.g. *You should have a shower, not a bath. A shower uses a lot less water than a bath.*
- When students have completed their posters, ask them to discuss their tips with a partner, saying which of the tips they already do at home, and which they are going to do in future.

3 Present your project.

Communication

- Put students into groups of three or four. Tell them that they are going to talk about their project with each other.
- Demonstrate by either holding up a completed poster, or using the example in the Student Book.
- Students talk in groups.
- Invite individual students to stand up and present their projects to the class.

Further practice
Workbook page 53
Online Practice • Science Time!

6 You've won a computer!

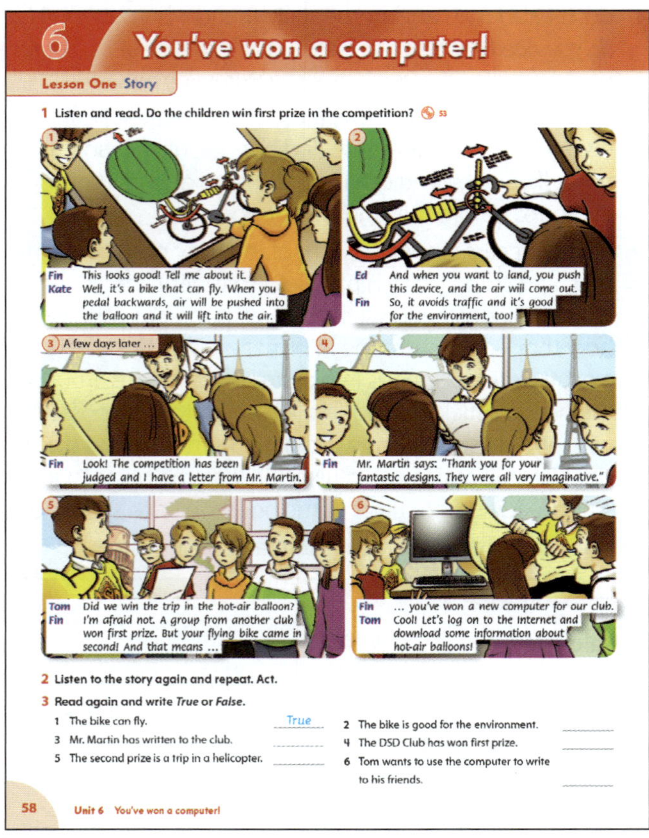
6 You've won a computer!

Lesson One Story

1 Listen and read. Do the children win first prize in the competition? 53

2 Listen to the story again and repeat. Act.

3 Read again and write *True* or *False*.

1 The bike can fly. True
2 The bike is good for the environment. ______
3 Mr. Martin has written to the club. ______
4 The DSD Club has won first prize. ______
5 The second prize is a trip in a helicopter. ______
6 Tom wants to use the computer to write to his friends. ______

58 Unit 6 You've won a computer!

Lesson One SB page 58

Story

Learning outcomes

To read and understand a story

To act out a story

Language

Introducing vocabulary through a story

Extra: *land (v), judge (v)*

Materials

CD 53

Oxford iTools Digital classroom • Unit 6 • Story

Warmer

- Ask students what they remember about the story. Ask questions, e.g. *Where did the children go? What did they see?*
- Ask *Do you think the children's idea is good? Do you think they will win the competition?*

1 Listen and read. Do the children win first prize in the competition? 53

- Play the recording. Students follow the story. Ask the gist question *Do the children win first prize in the competition?*

ANSWER

The children didn't win first prize in the competition, but they came second.

- Play it again. Ask comprehension questions, e.g. *What happens when you pedal the bike backwards? What did the children win?*

2 Listen to the story again and repeat. Act.

- Play the recording, pausing for students to repeat each line.
- Divide the class into groups of four to play Fin, Kate, Ed, and Tom.
- Ask students to look at the story frames and decide on actions for each one. Play the recording again. Students mime the actions as they listen.
- Let students practice acting out the story in their groups. Then ask one or two groups to act for the class.

Differentiation

Below level:

- Ask students to underline words in the story they don't know. Have them first guess the meaning with context clues. Then look the words up in a dictionary. Have students write the definitions in their own words in their notebooks.

At level:

- Write the dialogue from frame 4 on the board and read it with the students. Then play *Disappearing dialogue* (see page 9).

Above level:

- Extend the "at level" activity to include frames 3 and 4.

3 Read again and write *True* or *False*.

- Ask students to look at the example together. Ask them to find where in the story it says the bike can fly (Kate says it in frame 1).
- Ask students to read the rest of the story and write *True* or *False*.

ANSWERS

1. True 2. True 3. True 4. False 5. False 6. False

Further practice

Workbook page 54

Online Practice • Unit 6 • Story

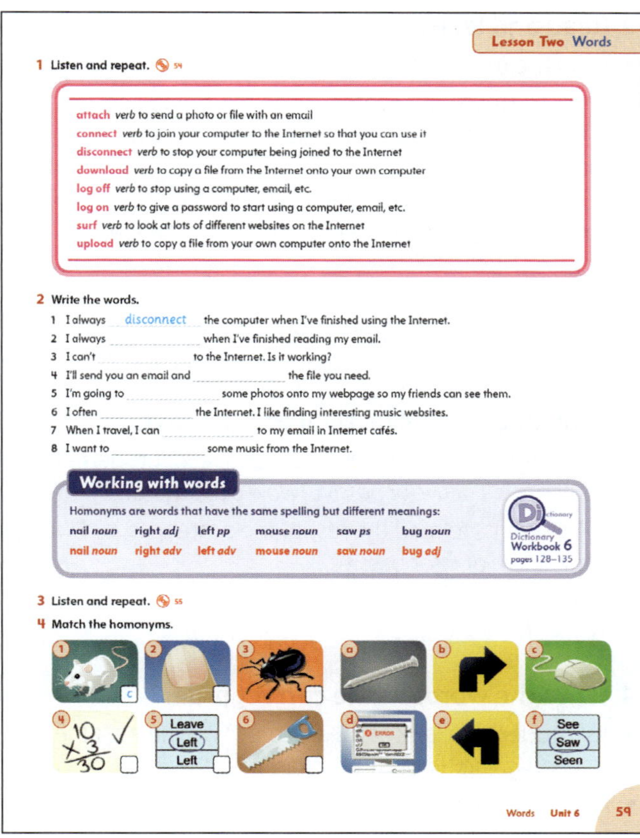

Lesson Two Words

1 Listen and repeat. 54

attach *verb* to send a photo or file with an email
connect *verb* to join your computer to the Internet so that you can use it
disconnect *verb* to stop your computer being joined to the Internet
download *verb* to copy a file from the Internet onto your own computer
log off *verb* to stop using a computer, email, etc.
log on *verb* to give a password to start using a computer, email, etc.
surf *verb* to look at lots of different websites on the Internet
upload *verb* to copy a file from your own computer onto the Internet

2 Write the words.

1 I always disconnect the computer when I've finished using the Internet.
2 I always ______ when I've finished reading my email.
3 I can't ______ to the Internet. Is it working?
4 I'll send you an email and ______ the file you need.
5 I'm going to ______ some photos onto my webpage so my friends can see them.
6 I often ______ the Internet. I like finding interesting music websites.
7 When I travel, I can ______ to my email in Internet cafés.
8 I want to ______ some music from the Internet.

Working with words

Homonyms are words that have the same spelling but different meanings:

nail *noun* right *adj* left *pp* mouse *noun* saw *ps* bug *noun*
nail *noun* right *adv* left *adv* mouse *noun* saw *noun* bug *adj*

Dictionary Workbook 6 pages 128–135

3 Listen and repeat. 55

4 Match the homonyms.

Words Unit 6 59

Lesson Two SB page 59

Words

Learning outcomes

To identify and use words related to computers

To identify different homonyms and use them in the correct context

Language

Words: *attach, connect, disconnect, download, log off, log on, surf, upload* (Student Book); *bug, chip, mouse, speaker* (Workbook)

Working with words: *nail (n), nail (n), right (adj), right (adv), left (pp), left (adv), match (n), match (n), saw (pp), saw (n), sweet (n), sweet (adj)*

Extra: *file*

Materials

CD 54–55 Dictionary Workbook pages 128–135

Oxford iTools Digital classroom • Unit 6 • Words

Warmer

- Discuss computers. Ask *Do you like computers? How often do you use a computer? What do you use a computer for?*

1 Listen and repeat. 54

- Ask students to look at the words and their definitions. Ask students to read them silently.
- Tell students you are going to play a recording for them to listen and repeat.
- Play the recording, pausing for students to repeat.
- Play again. Students listen and repeat.
- Ask individual students to say the words for the class.

2 Write the words.

- Read the instructions and the example together.
- Ask students to read the rest of the sentences and complete them.
- Go through the answers together. Ask different students to read aloud.

Differentiation

Below level:

- Play *Miming snap* (see page 8) with the new words. Exaggerate the actions for clarity.

At level:

- Play a game of *Guess the word* (see page 8) with the vocabulary from Exercise 1.

Above level:

- Ask students to use the new words to teach someone how to do something on the Internet, e.g. log on to an online account, send an email with an attachment.

ANSWERS

1. disconnect 2. log off 3. connect 4. attach
5. upload 6. surf 7. log on 8. download

3 Listen and repeat. 55

- Before doing the activity, focus students' attention on the *Working with words* section. Ask *What are homonyms?* Mime hitting a nail with a hammer. Ask *What am I hitting?* to elicit *a nail*. Hold up your hand and point to a fingernail. Ask *What's this?* to elicit the same answer. Tell students this is an example of a homonym.
- Ask students to read the list of homonyms.
- Play the recording. Students listen and repeat.
- Play the recording again. Students listen and repeat. Repeat as often as necessary.

4 Match the homonyms.

- Look at the example together. Ask *What's the word?* Ask students to point to the picture that shows the other meaning of *mouse*.
- Make sure students know to look at pictures 1–6 and match them with pictures a–f.

ANSWERS

1. c 2. a 3. d 4. b 5. e 6. f

Further practice

Workbook page 55

Online Practice • Unit 6 • Words

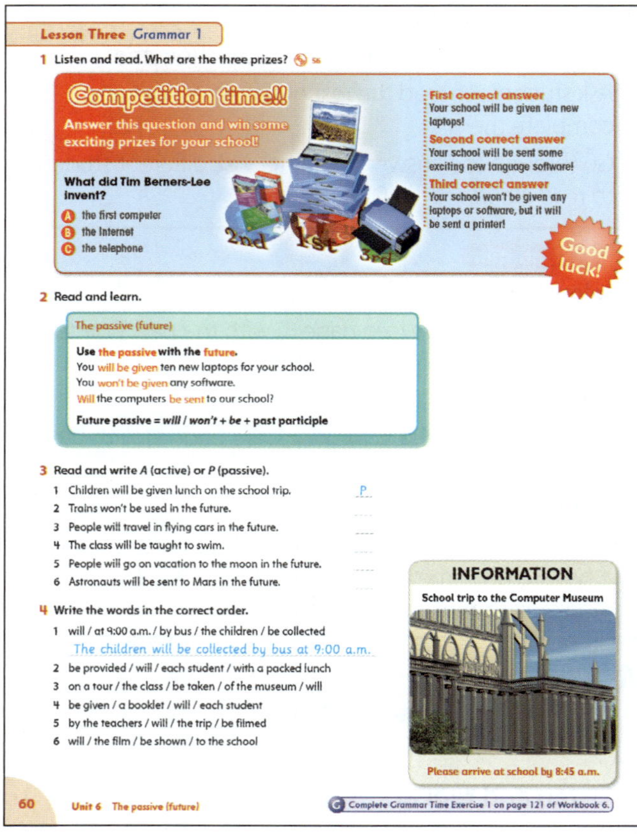
Lesson Three Grammar 1

1 Listen and read. What are the three prizes? 56

Competition time!!

Answer this question and win some exciting prizes for your school!

What did Tim Berners-Lee invent?

A the first computer
B the Internet
C the telephone

First correct answer
Your school will be given ten new laptops!

Second correct answer
Your school will be sent some exciting new language software!

Third correct answer
Your school won't be given any laptops or software, but it will be sent a printer!

2nd 1st 3rd

Good luck!

2 Read and learn.

The passive (future)

Use the passive with the future.
You will be given ten new laptops for your school.
You won't be given any software.
Will the computers be sent to our school?

Future passive = *will* / *won't* + *be* + past participle

3 Read and write *A* (active) or *P* (passive).

1 Children will be given lunch on the school trip. P
2 Trains won't be used in the future. ____
3 People will travel in flying cars in the future. ____
4 The class will be taught to swim. ____
5 People will go on vacation to the moon in the future. ____
6 Astronauts will be sent to Mars in the future. ____

4 Write the words in the correct order.

1 will / at 9:00 a.m. / by bus / the children / be collected
The children will be collected by bus at 9:00 a.m.
2 be provided / will / each student / with a packed lunch
3 on a tour / the class / be taken / of the museum / will
4 be given / a booklet / will / each student
5 by the teachers / will / the trip / be filmed
6 will / the film / be shown / to the school

INFORMATION

School trip to the Computer Museum

Please arrive at school by 8:45 a.m.

60 Unit 6 The passive (future)

Complete Grammar Time Exercise 1 on page 121 of Workbook 6.

Lesson Three SB page 60

Grammar 1

Learning outcomes

To use the passive with the future

Language

Core: *You will be given ten new laptops for your school. You won't be given any software. Will the computers be sent to our school?*

Extra: *laptop, software, Mars, packed lunch, booklet*

Materials

CD  56

Oxford iTools Digital classroom • Unit 6 • Grammar 1

Warmer

- Ask *Do you like to enter competitions? Have you ever won a competition? What would you most like to win?*

1 Listen and read. What are the three prizes?  56

- Play the recording. Students follow along. Ask the gist question *What are the three prizes?*

ANSWER

First prize is ten new laptops for your school, second prize is new language software for your school and third prize is a printer for your school.

- Play the recording again. Ask comprehension questions, e.g. *How many laptops do you get if you win first prize? Will your school get any software if you win third prize?*
- Focus on the competition question. Ask if anyone can tell you the correct answer (*B the Internet*).

2 Read and learn.

- Read the rules and examples in the box together.
- Write the following sentences on the board and ask students to help you complete them using the future passive.

You ___________ (teach) grammar in today's lesson.
You___________ (not give) any homework tonight.
___________ *the visitors* ____________ *(show) around the school?*

- Ask students to read the text from Exercise 1 again and find examples of future passive sentences.

3 Read and write *A* (active) or *P* (passive).

- Focus attention on the example and read it together. Ask students *Is it active or passive? How do you know?*
- Ask students to read the rest of the sentences and write *A* for active or *P* for passive.

ANSWERS

1. P 2. P 3. A 4. P 5. A 6. P

4 Write the words in the correct order.

- Ask students to look at the picture. Ask *Where are the students going?* Look at the example together.
- Ask students to reorder the words in the other sentences, using the future passive.

Differentiation

Below level:

- Put students in pairs and ask them to look at the word prompts on the board. Have them identify the verbs and write them in their notebooks in the future passive.

At level:

- Tell students to imagine their class is going on a trip to the chocolate factory. Write these prompts on the board. Students use them to make sentences in the future passive:
Children / collect / school bus
Children / show / the chocolate machines
Lunch / provide
Each student / give / a chocolate bar

Above level:

- Discuss school trips. Ask students where they would like to go, and take a vote to find the most popular place. Tell students to imagine that they are going on trip to this place. Put students in groups and ask them to prepare a note to parents. They must use the future passive when possible.

ANSWERS

1. The children will be collected by bus at 9:00 a.m.
2. Each student will be provided with a packed lunch.
3. The class will be taken on a tour of the museum.
4. Each student will be given a booklet.
5. The trip will be filmed by the teachers.
6. The film will be shown to the school.

Further practice
Grammar Time, Workbook page 121
Workbook page 56
Online Practice • Unit 6 • Grammar 1

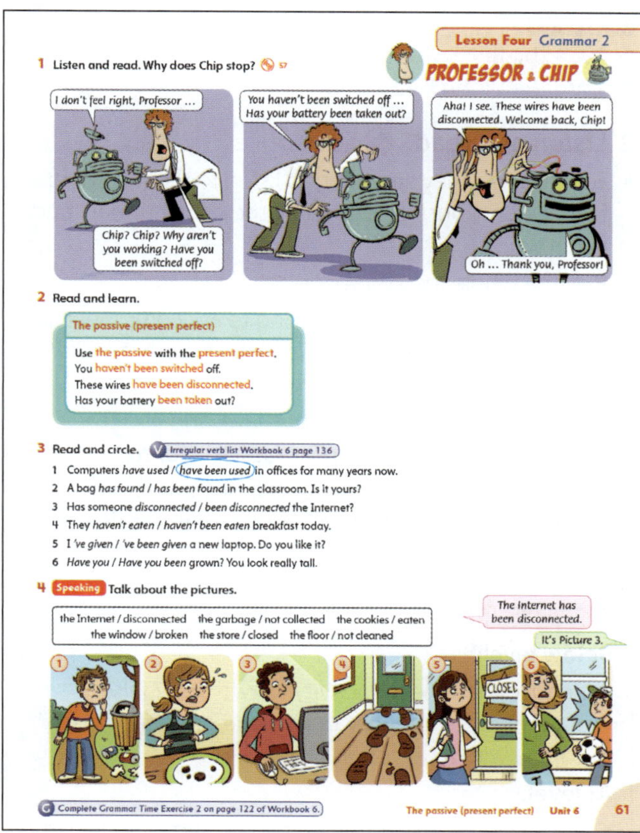
Lesson Four Grammar 2

PROFESSOR & CHIP

1 Listen and read. Why does Chip stop? 57

2 Read and learn.

The passive (present perfect)

Use the passive with the present perfect.
You haven't been switched off.
These wires have been disconnected.
Has your battery been taken out?

3 Read and circle. Irregular verb list Workbook 6 page 136

1 Computers *have used* / *have been used* in offices for many years now.
2 A bag *has found* / *has been found* in the classroom. Is it yours?
3 Has someone *disconnected* / *been disconnected* the Internet?
4 They *haven't eaten* / *haven't been eaten* breakfast today.
5 I *'ve given* / *'ve been given* a new laptop. Do you like it?
6 *Have you* / *Have you been* grown? You look really tall.

4 Speaking Talk about the pictures.

the Internet / disconnected the garbage / not collected the cookies / eaten
the window / broken the store / closed the floor / not cleaned

Complete Grammar Time Exercise 2 on page 122 of Workbook 6.

The passive (present perfect) Unit 6 61

Lesson Four SB page 61

Grammar 2

Learning outcomes

To use the passive with the present perfect

Speaking: using the passive with the present perfect to describe what has or hasn't happened

Language

Core: *These wires have been disconnected. You haven't been switched off. Has your battery been taken out?*

Extra: *wire*

Materials

CD 57

Oxford iTools Digital classroom • Unit 6 • Grammar 2

Warmer

- Ask students to suggest things that Professor has to do to keep Chip working properly. Ask students to suggest how Chip is powered. Does he run on gas?

1 Listen and read. Why does Chip stop? 57

- Play the recording. Students listen and follow along. Ask the gist question *Why does Chip stop?*

ANSWER

Chip stops because some of his wires have been disconnected.

- Play the recording again for students to follow along. Ask comprehension questions, e.g. *How does Chip feel? Does Professor find the problem?*

2 Read and learn.

- Read the rule and examples together.
- Write the following sentences on the board. Ask students to help you complete them using the passive with the present perfect form of the verbs in brackets:
  The machines ___________ (switch on).
  The windows ___________ (clean).
  We ___________ (not give) any lunch.
- Ask students to re-read the story and find more examples of the passive with the present perfect.

3 Read and circle.

- Ask students to look at the example, and ask *Is the sentence passive?* Establish that it is, so the passive form of the present perfect is needed.
- Students read the sentences and circle the correct words.

ANSWERS

1. have been used 2. has been found 3. disconnected
4. haven't eaten 5. 've been given 6. Have you

4 Talk about the pictures.

- Ask students to look at the pictures. Ask two students to read the speech bubbles aloud.
- Tell the class you are going to describe what's happened in one of the pictures and say which one it is. Say *The floor hasn't been cleaned*. Students should respond *It's Picture 4*.
- Put students in pairs. They take turns looking at the pictures and making sentences using the prompts. Their partner identifies which picture they are describing.

Differentiation

Below level:

- Look at the pictures with students. Ask *What happened?* and elicit responses. Together, practice making sentences in the passive (present perfect) with the words in the box. Then students complete the activity in pairs.

At level:

- Students complete the activity.

Above level:

- Play *Miming snap* (see page 8). Use sentences from the lesson or make up your own.

ANSWERS

Picture 1: The garbage hasn't been collected.
Picture 2: The cookies have been eaten.
Picture 3: The Internet has been disconnected.
Picture 4: The floor hasn't been cleaned.
Picture 5: The store has been closed.
Picture 6: The window has been broken.

Further practice

Grammar Time, Workbook page 122
Workbook page 57
Unit 6 Language practice worksheet, Assessment and Resource CD-ROM
Online Practice • Unit 6 • Grammar 2

Skills Time!

Lesson Five

Reading

1 Look at the text. What was invented on these dates? a) 1964 b) 1990

2 Listen and read. 58

Computers – Fun Facts

HOME NEWS FUN CONTACT US

Who invented the computer?
In 1833, a British inventor, Charles Babbage made plans for a math machine. It was the beginning of the first computer. Babbage spent 37 years trying to build his machine, but there were many complications and he died before he finished it. The first computer was finally created in 1946. It was called The Small-Scale Experimental Machine.

How big was the first computer?
The first computer was huge. It filled a large room and weighed the same as six adult male elephants! Luckily, as technology has improved, computers have gotten smaller.

Why is a mouse called a mouse?
The first computer mouse was invented by Douglas Engelbart in around 1964. It was a little wooden box on wheels that could move an on-screen cursor. It was called a mouse because the wire that connected it to the computer looked like a tail. Luckily, a computer mouse is much smaller now and it is usually made of plastic. However, it still looks like the first mouse that was made.

When did the World Wide Web begin?
The World Wide Web (WWW) was invented by Tim Berners-Lee and Robert Cailliau in 1990. It was immediately successful and in four years, 50 million people were using it! It is difficult to imagine life without it as the World Wide Web has changed the world!

How many computers are there in the world today?
In the early 1940s, the president of the computer company IBM said, "I think there is a world market for about five computers." However, today there are more than one billion computers in the world! Computers became much more important in the world than anyone ever expected!

3 Read again and match.

1 Charles Babbage [d]
2 The first computer [ ]
3 The first computer mouse [ ]
4 Two men [ ]
5 The World Wide Web [ ]
6 In the 1940s, the President of IBM [ ]

a was very, very heavy.
b became popular very quickly.
c invented the World Wide Web.
d never built a computer.
e didn't think computers would be popular.
f was a box on wheels.

62 Unit 6 Reading: a website article

Lesson Five SB page 62

Skills Time!

Skills development

Reading: read a website article

Language

Recycled: vocabulary and structures seen previously

Extra: *complications, created, experimental, huge, weigh (v), male, cursor, immediately, president, market*

Materials

CD 58

Oxford iTools Digital classroom • Unit 6 • Reading

Warmer

- Discuss websites together. Ask students which websites they look at regularly. What do they look at them for? Which ones are useful for finding out information?
- Tell students they are going to read a webpage about interesting computer facts. Ask what they would like to know about computers. Write students' suggestions on the board.

1 Look at the text. What was invented on these dates?

- Ask students to look at the pictures. Without reading the text, ask students what they think the pictures show.
- Ask students to skim the article, without reading in detail, to find the answer to the gist question. Go through the answers together.

ANSWER

a 1964 the first computer mouse
b 1990 the World Wide Web

2 Listen and read. 58

- Tell students they are going to listen to the recording and follow along, but not to worry if they don't understand every word.
- Play the whole recording.
- Play the recording again, pausing to ask comprehension questions, e.g. *What did Charles Babbage make plans for? How big was the first computer?*
- Answer any questions students have, and elicit the meanings of any unknown words from context.
- Ask students to look at the list on the board from the warmer. Did the text answer any of the students' questions?

Differentiation

Below level:

- Reduce the "at level" activity to two true / false statements. Students work in pairs, and then swap papers with a neighbor.

At level:

- Ask students to read the text again and write five true / false sentences. Ask different students to read their sentences for the class to respond *True* or *False*.

Above level:

- Extend the "at level" activity. Play *Wrong word* (see page 8) with the false sentences.

3 Read again and match.

- Ask students to look at the example. Read the full sentence together.
- Ask students to re-read the article and match the rest of the sentences.
- Ask students to read the sentences aloud.

ANSWERS

1. d 2. a 3. f 4. c 5. b 6. e

Further practice

Workbook page 58

Online Practice • Unit 6 • Reading

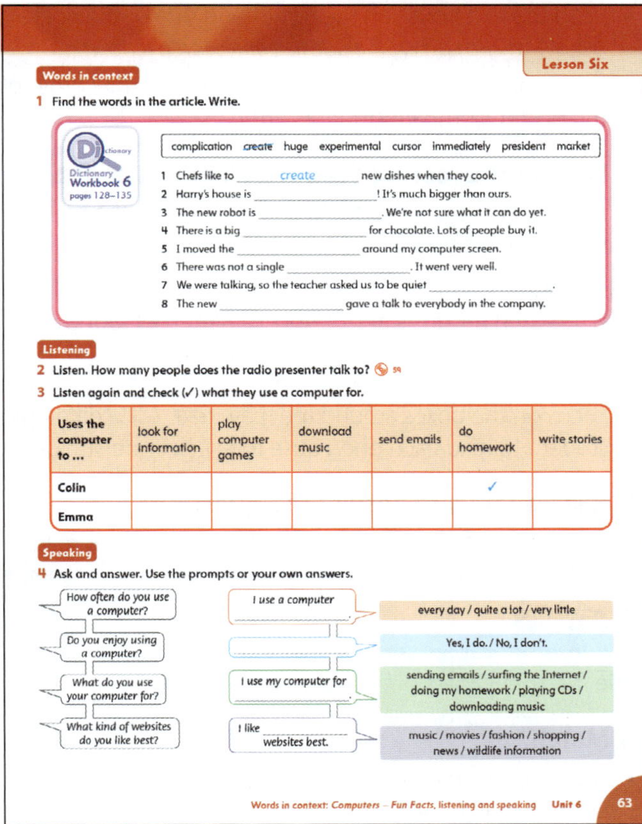

Lesson Six

Words in context

1 Find the words in the article. Write.

Dictionary Workbook 6 pages 128–135

complication create huge experimental cursor immediately president market

1 Chefs like to ___create___ new dishes when they cook.
2 Harry's house is ________! It's much bigger than ours.
3 The new robot is ________. We're not sure what it can do yet.
4 There is a big ________ for chocolate. Lots of people buy it.
5 I moved the ________ around my computer screen.
6 There was not a single ________. It went very well.
7 We were talking, so the teacher asked us to be quiet ________.
8 The new ________ gave a talk to everybody in the company.

Listening

2 Listen. How many people does the radio presenter talk to? 59

3 Listen again and check (✓) what they use a computer for.

Uses the computer to ...	look for information	play computer games	download music	send emails	do homework	write stories
Colin					✓	
Emma						

Speaking

4 Ask and answer. Use the prompts or your own answers.

Words in context: *Computers* – *Fun Facts*, listening and speaking Unit 6 63

Lesson Six SB page 63

Skills Time!

Skills development

Dictionary: discover meanings of words in context

Listening: listen for specific detail

Speaking: ask and answer questions about computers

Language

Words in context: *complication, create, cursor, experimental, huge, immediately, market, president* (Student Book); *public, available, expect, ordinary* (Workbook)

Materials

CD 59; Dictionary Workbook pages 128–135

Oxford iTools Digital classroom • Unit 6 • Words, Listening, Speaking

Warmer

- With books closed, ask students what they remember about the webpage from the previous lesson. Ask questions if necessary, e.g. *What did Charles Babbage do? What was the first computer like?*

NOTE: Remind students to consult the Dictionary pages in their Workbooks for Exercise 1.

1 Find the words in the article. Write.

- Ask the students to look at the definitions. Explain that the words are underlined in the text on page 62.
- Ask students to look at the webpage again and find the underlined words. They re-read the text and try to determine the meanings from context.

Differentiation

Below level:

- Ask students to close their Student Books, take out their Workbooks, and turn to page 128. Divide students into teams. Tell students you are going to say a word, and they have to find it in the dictionary. Whoever finds it first, gets a point. Say each of the vocabulary words. The team with the most points wins.

At level:

- Play *Smiley face* (see page 8) with the new vocabulary.

Above level:

- Ask students to write a sentence for each of the new words. If time permits, students share with the class.

ANSWERS

1. create 2. huge 3. experimental 4. market
5. cursor 6. complication 7. immediately
8. president

2 Listen. How many people does the radio presenter talk to? 59

- Tell students they are going to hear a radio interview about what people use a computer for, and to listen to find how many people the presenter talks to.
- Play the recording and elicit the answer from the class.

ANSWER

The presenter talks to two people.

3 Listen again and check (✓) what they use a computer for.

- Tell students to listen to the recording again. This time they must check the things in the chart that Colin and Emma use the computer for.
- Before you play the recording, allow time for students to read the activities in the chart.
- Play the recording, pausing for students to check activities.

ANSWERS

Uses the computer to ...	Colin	Emma
look for information	✓	
play computer games		✓
download music	✓	
send emails		✓
do homework	✓	
write stories		✓

4 Ask and answer. Use the prompts or your own answers.

- Ask students to look at the example. Choose a strong student and ask him / her the questions.
- Put students in pairs. Tell them to take turns asking their partner questions. Their partner must answer using the prompts or his / her own ideas.

Further practice

Workbook page 59

Unit 6 Speaking skills worksheet, Assessment and Resource CD-ROM

Online Practice • Unit 6 • Words in context, Listening, and Speaking

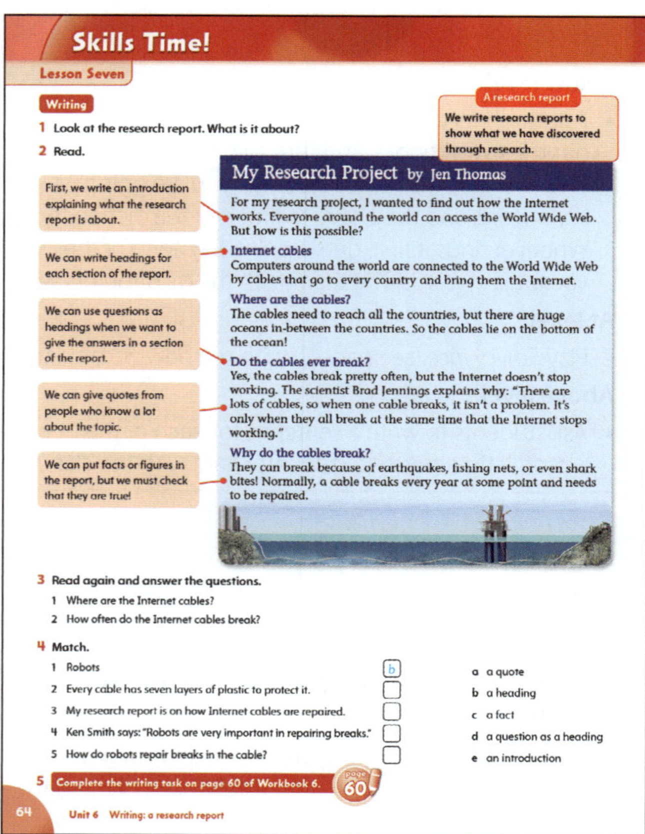

Skills Time!

Lesson Seven

Writing

1 Look at the research report. What is it about?

2 Read.

A research report
We write research reports to show what we have discovered through research.

First, we write an introduction explaining what the research report is about.

We can write headings for each section of the report.

We can use questions as headings when we want to give the answers in a section of the report.

We can give quotes from people who know a lot about the topic.

We can put facts or figures in the report, but we must check that they are true!

My Research Project by Jen Thomas

For my research project, I wanted to find out how the Internet works. Everyone around the world can access the World Wide Web. But how is this possible?

Internet cables
Computers around the world are connected to the World Wide Web by cables that go to every country and bring them the Internet.

Where are the cables?
The cables need to reach all the countries, but there are huge oceans in-between the countries. So the cables lie on the bottom of the ocean!

Do the cables ever break?
Yes, the cables break pretty often, but the Internet doesn't stop working. The scientist Brad Jennings explains why: "There are lots of cables, so when one cable breaks, it isn't a problem. It's only when they all break at the same time that the Internet stops working."

Why do the cables break?
They can break because of earthquakes, fishing nets, or even shark bites! Normally, a cable breaks every year at some point and needs to be repaired.

3 Read again and answer the questions.
1 Where are the Internet cables?
2 How often do the Internet cables break?

4 Match.
1 Robots [b]
2 Every cable has seven layers of plastic to protect it. [ ]
3 My research report is on how Internet cables are repaired. [ ]
4 Ken Smith says: "Robots are very important in repairing breaks." [ ]
5 How do robots repair breaks in the cable? [ ]

a a quote
b a heading
c a fact
d a question as a heading
e an introduction

5 Complete the writing task on page 60 of Workbook 6. page 60

64 Unit 6 Writing: a research report

Lesson Seven

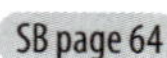

Skills Time!

Skills development
Writing focus: lay out a research report correctly
Writing outcome: write a research report

Language
Recycled: vocabulary and structures seen previously
Extra: *research, report (n), heading, quote, topic, access (v), possible, cable*

Materials
Writing poster 6; a copy of the text from poster 6, Assessment and Resource CD-ROM, for each student

Oxford iTools Digital classroom • Unit 6 • Writing

Warmer
- Tell students they are going to read a research report. Ask students *What do you think a research report is? What could you write a research report about? What do you think you need to include in a research report?* Write students' suggestions on the board.

Poster 6: A research report
- Hand out the photocopy of the poster text to each student.
- Ask the "Before reading" question. Students read silently. Then ask comprehension questions, e.g. *How many people use the Internet? Who first created a way to link networks?*
- Read the first and second text boxes to the class. Ask *Why do we write research reports? What do we write first?*
- Read the third text box. Ask *What do we do with each piece of information? What can we use as headings? Why?*
- Read the text boxes on the right-hand side of the poster. Ask *What else can we include in our research report?*
- Ask students the "After reading" questions in the corner of the poster. Compare students' answers.

1 Look at the research report. What is it about?
- Ask students to look at the pictures and skim the text. Ask the gist question *What is the research project about?*

ANSWER
The research report is about how the Internet works.

2 Read.
- Focus on the boxes around the main text. Ask a different student to read each one. Pause to check understanding.

3 Read again and answer the questions.
- Ask students to re-read the text to themselves. They read and answer the questions. Go through the answers together.

ANSWERS
The Internet cables are at the bottom of the ocean.
The Internet cables break quite often / every year.

4 Match.
- Ask students to look at descriptions a–e on the right. Tell them to match the correct description to the texts 1–5.
- Look at the example together. Ask *Is this a question?* (No, there isn't a question mark.) *Is this a quote?* (No, there are no quotation marks.) Establish that it is a heading, so the letter b has been written in the box.
- Ask students to complete the exercise.

Differentiation

Below level:
- Ask students to close their books. Write the headings on the board in random order: *Internet Cables / Where are the cables? / Do the cables ever break? / Why do the cables break?* Ask students to put the headings in order.

At level:
- Ask students to label a quote, a heading, a fact, a question as a heading, and the introduction in the text from Exercise 1.

Above level:
- Put students in groups and ask them to think of a topic they would like to research. Write a basic outline which includes the topic, section headers, and questions to answer. Monitor and help as needed.

ANSWERS
1. b 2. c 3. e 4. a 5. d

5 Complete the writing task on page 60 of Workbook 6.
- Refer students to the Workbook to complete the writing task. Go through the activity with them first.

Further practice
Workbook page 60
Unit 6 Writing skills worksheet, Assessment and Resource CD-ROM
Online Practice • Unit 6 • Writing

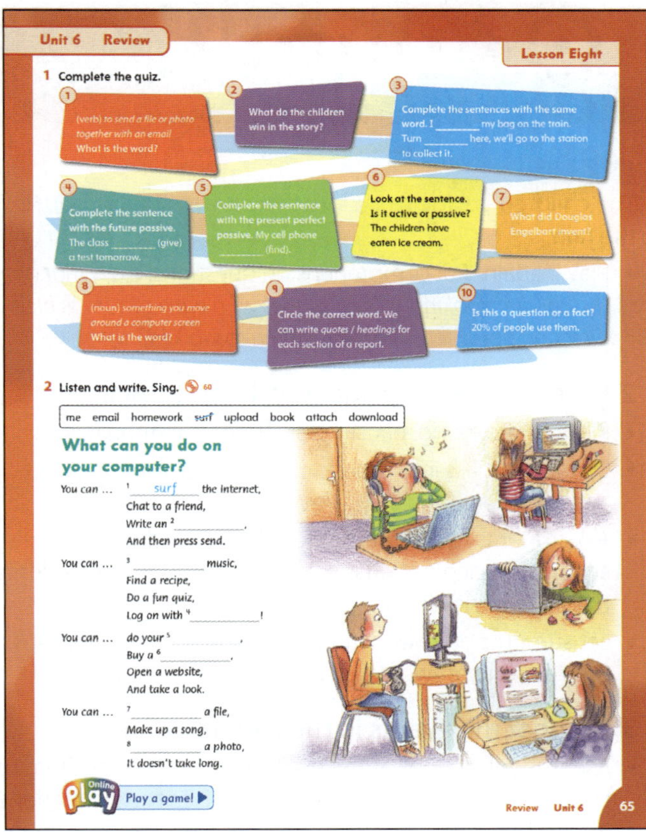
Unit 6 Review

Lesson Eight

1 Complete the quiz.

1 (verb) *to send a file or photo together with an email* What is the word?

2 What do the children win in the story?

3 Complete the sentences with the same word. I ______ my bag on the train. Turn ______ here, we'll go to the station to collect it.

4 Complete the sentence with the future passive. The class ______ (give) a test tomorrow.

5 Complete the sentence with the present perfect passive. My cell phone ______ (find).

6 Look at the sentence. Is it active or passive? The children have eaten ice cream.

7 What did Douglas Engelbart invent?

8 (noun) *something you move around a computer screen* What is the word?

9 Circle the correct word. We can write *quotes / headings* for each section of a report.

10 Is this a question or a fact? 20% of people use them.

2 Listen and write. Sing. 60

me email homework ~~surf~~ upload book attach download

What can you do on your computer?

You can ... [1] surf the Internet,
Chat to a friend,
Write an [2] ______,
And then press send.

You can ... [3] ______ music,
Find a recipe,
Do a fun quiz,
Log on with [4] ______!

You can ... do your [5] ______,
Buy a [6] ______,
Open a website,
And take a look.

You can ... [7] ______ a file,
Make up a song,
[8] ______ a photo,
It doesn't take long.

Online Play Play a game!

Review Unit 6 65

Lesson Eight SB page 65

Unit 6 Review

Learning outcomes

To review vocabulary and structures practiced previously

To use vocabulary and structures from the unit in the context of a song

Language

Recycled: vocabulary and structures seen previously

Materials

CD 60

Oxford iTools Digital classroom • Unit 6 • Review

Warmer

- Play *Book race* (see page 8) to review the unit.
- Read these sentences and give students 20 seconds to find each one:
  What did Tim Berners-Lee invent? (Lesson 3)
  Has your battery been taken out? (Lesson 4)
  The competition has been judged. (Lesson 1)
  However, today there are more than one billion computers in the world! (Lesson 5)
  I don't feel right, Professor. (Lesson 4)
  Why do the cables break? (Lesson 7)
  Your school will be given ten new laptops! (Lesson 3)
  We can give quotes from people who know a lot about the topic. (Lesson 7)

1 Complete the quiz.

- Tell students they are going to do a quiz based on this unit. They can work individually, in pairs, or in teams.
- Students work with books open to page 65. They may not refer back to the other lessons in the unit.

ANSWERS

1. attach 2. a computer for their club 3. left, left
4. will be given 5. has been found 6. active
7. the computer mouse 8. cursor 9. headings
10. a fact

2 Listen and write. Sing. 60

- Focus students' attention on the pictures. Ask *What are the people doing?*
- Play the song. Students listen and point to each line as they hear it.
- Play it again, pausing for students to write the correct word in each blank. Play the recording a third time, if necessary.
- Go through the answers. Ask students to read each line aloud, saying the missing word.
- Play the recording once more. Students sing along.

Differentiation

Below level:

- Put students into groups. Assign each group a phrase, e.g. *surf the Internet, do your homework*. Students decide on actions for their phrases. Then play the song. Students should stand and do their action when they hear their phrase. If time permits, switch phrases and play again.

At level:

- Write each verse on pieces of paper. Leave blanks for key words. Divide the class into three groups to play a memory game. Ask students to close their books. Ask students to work together to fill in the missing words. Play the song again to check answers.

Above level:

- Ask students to work in pairs to write a new verse. First, brainstorm ideas about what to include. Write suggestions on the board. Tell students that they must begin their verse with the line *You can ...*, as the original song. Students can use the ideas on the board or new ones to write the remaining three lines. Students practice their new verses.

ANSWERS

1. surf 2. email 3. Download 4. me 5. homework
6. book 7. Upload 8. Attach

Further practice

Workbook page 61
Unit 6 test, Assessment and Resource CD-ROM
Progress test 2, Assessment and Resource CD-ROM
Skills test 2, Assessment and Resource CD-ROM
Values 2 worksheet, Units 4–6, Assessment and Resource CD-ROM
Writing portfolio 2 worksheet, Assessment and Resource CD-ROM
Progress certificate, Assessment and Resource CD-ROM
Online Practice • Unit 6 • Review

7 Explorers for a day!

7 Explorers for a day!

Lesson One Story

1 Listen and read. Why do the children decide to go into the cave? 62

2 Listen to the story again and repeat. Act.

3 Number the events in the correct order.

a Each group gets a compass. ☐
b The children decide which flag to look for. ☐
c It starts raining. ☐
d They discover they're lost. ☐
e They go in a cave. ☐
f Fin gives instructions. 1

68 Unit 7 Explorers for a day!

Lesson One 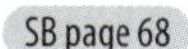 SB page 68

Story

Learning outcomes

To read and understand a story

To act out a story

Language

Introducing vocabulary through a story

Materials

CD 62

Oxford iTools Digital classroom • Unit 7 • Story

Warmer

- Ask students to tell you what they remember about the last episode of the story. Ask questions, e.g. *Did the children win first prize? What did the children win?*
- Tell students this is the first episode of a new story about the DSD Club. Tell them the topic of this unit is *Explorers*. Invite predictions about what might happen in the story.

1 Listen and read. Why do the children decide to go into the cave? 62

- Play the recording. Students follow the story. Ask the gist question *Why do the children decide to go into the cave?*

ANSWER

The children decide to go into the cave to shelter from the rain.

- Play it again. Ask comprehension questions, e.g. *What are the children looking for? Who goes with each group? Which direction does Libby tell the children to walk in?*

2 Listen to the story again and repeat. Act.

- Play the recording, pausing for students to repeat.
- Divide the class into groups of five to play Fin, Libby, Ed, Kate, and Tom.
- Ask students to look at the story frames and decide on actions for each one. Play the recording again for students to mime as they listen.
- Let students practice acting out the story in their groups, then ask one or two groups to act for the class.

3 Number the events in the correct order.

- Ask students to look at the example together. Ask them to find the place in the story where Fin gives the instructions (frame 1).
- Ask students to read the rest of the sentences and number them in order.

Differentiation

Below level:

- Ask students to read the sentences aloud and then work together to find the answers in the story. Monitor and help as needed.

At level:

- Students complete the activity.

Above level:

- Students write a short paragraph retelling the story. If time permits, students can share with the class.

ANSWERS

a. 2 b. 3 c. 5 d. 4 e. 6 f. 1

Further practice

Workbook page 62

Online Practice • Unit 7 • Story

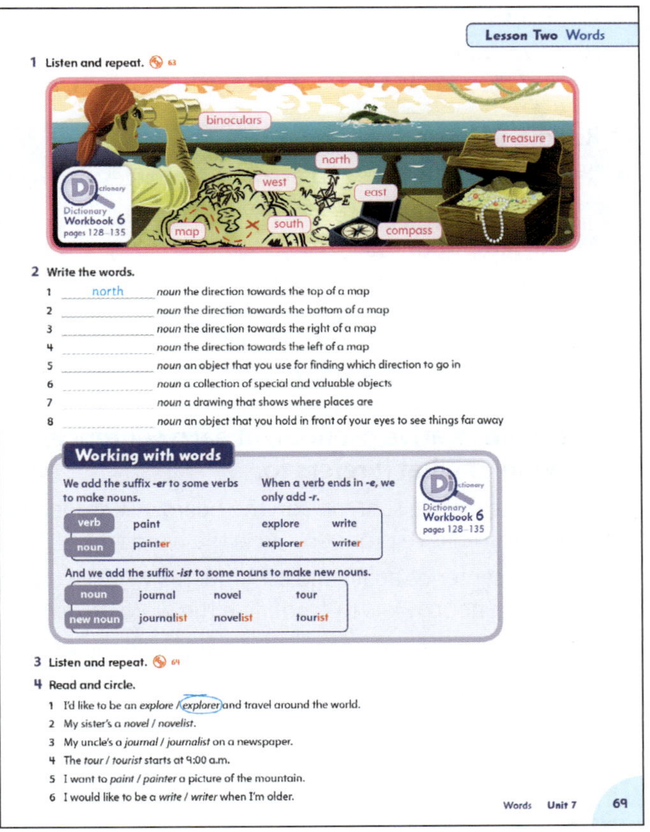

Lesson Two Words

1 Listen and repeat. 63

2 Write the words.

1 north *noun* the direction towards the top of a map
2 ________ *noun* the direction towards the bottom of a map
3 ________ *noun* the direction towards the right of a map
4 ________ *noun* the direction towards the left of a map
5 ________ *noun* an object that you use for finding which direction to go in
6 ________ *noun* a collection of special and valuable objects
7 ________ *noun* a drawing that shows where places are
8 ________ *noun* an object that you hold in front of your eyes to see things far away

Working with words

We add the suffix *-er* to some verbs to make nouns. When a verb ends in *-e*, we only add *-r*.

verb	paint	explore	write
noun	painter	explorer	writer

And we add the suffix *-ist* to some nouns to make new nouns.

noun	journal	novel	tour
new noun	journalist	novelist	tourist

Dictionary Workbook 6 pages 128–135

3 Listen and repeat. 64

4 Read and circle.

1 I'd like to be an *explore* / *explorer* and travel around the world.
2 My sister's a *novel* / *novelist*.
3 My uncle's a *journal* / *journalist* on a newspaper.
4 The *tour* / *tourist* starts at 9:00 a.m.
5 I want to *paint* / *painter* a picture of the mountain.
6 I would like to be a *write* / *writer* when I'm older.

Words Unit 7 69

Lesson Two SB page 69

Words

Learning outcomes

To identify and use words related to treasure hunting

To use suffix *-er* to make some verbs into nouns, and suffix *-ist* to make some nouns into new nouns

Language

Words: *binoculars, compass, map, treasure, north, south, east, west*

Working with words: *paint / painter, explore / explorer, write / writer, journal / journalist, novel / novelist, tour / tourist* (Student Book); *drive / driver, art / artist, build / builder, guitar / guitarist* (Workbook)

Materials

CD 63–64 Dictionary Workbook pages 128–135

Oxford iTools Digital classroom • Unit 7 • Words

Warmer

- Teach or elicit the word *treasure*. Tell children to imagine that there is some hidden treasure near their school. Ask *What equipment do you need to find it?* Encourage as many suggestions as possible and write them on the board.

1 Listen and repeat. 63

- Ask students to look at the words and the picture. Play the recording, pausing after each word for students to repeat.
- Play it again for students to listen and repeat. Repeat as often as necessary.

2 Write the words.

- Ask students to look at the example. Read the definition together. Ask students to find north on the map in the picture.
- Ask students to read the definitions and write the correct word from Exercise 1 for each one.

ANSWERS

1. north 2. south 3. east 4. west 5. compass
6. treasure 7. map 8. binoculars

3 Listen and repeat. 64

- Before doing the activity, focus students' attention on the *Working with words* section above.
- Read the explanations and examples together.
- Ask students *What happens when we add -*er *to these verbs?* Elicit that you make nouns. The nouns describe the person who does the action of the verb.
- Ask students *What happens when we add -*ist *to these nouns?* Elicit that you make new nouns.
- Ask *What is the name for someone who paints / writes / visits another country?* Explain any unknown words, for example, *journalist, novelist,* and *tourist*.
- Play the recording. Students listen and repeat the words.
- Play the recording again. Students listen and repeat. Repeat as often as necessary.

4 Read and circle.

- Look at the example together. Ask *Do we need a verb or a noun here?* Establish that we need a noun, so the word *explorer* is circled.
- Ask students to read the rest of the sentences and circle the correct words.

Differentiation

Below level:

- Tell students you are going to say some sentences. If what you read is true, they should touch their noses. If it's false, they shouldn't move. Say *I can be a (paint).* Continue, in random order, with each word in the box. Then students work in pairs to complete the activity.

At level:

- Students complete the activity.

Above level:

- After students complete the activity, ask them to write sentences using the uncircled words from the exercise, e.g. *I'd like to explore the Grand Canyon.*

ANSWERS

1. explorer 2. novelist 3. journalist 4. tour
5. paint 6. writer

Further practice

Workbook page 63

Online Practice • Unit 7 • Words

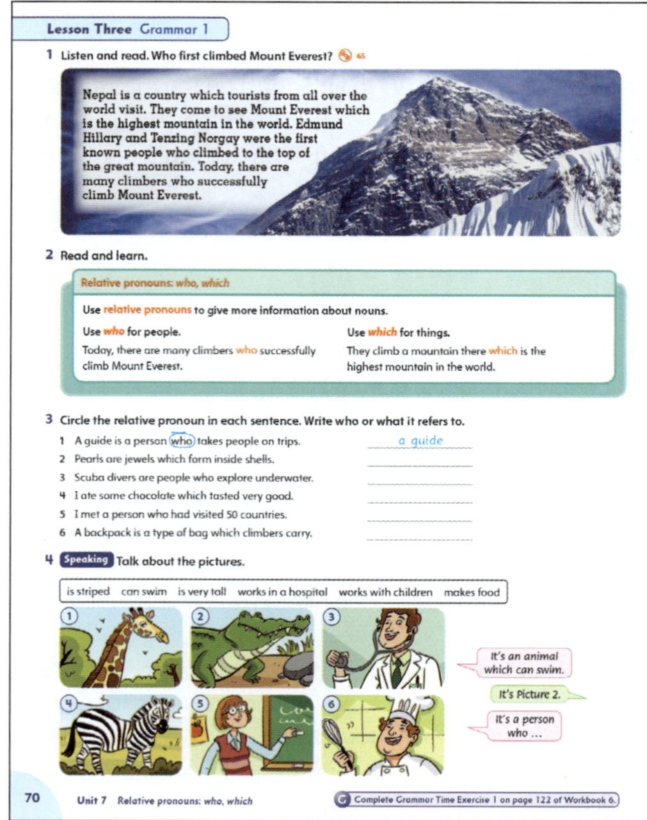
Lesson Three Grammar 1

1 Listen and read. Who first climbed Mount Everest? 65

Nepal is a country which tourists from all over the world visit. They come to see Mount Everest which is the highest mountain in the world. Edmund Hillary and Tenzing Norgay were the first known people who climbed to the top of the great mountain. Today, there are many climbers who successfully climb Mount Everest.

2 Read and learn.

Relative pronouns: *who, which*

Use relative pronouns to give more information about nouns.

Use *who* for people.	Use *which* for things.
Today, there are many climbers who successfully climb Mount Everest.	They climb a mountain there which is the highest mountain in the world.

3 Circle the relative pronoun in each sentence. Write who or what it refers to.

1 A guide is a person who takes people on trips. a guide
2 Pearls are jewels which form inside shells. ______
3 Scuba divers are people who explore underwater. ______
4 I ate some chocolate which tasted very good. ______
5 I met a person who had visited 50 countries. ______
6 A backpack is a type of bag which climbers carry. ______

4 Speaking Talk about the pictures.

is striped | can swim | is very tall | works in a hospital | works with children | makes food

1
2
3
4
5
6
It's an animal which can swim.
It's Picture 2.
It's a person who …

70 Unit 7 Relative pronouns: *who, which*

Complete Grammar Time Exercise 1 on page 122 of Workbook 6.

Lesson Three  SB page 70

Grammar 1

Learning outcomes

To use the relative pronouns *who* and *which* to describe people and things

Speaking: describing people and things using relative pronouns.

Language

Core: *Today, there are many climbers who successfully climb Mount Everest. They climb a mountain there which is the highest mountain in the world.*

Extra: scuba diver, carry

Materials

CD 65

 Oxford iTools Digital classroom • Unit 7 • Grammar 1

Warmer

- Elicit the word *mountain*, using a drawing or description, and write it on the board. Ask *Have you visited any mountains? Are there any mountains in our country? Which is the highest mountain in the world?* Write useful vocabulary on the board.

1 Listen and read. Who first climbed Mount Everest? 65

- Play the recording. Students follow along. Ask the gist question *Who first climbed Mount Everest?*

ANSWER

Edmund Hillary and Tenzing Norgay first climbed Mount Everest.

- Play it again. Ask comprehension questions, e.g. *Which country has the highest mountain? Do many people successfully climb Mount Everest today?*

2 Read and learn.

- Read through the rules and example sentences. Ask *Which relative pronoun do we use for people / things?*
- Ask students to complete these sentences:
  Ella is the girl ____ sits next to me.
  This is the book ______ we read in class.
  I like stories ______ are about adventures.
- Ask students to find *who* and *which* in Exercise 1.

3 Circle the relative pronoun in each sentence. Write who or what it refers to.

- Write the example sentence on the board. Ask students to tell you the relative pronoun. Circle the word *who*.
- Read the sentence again and ask students which word the relative pronoun refers to. Underline the word *guide*.
- Students read the rest of the sentences, circle the relative pronouns and write the people or things

ANSWERS

1. who, a guide
2. which, pearls
3. who, scuba divers
4. which, chocolate
5. who, a person
6. which, a backpack

4 Talk about the pictures.

- Ask students to look at the pictures. Ask *What can you see?*
- Focus on the speech bubbles. Choose a student and read the first speech bubble for the student to respond with the second speech bubble.
- Ask students to work in pairs. They take turns to describe the people and things using the correct relative pronouns and the words in the box.

Differentiation

Below level:

- Ask students to point to each picture and say *who* or *which*. Then ask *Which one (is striped)?* using the words in the box. Students say the number of the correct picture. Then put students in groups to complete the activity.

At level:

- Students complete the activity.

Above level:

- Ask students if they know the names of the people and animals in the pictures. Have students make sentences in pairs using these words, e.g. *A giraffe is an animal which is very tall.*

Further practice

Grammar Time, Workbook page 122

Workbook page 64

Online Practice • Unit 7 • Grammar 1

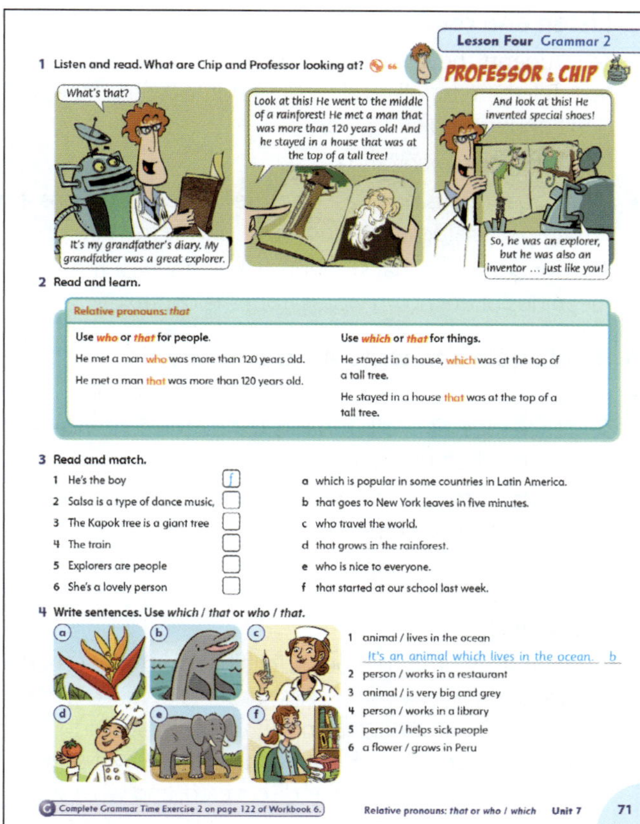

Lesson Four Grammar 2

PROFESSOR & CHIP

1 Listen and read. What are Chip and Professor looking at? 66

2 Read and learn.

Relative pronouns: that

Use **who** or **that** for people.	Use **which** or **that** for things.
He met a man who was more than 120 years old.	He stayed in a house, which was at the top of a tall tree.
He met a man that was more than 120 years old.	He stayed in a house that was at the top of a tall tree.

3 Read and match.

1 He's the boy [f]
2 Salsa is a type of dance music, [ ]
3 The Kapok tree is a giant tree [ ]
4 The train [ ]
5 Explorers are people [ ]
6 She's a lovely person [ ]

a which is popular in some countries in Latin America.
b that goes to New York leaves in five minutes.
c who travel the world.
d that grows in the rainforest.
e who is nice to everyone.
f that started at our school last week.

4 Write sentences. Use *which* / *that* or *who* / *that*.

1 animal / lives in the ocean
It's an animal which lives in the ocean. b
2 person / works in a restaurant
3 animal / is very big and grey
4 person / works in a library
5 person / helps sick people
6 a flower / grows in Peru

Complete Grammar Time Exercise 2 on page 122 of Workbook 6.

Relative pronouns: that or who / which Unit 7 71

Lesson Four SB page 71

Grammar 2

Learning outcomes

To use the relative pronoun *that* for people and things

To use relative pronouns to describe people or things

Language

Core: *He met a man who / that was more than 120 years old. He stayed in a house which / that was at the top of a tall tree.*

Materials

CD 66

 Digital classroom • Unit 7 • Grammar 2

Warmer

- Ask students to name any of Professor's inventions they can remember. Encourage them to look through their books if they are having difficulty. Write the inventions on the board.
- Invite students to make sentences describing the inventions using relative pronouns, for example: *He invented a car which cleans itself/ He invented a mechanical mop which cleans the floor.*

1 Listen and read. What are Chip and Professor looking at? 66

- Play the recording. Students listen and follow along. Ask the gist question and elicit the response.

ANSWER

Chip and Professor are looking at a diary which belonged to Professor's grandfather.

- Play it again for students to re-read the text. Ask comprehension questions, e.g. *Where did Professor's grandfather go? Who did he meet?*

2 Read and learn.

- Read the rules and examples in the box together. Ask *What do we use "who" / "which" / "that" for?*
- Ask students to re-read the story and find the sentences containing the relative pronoun *that*. For each one, ask *Which other word could we use here?*

3 Read and match.

- Ask students to look at the first part of the example. Ask students which relative pronouns the next part of the sentence could begin with (*which* or *that*). Read the complete sentence together.
- Ask students to match the rest of the sentence halves.

ANSWERS

1. f 2. a 3. d 4. b 5. c 6. e

4 Write sentences. Use *which / that* or *who / that*.

- Ask students to look at the pictures. Ask *What can you see?*
- Read the example together. Ask *Which other relative pronoun could you use in this sentence?*
- Ask students to look at the pictures and write sentences using the prompts and *which / that* or *who / that*, then match the sentences with the pictures.

Differentiation

Below level:

- Students first practice making sentences using *that* in pairs. Monitor and elicit as needed. Then switch the pairs for students to complete the activity using *who* or *which*.

At level:

- Students complete the activity.

Above level:

- After students finish, put them into pairs. Write the words for pictures a–f on the board. Have students play a guessing game using their sentences, e.g. *It's an animal which lives in the ocean. What is it? / It's a dolphin.* Make sure students take turns asking and guessing. Monitor and help as needed.

ANSWERS

1. It's an animal which / that lives in the ocean. (b)
2. It's a person who / that works in a restaurant. (d)
3. It's an animal which / that is very big and gray. (e)
4. It's a person who / that works in a library. (f)
5. It's a person who / that helps sick people. (c)
6. It's a flower which / that grows in Peru. (a)

Further practice

Grammar Time, Workbook page 122

Workbook page 65

Unit 7 Language practice worksheet, Assessment and Resource CD-ROM

Online Practice • Unit 7 • Grammar 2

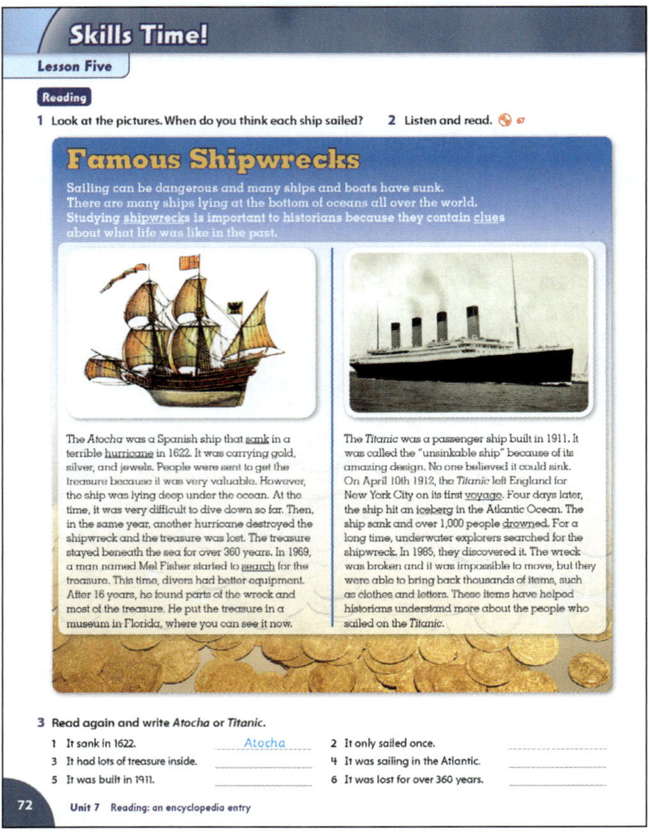

Skills Time!

Lesson Five

Reading

1 Look at the pictures. When do you think each ship sailed? 2 Listen and read. 67

Famous Shipwrecks

Sailing can be dangerous and many ships and boats have sunk. There are many ships lying at the bottom of oceans all over the world. Studying shipwrecks is important to historians because they contain clues about what life was like in the past.

The *Atocha* was a Spanish ship that sank in a terrible hurricane in 1622. It was carrying gold, silver, and jewels. People were sent to get the treasure because it was very valuable. However, the ship was lying deep under the ocean. At the time, it was very difficult to dive down so far. Then, in the same year, another hurricane destroyed the shipwreck and the treasure was lost. The treasure stayed beneath the sea for over 360 years. In 1969, a man named Mel Fisher started to search for the treasure. This time, divers had better equipment. After 16 years, he found parts of the wreck and most of the treasure. He put the treasure in a museum in Florida, where you can see it now.

The *Titanic* was a passenger ship built in 1911. It was called the "unsinkable ship" because of its amazing design. No one believed it could sink. On April 10th 1912, the *Titanic* left England for New York City on its first voyage. Four days later, the ship hit an iceberg in the Atlantic Ocean. The ship sank and over 1,000 people drowned. For a long time, underwater explorers searched for the shipwreck. In 1985, they discovered it. The wreck was broken and it was impossible to move, but they were able to bring back thousands of items, such as clothes and letters. These items have helped historians understand more about the people who sailed on the *Titanic*.

3 Read again and write *Atocha* or *Titanic*.

1 It sank in 1622. Atocha
2 It only sailed once. ______
3 It had lots of treasure inside. ______
4 It was sailing in the Atlantic. ______
5 It was built in 1911. ______
6 It was lost for over 360 years. ______

72 Unit 7 Reading: an encyclopedia entry

Lesson Five SB page 72

Skills Time!

Skills development

Reading: read a factual text

Language

Recycled: vocabulary and structures seen previously

Extra: *shipwreck, historian, clue, sank, hurricane, beneath, search, unsinkable, voyage, iceberg, drown*

Materials

CD 67

Oxford iTools Digital classroom • Unit 7 • Reading

Warmer

- Elicit the word *shipwreck*. Ask students to name any famous shipwrecks they know of. What things might they find if they discovered a shipwreck under the ocean?
- Ask *What can shipwrecks tell us about life in the past?*

1 Look at the pictures. When do you think each ship sailed?

- Ask students to look at the pictures. Without reading the text, ask when they think each ship sailed. Write their suggestions on the board.
- Ask students to skim the article briefly, without reading in detail, to find the answer to the gist question. Go through the answer together. Ask students to look at the guesses on the board. Who got closest to each date?

ANSWER

The *Atocha* sailed in 1622. The *Titanic* sailed in 1912.

2 Listen and read. 67

- Tell students they are going to listen to a recording of the text. Tell them to follow along, but not to worry if they don't understand every word.
- Play the whole recording once.
- Play it again, pausing to ask comprehension questions, e.g. *What was the Atocha carrying? Why was the treasure lost?*
- Answer questions that students have, and elicit the meanings of unknown words from the context.

3 Read again and write *Atocha* or *Titanic*.

- Ask students to look at the example. Read the full sentence together. Ask students to find the sentence that tells them when the *Atocha* sank.
- Ask students to read the article again and write *Atocha* or *Titanic* for the rest of the sentences.

Differentiation

Below level:

- Divide students into groups. Tell them to make a chart comparing the two ships. Ask students to make two columns, labeled *Atocha* and *Titanic*. They should include the year it sank, if it had treasure, why it sank, the year the shipwreck was discovered, and what was found in the shipwreck. If time permits, students share their charts.

At level:

- Divide the class into two teams. Each team writes six questions. One team writes about the *Atocha* and the other about the *Titanic*. Ask students to close their books. Each team selects a captain to ask the questions and give the answers. Then they take turns asking and answering. The students can discuss before the captain gives the answer. Keep score on the board. The team with the most points wins.

Above level:

- Ask students to write sentences comparing the two ships. Encourage students to use comparatives, e.g. *It took longer to find the Atocha than the Titanic*, or *before* and *after*, e.g. *The Atocha sank before the Titanic*. Review comparatives briefly, if needed. Monitor and help.

ANSWERS

1. Atocha 2. Titanic 3. Atocha 4. Titanic
5. Titanic 6. Atocha

Further practice

Workbook page 72

Online Practice • Unit 7 • Reading

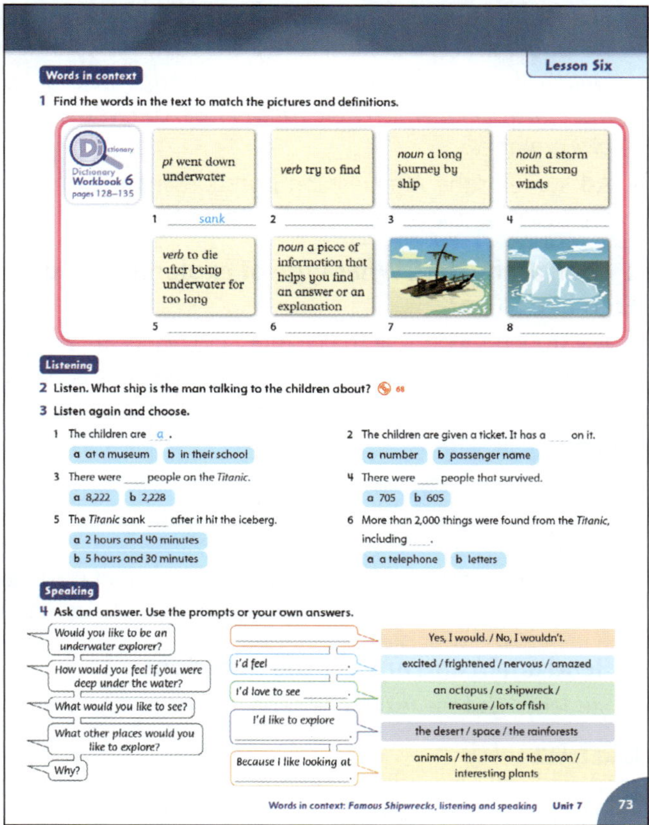
Lesson Six

Words in context

1 Find the words in the text to match the pictures and definitions.

Dictionary Workbook 6 pages 128–135

pt went down underwater — 1 sank
verb try to find — 2 ____
noun a long journey by ship — 3 ____
noun a storm with strong winds — 4 ____
verb to die after being underwater for too long — 5 ____
noun a piece of information that helps you find an answer or an explanation — 6 ____
7 ____
8 ____

Listening

2 Listen. What ship is the man talking to the children about? 68

3 Listen again and choose.

1 The children are a .
a at a museum b in their school

2 The children are given a ticket. It has a ____ on it.
a number b passenger name

3 There were ____ people on the *Titanic*.
a 8,222 b 2,228

4 There were ____ people that survived.
a 705 b 605

5 The *Titanic* sank ____ after it hit the iceberg.
a 2 hours and 40 minutes
b 5 hours and 30 minutes

6 More than 2,000 things were found from the *Titanic*, including ____.
a a telephone b letters

Speaking

4 Ask and answer. Use the prompts or your own answers.

Would you like to be an underwater explorer? — ____ — Yes, I would. / No, I wouldn't.
How would you feel if you were deep under the water? — I'd feel ____. — excited / frightened / nervous / amazed
What would you like to see? — I'd love to see ____. — an octopus / a shipwreck / treasure / lots of fish
What other places would you like to explore? — I'd like to explore ____. — the desert / space / the rainforests
Why? — Because I like looking at ____. — animals / the stars and the moon / interesting plants

Words in context: *Famous Shipwrecks*, listening and speaking Unit 7 73

Lesson Six SB page 73

Skills Time!

Skills development

Dictionary: discover meanings of words in context

Listening: listen for specific detail

Speaking: ask and answer questions about exploring

Language

Words in context: *sank, shipwreck, clue, hurricane, search, voyage, iceberg, drown* (Student Book); *harbor, on board, souvenirs, deck* (Workbook)

Materials

CD 68; Dictionary Workbook pages 128–135

Oxford iTools Digital classroom • Unit 7 • Words, Listening, Speaking

Warmer

- With books closed, ask students what they remember about the text from the previous lesson. Ask questions, e.g. *What did the Atocha carry? When did it sink?*

1 Find the words in the text to match the pictures and definitions.

- Ask the students to look at the definitions and pictures. Explain that all the words that students need are underlined in the text on page 72.
- Ask students to look at the article again and find all of the underlined words. They read the sentences that contain each word and try to determine the meaning from the context.
- Students then write the correct words below each definition and picture on page 73.

ANSWERS

1. sank 2. search 3. voyage 4. hurricane 5. drown 6. clue 7. shipwreck 8. Iceberg

2 Listen. What ship is the man talking to the children about? 68

- Tell students they are going to hear a recording. Explain that students have to listen to find out what ship the man is talking about.
- Play the whole recording.
- Elicit the answer from the class.

ANSWER

The man is talking about the *Titanic*.

3 Listen again and choose.

- Tell students to listen to the recording again. Read the instructions together and use the example to demonstrate how they should give the correct answers to the questions.
- Before you play the recording, allow time for students to read the questions and the two possible answers.
- Play the recording, pausing for students to answer.
- Play the recording again. Students complete their answers. Play the recording a third time if necessary.

ANSWERS

1. a 2. b 3. b 4. a 5. a 6. b

4 Ask and answer. Use the prompts or your own answers.

- Ask students to look at the example. Choose a strong student and ask him / her the questions.
- Put students in pairs. Tell them to take turns asking their partner questions. Their partner must answer using the prompts or his / her own ideas.
- If you wish, ask some of the pairs to ask and answer the questions in front of the class.

Differentiation

Below level:

- Read the questions aloud to the students. Pause after each one, and ask them to circle one of the prompts as their answer. Then put students in pairs to complete the activity.

At level:

- Students complete the activity.

Above level:

- After students finish, switch pairs. Ask students to ask and answer about the exploring the desert, space, or the rainforests instead. Monitor and elicit as needed.

Further practice

Workbook page 67

Unit 7 Speaking skills worksheet, Assessment and Resource CD-ROM

Online Practice • Unit 7 • Words in context, Listening, and Speaking

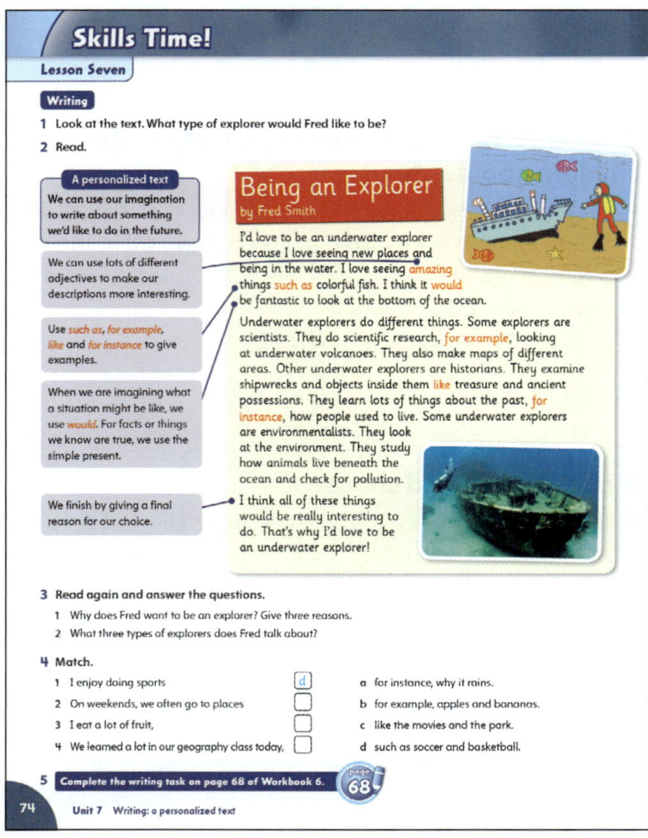

Skills Time!

Lesson Seven

Writing

1 Look at the text. What type of explorer would Fred like to be?

2 Read.

A personalized text

We can use our imagination to write about something we'd like to do in the future.

We can use lots of different adjectives to make our descriptions more interesting.

Use *such as*, *for example*, *like* and *for instance* to give examples.

When we are imagining what a situation might be like, we use *would*. For facts or things we know are true, we use the simple present.

We finish by giving a final reason for our choice.

Being an Explorer

by Fred Smith

I'd love to be an underwater explorer because I love seeing new places and being in the water. I love seeing amazing things such as colorful fish. I think it would be fantastic to look at the bottom of the ocean.

Underwater explorers do different things. Some explorers are scientists. They do scientific research, for example, looking at underwater volcanoes. They also make maps of different areas. Other underwater explorers are historians. They examine shipwrecks and objects inside them like treasure and ancient possessions. They learn lots of things about the past, for instance, how people used to live. Some underwater explorers are environmentalists. They look at the environment. They study how animals live beneath the ocean and check for pollution.

I think all of these things would be really interesting to do. That's why I'd love to be an underwater explorer!

3 Read again and answer the questions.

1 Why does Fred want to be an explorer? Give three reasons.

2 What three types of explorers does Fred talk about?

4 Match.

1 I enjoy doing sports [d]

2 On weekends, we often go to places [ ]

3 I eat a lot of fruit, [ ]

4 We learned a lot in our geography class today, [ ]

a for instance, why it rains.

b for example, apples and bananas.

c like the movies and the park.

d such as soccer and basketball.

5 Complete the writing task on page 68 of Workbook 6. page 68

74 Unit 7 Writing: a personalized text

Lesson Seven SB page 74

Skills Time!

Skills development
Writing focus: plan a personalized text
Writing outcome: write a personalized text

Language
Recycled: vocabulary and structures seen previously
Extra: *such as, for example, for instance*

Materials
Writing poster 7; a copy of the text from poster 7, Assessment and Resource CD-ROM, for each student

Oxford iTools Digital classroom • Unit 7 • Writing

Warmer

- Play a game of *Smiley face* (see page 8) to review the vocabulary from Lesson 6.

Poster 7: A personalized text

- Hand out a photocopy of the poster text to each student.
- Ask students the "Before reading" questions.
- Ask students to read silently. Ask comprehension questions, e.g. *Why would Emily love to be a jungle explorer? What do jungle explorers do?*
- Read the text boxes on the left-hand side of the text to the class. Ask *What do we say at the beginning? Which words do we use when we are imagining what a situation might be like? Which words do we use when we are imagining what might happen in a situation?*
- Read the text boxes on the right-hand side. Ask *What do we include to help the reader get a picture of what we are writing about? What do we use to make our descriptions more interesting? Which words and phrases can we use to give examples?*
- Ask students the "After reading" questions in the corner of the poster. Compare some of the students' answers.

1 Look at the text. What type of explorer would Fred like to be?

- Ask students to look at the pictures and glance through the text without reading it in detail. Ask the gist question *What type of explorer would Fred like to be?*

ANSWER

Fred would like to be an underwater explorer.

2 Read.

- Ask a different student to read each paragraph of the text to the class. Ask further questions to check understanding,

3 Read again and answer the questions.

- Students read the text silently and answer the questions.

ANSWERS

Fred wants to be an underwater explorer because he loves seeing new places and amazing things such as colorful fish. He also likes being in the water and thinks it would be fantastic to look at the bottom of the ocean.

Fred talks about scientists, historians, and environmentalists.

4 Match.

- Ask students to match the rest of the sentence halves.
- Ask them underline the phrases used to give examples.

Differentiation

Below level:

- Ask students to identify the general (e.g. *sports*) and specific words (e.g. *soccer* and *basketball*) in Exercise 4. Ask students to think of a few more general words and matching examples. Write them on the board. Work with students to make more sentences using *such as, for example, like,* and *for instance*. Monitor and help.

At level:

- Students complete the activity.

Above level:

- Ask students to write a paragraph about something they would like to do in the future.

ANSWERS

1. d 2. c 3. b 4. a

5 Complete the writing task on page 68 of Workbook 6.

- Refer students to the Workbook to complete the writing task. Go through the activity with them first.

Further practice

Workbook page 68

Unit 7 Writing skills worksheet, Assessment and Resource CD-ROM

Online Practice • Unit 7 • Writing

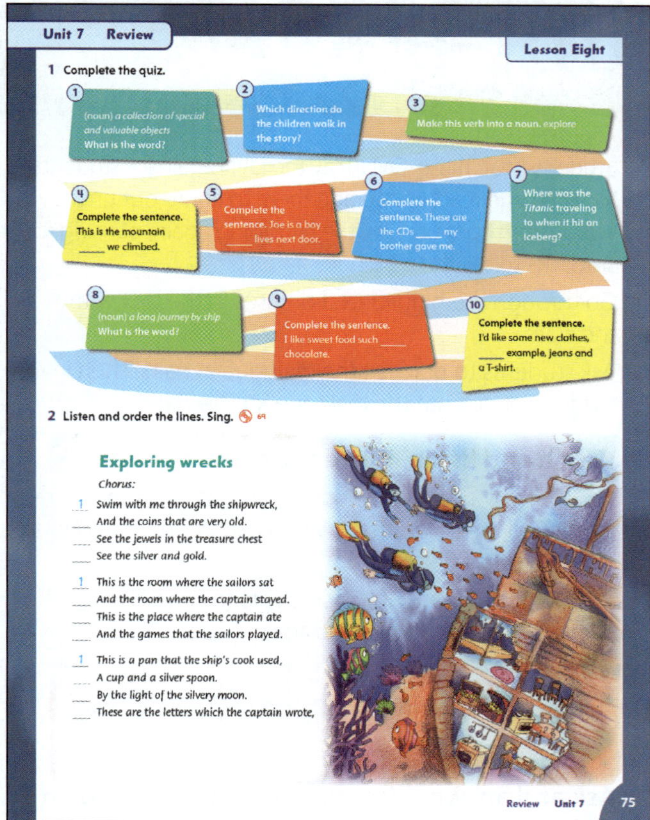
Unit 7 Review

Lesson Eight

1 Complete the quiz.

1. (noun) *a collection of special and valuable objects* What is the word?
2. Which direction do the children walk in the story?
3. Make this verb into a noun. explore
4. Complete the sentence. This is the mountain _____ we climbed.
5. Complete the sentence. Joe is a boy _____ lives next door.
6. Complete the sentence. These are the CDs _____ my brother gave me.
7. Where was the *Titanic* traveling to when it hit an iceberg?
8. (noun) *a long journey by ship* What is the word?
9. Complete the sentence. I like sweet food such _____ chocolate.
10. Complete the sentence. I'd like some new clothes, _____ example, jeans and a T-shirt.

2 Listen and order the lines. Sing. 69

Exploring wrecks

Chorus:

1 Swim with me through the shipwreck,
___ And the coins that are very old.
___ See the jewels in the treasure chest
___ See the silver and gold.

1 This is the room where the sailors sat
___ And the room where the captain stayed.
___ This is the place where the captain ate
___ And the games that the sailors played.

1 This is a pan that the ship's cook used,
___ A cup and a silver spoon.
___ By the light of the silvery moon.
___ These are the letters which the captain wrote,

Review Unit 7 75

Lesson Eight SB page 75

Unit 7 Review

Learning outcomes

To review vocabulary and structures practiced previously

To use vocabulary and structures from the unit in the context of a song

Language

Recycled: vocabulary and structures seen previously

Materials

CD 69

Oxford iTools Digital classroom • Unit 7 • Review

Warmer

- Play *Book race* (see page 8) to review words and structures from the unit.
- Read these sentences and give students 20 seconds to find the answer to each one:
  He invented special shoes. (Lesson 4)
  Nepal is a country which tourists from all over the world visit. (Lesson 3)
  The ship sank and over 1,000 people drowned. (Lesson 5)
  Some underwater explorers are environmentalists. (Lesson 7)
  We need to find shelter. (Lesson 1)
  My grandfather was a great explorer. (Lesson 4)
  We've been walking for a long time. (Lesson 1)
  The treasure stayed beneath the sea for over 360 years. (Lesson 5)

1 Complete the quiz.

- Tell students they are going to do a quiz based on the unit. Students can work individually, in pairs, or in teams.
- Students work with books open at page 75. They may not refer back to other lessons in the unit.

Differentiation

Below level:

- Play *Order the letters* (see page 9) using vocabulary words from pages 69 and 73.

At level:

- Divide the class into two teams. Tell students you have chosen a person or thing from the unit and describe it for them to guess, e.g. *He's the boy who wrote the personalized text about being an explorer.* The team who guesses correctly first gets a point, and the team with the most points wins.

Above level:

- Extend the "at level" game, and ask each student to choose one person or thing from the unit and write it down without showing anyone. Students write a sentence describing the person or thing, using a relative pronoun. Ask students to read their descriptions. The class guesses who or what it is. Monitor and help as needed.

ANSWERS

1. treasure 2. south 3. explorer 4. which / that
5. who / that 6. which / that
7. It was traveling to New York. 8. voyage
9. as 10. For

2 Listen and order the lines. Sing. 69

- Focus students' attention on the picture. Ask *Where are the divers going? What is on the shipwreck?*
- Tell students that the words to the song are in their books, but the lines are in the wrong order.
- Ask students to read the words silently.
- Play the song for the first time. Students listen and point to each line as they hear it.
- Play the song again, pausing for students to number the lines in order.
- Play it a third time. Students complete their answers.
- Go through the answers. Then play the recording again for students to sing along.

ANSWERS

Verse 1: 1, 4, 3, 2
Verse 2: 1, 4, 3, 2
Verse 3: 1, 2, 4, 3

Further practice

Workbook page 69
Unit 7 test, Assessment and Resource CD-ROM
Progress certificate, Assessment and Resource CD-ROM
Online Practice • Unit 7 • Review

Fluency Time! 3

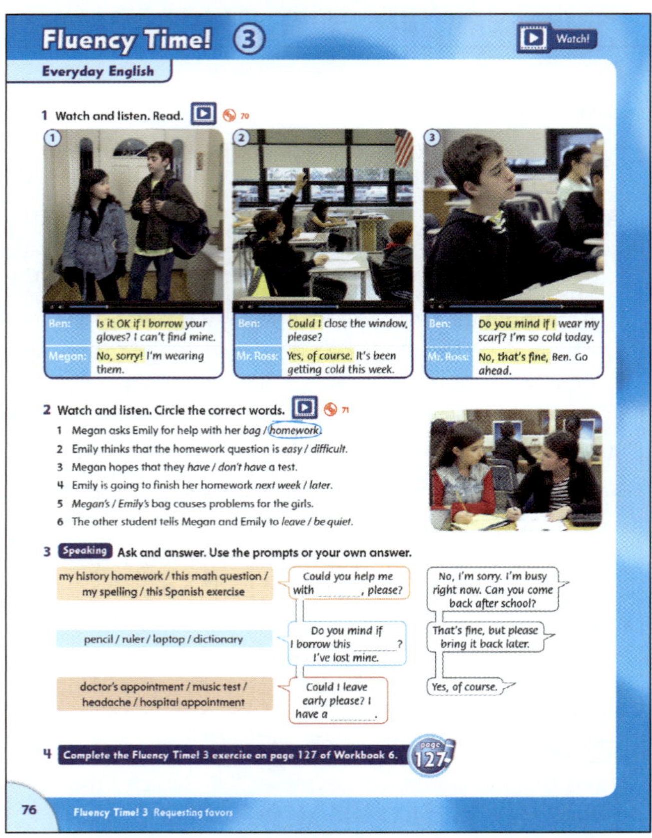

Fluency Time! 3

Watch!

Everyday English

1 Watch and listen. Read. 70

1
Ben: Is it OK if I borrow your gloves? I can't find mine.
Megan: No, sorry! I'm wearing them.

2
Ben: Could I close the window, please?
Mr. Ross: Yes, of course. It's been getting cold this week.

3
Ben: Do you mind if I wear my scarf? I'm so cold today.
Mr. Ross: No, that's fine, Ben. Go ahead.

2 Watch and listen. Circle the correct words. 71

1 Megan asks Emily for help with her *bag / homework*.
2 Emily thinks that the homework question is *easy / difficult*.
3 Megan hopes that they *have / don't have* a test.
4 Emily is going to finish her homework *next week / later*.
5 *Megan's / Emily's* bag causes problems for the girls.
6 The other student tells Megan and Emily to *leave / be quiet*.

3 Speaking Ask and answer. Use the prompts or your own answer.

my history homework / this math question / my spelling / this Spanish exercise
Could you help me with ________, please?
No, I'm sorry. I'm busy right now. Can you come back after school?

pencil / ruler / laptop / dictionary
Do you mind if I borrow this ________? I've lost mine.
That's fine, but please bring it back later.

doctor's appointment / music test / headache / hospital appointment
Could I leave early please? I have a ________.
Yes, of course.

4 Complete the Fluency Time! 3 exercise on page 127 of Workbook 6. page 127

76 Fluency Time! 3 Requesting favors

Everyday English SB page 76

Learning outcomes

To learn some useful language for requesting favors

Language

Is it OK if I borrow your gloves? No, sorry! / Yes, OK. / Sure! Do you mind if I wear my scarf? No, that's fine. Could I close the window, please? No, I'm sorry. / Yes, of course.

Materials

CD 70–71; Fluency DVD Fluency Time! 3

Oxford iTools Digital classroom • Fluency Time! 3 • Everyday English

Warmer

- Tell the class they are going to learn some useful language for requesting favors.
- Write the headings and phrases from the box in Exercise 1 on the board. Ask which phrases we use to request, grant, or refuse a favor. Ask students who they would use informal (*friends and family members*) and formal language with (*teachers, other adults, strangers*).

1 Watch and listen. Read. 70

- Focus on the pictures. Ask students who they see (*Ben, Megan, Ben's teacher, and classmates*), where they are (*at home / in a classroom*), and what they are doing (*getting ready for school / having a lesson*).
- Students watch the DVD. Play the DVD again for students to listen and read. Encourage them to figure out unknown words from context. Play the recording again, pausing for students to say the dialogue.
- Go through the highlighted phrases in the box with the class.
- Ask students to practice the dialogue in pairs. Then invite students to act out the dialogue for the class.

2 Watch and listen. Circle the correct words. 71

- Explain that students need to listen and circle the correct words. Tell the students to watch and listen for the details in the activity.
- Play the video, pausing for students to circle. Check answers by playing the video again.

ANSWERS

1. homework 2. difficult 3. don't have 4. later
5. Emily's 6. be quiet

3 Ask and answer. Use the prompts or your own answer.

- Put students in pairs to act out their own dialogues.
- Ask a volunteer to act out a dialogue with you.
- In pairs, students use the prompts, or their own answers, to act out dialogues with their partner.
- Ask some pairs to act for the class.

Differentiation

Below level:

- Break the dialogue up into three shorter exchanges. Have students practice the first question and answer a few times, then move on to the second and third ones. Make sure they switch roles for even practice.

At level:

- Put students into groups. Ask them to think of two more prompts for each blank in the dialogue. Call some students to the front and ask them to read their new dialogues.

Above level:

- Ask students to change the responses in the dialogue, e.g. *Sorry, I only have one pencil today.* Students can add more lines to the dialogue, if needed.

4 Complete the Fluency Time! 3 exercise on page 127 of Workbook 6.

- Refer students to the Workbook to complete the tasks. Review the activities with them first.

Further practice
Workbook page 70
Everyday English phrase bank, Workbook page 127
Fluency Time! 3, Fluency DVD
Online Practice • Fluency Time! 3

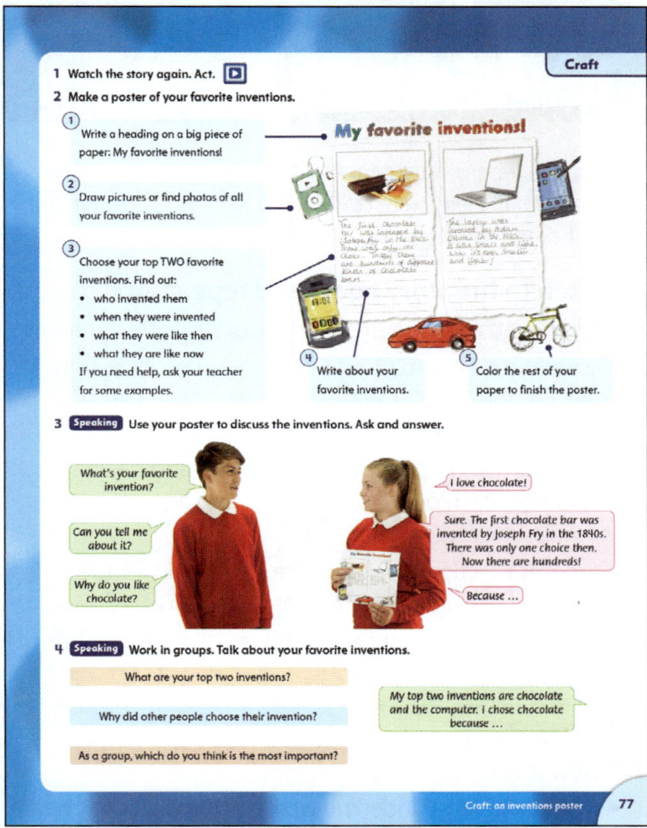

Craft

1 Watch the story again. Act.

2 Make a poster of your favorite inventions.

1 Write a heading on a big piece of paper: My favorite inventions!

2 Draw pictures or find photos of all your favorite inventions.

3 Choose your top TWO favorite inventions. Find out:

- who invented them
- when they were invented
- what they were like then
- what they are like now

If you need help, ask your teacher for some examples.

4 Write about your favorite inventions.

5 Color the rest of your paper to finish the poster.

My favorite inventions!

3 Speaking Use your poster to discuss the inventions. Ask and answer.

What's your favorite invention?

I love chocolate!

Can you tell me about it?

Sure. The first chocolate bar was invented by Joseph Fry in the 1840s. There was only one choice then. Now there are hundreds!

Why do you like chocolate?

Because …

4 Speaking Work in groups. Talk about your favorite inventions.

What are your top two inventions?

Why did other people choose their invention?

As a group, which do you think is the most important?

My top two inventions are chocolate and the computer. I chose chocolate because …

Craft: an inventions poster 77

Craft SB page 77

Learning outcomes

To make a poster of your favorite inventions

To practice discussing inventions

Language

What's your favorite invention? I love chocolate! Can you tell me about it? Sure. Why do you like chocolate? Because …

Materials

Fluency DVD Fluency Time! 3; Fluency Craft 3 (see Assessment and Resource CD-ROM) (a set of templates for each student); completed poster; colored pencils, scissors, and glue for each group

Oxford iTools Digital classroom • Fluency Time! 3 • Craft

1 Watch the story again. Act.

- Focus on the story in Exercise 1 on Student Book page 76. Ask students what they remember.
- Play the DVD Fluency Time! 3. If you don't have enough time, read the dialogue on page 76.
- Invite students to act out the dialogue. Encourage them to change details to make their own variations.

2 Make a poster of your favorite inventions.

- Focus on the picture. Ask students to say what the picture shows (*a poster about inventions*) and what inventions they can see on the poster.
- Hand out copies of the poster template and the inventions template (see Fluency Craft 3, Assessment and Resource CD-ROM).
- Read the instructions around the poster in Exercise 1. Show the class your completed poster. Ask *What inventions can you see? How many are there?*
- The students can use the inventions on the template, or find other inventions on the Internet or in books.
- Move around the class as students work, asking questions, e.g. *What's your favorite invention? Why do you like …?*

NOTE: If you do not have time, ask students to make their posters on a piece of paper.

3 Use your poster to discuss the inventions. Ask and answer.

- Focus on the photos. Tell students they are going to use their posters to act out dialogues with a friend. They will take turns asking about their partner's poster and request more information about different inventions.
- Act out the example with a volunteer, then let students talk in pairs.
- Encourage them to request and give more information.
- Ask some students to act for the class.

4 Work in groups. Talk about your favorite inventions.

- Ask a volunteer to read the speech bubble. Then invite students to tell the class about their favorite inventions. They can read the questions for help, or you can ask the questions as prompts.

Differentiation

Below level:

- Ask students to look at the poster on page 77. Put students in pairs. Have them ask and answer using the *Wh-* questions in Exeercise 2, e.g. *Who invented chocolate?* Monitor and help as needed.

At level:

- Divide the class into two teams. Ask a child from Team A to use a fact from their poster to ask a question, e.g. *Who invented the television?* Ask a child from Team B to answer. Teams alternate asking questions. Award one point for each correct answer. The team with the most points wins.

Above level:

- Ask students to switch groups and interview others. Ask them to find one person who has one of the same top inventions. Ask them to talk about why it's their favorite. Then they report back to the class, e.g. *We think airplanes are the top invention because …* Monitor and elicit as needed.

Further practice

Workbook page 71

Skills test 3 Fluency Time!, Assessment and Resource CD-ROM

Fluency Time! 3, Fluency DVD

Online Practice • Fluency Time! 3

8 It's a mystery!

8 It's a mystery!

Lesson One Story

1 Listen and read. What do the children find in the cave? 72

2 Listen to the story again and repeat. Act.

3 Read again and write the names. Ed Kate Libby Tom

1 Libby doesn't like the dark.
2 ________ and ________ explored a cave in Mexico.
3 ________ looks at the map.
4 ________ describes the weather.
5 ________ sees that the cave wall is coming down.
6 ________ sees the treasure chest.

78 Unit 8 It's a mystery!

Lesson One SB page 78

Story

Learning outcomes

To read and understand a story

To act out a story

Language

Introducing core vocabulary (Lesson 2) through a story

Extra: *entrance, come down, stand back*

Materials

CD 72

Oxford **iTools** Digital classroom • Unit 8 • Story

Warmer

- Ask students to tell you what they remember about the last episode. If necessary, ask questions, e.g. *What were the children doing? Where did they go to shelter from the rain?*

1 Listen and read. What do the children find in the cave? 72

- Play the recording. Students listen and follow along.
- Ask the gist question *What do the children find in the cave?*

ANSWER

The children find a treasure chest in the cave.

- Play the recording again. Ask comprehension questions, e.g. *What is it like in the cave? What is coming through the back of the cave?*

2 Listen to the story again and repeat. Act.

- Play the recording again, pausing for students to repeat.
- Divide the class into groups of five to play Libby, Tom, Kate, Ed, and Dad. If the class doesn't divide exactly, students can have more than one role.
- Ask students to look at the story frames and decide on actions for each one. Play the recording again. Students mime as they listen.
- Students practice acting out the story. Monitor the activity, checking for correct pronunciation.
- If you wish, ask one or two groups to come to the front of the class to act out the story.

Differentiation

Below level:

- Ask students to underline words in the dialogue they don't know. Have them first guess the meanings with context clues. Then look the words up in a dictionary. Ask students to write the definitions in their own words in their notebooks.

At level:

- Put students in pairs. Everyone re-reads the story and writes three true / false statements without showing their partner. Students swap notebooks and write *True* or *False* without looking at the story. Students check answers in their book.

Above level:

- Extend the "at level" activity to six statements.

3 Read again and write the names.

- Ask students to look at the example together. Ask them to find where we learn that Libby doesn't like the dark (frame 1).
- Ask students to read the rest of the story again and write the names. Review answers together.

ANSWERS

1. Libby 2. Kate, Ed 3. Tom 4. Libby 5. Tom 6 Tom

Further practice

Workbook page 72

Online Practice • Unit 8 • Story

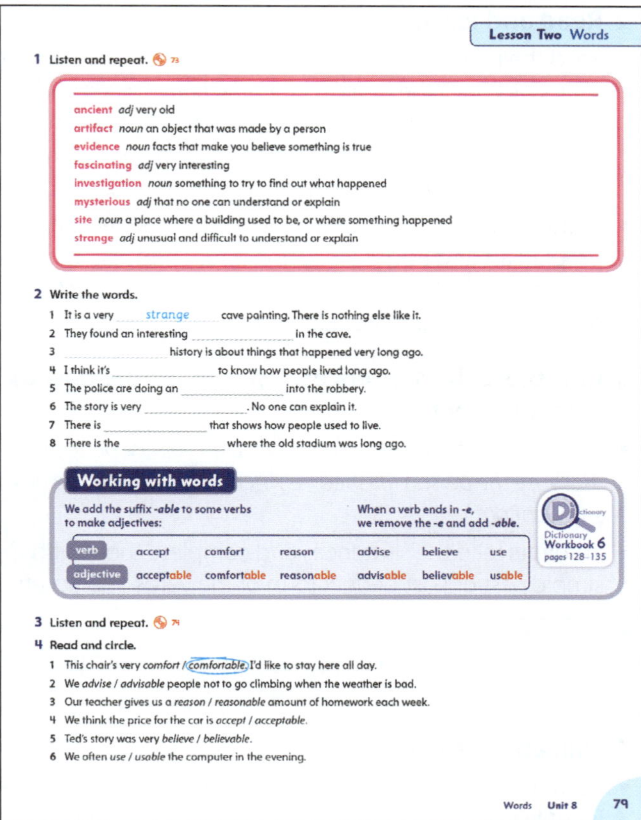

Lesson Two Words

1 Listen and repeat. 73

ancient *adj* very old
artifact *noun* an object that was made by a person
evidence *noun* facts that make you believe something is true
fascinating *adj* very interesting
investigation *noun* something to try to find out what happened
mysterious *adj* that no one can understand or explain
site *noun* a place where a building used to be, or where something happened
strange *adj* unusual and difficult to understand or explain

2 Write the words.

1 It is a very ___strange___ cave painting. There is nothing else like it.
2 They found an interesting ________ in the cave.
3 ________ history is about things that happened very long ago.
4 I think it's ________ to know how people lived long ago.
5 The police are doing an ________ into the robbery.
6 The story is very ________. No one can explain it.
7 There is ________ that shows how people used to live.
8 There is the ________ where the old stadium was long ago.

Working with words

We add the suffix *-able* to some verbs to make adjectives:

When a verb ends in *-e*, we remove the *-e* and add *-able*.

verb	accept	comfort	reason	advise	believe	use
adjective	acceptable	comfortable	reasonable	advisable	believable	usable

Dictionary Workbook 6 pages 128–135

3 Listen and repeat. 74

4 Read and circle.

1 This chair's very *comfort* / *comfortable*. I'd like to stay here all day.
2 We *advise* / *advisable* people not to go climbing when the weather is bad.
3 Our teacher gives us a *reason* / *reasonable* amount of homework each week.
4 We think the price for the car is *accept* / *acceptable*.
5 Ted's story was very *believe* / *believable*.
6 We often *use* / *usable* the computer in the evening.

Words Unit 8 79

Lesson Two SB page 79

Words

Learning outcomes

To identify and use words related to mystery and archeology

To use the suffix *-able* to make adjectives from certain verbs

Language

Words: *ancient, artifact, evidence, fascinating, investigation, mysterious, site, strange*

Working with words: *accept / acceptable, comfort / comfortable, reason / reasonable, advise / advisable, believe / believable, use / usable* (Student Book); *enjoy / enjoyable, break / breakable, prefer / preferable, understand / understandable* (Workbook)

Materials

CD 73–74 Dictionary Workbook pages 128–135

Oxford iTools Digital classroom • Unit 8 • Words

Warmer

- Ask students to look at the last frame in the story on page 78. Ask *Which word does Ed use to describe the treasure chest?* Ask students if they have ever found anything ancient. Do they know of any ancient artifacts in their local museum? Discuss.

1 Listen and repeat. 73

- Ask students to look at the words and their definitions. Ask them to read the definitions for each word silently.
- Play the recording, pausing for students to repeat.
- Play the recording again. Students listen and repeat. Repeat as often as necessary.
- Ask individual students to say the words for the class.

2 Write the words.

- Ask students to look at the example. Read it together.
- Ask students to read the sentences and complete them with the words from Exercise 1.
- Ask different students to read the sentences aloud.

ANSWERS
1. strange 2. artifact 3. Ancient 4. fascinating
5. investigation 6. mysterious 7. evidence 8. site

3 Listen and repeat. 74

- Before doing the activity, focus students' attention on the *Working with words* section.
- Ask students *What happens when we add '-able' to the end of these verbs?*
- Ask students to read the verbs and adjectives. Ask *What do we do when a verb ends in "e"?*
- Play the recording. Students listen and repeat.
- Play it again. Students listen and repeat. Repeat as often as necessary.
- Ask individual students to say the words aloud.

4 Read and circle.

- Look at the example together. Ask *Do we need a verb or an adjective here?* Establish that we need an adjective so *comfortable* is circled.
- Ask students to read the sentences and circle the correct words.
- Review answers together.

Differentiation

Below level:

- Tell students you are going to read some sentences. When they hear a verb, they should wave their arms. For adjectives ending in *-able*, they should sit still. Read these: *I accept your apology. / That chair is comfortable. / The principal reasoned with him. / It's advisable to study before a test. / I believe you. / This desk is unusable.* Then students complete the activity.

At level:

- Students complete the activity.

Above level:

- After students complete the activity, ask them to write sentences using the uncircled words from the exercise, e.g. *Mom comforts me when I'm sick.*

ANSWERS
1. comfortable 2. advise 3. reasonable
4. acceptable 5. believable 6. use

Further practice
Workbook page 73
Online Practice • Unit 8 • Words

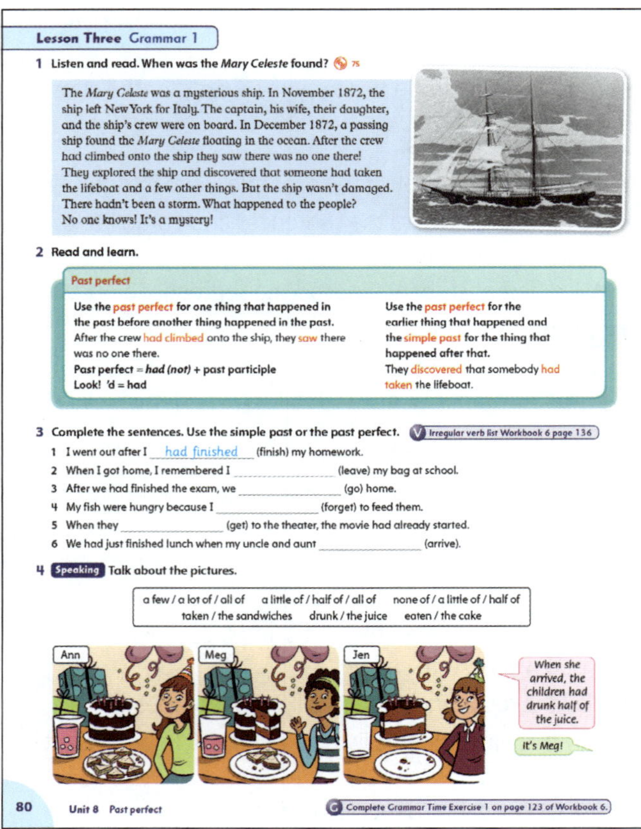

Lesson Three Grammar 1

1 Listen and read. When was the *Mary Celeste* found? 75

The *Mary Celeste* was a mysterious ship. In November 1872, the ship left New York for Italy. The captain, his wife, their daughter, and the ship's crew were on board. In December 1872, a passing ship found the *Mary Celeste* floating in the ocean. After the crew had climbed onto the ship they saw there was no one there! They explored the ship and discovered that someone had taken the lifeboat and a few other things. But the ship wasn't damaged. There hadn't been a storm. What happened to the people? No one knows! It's a mystery!

2 Read and learn.

Past perfect

Use the past perfect for one thing that happened in the past before another thing happened in the past.
After the crew had climbed onto the ship, they saw there was no one there.
Past perfect = *had (not)* + past participle
Look! 'd = had

Use the past perfect for the earlier thing that happened and the simple past for the thing that happened after that.
They discovered that somebody had taken the lifeboat.

3 Complete the sentences. Use the simple past or the past perfect. Irregular verb list Workbook 6 page 136

1 I went out after I had finished (finish) my homework.
2 When I got home, I remembered I ______ (leave) my bag at school.
3 After we had finished the exam, we ______ (go) home.
4 My fish were hungry because I ______ (forget) to feed them.
5 When they ______ (get) to the theater, the movie had already started.
6 We had just finished lunch when my uncle and aunt ______ (arrive).

4 Speaking Talk about the pictures.

a few / a lot of / all of taken / the sandwiches
a little of / half of / all of drunk / the juice
none of / a little of / half of eaten / the cake

80 Unit 8 Past perfect
Complete Grammar Time Exercise 1 on page 123 of Workbook 6.

Lesson Three SB page 80

Grammar 1

Learning outcomes

To use the past perfect to show that one thing happened before another in the past

Speaking: using the past perfect to describe past events

Language

Core: *After the crew had climbed onto the ship, they saw there was no one there. They discovered that somebody had taken the lifeboat.*

Extra: *Italy, on board*

Materials

CD 75

Oxford iTools Digital classroom • Unit 8 • Grammar 1

Warmer

- Discuss the *Atocha* and the *Titanic*. Ask *What were they carrying? Why did they sink? What happened to the people?*
- Tell students they are going to read about another ship called the *Mary Celeste*. Ask if they have heard of this ship.

1 Listen and read. When was the Mary Celeste found? 75

- Play the recording. Students follow along. Ask the gist question *When was the Mary Celeste found?*

ANSWER

The Mary Celeste was found in 1872.

- Play the recording again. Ask comprehension questions, e.g. *Where was the Mary Celeste traveling to? Who went onto the ship when it was found?*

2 Read and learn.

- Read the rules and example sentences. Copy the example sentences onto the board. Underline *had climbed* and *saw* in the first sentence. Ask *Which action happened first?* Underline *discovered* and *had taken* in the second sentence and ask the question again.
- Write these sentences. Underline the past perfect and simple past and ask which action happened first. *When we arrived at school, the lesson had already started. After they had eaten lunch, they went to the park.*

3 Complete the sentences. Use the simple past or the past perfect.

- Read the example. Ask *Why do we use the past perfect? (Because the person finished his / her homework before he / she went out.)*
- Students read the sentences and complete them with the simple past or past perfect form of the verbs in brackets.

ANSWERS

1. had finished 2. had left 3. went 4. had forgotten 5. got 6. arrived

4 Talk about the pictures.

- Focus on the pictures. Ask *What are the names of the girls?* Identify some of the differences between the pictures.
- Tell students the three girls went to the same party but arrived at different times. Different things had happened by the time each girl got there.
- Read the example aloud and demonstrate how to make sentences with the prompts.
- Ask students to work in pairs. They take turns to choose a picture and describe what had happened. Their partner finds the picture and says the name of the girl.

Differentiation

Below level:

- Draw three clocks on the board (1:00, 2:00, and 3:00), and write the three girls' names beneath. Ask students to look at the first picture. Ask *What did the children do? (took a few sandwiches*, etc.). Then ask what time Ann arrived? (1:00.) Ask *Which happened first? (The children ate and drank.)* Build a few sentences together using the example on the page. Then students complete the activity in pairs.

At level:

- Students complete the activity.

Above level:

- Ask students to think about what happened after the girls arrived and to write sentences, e.g. *After (Ann) had arrived, …* If time permits, students share with the class.

Further practice

Grammar Time, Workbook pages 122–123
Workbook page 74
Online Practice • Unit 8 • Grammar 1

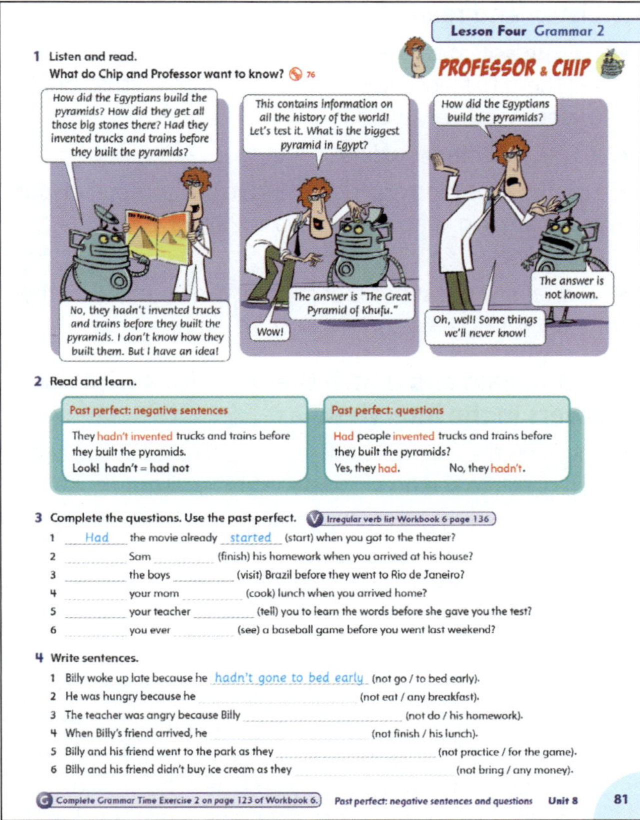

Lesson Four Grammar 2

PROFESSOR & CHIP

1 Listen and read.
What do Chip and Professor want to know? 76

2 Read and learn.

Past perfect: negative sentences
They hadn't invented trucks and trains before they built the pyramids.
Look! hadn't = had not

Past perfect: questions
Had people invented trucks and trains before they built the pyramids?
Yes, they had. No, they hadn't.

3 Complete the questions. Use the past perfect. Irregular verb list Workbook 6 page 136

1 Had the movie already started (start) when you got to the theater?
2 ______ Sam ______ (finish) his homework when you arrived at his house?
3 ______ the boys ______ (visit) Brazil before they went to Rio de Janeiro?
4 ______ your mom ______ (cook) lunch when you arrived home?
5 ______ your teacher ______ (tell) you to learn the words before she gave you the test?
6 ______ you ever ______ (see) a baseball game before you went last weekend?

4 Write sentences.

1 Billy woke up late because he hadn't gone to bed early (not go / to bed early).
2 He was hungry because he ______ (not eat / any breakfast).
3 The teacher was angry because Billy ______ (not do / his homework).
4 When Billy's friend arrived, he ______ (not finish / his lunch).
5 Billy and his friend went to the park as they ______ (not practice / for the game).
6 Billy and his friend didn't buy ice cream as they ______ (not bring / any money).

Complete Grammar Time Exercise 2 on page 123 of Workbook 6. Past perfect: negative sentences and questions Unit 8 81

Lesson Four SB page 81

Grammar 2

Learning outcomes

To use the past perfect in negative sentences and questions

Language

Core: *They hadn't invented trucks and trains before they built the Pyramids. Had people invented trucks and trains before they built the Pyramids?*

Materials

CD 76

Oxford iTools Digital classroom • Unit 8 • Grammar 2

Warmer

- Tell students that Professor and Chip are talking about one of the most famous groups of ancient monuments in the world. Ask students to guess its name.

1 Listen and read. What do Chip and Professor want to know? 76

- Ask students to look at the pictures. Ask *What is Professor holding? What are Professor and Chip talking about?* Did any of the students guess correctly?
- Play the recording. Students follow along. Ask the gist question *What do Professor and Chip want to know?*

ANSWER

Chip and Professor want to know who built the Pyramids.

- Play the recording again. Ask comprehension questions, e.g. *What is Professor's idea? Does Chip tell Professor who built the Pyramids?*

2 Read and learn.

- Read the first box together. Ask students to help you complete the following sentences with the negative past perfect form of the verbs in brackets:
  I ________ (not eat) my lunch before Lucy arrived.
  Alex ________ (not visit) France before he went on vacation to Paris.
- Read the second box together. Write these questions and ask students to complete them.
  ________ you ________ (do) your homework before you went out?
  _______ Jasmine _______ (meet) Emily before she joined the club?

3 Complete the questions. Use the past perfect.

- Write the example on the board and ask students complete it.
- Ask students to look at the exercise. They read and complete the questions with the past perfect form of the verbs in brackets.

ANSWERS

1. Had, started 2. Had, finished 3. Had, visited
4. Had, cooked 5. Had, told 6. Had, seen

4 Write sentences.

- Focus on the example. Read it together.
- Ask students to read the sentences and complete them using the prompts in brackets.

Differentiation

Below level:

- Play *Target words TPR* (see page 8). Assign students *hadn't* or a past participle verbs as targets. Make sentences in the negative simple past (e.g. *We didn't go….*) or the negative past perfect (*They hadn't gone…*) until students become comfortable. Then students complete the activity.

At level:

- Students complete the activity.

Above level:

- Play *Miming snap* (see page 8). Ask students to close their books. Use sentences from the lesson or make up your own.

ANSWERS

1. Billy woke up late because he hadn't gone to bed early.
2. He was hungry because he hadn't eaten any breakfast.
3. The teacher was angry because Billy hadn't done his homework.
4. When Billy's friend arrived, he hadn't finished his lunch.
5. Billy and his friend went to the park as they hadn't practiced for the game.
6. Billy and his friend didn't buy ice cream as they hadn't brought any money.

Further practice

Grammar Time, Workbook pages 122–123
Workbook page 75
Unit 8 Language practice worksheet, Assessment and Resource CD-ROM
Online Practice • Unit 8 • Grammar 2

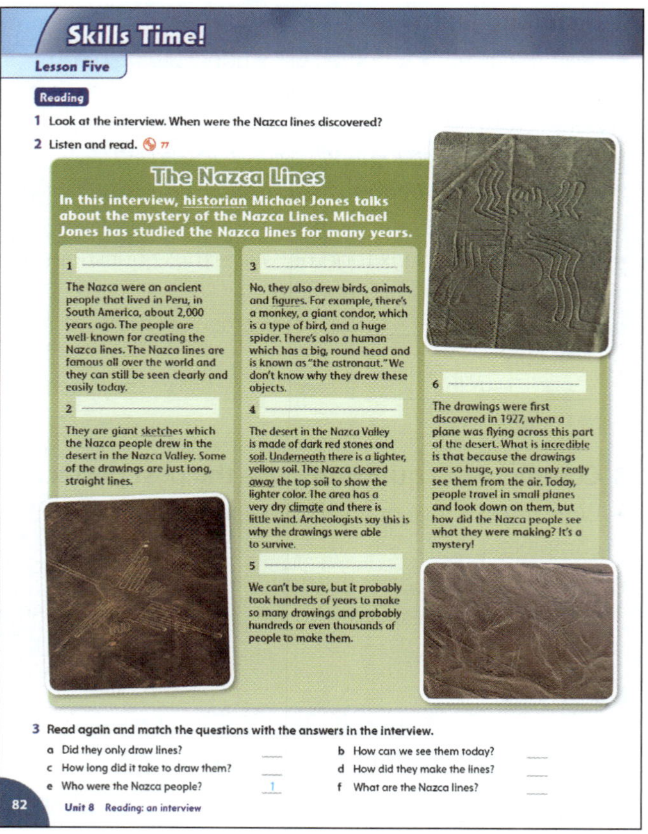

Skills Time!

Lesson Five

Reading

1 Look at the interview. When were the Nazca lines discovered?

2 Listen and read. 77

The Nazca Lines

In this interview, historian Michael Jones talks about the mystery of the Nazca Lines. Michael Jones has studied the Nazca lines for many years.

1 ______

The Nazca were an ancient people that lived in Peru, in South America, about 2,000 years ago. The people are well-known for creating the Nazca lines. The Nazca lines are famous all over the world and they can still be seen clearly and easily today.

2 ______

They are giant sketches which the Nazca people drew in the desert in the Nazca Valley. Some of the drawings are just long, straight lines.

3 ______

No, they also drew birds, animals, and figures. For example, there's a monkey, a giant condor, which is a type of bird, and a huge spider. There's also a human which has a big, round head and is known as "the astronaut." We don't know why they drew these objects.

4 ______

The desert in the Nazca Valley is made of dark red stones and soil. Underneath there is a lighter, yellow soil. The Nazca cleared away the top soil to show the lighter color. The area has a very dry climate and there is little wind. Archeologists say this is why the drawings were able to survive.

5 ______

We can't be sure, but it probably took hundreds of years to make so many drawings and probably hundreds or even thousands of people to make them.

6 ______

The drawings were first discovered in 1927, when a plane was flying across this part of the desert. What is incredible is that because the drawings are so huge, you can only really see them from the air. Today, people travel in small planes and look down on them, but how did the Nazca people see what they were making? It's a mystery!

3 Read again and match the questions with the answers in the interview.

a Did they only draw lines? ___
b How can we see them today? ___
c How long did it take to draw them? ___
d How did they make the lines? ___
e Who were the Nazca people? 1
f What are the Nazca lines? ___

82 Unit 8 Reading: an interview

Lesson Five SB page 82

Skills Time!

Skills development

Reading: read an interview

Language

Recycled: vocabulary and structures seen previously

Extra: *Peru, South America, well-known, sketch (n), figure, human, soil, underneath, clear away, climate, incredible*

Materials

CD 77

Oxford **iTools** Digital classroom • Unit 8 • Reading

Warmer

- Ask students what Professor and Chip were talking about in the previous lesson. Ask students to suggest ideas about how the Egyptians built the Pyramids. Do they know of any other famous mysteries from around the world? Discuss these together.

1 Look at the interview. When were the Nazca lines discovered?

- Ask students to look at the pictures. Ask *What can you see?*
- Ask students to skim the article, without reading in detail, to find the answer to the gist question.

ANSWER

The Nazca lines were discovered in 1927.

2 Listen and read. 77

- Tell students they are going to listen to an interview. Tell them to follow along, but not to worry if they don't understand every word.
- Play the whole recording.
- Play the recording again, pausing to ask comprehension questions, e.g. *Who were the Nazca? What are the Nazca lines?*
- Answer any questions that students have, and elicit the meanings of unknown words from context.

3 Read again and match the questions with the answers in the interview.

- Focus on the example. Ask students to re-read the first paragraph to see how it answers the question.
- Ask students to read the interview again and match the questions to the paragraphs.

Differentiation

Below level:

- Have a spelling bee with words from the lesson. Have students stand in a row at the front of the classroom. Say a word for the first student to spell. If correct, he / she stays at the front. If incorrect, he / she sits down, and the next student tries. Continue until there is only one student left. That student is the winner.

At level:

- Ask students to close their books. Write the following words on the board: *Peru / astronaut / desert / plane / discovered / mystery.*
- Ask a student to stand, choose a word, and use it in a sentence about the Nazca lines. If the sentence is factually correct, cross the word out. Continue with other students until you have used all the words.

Above level:

- Ask *How do you think the Nazca lines were drawn?* Put students into groups to discuss. Ask one person from each group to share their ideas with the rest of the class.

ANSWERS

a. 3 b. 6 c. 5 d. 4 e. 1 f. 2

Further practice

Workbook page 76

Online Practice • Unit 8 • Reading

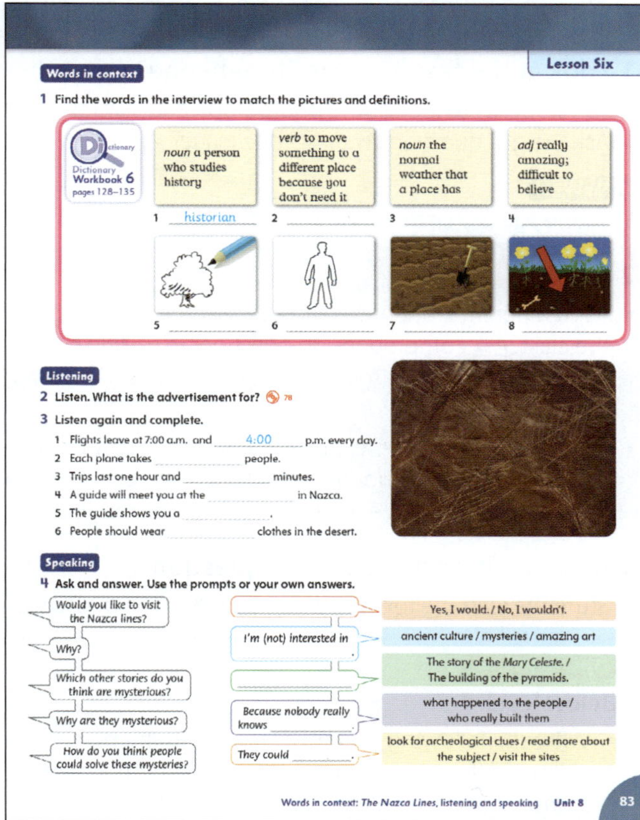

Lesson Six

Words in context

1 Find the words in the interview to match the pictures and definitions.

Dictionary Workbook 6 pages 128–135

noun a person who studies history
1 historian

verb to move something to a different place because you don't need it
2 ______

noun the normal weather that a place has
3 ______

adj really amazing; difficult to believe
4 ______

5 ______ 6 ______ 7 ______ 8 ______

Listening

2 Listen. What is the advertisement for? 78

3 Listen again and complete.

1 Flights leave at 7:00 a.m. and 4:00 p.m. every day.
2 Each plane takes ______ people.
3 Trips last one hour and ______ minutes.
4 A guide will meet you at the ______ in Nazca.
5 The guide shows you a ______.
6 People should wear ______ clothes in the desert.

Speaking

4 Ask and answer. Use the prompts or your own answers.

Would you like to visit the Nazca lines? — ______ — Yes, I would. / No, I wouldn't.
Why? — I'm (not) interested in ______. — ancient culture / mysteries / amazing art
Which other stories do you think are mysterious? — ______ — The story of the *Mary Celeste*. / The building of the pyramids.
Why are they mysterious? — Because nobody really knows ______. — what happened to the people / who really built them
How do you think people could solve these mysteries? — They could ______. — look for archeological clues / read more about the subject / visit the sites

Words in context: *The Nazca Lines*, listening and speaking Unit 8 83

Lesson Six SB page 83

Skills Time!

Skills development

Dictionary: discover meanings of words in context

Listening: listen for specific detail

Speaking: ask and answer questions about mysteries

Language

Words in context: *historian, sketch (n), figure, soil, underneath, clear away, climate, incredible* (Student Book); *quarry, erupt, statue, platform* (Workbook)

Materials

CD 78; Dictionary Workbook pages 128–135

Oxford iTools Digital classroom • Unit 8 • Words, Listening, Speaking

Warmer

- With books closed, ask students what they remember about the interview from the previous lesson. Ask questions if necessary, e.g. *What are the Nazca lines? When were they made?*

NOTE: Remind students to consult the Dictionary pages in their Workbooks when completing Exercise 1.

1 Find the words in the interview to match the pictures and definitions.

- Ask students to look at the definitions and pictures. Explain that all the words needed are underlined in the text on page 82.
- Ask students to look at the article again and find all the underlined words. They read the sentences that contain each word and try to determine the meaning from context.
- Students then write the correct words below each definition and picture on page 83.

Differentiation

Below level:

- Ask students to close their Student Books, take out their Workbooks, and turn to page 128. Divide students into teams. Tell students you are going to say a word, and they have to find it in the dictionary. Whoever finds it first, gets a point. Say each of the vocabulary words. The team with the most points wins.

At level:

- Play *Time's up!* (see page 9) with the new vocabulary.

Above level:

- Ask students to write a sentence for each of the new words. If time permits, students share with the class.

ANSWERS

1. historian 2. clear away 3. climate 4. incredible 5. sketch 6. figure 7. soil 8. underneath

2 Listen. What is the advertisement for? 78

- Tell students they are going to hear an advertisement. Ask students to listen to find out what it is for.
- Play the whole recording. Then elicit the answer.

ANSWER

The advertisement is for a plane trip to see the Nazca lines.

3 Listen again and complete.

- Tell students they are going to listen again. This time they must complete the sentences.
- Before playing the recording, allow time for students to read the sentences.
- Play the recording, pausing for students to write the missing words.
- Play the recording again. Students complete their answers. Play it a third time if necessary.

ANSWERS

1. 4 2. six 3. thirty 4. airport 5. movie 6. light

4 Ask and answer. Use the prompts or your own answers.

- Ask students to look at the example. Choose a strong student and ask the questions for him / her to answer.
- Ask students to work in pairs. Tell them to take turns asking their partner questions. Their partner answers using the prompts or his / her own ideas.
- Ask some of the pairs to ask and answer in front of the class.

Further practice

Workbook page 77

Unit 8 Speaking skills worksheet, Assessment and Resource CD-ROM

Online Practice • Unit 8 • Words in context, Listening, and Speaking

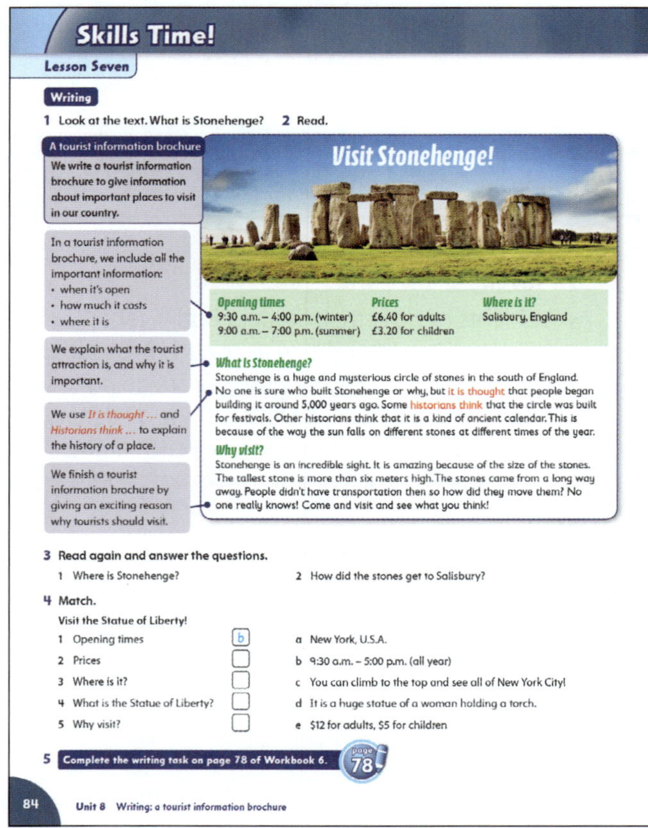

Skills Time!

Lesson Seven

Writing

1 Look at the text. What is Stonehenge? 2 Read.

A tourist information brochure

We write a tourist information brochure to give information about important places to visit in our country.

In a tourist information brochure, we include all the important information:
- when it's open
- how much it costs
- where it is

We explain what the tourist attraction is, and why it is important.

We use *It is thought …* and *Historians think …* to explain the history of a place.

We finish a tourist information brochure by giving an exciting reason why tourists should visit.

Visit Stonehenge!

Opening times	Prices	Where is it?
9:30 a.m. – 4:00 p.m. (winter) 9:00 a.m. – 7:00 p.m. (summer)	£6.40 for adults £3.20 for children	Salisbury, England

What is Stonehenge?

Stonehenge is a huge and mysterious circle of stones in the south of England. No one is sure who built Stonehenge or why, but it is thought that people began building it around 5,000 years ago. Some historians think that the circle was built for festivals. Other historians think that it is a kind of ancient calendar. This is because of the way the sun falls on different stones at different times of the year.

Why visit?

Stonehenge is an incredible sight. It is amazing because of the size of the stones. The tallest stone is more than six meters high. The stones came from a long way away. People didn't have transportation then so how did they move them? No one really knows! Come and visit and see what you think!

3 Read again and answer the questions.

1 Where is Stonehenge? 2 How did the stones get to Salisbury?

4 Match.

Visit the Statue of Liberty!

1 Opening times [b] a New York, U.S.A.
2 Prices [ ] b 9:30 a.m. – 5:00 p.m. (all year)
3 Where is it? [ ] c You can climb to the top and see all of New York City!
4 What is the Statue of Liberty? [ ] d It is a huge statue of a woman holding a torch.
5 Why visit? [ ] e $12 for adults, $5 for children

5 Complete the writing task on page 78 of Workbook 6. page 78

84 Unit 8 Writing: a tourist information brochure

Lesson Seven SB page 84

Skills Time!

Skills development

Writing focus: lay out a tourist information brochure

Writing outcome: write a tourist information brochure

Language

Recycled: vocabulary and structures seen previously

Extra: *attraction*

Materials

Writing poster 8; a copy of the text from poster 8, Assessment and Resource CD-ROM, for each student; paper and colored pencils (optional)

Oxford iTools Digital classroom • Unit 8 • Writing

Warmer

- Tell students they are going to look at a tourist information brochure for a very famous world attraction. Ask what information they think should be included.

Poster 8: A tourist information brochure

- Give a copy of the poster to each student. Display your copy, and ask the "Before reading" question.
- Ask students to read the text silently. Ask comprehension questions, e.g. *Where is the Great Wall of China? How old is it?*
- Read the text boxes on the left-hand side of the brochure. Ask *Why do we write tourist information brochures? What information should we include? What phrases can we use to explain the history of the place?*
- Read the text boxes on the right. Ask *Why should we include a photo? What can we use to persuade the reader to visit? How do we finish the brochure?*
- Ask the "After reading" questions. Discuss students' answers.

1 Look at the text. What is Stonehenge?

- Ask students to look at the photograph and skim the text. Ask the gist question *What is Stonehenge?*

ANSWER

Stonehenge is a circle of stones in the south of England.

2 Read.

- Ask a different student to read each section of text to the class. Ask comprehension questions, e.g. *Who built Stonehenge? What do some historians think it is? Where did the stones come from?*
- Draw attention to the text boxes around the main text. Choose a different student to read each text box to the class. Pause between each and check understanding.

3 Read again and answer the questions.

- Students read the text silently and answer the questions.

Differentiation

Below level:

- Write the following sentence starters on the board and ask different students to complete them: *In winter, Stonehenge is open from / It costs £6.40 / Stonehenge is a huge and mysterious / It is thought that people began building it / The tallest stone / The stones came from*

At level:

- Put students in groups to make a tourist brochure for the Statue of Liberty, using the information in Exercise 4. Give each group paper and colored pencils. If time permits, students can share with the class.

Above level:

- Put students in groups and ask them to think of a place in their country for tourists to visit. Give each group paper and colored pencils. Tell students they are in charge of advertising the attraction and to compile a list of exciting reasons that people should visit. If time permits, students can share with the class.

ANSWERS

1. Stonehenge is in Salisbury, England.
2. No one know how the stones got to Salisbury.

4 Match.

- Ask students to look at the pieces of text on the left. Tell them they are section headings from a tourist information brochure for the Statue of Liberty. Students match the headings to the items on the right.

ANSWERS

1. b 2. e 3. a 4. d 5. c

5 Complete the writing task on page 78 of Workbook 6.

- Refer students to the Workbook to complete the writing task. Go through the activity with them first.

Further practice

Workbook page 78

Unit 8 Writing skills worksheet, Assessment and Resource CD-ROM

Online Practice • Unit 8 • Writing

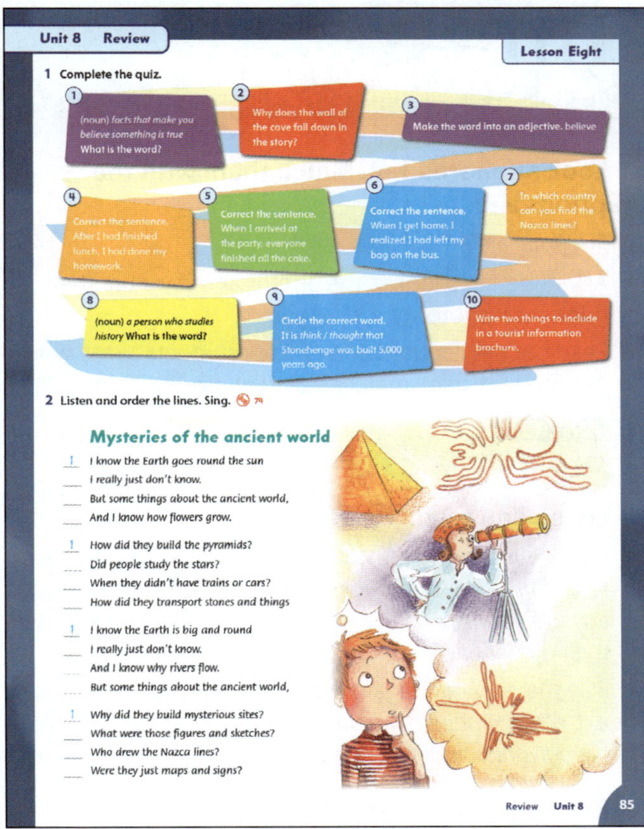
Unit 8 Review

Lesson Eight

1 Complete the quiz.

1 (noun) facts that make you believe something is true What is the word?

2 Why does the wall of the cave fall down in the story?

3 Make the word into an adjective. believe

4 Correct the sentence. After I had finished lunch, I had done my homework.

5 Correct the sentence. When I arrived at the party, everyone finished all the cake.

6 Correct the sentence. When I get home, I realized I had left my bag on the bus.

7 In which country can you find the Nazca lines?

8 (noun) a person who studies history What is the word?

9 Circle the correct word. It is *think* / *thought* that Stonehenge was built 5,000 years ago.

10 Write two things to include in a tourist information brochure.

2 Listen and order the lines. Sing. 79

Mysteries of the ancient world

1 I know the Earth goes round the sun
___ I really just don't know.
___ But some things about the ancient world,
___ And I know how flowers grow.

1 How did they build the pyramids?
___ Did people study the stars?
___ When they didn't have trains or cars?
___ How did they transport stones and things

1 I know the Earth is big and round
___ I really just don't know.
___ And I know why rivers flow.
___ But some things about the ancient world,

1 Why did they build mysterious sites?
___ What were those figures and sketches?
___ Who drew the Nazca lines?
___ Were they just maps and signs?

Review Unit 8 85

Lesson Eight SB page 85

Unit 8 Review

Learning outcomes

To review vocabulary and structures practiced previously

To use vocabulary and structures from the unit in the context of a song

Language

Recycled: vocabulary and structures seen previously

Materials

CD 79

Oxford iTools Digital classroom • Unit 8 • Review

Warmer

- Play *Book race* (see page 8) to review the unit.
- Read the sentences below and give students 20 seconds to find each one.
  Stonehenge is an incredible sight. (Lesson 7)
  The Mary Celeste was a mysterious ship. (Lesson 3)
  The answer is not known. (Lesson 4)
  Look out! The cave wall is coming down! (Lesson 1)
  The people are well-known for creating Nazca lines. (Lesson 5)
  The answer is 'The Great Pyramid of Khufu.' (Lesson 4)
  There hadn't been a storm. (Lesson 3)
  It's very mysterious! (Lesson 1)

1 Complete the quiz.

- Tell students they are going to do a quiz based on this unit. Students can work individually, in pairs, or in teams.
- Students work with books open at page 85. They may not refer back to other lessons in the unit.

ANSWERS

1. evidence 2. Because water is coming through it. 3. believable 4. After I had finished lunch, I did my homework. 5. When I arrived at the party, everyone had finished all the cake. 6. When I got home, I realized I had left my bag on the bus. 7. You can find the Nazca lines in Peru. 8. historian 9. thought 10. Possible answers: when it's open; how much it costs; where it is.

2 Listen and order the lines. Sing. 79

- Focus students' attention on the picture. Ask *What can you see? What is the boy doing?*
- Tell students the words to the song are in their books, but the lines are in the wrong order.
- Ask students to read the words silently.
- Play the song. Students listen and point to each line as they hear it.
- Play it again, pausing for students to number the lines.
- Play the song a third time. Students check answers.
- Ask a different student to read each line in order.
- Play the recording for students to sing along.

Differentiation

Below level:

- Put students into groups. Assign each group a phrase, e.g. *how flowers grow, build the pyramids*. Students decide on actions for their phrases. Then play the song. Students stand and do their action when they hear their phrase. If time permits, switch phrases and play again.

At level:

- Write each verse on pieces of paper. Leave blanks for key words. Divide the class into three groups to play a memory game. Ask students to close their books. Ask students to work together to fill in the words. Play the song again to check answers.

Above level:

- Put students into groups. Ask them to brainstorm mysteries they want to know about. Give out paper to write their ideas down. Students use their ideas to write a new verse for the song.

ANSWERS

Verse 1: 1, 4, 3, 2
Verse 2: 1, 2, 4, 3
Verse 3: 1, 3, 4, 2
Verse 4: 1, 3, 2, 4

Further practice

Workbook page 79
Unit 8 test, Assessment and Resource CD-ROM
Progress certificate, Assessment and Resource CD-ROM
Online Practice • Unit 8 • Review

History Time!

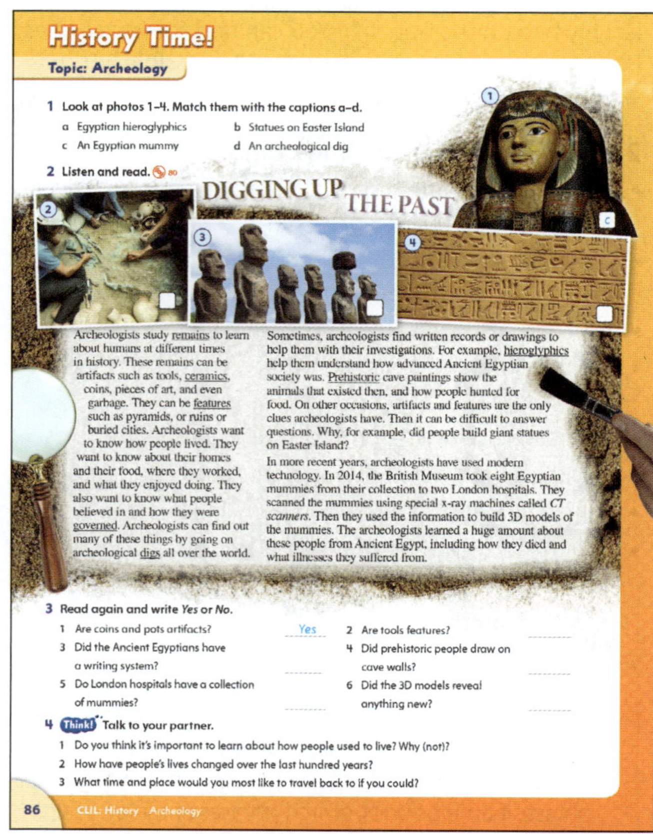

History Time!

Topic: Archeology

1 Look at photos 1–4. Match them with the captions a–d.

a Egyptian hieroglyphics
b Statues on Easter Island
c An Egyptian mummy
d An archeological dig

2 Listen and read. 80

DIGGING UP THE PAST

Archeologists study remains to learn about humans at different times in history. These remains can be artifacts such as tools, ceramics, coins, pieces of art, and even garbage. They can be features such as pyramids, or ruins or buried cities. Archeologists want to know how people lived. They want to know about their homes and their food, where they worked, and what they enjoyed doing. They also want to know what people believed in and how they were governed. Archeologists can find out many of these things by going on archeological digs all over the world.

Sometimes, archeologists find written records or drawings to help them with their investigations. For example, hieroglyphics help them understand how advanced Ancient Egyptian society was. Prehistoric cave paintings show the animals that existed then, and how people hunted for food. On other occasions, artifacts and features are the only clues archeologists have. Then it can be difficult to answer questions. Why, for example, did people build giant statues on Easter Island?

In more recent years, archeologists have used modern technology. In 2014, the British Museum took eight Egyptian mummies from their collection to two London hospitals. They scanned the mummies using special x-ray machines called *CT scanners*. Then they used the information to build 3D models of the mummies. The archeologists learned a huge amount about these people from Ancient Egypt, including how they died and what illnesses they suffered from.

3 Read again and write *Yes* or *No*.

1 Are coins and pots artifacts? Yes
2 Are tools features? ____
3 Did the Ancient Egyptians have a writing system? ____
4 Did prehistoric people draw on cave walls? ____
5 Do London hospitals have a collection of mummies? ____
6 Did the 3D models reveal anything new? ____

4 Think! Talk to your partner.

1 Do you think it's important to learn about how people used to live? Why (not)?
2 How have people's lives changed over the last hundred years?
3 What time and place would you most like to travel back to if you could?

86 CLIL: History Archeology

Topic: Archeology SB page 86

Learning outcomes

To learn some useful content and language about archeology

Language

Core: *remains, ceramic, features, governed, digs, hieroglyphics, prehistoric*

Extra: *archeologists, artifacts, ruins, records, investigations, scanned, suffered*

Materials

CD 80

Oxford iTools Digital classroom • History Time! • Archeology

Warmer

Critical Thinking

- Ask students to say whether they enjoy learning about history or not, and to give reasons for their answers. Ask them how we can find out about life in the past.

Lead-in

- Tell students that they are going to learn about history in this lesson. Ask students which periods / groups of people in history they know about (e.g. *Ancient Egypt / Ancient Rome / the Ancient Mayans*) and what they know about each period / group of people (e.g. *The Ancient Egyptians built pyramids / Julius Caesar lived in Ancient Rome. / The Ancient Mayans lived 2,000 years ago.*).

1 Look at photos 1–4. Match them with the captions a–d.

Critical Thinking

- Ask students to look at the photos and say what they think each photo shows.
- Read out the captions a–d and ask students to say which caption they think matches each photo.

ANSWERS

1. c 2. d 3. b 4. a

2 Listen and read. 80

- Play the recording for students to listen and follow the text in their Student Books. Elicit / Teach the meanings of any unknown words, or ask students to find the words in their dictionaries.
- Play the recording again. Ask comprehension questions, e.g. *What remains do archeologists study? How do hieroglyphics help archeologists?*

3 Read again and write *Yes* or *No*.

- Explain that students need to find information in the text to answer the questions. Read out the first question and allow students time to look at the text and find the answer.
- Students complete the rest of the activity individually.

ANSWERS

1. Yes 2. No 3. Yes 4. Yes 5. No 6. Yes

4 Think! Talk to your partner.

Critical Thinking

- Read out the questions and elicit suggestions from students around the class.

Collaboration

- Put students in pairs to discuss their answers.
- Have pairs report back to the class.

Differentiation

Below level:

- Divide the class into three groups. Assign one question to each group. Students talk together to decide on the best answer to their question.
- Invite students from each group to report their answer to the class.

At level:

- Students complete the activity.

Above level:

- When students have finished the exercise, ask them to choose a period in history and imagine what a day in their life would be like if they were alive then.
- Invite students to tell the class about their day in history.

Further practice
Workbook page 80
Online Practice • History Time!

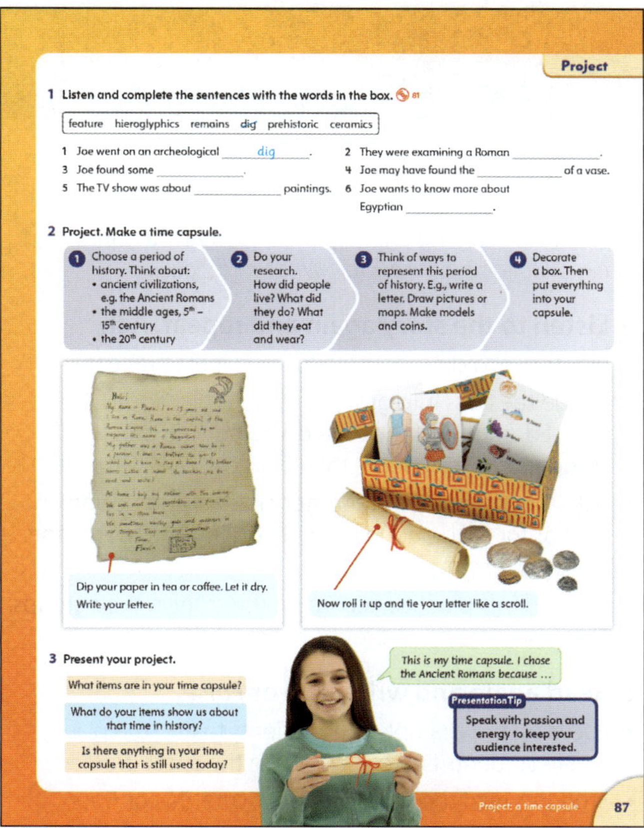

Project

1 Listen and complete the sentences with the words in the box. 81

feature hieroglyphics remains dig prehistoric ceramics

1 Joe went on an archeological _dig_.
2 They were examining a Roman ________.
3 Joe found some ________.
4 Joe may have found the ________ of a vase.
5 The TV show was about ________ paintings.
6 Joe wants to know more about Egyptian ________.

2 Project. Make a time capsule.

1 Choose a period of history. Think about:
• ancient civilizations, e.g. the Ancient Romans
• the middle ages, 5th – 15th century
• the 20th century

2 Do your research. How did people live? What did they do? What did they eat and wear?

3 Think of ways to represent this period of history. E.g., write a letter. Draw pictures or maps. Make models and coins.

4 Decorate a box. Then put everything into your capsule.

Dip your paper in tea or coffee. Let it dry. Write your letter.

Now roll it up and tie your letter like a scroll.

3 Present your project.

What items are in your time capsule?

What do your items show us about that time in history?

Is there anything in your time capsule that is still used today?

This is my time capsule. I chose the Ancient Romans because …

Presentation Tip

Speak with passion and energy to keep your audience interested.

Project: a time capsule 87

Project SB page 87

Learning outcomes

To listen and complete sentences with words from a box

To make a time capsule

Language

This is my time capsule. I chose the Ancient Romans because …

Materials

CD 81; shoeboxes; paper; tea or coffee in a large container; modelling clay; colored pens or pencils; scissors; glue

Oxford iTools Digital classroom • History Time! • Project

Warmer

- Ask students what they can remember about the text on Student Book page 86. Ask them to say what their favorite period in history is and why.

1 Listen and complete the sentences with the words in the box. 81

- Play the recording. Students need to listen and complete the sentences with the words in the box.
- Play the recording once through. Play it again, pausing after each answer is mentioned so that students have time to think about their answers.
- Check answers with the class.

ANSWERS

1. dig 2. feature 3. ceramics 4. remains
5. prehistoric 6. hieroglyphics

2 Project. Make a time capsule.

Creativity

- Explain that students are going to make a time capsule for a period in history. Ask *What do you need to make a time capsule?* Elicit / Teach *shoebox, modelling clay, tea/coffee, paper, colored pens or pencils, scissors, glue.*
- Focus on the instructions. Ask a student to read out the instructions to the class.
- Before students begin the project, dip their sheets of paper in a bowl of cold tea or coffee and let the paper dry.
- Students work in pairs to choose a period in history for their time capsule and research on the Internet or in history books to find out the information they need.
- Hand out shoeboxes, modelling clay, paper, scissors, and glue to each pair. Have students work in pairs to make their time capsules.

NOTE: To save time in class, prepare the sheets of paper dipped in tea or coffee before the lesson.

Differentiation

Below level:

- Choose a period in history. Ask questions about it, e.g. *Where did people live? What did they wear? What things did they have? What did they eat? What did they do?* Elicit answers and write them on the board. Children can use history books or the Internet to find the answers.
- Children work in their groups to make their time capsules. They draw pictures, make things with modelling clay, and write a letter to put in their box.

At level:

- Students complete the activity.

Above level:

- When students have made their time capsules, demonstrate a memory game with one of the time capsules. Place the items on a desk, and tell students to look at them for one minute.
- Tell students to close their eyes. Replace all the items in the box. Students open their eyes and try to remember all of the items.
- Students can then play this game in pairs, using their own time capsules.

3 Present your project.

Communication

- Put students into groups of three or four. Tell them that they are now going to talk about their project with each other.
- Demonstrate by either holding up a completed time capsule, or using the example in the Student Book. Talk about the time capsule, as in the example. Point to different items as you mention them.
- Students talk in groups.
- Invite individual students to stand up and present their projects to the class.

Further practice

Workbook page 81

Online Practice • History Time!

9 Survival!

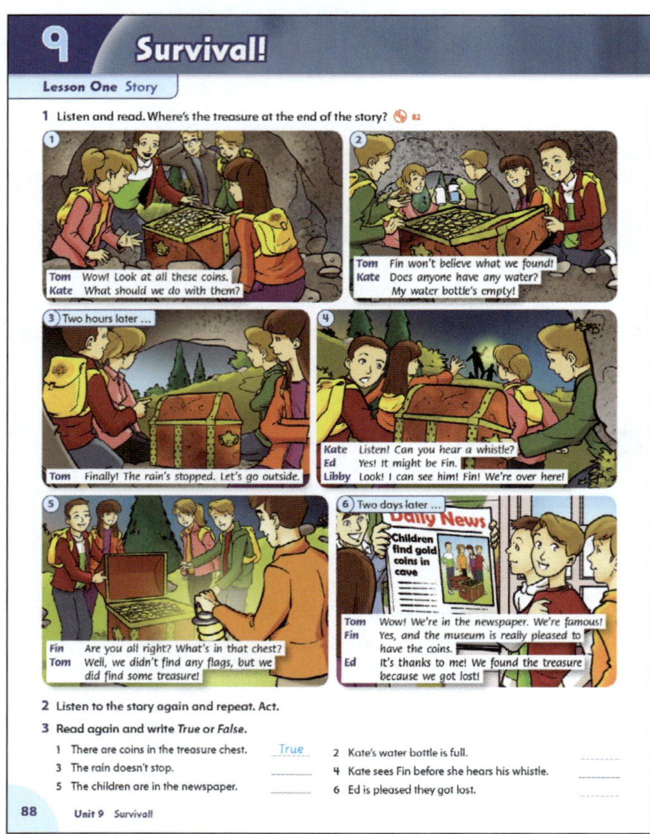

9 Survival!

Lesson One Story

1 Listen and read. Where's the treasure at the end of the story? 82

2 Listen to the story again and repeat. Act.

3 Read again and write *True* or *False*.

1 There are coins in the treasure chest. True
2 Kate's water bottle is full. ______
3 The rain doesn't stop. ______
4 Kate sees Fin before she hears his whistle. ______
5 The children are in the newspaper. ______
6 Ed is pleased they got lost. ______

88 Unit 9 Survival!

Lesson One 

SB page 88

Story

Learning outcomes

To read and understand a story

To act out a story

Language

Introducing vocabulary through a story

Materials

CD 82

Oxford iTools Digital classroom • Unit 9 • Story

Warmer

- Ask what students remember about the last episode of the story. Ask questions, e.g. *Where were the children? What happened in the cave?*
- Ask students to say what they think is in the chest. Write their suggestions on the board.

1 Listen and read. Where is the treasure at the end of the story? 82

- Ask students to look at the pictures and see what is in the chest. Did anyone guess correctly?
- Play the recording. Students listen and follow along. Ask the gist question *Where is the treasure at the end of the story?*

ANSWER

The treasure is in the museum at the end of the story.

- Play the recording again. Ask comprehension questions, e.g. *What does Kate ask for? What is Ed's joke?*

2 Listen to the story again and repeat. Act.

- Play the recording, pausing for students to repeat.
- Divide the class into groups of five to play Tom, Libby, Kate, Ed, and Fin. If the class doesn't divide exactly, students can have more than one role.
- Ask students to look at the story frames and decide on actions for each one. Play the recording again. Students mime as they listen.
- Let students practice acting out the story in their groups. Then ask one or two groups to act for the class.

3 Read again and write *True* or *False*.

- Focus on the example. Ask students to find the place where students find out what is in the chest (frame 1).
- Students read the sentences and write *True* or *False*.

Differentiation

Below level:

- Ask students to underline words in the story they don't know. Have them first guess the meaning with context clues. Then look the words up in a dictionary, in their Workbook or elsewhere. Have students take out their notebooks and write the definitions in their own words.

At level:

- Put students in pairs. Everyone re-reads the story and writes three true / false statements in his / her notebook without showing their partner what they written. Students swap notebooks and write *True* or *False* without checking. Students check answers by looking back at the story.

Above level:

- Extend the "at level" activity to six statements.

ANSWERS

1. True 2. False 3. False 4. False 5. True 6. True

Further practice

Workbook page 82

Online Practice • Unit 9 • Story

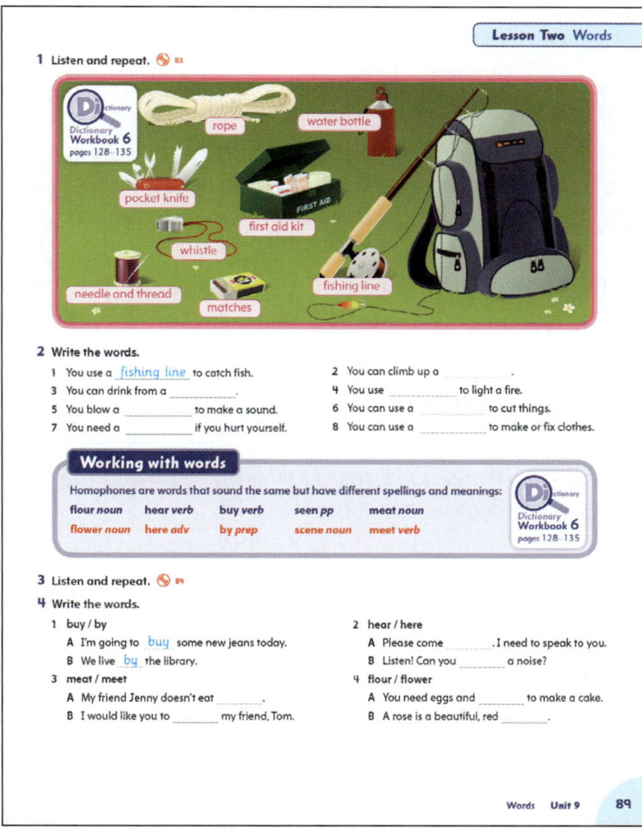

Lesson Two Words

1 Listen and repeat. 83

2 Write the words.

1 You use a fishing line to catch fish.
2 You can climb up a ______.
3 You can drink from a ______.
4 You use ______ to light a fire.
5 You blow a ______ to make a sound.
6 You can use a ______ to cut things.
7 You need a ______ if you hurt yourself.
8 You can use a ______ to make or fix clothes.

Working with words

Homophones are words that sound the same but have different spellings and meanings:

flour *noun*	hear *verb*	buy *verb*	seen *pp*	meat *noun*
flower *noun*	here *adv*	by *prep*	scene *noun*	meet *verb*

Dictionary Workbook 6 pages 128–135

3 Listen and repeat. 84

4 Write the words.

1 buy / by
A I'm going to buy some new jeans today.
B We live by the library.

2 hear / here
A Please come ______. I need to speak to you.
B Listen! Can you ______ a noise?

3 meat / meet
A My friend Jenny doesn't eat ______.
B I would like you to ______ my friend, Tom.

4 flour / flower
A You need eggs and ______ to make a cake.
B A rose is a beautiful, red ______.

Words Unit 9 89

Lesson Two SB page 89

Words

Learning outcomes

To identify and use words related to survival

To identify different homophones and use them in the correct context

Language

Words: *pocket knife, water bottle, fishing line, whistle, needle and thread, rope, matches, first aid kit*

Working with words: *flour (n) / flower (n), hear (vb) / here (adv), buy (vb) / by (prep), seen (pp) / scene (n), meat (n) / meet (v), sea (n), see (v)* (Student Book); *whether / weather, brake / break, sum / some* (Workbook)

Materials

CD 83–84 Dictionary Workbook pages 128–135; paper and colored pencils (optional)

Oxford iTools Digital classroom • Unit 9 • Words

Warmer

- Tell students to imagine that they are going to go on an expedition for two days. Ask *What do you need to pack in your backpack?* Write students' ideas on the board.

1 Listen and repeat. 83

- Ask students to look at the words and the pictures in their books. Did students suggest any of these things?
- Play the recording, pausing for students to repeat.
- Play it again. Students to listen and repeat.
- Ask individual students to say the words for the class.

2 Write the words.

- Ask students to look at the example and read the sentence together.
- Ask students to read the sentences and complete them with the correct words from Exercise 1.

ANSWERS

1. fishing line 2. rope 3. water bottle 4. matches
5. whistle 6. pocket knife 7. first aid kit
8. needle and thread

3 Listen and repeat. 84

- Before doing the activity, focus students' attention on the *Working with words* section.
- Read the explanations and examples together. Ask *What is a homophone?*
- Play the recording for students to listen and repeat.
- Play the recording again. Students listen and repeat. Repeat as often as necessary.
- Ask individual students to say the words for the class.

Differentiation

Below level:

- Tell students to draw the words you read and spell. Give each student paper and colored pencils. Use the words in the box on page 89. Check the students' drawings and display them around the room.

At level:

- Tell students you are going to read some sentences aloud. They must listen and write the correct spelling of the homophones they hear. Read these, pausing between each one to for students to write: *How long have you been waiting here? / Look at that beautiful flower in the yard. / I've never seen a famous person. / I love going to the sea. / Can you buy me some milk, please? / It's nice to meet you.*

Above level:

- Extend the "at level" activity by asking students to write sentences for each homophone they wrote. Check answers together.

4 Write the words.

- Look at the example together. Focus on the words *sea* and *see*. Ask *Which is a noun and which is a verb?* Read each sentence and ask *Do we need a noun or a verb here?*
- Ask students to read the rest of the pairs of sentences and complete them with the correct words.

ANSWERS

1. A buy B by
2. A here B hear
3. A meat B meet
4. A flour B flower

Further practice

Workbook page 83

Online Practice • Unit 9 • Words

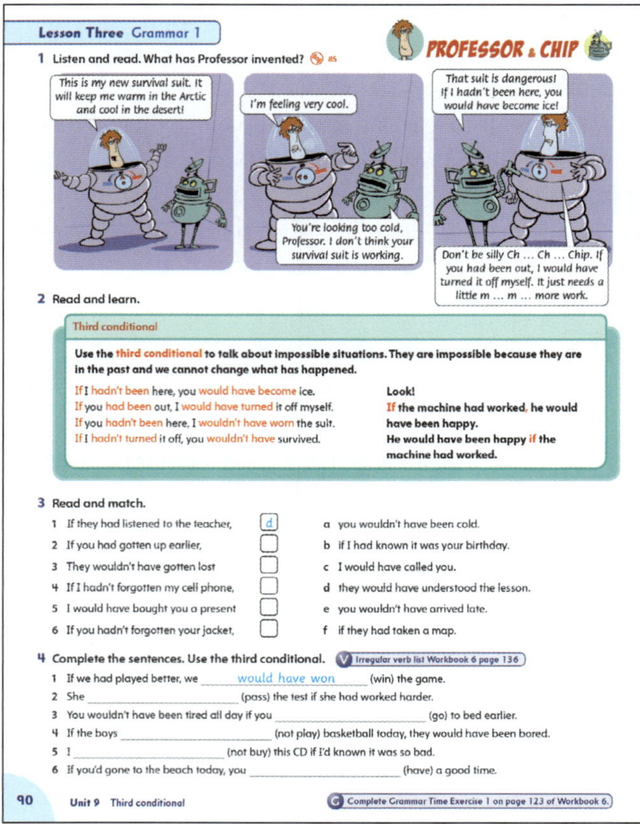
Lesson Three Grammar 1

PROFESSOR & CHIP

1 Listen and read. What has Professor invented? 85

2 Read and learn.

Third conditional

Use the third conditional to talk about impossible situations. They are impossible because they are in the past and we cannot change what has happened.

If I hadn't been here, you would have become ice.
If you had been out, I would have turned it off myself.
If you hadn't been here, I wouldn't have worn the suit.
If I hadn't turned it off, you wouldn't have survived.

Look!
If the machine had worked, he would have been happy.
He would have been happy if the machine had worked.

3 Read and match.

1 If they had listened to the teacher, [d]
2 If you had gotten up earlier, [ ]
3 They wouldn't have gotten lost [ ]
4 If I hadn't forgotten my cell phone, [ ]
5 I would have bought you a present [ ]
6 If you hadn't forgotten your jacket, [ ]

a you wouldn't have been cold.
b if I had known it was your birthday.
c I would have called you.
d they would have understood the lesson.
e you wouldn't have arrived late.
f if they had taken a map.

4 Complete the sentences. Use the third conditional. Irregular verb list Workbook 6 page 136

1 If we had played better, we ___would have won___ (win) the game.
2 She ________ (pass) the test if she had worked harder.
3 You wouldn't have been tired all day if you ________ (go) to bed earlier.
4 If the boys ________ (not play) basketball today, they would have been bored.
5 I ________ (not buy) this CD if I'd known it was so bad.
6 If you'd gone to the beach today, you ________ (have) a good time.

90 Unit 9 Third conditional

Complete Grammar Time Exercise 1 on page 123 of Workbook 6.

Lesson Three SB page 90

Grammar 1

Learning outcomes

To use the third conditional to talk about impossible situations

Language

Core: *If you had been out, I would have turned it off myself. If I hadn't been here, you would have become ice. If you hadn't been here, I wouldn't have worn the suit. If I hadn't turned it off, you wouldn't have survived.*

Materials

CD 85

Oxford iTools Digital classroom • Unit 9 • Grammar 1

Warmer

- Play *Order the letters* (see page 9) to review the vocabulary from the previous two lessons.

1 Listen and read. What has Professor invented? 85

- Play the recording. Students follow along. Ask the gist question *What has Professor invented?*

ANSWER

The Professor has invented a survival suit.

- Play the recording again. Ask comprehension questions, e.g. *What will Professor's survival suit do? Is the suit working?*

2 Read and learn.

- Read the rules and examples in the box together. Ask *What do we use the third conditional for?*
- Point out that the sentences have two parts (the *if* clause and the main clause). Copy an example from the box, separating the two parts:
  If I hadn't been here, / you would have become ice.
- Ask students *Which tense do we use in the first part of the sentence?* to elicit the answer *the past perfect*. Ask *What do we use in the second part of the sentence?* Elicit *would have* + past participle.
- Tell students the two parts of the sentence can go either way around, and rewrite the sentence with the main clause first: *You would have become ice if I hadn't been here.*

3 Read and match.

- Look at the example together. Ask *What would have happened if they had listened to the teacher?* Read the complete sentence together.
- Ask students to match the rest of the sentence halves.
- Review answers together. Ask individual students to read the sentences aloud.

ANSWERS

1. d 2. e 3. f 4. c 5. b 6. a

NOTE: Remind students to use the Irregular verb list in their Workbooks when they are completing Exercise 4.

4 Complete the sentences. Use the third conditional.

- Before students look at the exercise, copy the example onto the board. Ask students to help you complete it with the correct form of the verb in brackets.
- Ask students to look at the exercise and complete the third conditional sentences.
- Review answers together. Ask individual students to read the sentences aloud.

Differentiation

Below level:

- Have students look at Workbook page 136 to review how to form the past participle. Elicit the past participles for the verbs in parentheses. Practice forming the conditional aloud. Then students complete the activity.

At level:

- Write the following sentence starters on the board for students to complete with their own ideas: *If my alarm clock hadn't gone off this morning, … If I had forgotten to do my homework last night, … I would have been hungry if … My mom would have been angry if …*

Above level:

- Have students switch the order of the clauses and rewrite the sentences, e.g. *We would have won the game if we had played better.* If time permits, students can share with the class.

ANSWERS

1. would have won 2. would have passed 3. had gone 4. hadn't played 5. wouldn't have bought 6. would have had

Further practice

Grammar Time, Workbook page 123
Workbook page 84
Online Practice • Unit 9 • Grammar 1

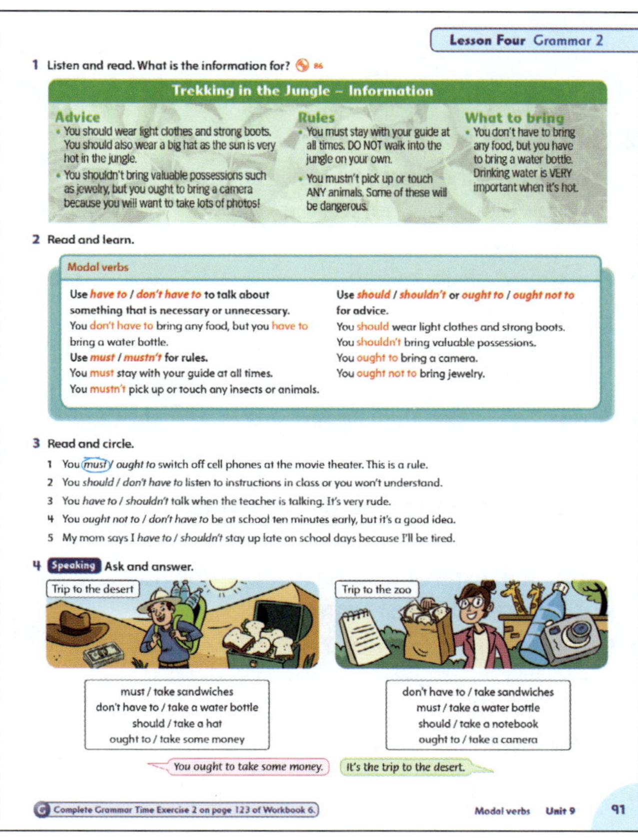

Lesson Four Grammar 2

1 Listen and read. What is the information for? 86

Trekking in the Jungle – Information

Advice
- You should wear light clothes and strong boots. You should also wear a big hat as the sun is very hot in the jungle.
- You shouldn't bring valuable possessions such as jewelry, but you ought to bring a camera because you will want to take lots of photos!

Rules
- You must stay with your guide at all times. DO NOT walk into the jungle on your own.
- You mustn't pick up or touch ANY animals. Some of these will be dangerous.

What to bring
- You don't have to bring any food, but you have to bring a water bottle. Drinking water is VERY important when it's hot.

2 Read and learn.

Modal verbs

Use *have to* / *don't have to* to talk about something that is necessary or unnecessary.
You don't have to bring any food, but you have to bring a water bottle.
Use *must* / *mustn't* for rules.
You must stay with your guide at all times.
You mustn't pick up or touch any insects or animals.

Use *should* / *shouldn't* or *ought to* / *ought not to* for advice.
You should wear light clothes and strong boots.
You shouldn't bring valuable possessions.
You ought to bring a camera.
You ought not to bring jewelry.

3 Read and circle.

1 You *must* / *ought to* switch off cell phones at the movie theater. This is a rule.
2 You *should* / *don't have to* listen to instructions in class or you won't understand.
3 You *have to* / *shouldn't* talk when the teacher is talking. It's very rude.
4 You *ought not to* / *don't have to* be at school ten minutes early, but it's a good idea.
5 My mom says I *have to* / *shouldn't* stay up late on school days because I'll be tired.

4 Speaking Ask and answer.

must / take sandwiches
don't have to / take a water bottle
should / take a hat
ought to / take some money

don't have to / take sandwiches
must / take a water bottle
should / take a notebook
ought to / take a camera

You ought to take some money.
It's the trip to the desert.

Complete Grammar Time Exercise 2 on page 123 of Workbook 6.

Modal verbs Unit 9 91

Lesson Four SB page 91

Grammar 2

Learning outcomes

To use *have to / don't have to* to talk about things which are necessary or unnecessary

To use *must / mustn't* for rules

To use *should / shouldn't* or *ought to / ought not to* for advice

Speaking: talking about things which are necessary or unnecessary and giving advice using modal verbs

Language

Core: *You don't have to bring any food, but you have to bring a water bottle. You must stay with your guide at all times. You mustn't pick up or touch any insects or animals. You should wear light clothes and strong boots. You shouldn't bring valuable possessions. You ought to bring a camera. You ought not to bring jewelry.*

Extra: *trekking, possessions*

Materials

CD 86

Oxford iTools Digital classroom • Unit 9 • Grammar 2

Warmer

- Play *Twenty, twenty* with the word *jungle* (see page 9). Tell students *It's a type of place* before you start the game.
- Ask the class if anyone has ever been to a jungle. Ask *How do you survive in the jungle? What do you need?*

1 Listen and read. What is the information for? 86

- Play the recording. Students follow along. Ask the gist question *What is the information for?*

ANSWER

The information is for trekking in the jungle.

- Play the recording for students to read again. Ask comprehension questions, e.g. *What should you wear in the jungle? What should you bring?*

2 Read and learn.

- Read the rules and examples in the box together. Ask *What do we use "have to" / "don't have to" for? What do we use "must" / "mustn't" for? What do we use "should" / "shouldn't" or "ought" / "ought not to" for?*
- Ask students to reread the text from Exercise 1 and find examples of the words.

3 Read and circle.

- Ask students to look at the first part of the example sentence. Ask *Why do we use "must" here?* (Because it's a rule.
- Ask students to read the sentences and circle the correct words.

ANSWERS

1. must 2. should 3. shouldn't 4. don't have to 5. shouldn't

4 Ask and answer.

- Ask students to look at the pictures. Ask *Where are the people?*
- Ask a pair of students to read the speech bubbles to the class.
- Ask students to work in pairs. They take turns making statements about a place for their partner to guess. They use the word prompts with the modal verbs.
- Monitor the activity and help where necessary.
- Review answers. If you wish, ask some of the students to make a statement for the class to say the place.

Differentiation

Below level:

- Write this model sentence on the board: *You ___ take ___*. Call students to the board to make sentences using the words in the box. Then put students in pairs to complete the activity. Monitor and elicit as needed.

At level:

- Students complete the activity.

Above level:

- Ask students to think about a third trip. Have them write sentences about the place using modal verbs, using Exercise 4 as a model. Put students in pairs to guess their partner's place. Monitor and help as needed.

Further practice

Grammar Time, Workbook page 123
Workbook page 85
Unit 9 Language practice worksheet, Assessment and Resource CD-ROM
Online Practice • Unit 9 • Grammar 2

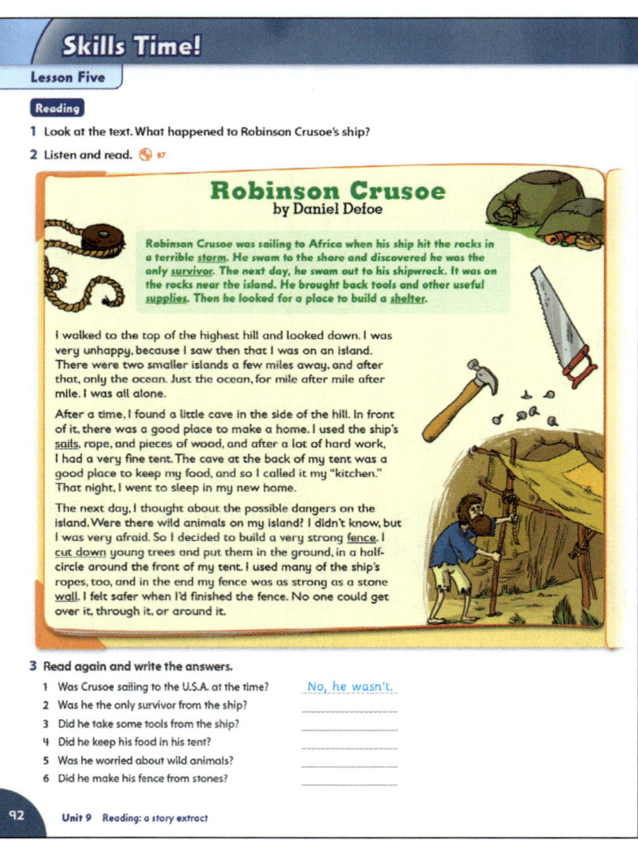

Skills Time!

Lesson Five

Reading

1 Look at the text. What happened to Robinson Crusoe's ship?

2 Listen and read. 87

Robinson Crusoe
by Daniel Defoe

Robinson Crusoe was sailing to Africa when his ship hit the rocks in a terrible storm. He swam to the shore and discovered he was the only survivor. The next day, he swam out to his shipwreck. It was on the rocks near the island. He brought back tools and other useful supplies. Then he looked for a place to build a shelter.

I walked to the top of the highest hill and looked down. I was very unhappy, because I saw then that I was on an island. There were two smaller islands a few miles away, and after that, only the ocean. Just the ocean, for mile after mile after mile. I was all alone.

After a time, I found a little cave in the side of the hill. In front of it, there was a good place to make a home. I used the ship's sails, rope, and pieces of wood, and after a lot of hard work, I had a very fine tent. The cave at the back of my tent was a good place to keep my food, and so I called it my "kitchen." That night, I went to sleep in my new home.

The next day, I thought about the possible dangers on the island. Were there wild animals on my island? I didn't know, but I was very afraid. So I decided to build a very strong fence. I cut down young trees and put them in the ground, in a half-circle around the front of my tent. I used many of the ship's ropes, too, and in the end my fence was as strong as a stone wall. I felt safer when I'd finished the fence. No one could get over it, through it, or around it.

3 Read again and write the answers.

1 Was Crusoe sailing to the U.S.A. at the time? No, he wasn't.
2 Was he the only survivor from the ship? ______
3 Did he take some tools from the ship? ______
4 Did he keep his food in his tent? ______
5 Was he worried about wild animals? ______
6 Did he make his fence from stones? ______

92 Unit 9 Reading: a story extract

Lesson Five SB page 92

Skills Time!

Skills development

Reading: read an extract from a novel

Language

Recycled: vocabulary and structures seen previously

Extra: *storm, survivor, supplies, shelter, sails, fence, cut down, wall*

Materials

CD 87

Oxford iTools Digital classroom • Digital classroom • Unit 9 • Reading

Warmer

- Ask students to imagine being stranded on a desert island. Ask *What would you do? What would you eat? Where would you sleep? How would you keep safe?*
- Tell students they are going to read an excerpt from a famous book about a man called *Robinson Crusoe* who is stranded on a desert island. Ask students if they know the book. Can they tell you anything about it?

1 Look at the text. What happened to Robinson Crusoe's ship?

- Ask students to look at the pictures. Ask *What can you see? Where is the man? What has he made?*
- Ask students to skim the article briefly, without reading in detail, to find the answer to the gist question.

ANSWER

Robinson Crusoe's ship was wrecked when it hit the rocks in a terrible storm.

2 Listen and read. 87

- Tell students they are going to listen to the text. Tell them to follow along, but not to worry if they don't understand every word.
- Play the whole recording.
- Play the recording again, pausing to ask comprehension questions, e.g. *How does Robinson Crusoe feel when he realizes he's on an island? Where does he make his home?*
- Answer questions that students have, and elicit the meanings of unknown words from context.

3 Read again and write the answers.

- Ask students to look at the example. Ask them to find the part of the text that tells them where Robinson Crusoe was sailing to (the first sentence).
- Students re-read the text and write short answers.

Differentiation

Below level:

- Play *Miming snap* (see page 8) using the new words from the text. Encourage students to come up and mime.

At level:

- Play *Wrong word* (see page 8) with these sentences: *Robinson Crusoe decided to buy a little house. / He found a little tent in the side of the hill. / He used the ship's sails, rope, and pieces of metal. / The cave was a good place to keep his tools. / Crusoe was afraid of wild animals on his ship. / He built a sail around his tent to make it safe.*

Above level:

- Extend the "at level" activity by asking students to write their own sentences to add to the *Wrong word* game. Monitor and help as needed

ANSWERS

1. No, he wasn't. 2. Yes, he was. 3. Yes, he did.
4. No, he didn't. 5. Yes, he was. 6. No, he didn't.

Further practice

Workbook page 86

Online Practice • Unit 9 • Reading

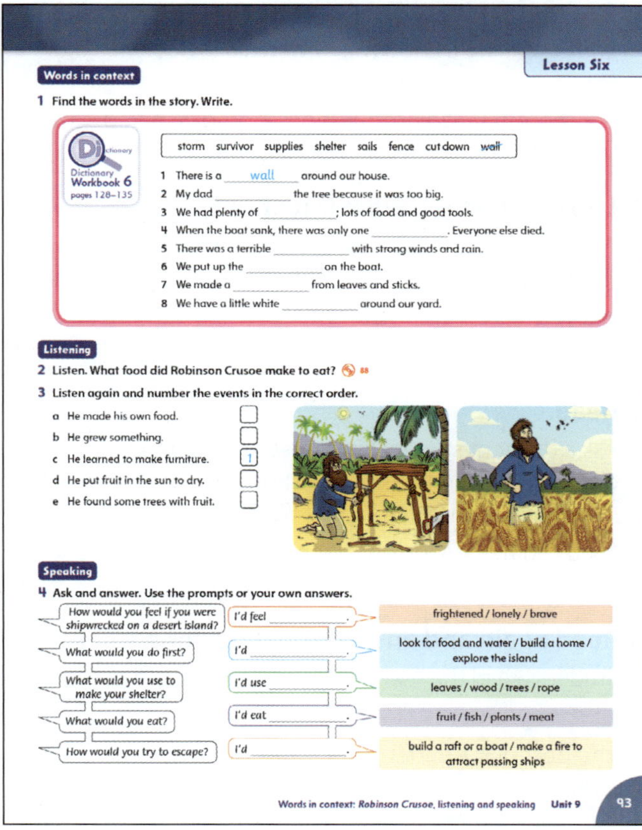

Lesson Six

Words in context

1 Find the words in the story. Write.

Dictionary Workbook 6 pages 128–135

storm survivor supplies shelter sails fence cut down wall

1 There is a wall around our house.
2 My dad ________ the tree because it was too big.
3 We had plenty of ________; lots of food and good tools.
4 When the boat sank, there was only one ________. Everyone else died.
5 There was a terrible ________ with strong winds and rain.
6 We put up the ________ on the boat.
7 We made a ________ from leaves and sticks.
8 We have a little white ________ around our yard.

Listening

2 Listen. What food did Robinson Crusoe make to eat? 88

3 Listen again and number the events in the correct order.

a He made his own food. ☐
b He grew something. ☐
c He learned to make furniture. 1
d He put fruit in the sun to dry. ☐
e He found some trees with fruit. ☐

Speaking

4 Ask and answer. Use the prompts or your own answers.

How would you feel if you were shipwrecked on a desert island?	I'd feel ________.	frightened / lonely / brave
What would you do first?	I'd ________.	look for food and water / build a home / explore the island
What would you use to make your shelter?	I'd use ________.	leaves / wood / trees / rope
What would you eat?	I'd eat ________.	fruit / fish / plants / meat
How would you try to escape?	I'd ________.	build a raft or a boat / make a fire to attract passing ships

Words in context: *Robinson Crusoe*, listening and speaking Unit 9 93

Lesson Six SB page 93

Skills Time!

Skills development

Dictionary: discover meaning of words in context
Listening: listen for specific detail

Speaking: ask and answer questions about being shipwrecked on a desert island

Language

Words in context: *storm, survivor, supplies, shelter, sails, fence, cut down, wall* (Student Book); *hunt, hut, alone, seal* (Workbook)

Extra: frightened

Materials

CD 88; Dictionary Workbook pages 128–135; paper and colored pencils

Oxford iTools Digital classroom • Unit 9 • Words, Listening, Speaking

Warmer

- With books closed, ask students what they remember about the story from the previous lesson. Ask questions, e.g. *What happened to Robinson Crusoe's ship? What did he build on the island?*

NOTE: Remind students to consult the Dictionary pages in their Workbooks when completing Exercise 1.

1 Find the words in the story. Write.

- Ask students to look at the words in the box. Explain that all the words are underlined in the text on page 92.
- Ask students to look at the text again and find all of the underlined words. They read the sentences that contain each word and try to determine the meaning from the context.
- Students then complete the sentences on page 93.

Differentiation

Below level:

- Ask each student to look up one word in the Dictionary in their Workbooks. Give out paper and colored pencils. Tell children to write the definition on one side and draw a picture on the other. When students are finished, have each child hold up the picture for others to guess the word.

At level:

- Students complete the activity.

Above level:

- Play *Whispers* (see page 9).

ANSWERS

1. wall 2. cut down 3. supplies 4. survivor
5. storm 6. sails 7. shelter 8. fence

2 Listen. What food did Robinson Crusoe make to eat? 88

- Tell students they are going to hear a recording from *Robinson Crusoe*. Explain that they should listen and find out what food Crusoe made to eat.
- Play the whole recording. Then elicit the answer from the class.

ANSWER

He made bread from the corn he grew.

3 Listen again and number the events in the correct order.

- Ask students to look at the pictures. Point to each one and ask *What has Robinson Crusoe done?*
- Ask students to read the list of events. Tell them to listen again. This time they must listen and number the events.
- Play the recording, pausing for students to number the events.

ANSWERS

a. 5 b. 4 c. 1 d. 3 e. 2

4 Ask and answer. Use the prompts or your own answers.

- Ask students to look at the example dialogue. Choose a strong student and ask the questions for him / her to answer.
- Ask students to work in pairs. Tell them they are going to take turns to ask the questions to their partner. Their partner must answer using the prompts given or his / her own ideas.

Further practice

Workbook page 87

Unit 9 Speaking skills worksheet, Assessment and Resource CD-ROM

Online Practice • Unit 9 • Words in context, Listening, and Speaking

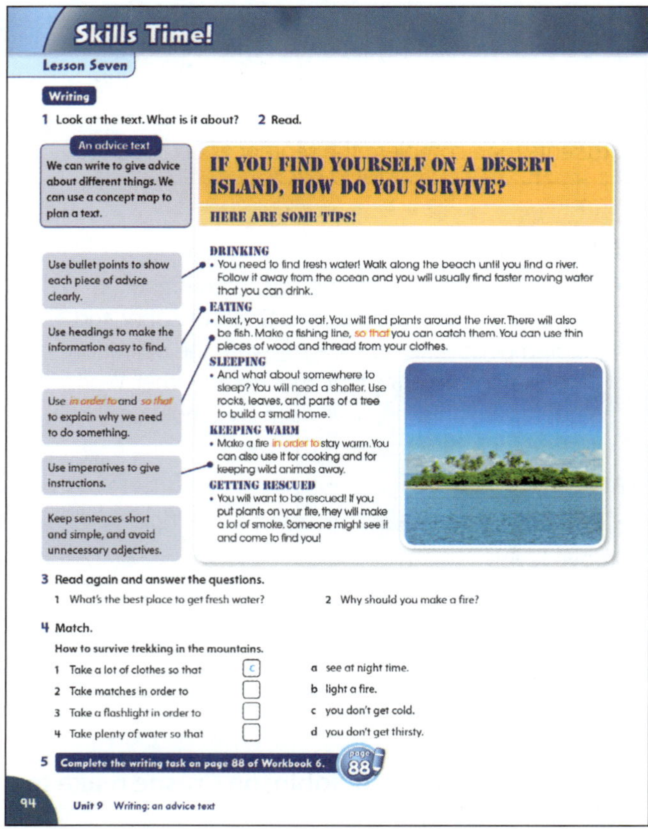

Skills Time!

Lesson Seven

Writing

1 Look at the text. What is it about? 2 Read.

An advice text

We can write to give advice about different things. We can use a concept map to plan a text.

Use bullet points to show each piece of advice clearly.

Use headings to make the information easy to find.

Use *in order to* and *so that* to explain why we need to do something.

Use imperatives to give instructions.

Keep sentences short and simple, and avoid unnecessary adjectives.

IF YOU FIND YOURSELF ON A DESERT ISLAND, HOW DO YOU SURVIVE?

HERE ARE SOME TIPS!

DRINKING
- You need to find fresh water! Walk along the beach until you find a river. Follow it away from the ocean and you will usually find faster moving water that you can drink.

EATING
- Next, you need to eat. You will find plants around the river. There will also be fish. Make a fishing line, so that you can catch them. You can use thin pieces of wood and thread from your clothes.

SLEEPING
- And what about somewhere to sleep? You will need a shelter. Use rocks, leaves, and parts of a tree to build a small home.

KEEPING WARM
- Make a fire in order to stay warm. You can also use it for cooking and for keeping wild animals away.

GETTING RESCUED
- You will want to be rescued! If you put plants on your fire, they will make a lot of smoke. Someone might see it and come to find you!

3 Read again and answer the questions.

1 What's the best place to get fresh water? 2 Why should you make a fire?

4 Match.

How to survive trekking in the mountains.

1 Take a lot of clothes so that [c] a see at night time.
2 Take matches in order to [ ] b light a fire.
3 Take a flashlight in order to [ ] c you don't get cold.
4 Take plenty of water so that [ ] d you don't get thirsty.

5 Complete the writing task on page 88 of Workbook 6. page 88

94 Unit 9 Writing: an advice text

Lesson Seven 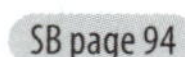

Skills Time!

Skills development
Writing focus: lay out an advice text
Writing outcome: write an advice text

Language
Recycled: vocabulary and structures seen previously
Extra: *advice, bullet point, in order to, so that*

Materials
Writing poster 9; a copy of the text from poster 9, Assessment and Resource CD-ROM, for each student

Oxford **iTools** Digital classroom • Unit 9 • Writing

Warmer
- Discuss the Robinson Crusoe texts from Lessons 5 and 6. Ask *What does Robinson Crusoe do to survive on the island?*

Poster 9: An advice text
- Give a photocopy of the poster text to each student.
- Point to the title. Explain that this is called a slogan. Ask *Why is it important to have a catchy slogan?* Read the corresponding text box (above the text) together.
- Ask students the "Before reading" question in the corner of the poster. Encourage them to discuss their ideas.
- Ask students to read the text silently. Ask comprehension questions, e.g. *What should you do before you go walking in the mountains? What should you take with you?*
- Read the text boxes on the left. Ask comprehension questions, e.g. *What can we use to help us plan an advice text? What do we use to show each piece of advice clearly?*
- Read the text boxes on the right-hand side. Ask *Which phrases can we use to say why we need to do something? How can we give people a choice of things to do?*
- Ask the "After reading" questions. Compare and discuss some of the students' answers together.

1 Look at the text. What is it about?
- Ask students to look at the pictures and glance through the text without reading it in detail. Ask the gist question.

ANSWER
The text is about how to survive on a desert island.

2 Read.
- Ask a different student to read each paragraph to the class. Ask comprehension questions, e.g. *How can you find fresh water? How can you catch fish?*
- Focus on the text boxes to the left. Choose a different student to read each text box to the class.

3 Read again and answer the questions.
- Students read the text silently and answer the questions.

ANSWERS
1. The best place to get fresh water is from a fast-moving river.
2. You should make a fire to stay warm, use it for cooking and for keeping wild animals away. Also someone might see the smoke and come and find you.

4 Match.
- Look at the example, then let students match the sentence halves. Ask students to read out the complete sentences.

Differentiation

Below level:
- Play *Miming snap* (see page 8) with the song vocabulary.

At level:
- Write the following sentence starters on the board: *1. You should make a fire … 2. Put plants on the fire … 3. Make a fishing line … 4. Find a river …* Point to the first sentence and ask *Why should you make a fire?* Elicit *To stay warm.* Ask students to link the ideas together using *in order to* or *so that*. For example: *You should make a fire in order to stay warm. / You should make a fire so that you can stay warm.* Ask students to complete the remaining sentences.

Above level:
- Put children into groups. Ask them to think of something can do well and give advice about. Have them make a concept map to plan their writing.

ANSWERS
1. c 2. b 3. a 4. d

5 Complete the writing task on page 88 of Workbook 6.
- Refer students to the Workbook to complete the writing task. Go through the activity with them first.

Further practice
Workbook page 88
Unit 9 Writing skills worksheet, Assessment and Resource CD-ROM
Online Practice • Unit 9 • Writing

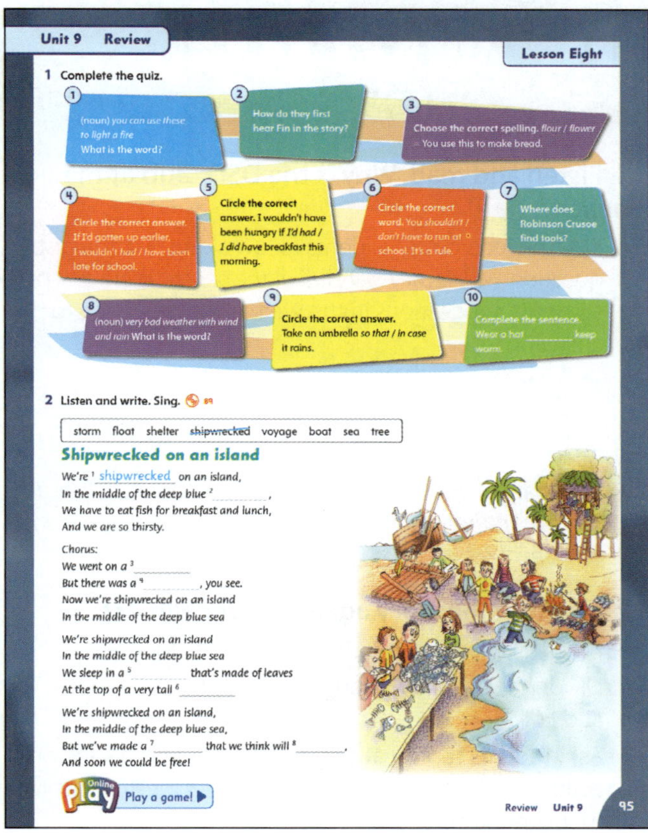

Unit 9 Review

Lesson Eight

1 Complete the quiz.

1 (noun) *you can use these to light a fire* What is the word?

2 How do they first hear Fin in the story?

3 Choose the correct spelling. *flour / flower* – You use this to make bread.

4 Circle the correct answer. If I'd gotten up earlier, I wouldn't *had / have* been late for school.

5 Circle the correct answer. I wouldn't have been hungry if *I'd had / I did have* breakfast this morning.

6 Circle the correct word. You *shouldn't / don't have to* run at school. It's a rule.

7 Where does Robinson Crusoe find tools?

8 (noun) *very bad weather with wind and rain* What is the word?

9 Circle the correct answer. Take an umbrella *so that / in case* it rains.

10 Complete the sentence. Wear a hat ________ keep warm.

2 Listen and write. Sing. 89

storm float shelter ~~shipwrecked~~ voyage boat sea tree

Shipwrecked on an island

We're [1] shipwrecked on an island,
In the middle of the deep blue [2] ________,
We have to eat fish for breakfast and lunch,
And we are so thirsty.

Chorus:
We went on a [3] ________
But there was a [4] ________, you see.
Now we're shipwrecked on an island
In the middle of the deep blue sea

We're shipwrecked on an island
In the middle of the deep blue sea
We sleep in a [5] ________ that's made of leaves
At the top of a very tall [6] ________

We're shipwrecked on an island,
In the middle of the deep blue sea,
But we've made a [7] ________ that we think will [8] ________,
And soon we could be free!

Online Play Play a game!

Review Unit 9 95

Lesson Eight SB page 95

Unit 9 Review

Learning outcomes

To review vocabulary and structures practiced previously

To use vocabulary and structures from the unit in the context of a song

Language

Recycled: vocabulary and structures seen previously

Materials

CD 89

Oxford **iTools** Digital classroom • Unit 9 • Review

Warmer

- Play *Book race* (see page 8) to review the unit.
- Read the sentences below and give students 20 seconds to find each one.
  You will need a shelter. (Lesson 7)
  Can you hear a whistle? (Lesson 1)
  That suit is dangerous! (Lesson 3)
  You must stay with your guide at all times. (Lesson 4)
  I'm feeling very cool. (Lesson 3)
  That night, I went to sleep in my new home. (Lesson 5)
  My water bottle's empty. (Lesson 1)
  Drinking water is very important when it's hot. (Lesson 4)

1 Complete the quiz.

- Tell students they are going to do a quiz based on this unit. Students can work individually, in pairs, or in teams.
- Students work with books open at page 95. They may not refer back to other lessons in the unit.

ANSWERS

1. matches 2. They hear a whistle. 3. flour
4. have 5. I'd had 6. shouldn't
7. Robinson Crusoe finds tools on his ship.
8. storm 9. in case 10. in order to

2 Listen and write. Sing. 89

- Focus students' attention on the picture. Ask *What can you see? What has happened? What are the children doing?*
- Play the whole song. Students follow along.
- Play the song again, pausing for students to write the words.
- Play the recording a third time if necessary.
- Go through the answers. Ask students to read each line aloud saying the missing word.
- Play the recording. Students sing along.

Differentiation

Below level:

- Play *Time's up!* (see page 9) to practice the vocabulary from the song. You may also wish to include the words on pages 89 and 93.

At level:

- Tell students that they are going to play a memory game about the song. Divide the class into two groups and ask them to close their books. Ask students to choose a team captain. Teams can discuss their ideas together before the team captain gives the answer. Ask these questions, alternating between teams: *What has happened to the children? / Where is the island? / What do the children eat for breakfast and lunch? / What do they eat for tea? / What was the weather like at sea? / Where do the children sleep? / Where is the shelter? / What have the children made?*
- Give one point for each correct answer. Keep score on the board. Add up the scores to find the winning team.

Above level:

- Ask students to turn the song into a story. Have them write a few sentences or a paragraph about what happened. If time permits, students can share with the class.

ANSWERS

1. shipwrecked 2. sea 3. voyage 4. storm
5 shelter 6. tree 7. boat 8. float

Further practice

Workbook page 89
Unit 9 test, Assessment and Resource CD-ROM
Progress test 3, Assessment and Resource CD-ROM
Skills test 3, Assessment and Resource CD-ROM
Values 3 worksheet, Units 7–9, Assessment and Resource CD-ROM
Writing portfolio 3 worksheet, Assessment and Resource CD-ROM
Progress certificate, Assessment and Resource CD-ROM
Online Practice • Unit 9 • Review

10 Around the world!

10 Around the world!

Lesson One Story

1 Listen and read. Why is the DSD Club at the beach? 91

2 Listen to the story again and repeat. Act.

3 Read again and circle.

1 Fin wants everyone to meet at the *horse / car* sculpture.
2 The children look at the *elephant / giraffe* sculpture first.
3 The horse sculpture was made by a *French / English* person.
4 Tom can speak English and *French / Chinese*.
5 The children are meeting Fin at *five / six* o'clock.
6 The children think the animal is *an octopus / a shark*.

98 Unit 10 Around the world!

Lesson One

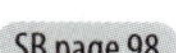

Story

Learning outcomes

To read and understand a story

To act out a story

Language

Introducing vocabulary through a story

Extra: French, discovery

Materials

CD 91

Oxford iTools Digital classroom • Unit 10 • Story

Warmer

- Ask students what they remember about the last story. Ask questions, e.g. *Where were the children sheltering? What was in the chest?*
- Tell students they are going to read the first episode of a new story. Tell them that today the DSD Club is at the beach. Ask *What do you think the children are doing there?*

1 Listen and read. Why is the DSD Club at the beach? 91

- Play the recording. Students follow along. Ask the gist question *Why is the DSD Club at the beach?* Were any of the students' suggestions in the warmer activity close to the answer?

ANSWER

The DSD Club is at the beach to see a sand sculpture competition.

- Play it again. Ask comprehension questions, e.g. *Which sand sculptures do the children see? Which languages does Tom speak?*

2 Listen to the story again and repeat. Act.

- Play the recording, pausing for students to repeat.
- Divide the class into groups of five to Fin, Kate, Libby, Tom, and Ed.
- Ask students to look at the story frames and decide on actions for each one. Play the recording for students to mime as they listen.
- Let students practice acting out the story in their groups. Then ask one or two groups to act for the class.

Differentiation

Below level:

- Ask students to underline words in the story they don't know. Have them first guess the meaning with context clues. Then look the words up in a dictionary. Have students write the definitions in their own words in their notebooks.

At level:

- Write the dialogue from frame 4 on the board and read it with the students. Then play *Disappearing dialogue* (see page 9).

Above level:

- Extend the "at level" activity to include frames 3 and 4.

3 Read again and circle.

- Focus on the example. Ask students to find the place that tells us the children have to meet at the car sculpture (frame 1).
- Ask students to re-read the story and circle the correct answers.

ANSWERS

1. car 2. elephant 3. French 4. French
5. six 6. a shark

Further practice

Workbook page 90

Online Practice • Unit 10 • Story

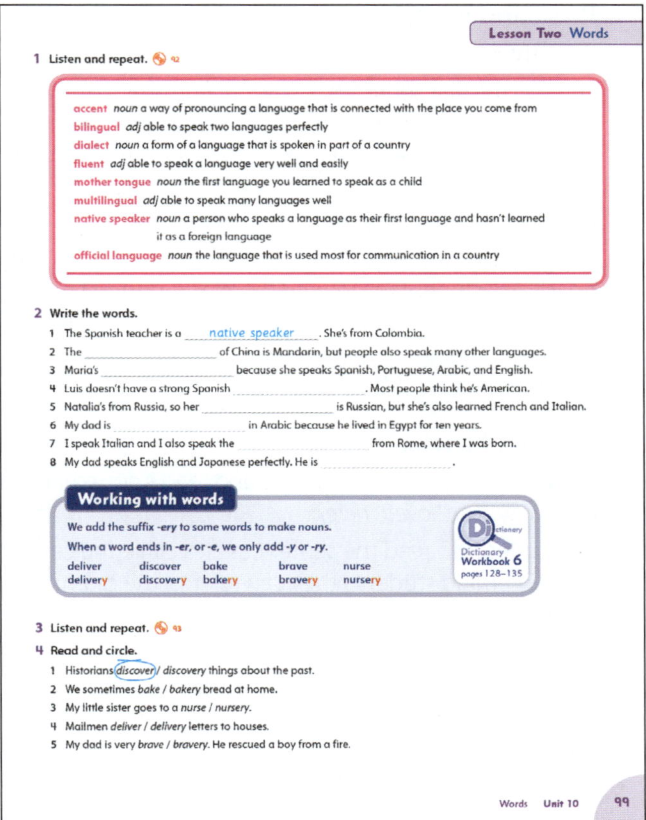

Lesson Two Words

1 Listen and repeat. 92

accent *noun* a way of pronouncing a language that is connected with the place you come from
bilingual *adj* able to speak two languages perfectly
dialect *noun* a form of a language that is spoken in part of a country
fluent *adj* able to speak a language very well and easily
mother tongue *noun* the first language you learned to speak as a child
multilingual *adj* able to speak many languages well
native speaker *noun* a person who speaks a language as their first language and hasn't learned it as a foreign language
official language *noun* the language that is used most for communication in a country

2 Write the words.

1 The Spanish teacher is a ___native speaker___. She's from Colombia.
2 The ______ of China is Mandarin, but people also speak many other languages.
3 Maria's ______ because she speaks Spanish, Portuguese, Arabic, and English.
4 Luis doesn't have a strong Spanish ______. Most people think he's American.
5 Natalia's from Russia, so her ______ is Russian, but she's also learned French and Italian.
6 My dad is ______ in Arabic because he lived in Egypt for ten years.
7 I speak Italian and I also speak the ______ from Rome, where I was born.
8 My dad speaks English and Japanese perfectly. He is ______.

Working with words

We add the suffix *-ery* to some words to make nouns.
When a word ends in *-er*, or *-e*, we only add *-y* or *-ry*.

deliver	discover	bake	brave	nurse
delivery	discovery	bakery	bravery	nursery

Dictionary Workbook 6 pages 128–135

3 Listen and repeat. 93

4 Read and circle.

1 Historians *discover* / *discovery* things about the past.
2 We sometimes *bake* / *bakery* bread at home.
3 My little sister goes to a *nurse* / *nursery*.
4 Mailmen *deliver* / *delivery* letters to houses.
5 My dad is very *brave* / *bravery*. He rescued a boy from a fire.

Words Unit 10 99

Lesson Two 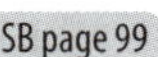

Words

Learning outcomes

To identify and use words related to language

To use the suffix *-ery* to make certain words into nouns

Language

Words: *official language, bilingual, multilingual, native speaker, accent, mother tongue, dialect, fluent*

Working with words: *deliver / delivery, discover / discovery, brave / bravery, nurse / nursery, bake / bakery* (Student Book); *machine / machinery, forge / forgery, rob / robbery, recover / recovery* (Workbook)

Extra: *pronounce, Mandarin, Spanish, Arabic, Russian*

Materials

CD 92–93 Dictionary Workbook pages 128–135

Oxford iTools Digital classroom • Unit 10 • Words

Warmer

- Ask students what they remember about the story from last lesson. Ask *Where were the children? What did they see? How many languages can Tom speak?*

1 Listen and repeat. 92

- Ask students to look at the words and their definitions. Ask them to read the definitions silently.
- Play the recording, pausing for students to repeat.
- Play the recording again. Students listen and repeat. Repeat as often as necessary.
- Ask individual students to say the words for the class.

2 Write the words.

- Ask students to look at the example. Read it together.
- Ask students to read the sentences and complete them with the words from Exercise 1.
- Ask different students to read complete sentences aloud.

ANSWERS

1. native speaker 2. official language 3. multilingual 4. accent 5. mother tongue 6. fluent 7. dialect 8. bilingual

3 Listen and repeat. 93

- Before doing the activity, focus students' attention on the *Working with words* section.
- Ask students *What happens when we add -ery to the end of these words?*
- Play the recording. Students listen and repeat. Repeat as often as necessary.
- Ask individual students to say the words for the class.

4 Read and circle.

- Look at the example together. Ask *Do we need a verb or a noun here?* Establish that we need a verb.
- Students read the sentences and circle the correct words.

Differentiation

Below level:

- Play *Miming snap* (see page 8) with the new words. Be sure to exaggerate the actions for clarity.

At level:

- Play a quiz with the words from Exercise 3. Divide the class into two teams. Ask the following questions, alternating between the two teams: *Where do young children sometimes go while their parents are at work? What do mailmen do with letters? What is the name of a building where people bake bread? If you find out something new, what do you make? What is the word for someone who does dangerous things to help other people?* Give one point for each correct answer. Keep score on the board and count the points to find the winner.

Above level:

- Put students in pairs. Ask them to interview each other, using these questions: *Are you bilingual? / What languages are you fluent in? / Do you think you have an accent? / Can you think of any dialects in (your country)? / What is the official language in (your country)? / Is anyone in your family multilingual? / What is your mother tongue?* Monitor and help as needed. If time permits, students can share what they learned with the class.

ANSWERS

1. discover 2. bake 3. nursery 4. deliver 5. brave

Further practice

Workbook page 91

Online Practice • Unit 10 • Words

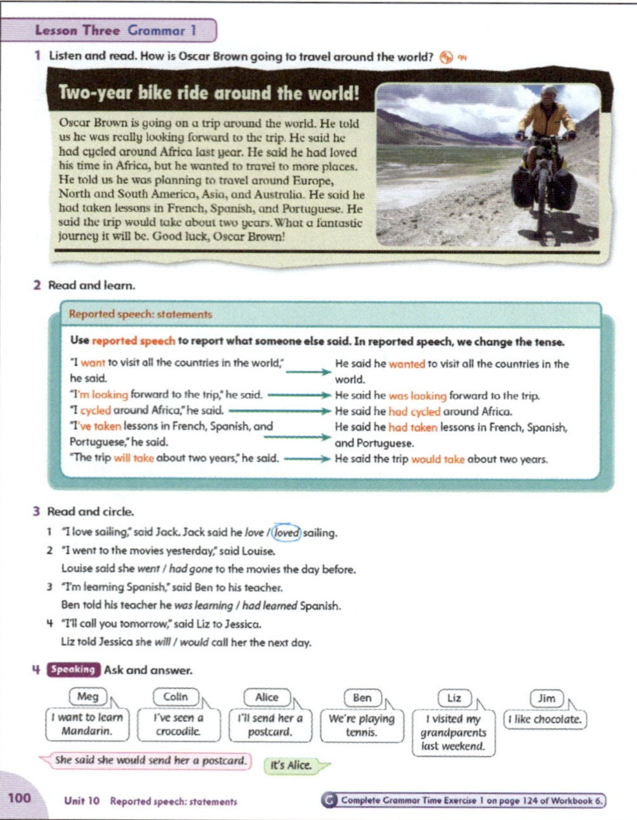

Lesson Three Grammar 1

1 Listen and read. How is Oscar Brown going to travel around the world? 94

Two-year bike ride around the world!

Oscar Brown is going on a trip around the world. He told us he was really looking forward to the trip. He said he had cycled around Africa last year. He said he had loved his time in Africa, but he wanted to travel to more places. He told us he was planning to travel around Europe, North and South America, Asia, and Australia. He said he had taken lessons in French, Spanish, and Portuguese. He said the trip would take about two years. What a fantastic journey it will be. Good luck, Oscar Brown!

2 Read and learn.

Reported speech: statements

Use reported speech to report what someone else said. In reported speech, we change the tense.

"I want to visit all the countries in the world," he said. →	He said he wanted to visit all the countries in the world.
"I'm looking forward to the trip," he said. →	He said he was looking forward to the trip.
"I cycled around Africa," he said. →	He said he had cycled around Africa.
"I've taken lessons in French, Spanish, and Portuguese," he said. →	He said he had taken lessons in French, Spanish, and Portuguese.
"The trip will take about two years," he said. →	He said the trip would take about two years.

3 Read and circle.

1 "I love sailing," said Jack. Jack said he *love* / *loved* sailing.
2 "I went to the movies yesterday," said Louise. Louise said she *went* / *had gone* to the movies the day before.
3 "I'm learning Spanish," said Ben to his teacher. Ben told his teacher he *was learning* / *had learned* Spanish.
4 "I'll call you tomorrow," said Liz to Jessica. Liz told Jessica she *will* / *would* call her the next day.

4 Speaking Ask and answer.

Meg: I want to learn Mandarin.
Colin: I've seen a crocodile.
Alice: I'll send her a postcard.
Ben: We're playing tennis.
Liz: I visited my grandparents last weekend.
Jim: I like chocolate.

She said she would send her a postcard.
It's Alice.

100 Unit 10 Reported speech: statements

Complete Grammar Time Exercise 1 on page 124 of Workbook 6.

Lesson Three SB page 100

Grammar 1

Learning outcomes

To use reported speech to report what someone else said

Speaking: reporting what someone has said

Language

Core: *He said he wanted to visit all the countries in the world. He said he was looking forward to the trip. He said he had cycled around Africa. He said he had taken lessons in French, Spanish, and Portuguese. He said the trip would take about two years.*

Extra: *Africa, Asia*

Materials

CD 94

 Digital classroom • Unit 10 • Grammar 1

Warmer

- Discuss around-the-world trips together. Ask children which type of transportation they would choose if they were going to travel around the world.

1 Listen and read. How is Oscar Brown going to travel around the world? 94

- Play the recording. Students follow along. Ask the gist question.

ANSWER

Oscar Brown is going to travel around the world by bike.

- Play the recording again. Ask comprehension questions, e.g. *How does Oscar Brown feel about his trip? Has he traveled by bike before?*

2 Read and learn.

- Read the rules and examples together.
- Point to the first sentence. Ask *What happens to the verb?* (it changes from simple present to simple past). Repeat with the rest of the sentences. Ask students to give you a general rule about what happens to the verbs with reported speech (they move back one tense).
- Practice further examples. Write these sentences on the board. Ask students to rewrite them as reported speech: *"I need to buy some eggs," Mom said. / "I'm thinking about my holiday," Zara said. / "I went to France last year," Lucas said. / "I'll be home at six o'clock," Dad said.*

3 Read and circle.

- Focus attention on the example and read it together. Ask *Why do we use "loved" here?*
- Ask students to read the sentences and circle the correct words. Remind students they can refer to the grammar box to see how the verbs change.

ANSWERS

1. loved 2. had gone 3. was learning 4. would

4 Ask and answer.

- Ask two students to read the example aloud. Ask students to look at the speech bubbles and compare Alice's actual speech with the reported speech.
- Students work in pairs, taking turns to ask and answer. Explain that the first student should report what has been said, and the other student must look at the speech bubbles and identify who said it.

Differentiation

Below level:

- In pairs, students look at the word prompts on the board. Have them identify the verbs and alter them in their notebooks by moving them back one tense.

At level:

- Tell students to imagine they are planning a trip around the world by bike. On the board, write: *Which countries do you want to visit? / What are you looking forward to about your trip? / Have you cycled around any countries before? / Have you taken any language lessons? / How long will your trip take?* Then ask students to work in pairs, taking turns to interview each other about the trip and note down each other's answers. Ask some of the students to tell the class what their partner said, using reported speech.

Above level:

- Put students in groups and ask them to plan a trip somewhere. Give students paper. Ask them to draw a concept map with their destination as the topic. Ask them to think about these questions: *Where are you going? / What do you want to see there? / How will you get there? / How long will your trip take?* Ask students to share their group's ideas using *We said we …*

Further practice

Grammar Time, Workbook page 124

Workbook page 92

Online Practice • Unit 10 • Grammar 1

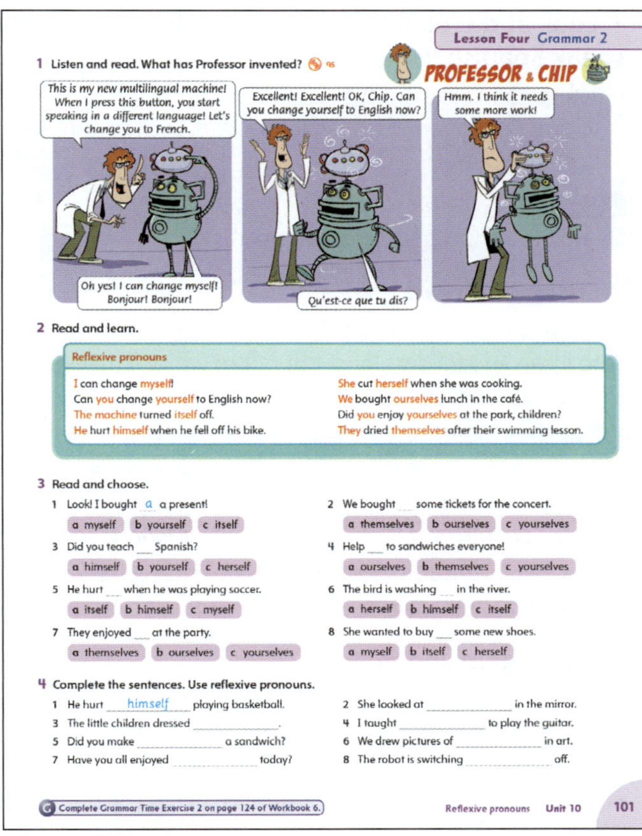

Lesson Four Grammar 2

1 Listen and read. What has Professor invented? 95

2 Read and learn.

Reflexive pronouns

I can change myself!
Can you change yourself to English now?
The machine turned itself off.
He hurt himself when he fell off his bike.
She cut herself when she was cooking.
We bought ourselves lunch in the café.
Did you enjoy yourselves at the park, children?
They dried themselves after their swimming lesson.

3 Read and choose.

1 Look! I bought _a_ a present!
a myself b yourself c itself

2 We bought __ some tickets for the concert.
a themselves b ourselves c yourselves

3 Did you teach __ Spanish?
a himself b yourself c herself

4 Help __ to sandwiches everyone!
a ourselves b themselves c yourselves

5 He hurt __ when he was playing soccer.
a itself b himself c myself

6 The bird is washing __ in the river.
a herself b himself c itself

7 They enjoyed __ at the party.
a themselves b ourselves c yourselves

8 She wanted to buy __ some new shoes.
a myself b itself c herself

4 Complete the sentences. Use reflexive pronouns.

1 He hurt _himself_ playing basketball.
2 She looked at ________ in the mirror.
3 The little children dressed ________.
4 I taught ________ to play the guitar.
5 Did you make ________ a sandwich?
6 We drew pictures of ________ in art.
7 Have you all enjoyed ________ today?
8 The robot is switching ________ off.

Complete Grammar Time Exercise 2 on page 124 of Workbook 6.

Reflexive pronouns Unit 10 101

Lesson Four SB page 101

Grammar 2

Learning outcomes

To use reflexive pronouns when the object of a sentence is the same as the subject

Language

Core: *I can change myself. Can you change yourself to English now? It turned itself off. He hurt himself when he fell off his bike. She cut herself when she was cooking. We bought ourselves lunch in the café. Did you enjoy yourselves at the park, children? They dried themselves after their swimming lesson.*

Materials

CD 95

Oxford iTools Digital classroom • Unit 10 • Grammar 2

Warmer

- Ask *What did Professor invent in the last story?* (a survival suit) *Did the suit work? What did Chip say about the suit? What did Professor say?* Check students use reported speech correctly.

1 Listen and read. What has the Professor invented? 95

- Play the recording. Students follow along. Ask the gist question *What has Professor invented?*

ANSWER

Professor has invented a multilingual machine.

- Play it again for students to re-read the text. Ask comprehension questions, e.g. *What language does Chip speak? Does Professor press the button?*
- Check that students understand the joke. Ask *Why can't Chip change himself back to English?* (Because he is set to French and can't understand what Professor is saying).

2 Read and learn.

- Read the sentences in the box together. Write the personal pronouns on the board and ask students to tell you the reflexive pronouns. Write these alongside the appropriate words.
- Write sentences on the board for students to complete, e.g.
  I made ________ a sandwich.
  We bought ________ a new computer.

3 Read and choose.

- Write the example on the board and ask students what should go in the blank.
- Ask students to look at the exercise in their books. They read the sentences and choose the correct word from the list of options for each one.
- Review answers together. Ask individual students to read the sentences to the class.

ANSWERS

1. a 2. b 3. b 4. c 5. b 6. c 7. a 8. c

4 Complete the sentences. Use reflexive pronouns.

- Focus on the example and read it together.
- Ask students to read the rest of the sentences and complete them with the correct reflexive pronouns.

Differentiation

Below level:

- Look at the pictures with students. Ask *What happened?* and elicit responses. Together, practice making sentences using the reflexive pronouns in the box. Then students complete the activity in pairs.

At level:

- Students complete the activity.

Above level:

- After students finish, play *True or false?* (see page 9). Use sentences from the lesson or make up your own.

ANSWERS

1. himself 2. herself 3. themselves 4. myself
5. yourself / yourselves 6. ourselves 7. yourselves
8. itself

Further practice

Grammar Time, Workbook page 124
Workbook page 93
Unit 10 Language practice worksheet, Assessment and Resource CD-ROM
Online Practice • Unit 10 • Grammar 2

Skills Time!

Lesson Five

Reading

1 Look at the text. How many people in the world speak Spanish?

2 Listen and read. 96

Languages of the World

Q How many languages are there in the world?

A There are around 7,000 languages spoken in the world. Some of these languages have almost disappeared and only have a few speakers left, but others are still spoken by millions of people! There are many languages which were widely spoken in the past and which no one speaks anymore, for example, Latin or Ancient Greek.

Q What's the most widely spoken language in the world?

A Mandarin is the most widely spoken language in the world. It's the official language of China and about 900 million people living there speak it as their native language. Mandarin is also spoken in other Asian countries such as Singapore, Malaysia, Indonesia, and Thailand. So, altogether, Mandarin is spoken by almost 15% of the world's population!

Q What are the next most widely spoken languages in the world?

A Hindi, English, and Spanish are each spoken by over 300 million native speakers. Portuguese, Russian, Arabic, Japanese, German, and French each have 100 – 300 million speakers. That's a lot of people!

Q More people speak Chinese than English, so why is English the international language?

A The reason is perhaps because English is spoken on so many different continents. People in the U.S.A., the U.K., Australia, Canada, Ireland, and New Zealand speak English as their first language. It's also recognized as an official language in more than 70 countries around the world!

Q Why do some languages disappear?

A International companies often have businesses in different countries. This is one reason why young people in these countries may learn the more dominant languages of the world and stop learning their own languages.

Q How many languages will there be in the future?

A Some scientists predict that half of the languages spoken in the world today will disappear by the end of the century, as young people stop learning the language of the country they come from.

Bonjour Namaste Aloha Guten Tag Hello Dobry den Terve Hola

3 Read again and match.

1 7,000 [e]
2 900 million
3 15%
4 over 300 million
5 more than 70

a The number of people that speak Hindi, English, and Spanish.
b The number of countries where English is an official language.
c The percentage of the world's population that speaks Mandarin.
d The number of people that speak Mandarin in China.
e The number of languages spoken in the world.

102 Unit 10 Reading: a question and answer text

Lesson Five SB page 102

Skills Time!

Skills development

Reading: read a Question and Answer text

Language

Recycled: vocabulary and structures seen previously

Extra: *disappear, altogether, population, Hindi, Japanese, continent, international, business, dominant, predict, century*

Materials

CD 96

Oxford iTools Digital classroom • Unit 10 • Reading

Warmer

- Discuss languages to review the Lesson 2 vocabulary and prepare for the reading text. Ask individual students *What is your mother tongue? Do you speak any other languages? Are you fluent? Do you know anyone who is bilingual? Which languages does he / she speak?*
- Ask students to predict the answers to the following questions from the text:
  How many languages are there in the world? What is the most widely spoken language?
- Write students' predictions on the board.

1 Look at the text. How many people in the world speak Spanish?

- Ask students to skim the article, without reading in detail, to find the answer to the gist question. Elicit the answer from the class.

ANSWER

Over 300 million people speak Spanish.

2 Listen and read. 96

- Tell students they are going to listen to the text. Tell them to listen and follow along, but not to worry if they don't understand every word.
- Play the whole recording.
- Play it again, pausing to ask comprehension questions, e.g. *What has happened to some of the world's languages? Which country has Mandarin as its official language?*
- Answer any questions students have and elicit the meanings of unknown words from context.

3 Read again and match.

- Focus on the example. Ask students to re-read the first paragraph and find the sentence that tells them what 7,000 relates to.
- Ask students to re-read the text and match the numbers with the items on the right.

Differentiation

Below level:

- Reduce the "at level" activity to two true / false statements. Students work in pairs. Then swap papers with neighbors.

At level:

- Ask students to re-read the text and write five true / false sentences about languages. Monitor the activity and help where necessary. Ask different students to read their sentences for the class to respond *True* or *False*.

Above level:

- Play *Talk!* (see page 9) on the subject of languages.

ANSWERS

1. e 2. d 3. c 4. a 5. b

Further practice

Workbook page 94

Online Practice • Unit 10 • Reading

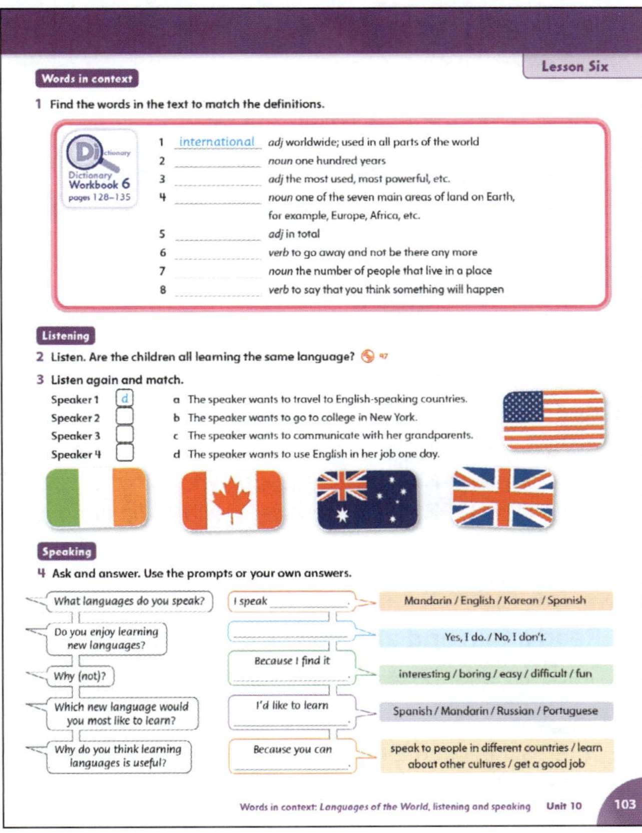
Lesson Six

Words in context

1 Find the words in the text to match the definitions.

Dictionary Workbook 6 pages 128–135

1 international *adj* worldwide; used in all parts of the world
2 .... *noun* one hundred years
3 .... *adj* the most used, most powerful, etc.
4 .... *noun* one of the seven main areas of land on Earth, for example, Europe, Africa, etc.
5 .... *adj* in total
6 .... *verb* to go away and not be there any more
7 .... *noun* the number of people that live in a place
8 .... *verb* to say that you think something will happen

Listening

2 Listen. Are the children all learning the same language? 97

3 Listen again and match.

Speaker 1 d
Speaker 2
Speaker 3
Speaker 4

a The speaker wants to travel to English-speaking countries.
b The speaker wants to go to college in New York.
c The speaker wants to communicate with her grandparents.
d The speaker wants to use English in her job one day.

Speaking

4 Ask and answer. Use the prompts or your own answers.

What languages do you speak? — I speak ... — Mandarin / English / Korean / Spanish
Do you enjoy learning new languages? — ... — Yes, I do. / No, I don't.
Why (not)? — Because I find it ... — interesting / boring / easy / difficult / fun
Which new language would you most like to learn? — I'd like to learn ... — Spanish / Mandarin / Russian / Portuguese
Why do you think learning languages is useful? — Because you can ... — speak to people in different countries / learn about other cultures / get a good job

Words in context: Languages of the World, listening and speaking Unit 10 103

Lesson Six SB page 103

Skills Time!

Skills development

Dictionary: discover meaning of words in context
Listening: listen for specific detail
Speaking: ask and answer questions about languages

Language

Words in context: *disappear, altogether, population, continent, international, dominant, predict, century* (Student Book); *isolated, tribe, communicate, inhabitants* (Workbook)
Extra: *worldwide, in total, go away, college*

Materials

CD 97; Dictionary Workbook pages 128–135

Oxford iTools Digital classroom • Unit 10 • Words, Listening, Speaking

Warmer

- With books closed, ask students what they remember about the text from the previous lesson.
- Ask questions if necessary, e.g. *How many languages are there in the world? Why is English an international language?*

1 Find the words in the text to match the definitions.

- Ask the students to look at the definitions. Explain that all the words students need are underlined in the text on page 102.
- Ask students to look at the article again and find all the underlined words. They read the sentences that contain each word and try to determine the meaning from the context.
- Students write the correct words for each definition on page 103.

ANSWERS
1. international 2. century 3. dominant
4. continent 5. altogether 6. disappear
7. population 8. predict

2 Listen. Are the children all learning the same language? 97

- Tell students they are going to hear four children talking about the languages they are learning. Students listen and find out whether it's the same language.
- Play the whole recording. Then elicit the answer.

Differentiation

Below level:

- Ask students to close their Student Books, take out their Workbooks, and turn to page 128. Divide students into teams. Tell students you are going to say a word, and they have to find it in the dictionary. Whoever finds it first, gets a point. Say each of the vocabulary words. The team with the most points wins.

At level:

- Ask students to close their books. Then play *Definitions* (see page 9) with the new words.

Above level:

- Ask students to write a sentence for each of the new words. If time permits, students share with the class.

ANSWER
Yes, the children are all learning the same language – English.

3 Listen again and match.

- Tell students they are going to listen again. This time they must match each speaker to the correct sentence.
- Before you play the recording, allow time for students to read the sentences.
- Play the recording as many times as necessary, pausing for students to write the letters in the boxes.

ANSWERS
1. d 2. a 3. b 4. c

4 Ask and answer. Use the prompts or your own answers.

- Ask students to look at the example. Choose a strong student and ask him / her questions.
- Ask students to work in pairs. Tell them to take turns to ask their partner questions. Their partner must answer using the prompts or his / her own ideas.

Further practice
Workbook page 95
Unit 10 Speaking skills worksheet, Assessment and Resource CD-ROM
Online Practice • Unit 10 • Words in context, Listening, and Speaking

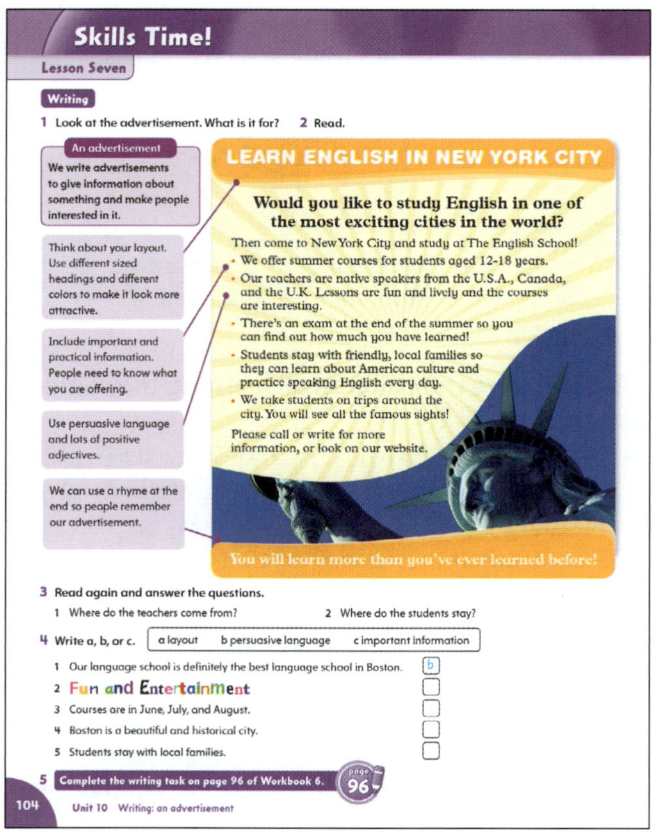

Skills Time!

Lesson Seven

Writing

1 Look at the advertisement. What is it for? 2 Read.

An advertisement

We write advertisements to give information about something and make people interested in it.

Think about your layout. Use different sized headings and different colors to make it look more attractive.

Include important and practical information. People need to know what you are offering.

Use persuasive language and lots of positive adjectives.

We can use a rhyme at the end so people remember our advertisement.

LEARN ENGLISH IN NEW YORK CITY

Would you like to study English in one of the most exciting cities in the world?

Then come to New York City and study at The English School!

- We offer summer courses for students aged 12-18 years.
- Our teachers are native speakers from the U.S.A., Canada, and the U.K. Lessons are fun and lively and the courses are interesting.
- There's an exam at the end of the summer so you can find out how much you have learned!
- Students stay with friendly, local families so they can learn about American culture and practice speaking English every day.
- We take students on trips around the city. You will see all the famous sights!

Please call or write for more information, or look on our website.

You will learn more than you've ever learned before!

3 Read again and answer the questions.

1 Where do the teachers come from? 2 Where do the students stay?

4 Write a, b, or c. a layout b persuasive language c important information

1 Our language school is definitely the best language school in Boston. b
2 Fun and Entertainment
3 Courses are in June, July, and August.
4 Boston is a beautiful and historical city.
5 Students stay with local families.

5 Complete the writing task on page 96 of Workbook 6. page 96

104 Unit 10 Writing: an advertisement

Lesson Seven SB page 104

Skills Time!

Skills development

Writing focus: lay out an advertisement; identify important information and persuasive language

Writing outcome: write an advertisement

Language

Recycled: vocabulary and structures seen previously

Extra: *layout, practical, persuasive, positive, lively, sights*

Materials

Writing poster 10; a copy of the text from poster 10, Assessment and Resource CD-ROM, for each student

Oxford iTools Digital classroom • Unit 10 • Writing

Warmer

- Tell students they are going to look at an advertisement. Ask what information should be included in an advertisement.

Poster 10: An advertisement

- Hand out a photocopy of the poster text to each student. Ask students the "Before reading" question.
- Ask students to read the text silently. Ask comprehension questions, e.g. *What will you do at the club? Who is the Level 1 class for?*
- Ask the class to look at the introduction. Ask *Why do we use questions here?* Then read the text box above together.
- Read the text boxes on the left-hand side to the class. Ask *Why do we write advertisements? What can we use to make people remember our ad?*
- Read the text boxes on the right to the class. Ask *What important and practical information should we include? What kind of persuasive language can we use?*
- Ask students the "After reading" questions.

1 Look at the advertisement. What is it for?

- Ask students to look at the picture and skim through the text. Ask the gist question *What is it for?*

ANSWER

The advertisement is for a language school in New York called *The English School*.

2 Read.

- Ask a different student to read each section of the text. Ask comprehension questions, e.g. *Who can go to the English School? What happens at the end of the summer?*
- Focus on the text boxes around the main text. Choose a different student to read each one.

3 Read again and answer the questions.

- Students read the text silently and answer the questions.

ANSWERS

1. The teachers come from the U.S.A., Canada, and the U.K.
2. The students stay with local families.

4 Write a, b, or c.

- Ask students to look at the example. Ask *What has the writer used to make the language persuasive?*
- Ask students to look at the remaining pieces of text and label them a, b, or c.

Differentiation

Below level:

- Ask students to close their books. On the board, write *heading, different colors, important information, extra details, big words, persuasive language, negative adjectives, and rhyme.* Ask students to circle what belongs in an advertisement and cross out what doesn't.

At level:

- Students complete the activity.

Above level:

- Put students in groups and ask them to imagine they are selling something. Write a basic outline for an advertisement, including the name of the product or service, a few positive adjectives, who will buy it, why, and what it does.

ANSWERS

1. b 2. a 3. c 4. b 5. c

5 Complete the writing task on page 96 of Workbook 6.

- Refer students to the Workbook to complete the writing task. Go through the activity with them first.

Further practice

Workbook page 96

Unit 10 Writing skills worksheet, Assessment and Resource CD-ROM

Online Practice • Unit 10 • Writing

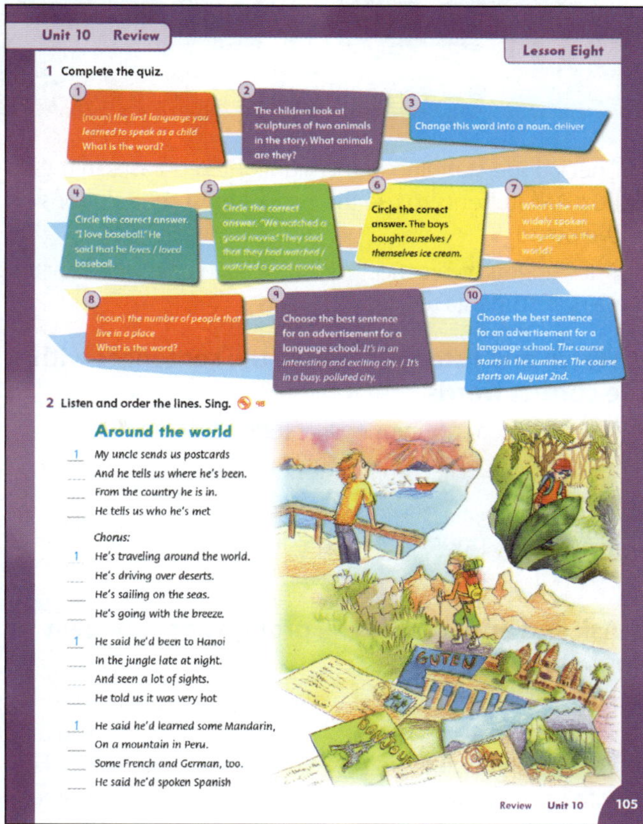
Unit 10 Review

Lesson Eight

1 Complete the quiz.

1 (noun) *the first language you learned to speak as a child* What is the word?

2 The children look at sculptures of two animals in the story. What animals are they?

3 Change this word into a noun. deliver

4 Circle the correct answer. "I love baseball." He said that he *loves / loved* baseball.

5 Circle the correct answer. "We watched a good movie." They said that they *had watched / watched a good movie.*

6 **Circle the correct answer.** The boys bought *ourselves / themselves ice cream.*

7 What's the most widely spoken language in the world?

8 (noun) *the number of people that live in a place* What is the word?

9 Choose the best sentence for an advertisement for a language school. *It's in an interesting and exciting city. / It's in a busy, polluted city.*

10 Choose the best sentence for an advertisement for a language school. *The course starts in the summer. The course starts on August 2nd.*

2 Listen and order the lines. Sing. 98

Around the world

1 *My uncle sends us postcards*
___ *And he tells us where he's been.*
___ *From the country he is in.*
___ *He tells us who he's met*

Chorus:
1 *He's traveling around the world.*
___ *He's driving over deserts.*
___ *He's sailing on the seas.*
___ *He's going with the breeze.*

1 *He said he'd been to Hanoi*
___ *In the jungle late at night.*
___ *And seen a lot of sights.*
___ *He told us it was very hot*

1 *He said he'd learned some Mandarin,*
___ *On a mountain in Peru.*
___ *Some French and German, too.*
___ *He said he'd spoken Spanish*

Review Unit 10 105

Lesson Eight SB page 105

Unit 10 Review

Learning outcomes

To review vocabulary and structures practiced previously

To use vocabulary and structures from the unit in the context of a song

Language

Recycled: vocabulary and structures seen previously

Extra: *breeze*

Materials

CD 98

Oxford iTools Digital classroom • Unit 10 • Review

Warmer

- Play *Book race* (see page 8) to review the unit. Read the sentences below and give students 20 seconds to find each one:
  Can you change yourself to English now? (Lesson 4)
  That's a discovery! (Lesson 1)
  International companies often have businesses in different countries. (Lesson 5)
  You will see all the famous sights! (Lesson 7)
  He said he had cycled around Africa last year. (Lesson 3)
  You will learn more than you've ever learned before! (Lesson 7)
  Good luck, Oscar Brown! (Lesson 3)
  I think it's a shark! (Lesson 1)

1 Complete the quiz.

- Tell students they are going to do a quiz based on the unit. Students can work individually, in pairs, or in teams.
- Students work with books open to page 105. They may not refer to other lessons in the unit.

ANSWERS

1. mother tongue 2. an elephant and a horse
3. delivery 4. loved 5. had watched 6. themselves
7. Mandarin 8. population
9. It's in an interesting and exciting city.
10. The course starts on August 2nd.

2 Listen and order the lines. Sing. 98

- Focus students' attention on the picture. Ask *What is the man doing? Which countries has he been to?*
- Tell students the words to the song are in their books, but the lines are in the wrong order.
- Ask students to read the words silently.
- Play the song. Students listen and point to each line as they hear it sung.
- Play the song again, pausing for students to number the lines in order.
- Play the recording again. Students complete their answers.
- Review answers. Ask a different student to read each line in order.
- Play the recording once more. Students sing along.

Differentiation

Below level:

- Put students into groups. Assign each group a phrase, e.g. *sends us postcards, driving over deserts*. Students decide on actions for their phrases. Then play the song. Students stand and do their action when they hear their phrase.

At level:

- Ask students to close their books. Write the following statements on the board. Students to write *True* or *False* from memory: *The uncle sends emails. / The uncle is driving over deserts. / He's sailing on the seas. / It's warm in the desert at night. / The uncle has been to Peru. / He can speak French, German, and Spanish.* Ask students to open their books and check their answers. Give one point for each correct answer. Keep score on the board. Add up the scores to find the winning team.

Above level:

- Ask students to work in pairs to write a new verse. First, brainstorm ideas about what to include. Write suggestions on the board. Tell students they must use reported speech. Students practice their new verses.

ANSWERS

Verse 1: 1, 4, 2, 3
Verse 2: 1, 3, 2, 4
Verse 3: 1, 4, 2, 3
Verse 4: 1, 4, 2, 3

Further practice

Workbook page 97
Unit 10 test, Assessment and Resource CD-ROM
Progress certificate, Assessment and Resource CD-ROM
Online Practice • Unit 10 • Review

Fluency Time! 4

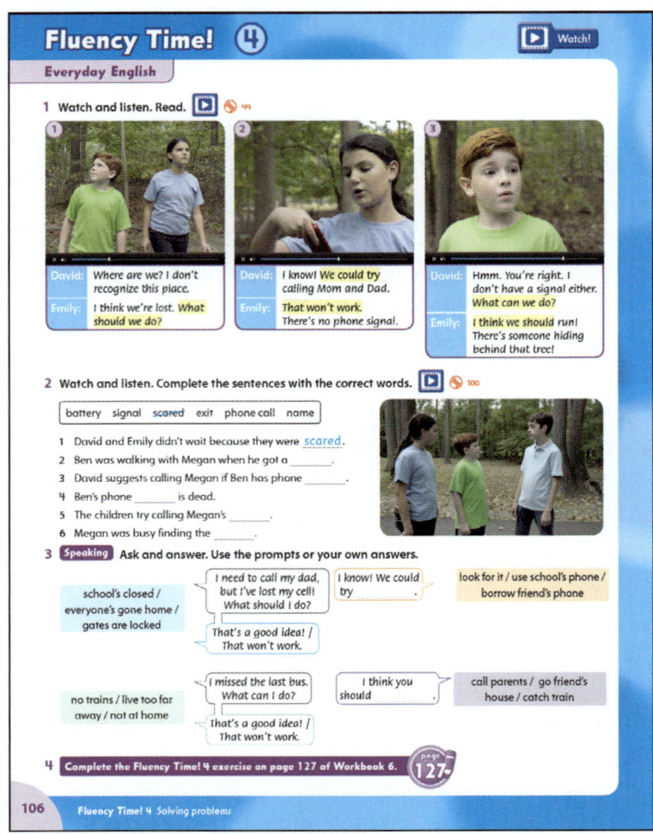

Fluency Time! 4

Watch!

Everyday English

1 Watch and listen. Read. 99

1

David: Where are we? I don't recognize this place.

Emily: I think we're lost. What should we do?

2

David: I know! We could try calling Mom and Dad.

Emily: That won't work. There's no phone signal.

3

David: Hmm. You're right. I don't have a signal either. What can we do?

Emily: I think we should run! There's someone hiding behind that tree!

2 Watch and listen. Complete the sentences with the correct words. 100

battery signal scared exit phone call name

1 David and Emily didn't wait because they were scared.
2 Ben was walking with Megan when he got a ______.
3 David suggests calling Megan if Ben has phone ______.
4 Ben's phone ______ is dead.
5 The children try calling Megan's ______.
6 Megan was busy finding the ______.

3 Speaking Ask and answer. Use the prompts or your own answers.

school's closed / everyone's gone home / gates are locked

I need to call my dad, but I've lost my cell! What should I do?

I know! We could try ______.

look for it / use school's phone / borrow friend's phone

That's a good idea! / That won't work.

no trains / live too far away / not at home

I missed the last bus. What can I do?

I think you should ______.

call parents / go friend's house / catch train

That's a good idea! / That won't work.

4 Complete the Fluency Time! 4 exercise on page 127 of Workbook 6. page 127

106 Fluency Time! 4 Solving problems

Everyday English SB page 106

Learning outcomes

To learn some useful language for solving problems

Language

What shall we do? What can we do? What do you think we should do? I know! We could try calling Mom and Dad. I think we should run! That won't work! / That's a good idea! / I'm not so sure.

Materials

CD 99–100; Fluency DVD Fluency Time 4

Oxford iTools Digital classroom • Fluency Time! 4 • Everyday English

Warmer

- Tell students they are going to learn some useful language for solving problems. Ask what they would do if they had a problem e.g. they were lost, missed the bus home, or felt sick at school. Write their ideas on the board.

1 Watch and listen. Read. 99

- Focus on the pictures. Ask students who they see (*Emily and David*), where they are (*in the park*), and what the problem is (*they're lost*).
- Students watch the DVD. Play the recording for students to listen and read. Answer any questions, then play the DVD again, pausing for students to say the dialogue.
- Check understanding of the highlighted phrases in the box. Ask students to use them to suggest the solutions on the board.
- Ask students to practice the dialogue in pairs, then invite pairs of students to act for the class.

2 Watch and listen. Complete the sentences with the correct words. 100

- Play the recording, pausing for students to write. Play it again for students to check their answers.

ANSWERS

1. scared 2. phone call 3. signal 4. battery
5. name 6. exit

3 Ask and answer. Use the prompts or your own answers.

- Ask a volunteer to act out a dialogue with you. Ask the volunteer to read the speech bubbles on the left. You read the speech bubbles on the right, completing the blanks with prompts from the boxes on the right. The volunteer looks at the prompts on the left and chooses responses to your suggestions.
- In pairs, students use the prompts, or their own answers, to act out dialogues with their partner.
- Ask some pairs to act for the class.

Differentiation

Below level:

- Break the dialogue up into two shorter exchanges. Have students practice the first question and answer a few times, then move on to the second one. Make sure students switch roles for even practice.

At level:

- Write the following problems on the board: *I'm locked out of my house. / I forgot my friend's birthday. / I don't have any money for lunch. / I left my P.E. clothes at home. / I've left my school bag on the bus. / I can't find my pen. / I don't know where my next lesson is. / I'm cold.*
- Divide the class into two teams. A student from Team A presents a problem to a student from Team B, who suggests a solution. Encourage students to use the new phrases.

Above level:

- Ask students to think of more problems to solve. Give them paper to brainstorm ideas. Then have them practice the dialogue with their ideas. If time permits, share them with the class.

Further practice

Workbook page 98
Everyday English phrase bank, Workbook page 127
Fluency Time! 4, Fluency DVD
Online Practice • Fluency Time! 4

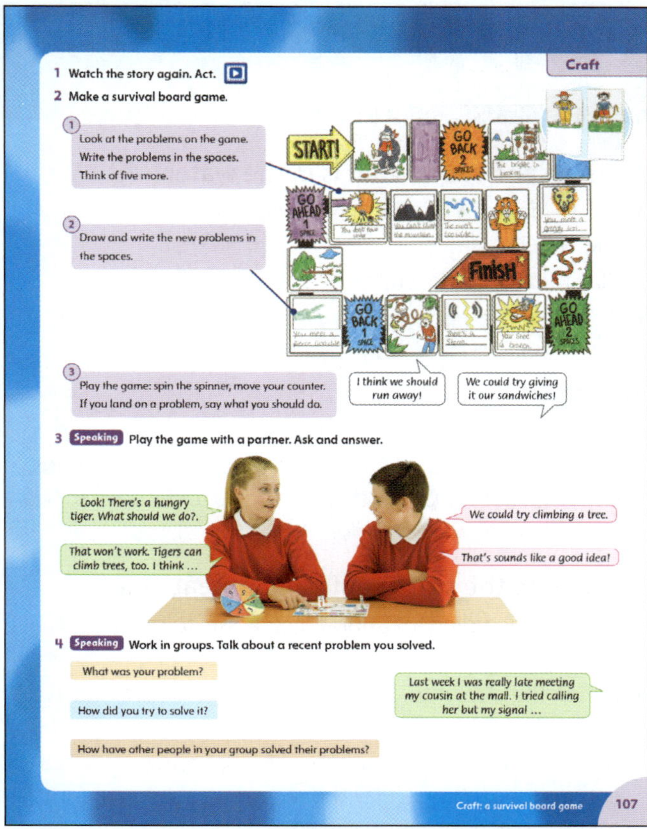

Craft

1 Watch the story again. Act.

2 Make a survival board game.

1 Look at the problems on the game. Write the problems in the spaces. Think of five more.

2 Draw and write the new problems in the spaces.

3 Play the game: spin the spinner, move your counter. If you land on a problem, say what you should do.

3 Speaking Play the game with a partner. Ask and answer.

4 Speaking Work in groups. Talk about a recent problem you solved.

What was your problem?

How did you try to solve it?

How have other people in your group solved their problems?

Craft: a survival board game 107

Craft SB page 107

Learning outcomes

To make a survival board game

To play the survival board game

Language

Look! There's a … What shall we do? We could try … That won't work. Tigers can climb trees, too. I think … That's sounds like a good idea!

Materials

Fluency DVD Fluency Time! 4 ; Fluency Craft 4 (see Assessment and Resource CD-ROM) (templates for each student, photocopied onto thin cardboard if possible); completed survival board game, counters and spinner; colored pencils and scissors for each group; thin cardboard (optional)

Oxford iTools Digital classroom • Fluency Time! 4 • Craft

1 Watch the story again. Act.

- Focus on the story in Exercise 1 of the Everyday English lesson on Student Book page 106. Ask students what they can remember about the story.
- Play Fluency Time! 4 Everyday English. If you don't have time for the DVD, read the dialogue on Student Book page 106.
- Invite pairs to act out the dialogue. Encourage them to change details to make their own variations.

2 Make a survival board game.

- Focus on the picture. Ask students to say what the picture shows (*a board game*) and what they see in the board game squares (*different problems*).
- Hand out the templates for the board game and the spinner and counters (see Fluency Craft 4, Assessment and Resource CD-ROM).
- Read the tips in Exercise 1. Show the class your completed board game and spinner. Demonstrate how to push a pencil through the middle of the spinner to make it spin.
- Ask questions as students work, e.g. *What problem is this? What does this picture show?*

NOTE: If you do not have time to use photocopies, ask students to write problems on paper. Then use them to play a quiz game in two teams, with students from each team giving problems for the other team to solve.

3 Play the game with a partner. Ask and answer.

- Focus on the photos. Tell students they are going to play their board games with a partner.
- The students place their counters on the *Start* arrow. They take turns spinning, then move their counter the correct number of squares. They must solve the problem on the square they land on. Their partner must decide if the solution will work or not. The first child to reach the *Finish* square is the winner.

Differentiation

Below level:

- Switch partners and play the game again.

At level:

- To make sure that all the problems on the board games are used, ask students to play in groups of six. Assign each student a number from 1–6. Each one holds their board game. Student 1 spins the spinner. The student with the number that the spinner lands on reads a problem from their game. The rest of the students suggest different solutions. Student 2 spins the spinner to continue the game.

Above level:

- Ask students to pick one of the problems on the board and draw a solution to it. Give out paper and colored pencils. Call pairs to the front of the class. Ask them to talk about their problem and solution.

4 Work in groups. Talk about a recent problem you solved.

- Ask a volunteer to read the speech bubble, then invite students to tell the class about a recent problem they had and solved. Encourage students to use language from the lesson.

Further practice

Workbook page 99

Skills test 4 Fluency Time!, Assessment and Resource CD-ROM

Fluency Time! 4, Fluency DVD

Online Practice • Fluency Time! 4

11 Space travel!

11 Space travel!

Lesson One Story

1 Listen and read. What is in the water? 101

2 Listen to the story again and repeat. Act.

3 Read again and write *True* or *False*.

1 Ed sees first that it is a dolphin. True

2 The water is too deep for the dolphin. ______

3 Kate and Tom go and tell Fin. ______

4 Libby saw an interview about dolphins. ______

5 Libby is interested in the stars. ______

6 Tom tries to carry the dolphin by himself. ______

108 Unit 11 Space travel!

Lesson One SB page 108

Story

Learning outcomes

To read and understand a story

To act out a story

Language

Introducing vocabulary through a story

Extra: *expert, explain*

Materials

CD 101

Oxford iTools Digital classroom • Unit 11 • Story

Warmer

- Ask students to tell you what they remember about the last episode of the story. If necessary, ask questions such as, *Where were the children? What were they looking at? What did they think was in the water?*
- Ask students to predict what was in the sea. Ask *Was it a shark or something else?* Write students' suggestions on the board.

1 Listen and read. What is in the water?  101

- Ask students to look at the pictures and see what is in the water.
- Play the recording. Students listen and follow along.
- Ask the gist question *What is in the water? Did anyone guess correctly in the warmer activity?*

ANSWER

The animal in the water is a dolphin.

- Play the recording again. Ask comprehension questions, e.g. *What does Libby say they have to do to the dolphin? How does Libby know what to do?*

2 Listen to the story again and repeat. Act.

- Play the recording, pausing for students to repeat each line.
- Divide the class into groups of four to play Kate, Tom, Ed, and Libby.
- Ask students to look at the story frames and decide on actions for each one. Play the recording again. Students mime the actions as they listen.
- Let students practice acting out the story in their groups. Then ask one or two groups to act for the class.

3 Read again and write *True* or *False*.

- Ask students to look at the example together. Ask them to find where in the story Ed sees that the animal is a dolphin (frame 2).
- Ask students to read the rest of the sentences and write *True* or *False*.
- Review answers together.

Differentiation

Below level:

- Ask students to read the sentences aloud and then work together to find the answers in the story. Monitor and help as needed.

At level:

- Students complete the activity.

Above level:

- After students finish, they rewrite the false sentences to make them true. Check answers together.

ANSWERS

1. True 2. False 3. False 4. True 5. False 6. False

Further practice

Workbook page 100

Online Practice • Unit 11 • Story

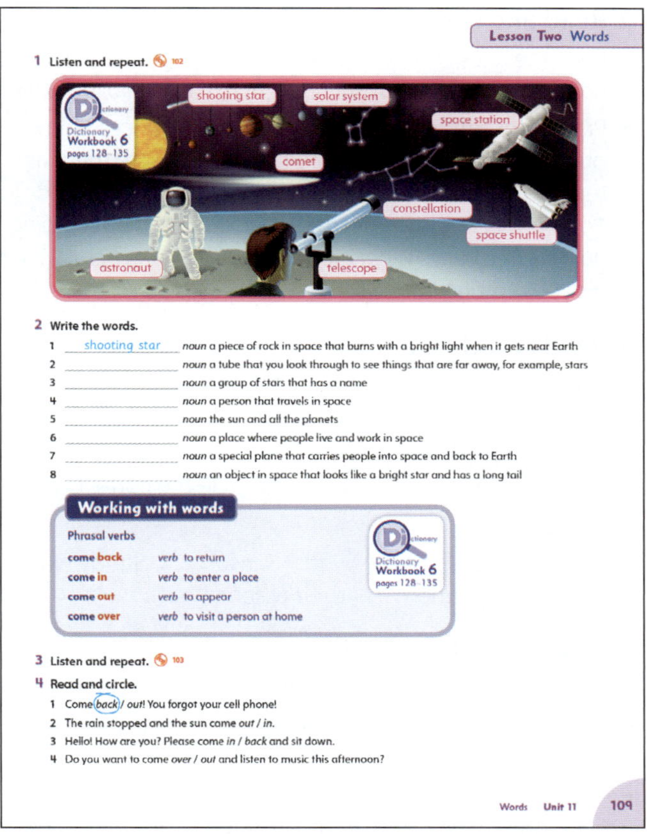

Lesson Two Words

1 Listen and repeat. 102

2 Write the words.

1 shooting star *noun* a piece of rock in space that burns with a bright light when it gets near Earth
2 ______ *noun* a tube that you look through to see things that are far away, for example, stars
3 ______ *noun* a group of stars that has a name
4 ______ *noun* a person that travels in space
5 ______ *noun* the sun and all the planets
6 ______ *noun* a place where people live and work in space
7 ______ *noun* a special plane that carries people into space and back to Earth
8 ______ *noun* an object in space that looks like a bright star and has a long tail

Working with words

Phrasal verbs

come back *verb* to return
come in *verb* to enter a place
come out *verb* to appear
come over *verb* to visit a person at home

Dictionary Workbook 6 pages 128–135

3 Listen and repeat. 103

4 Read and circle.

1 Come *back* / *out*! You forgot your cell phone!
2 The rain stopped and the sun came *out* / *in*.
3 Hello! How are you? Please come *in* / *back* and sit down.
4 Do you want to come *over* / *out* and listen to music this afternoon?

Words Unit 11 109

Lesson Two SB page 109

Words

Learning outcomes

To identify and use words related to space and space travel

To understand the meanings of different phrasal verbs with come

Language

Words: *shooting star, solar system, space station, comet, constellation, astronaut, telescope, space shuttle*

Working with words: *come back, come in, come out, come over* (Student Book); *come off, come across, come on, come up* (Workbook)

Materials

CD 102–103 Dictionary Workbook pages 128–135

Oxford iTools Digital classroom • Unit 11 • Words

Warmer

- Ask students *What time of day was it at the end of the story? How do you know? What did Tom see in the sky?*
- Ask students what they see in the night sky. Encourage as many ideas as possible and write them on the board.

1 Listen and repeat. 102

- Ask students to look at the words and the picture. Did students suggest any of these things?
- Tell students you are going to play a recording for them to listen and repeat.
- Play the recording, pausing for students to repeat.
- Play the recording again. Students listen and repeat. Repeat as often as necessary.
- Ask individual students to say the words for the class.

2 Write the words.

- Ask students to look at the example and read the definition together.
- Ask students to read the definitions and write the correct words from Exercise 1.
- Review answers together.

ANSWERS

1. shooting star 2. telescope 3. constellation
4. astronaut 5. solar system 6. space station
7. space shuttle 8. comet

3 Listen and repeat. 103

- Before doing the activity, focus students' attention on the *Working with words* section. Ask students to read the list of phrasal verbs and their meanings.
- Ask students *What is the original verb in all of these phrasal verbs? Does this help to figure out the meaning?* Remind students that sometimes we can figure out the meanings but often we have to learn them.
- Play the recording. Students listen and repeat.
- Play it again for students to listen and repeat.
- Ask individual students to say the words for the class.

Differentiation

Below level:

- Write *back, in, out,* and *over* on the board in one column. Ask children to say or mime what each one means. Then write come before each preposition. Explain that now the meanings have changed. Write these fill-in-the-blank sentences on the board: *Mom said to (come back) before dinner. / Please (come in) the back door. / Can you (come out) and play? / Can you (come over) on Saturday?* Ask students to write the answers. Then students complete the activity independently.

At level:

- Students complete the activity.

Above level:

- After students finish, ask them to write sentences of their own using the phrasal verbs.

4 Read and circle.

- Look at the example together and read it together. Ask students *What does "come back" mean?*
- Ask students to read the sentences and circle the correct words.
- Review answers together. Ask students to read the complete sentences aloud.

ANSWERS

1. back 2. out 3. in 4. over

Further practice

Workbook page 101

Online Practice • Unit 11 • Words

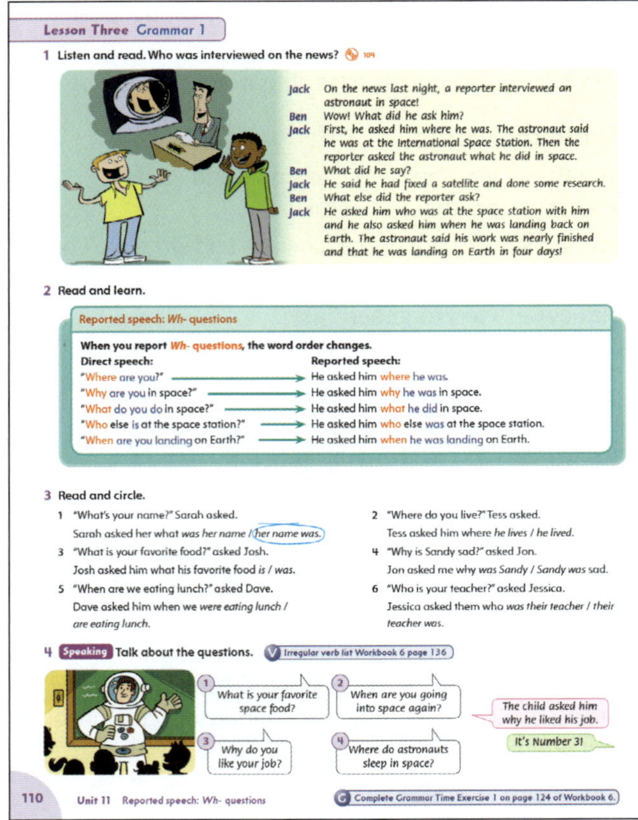

Lesson Three Grammar 1

1 Listen and read. Who was interviewed on the news? 104

Jack On the news last night, a reporter interviewed an astronaut in space!
Ben Wow! What did he ask him?
Jack First, he asked him where he was. The astronaut said he was at the International Space Station. Then the reporter asked the astronaut what he did in space.
Ben What did he say?
Jack He said he had fixed a satellite and done some research.
Ben What else did the reporter ask?
Jack He asked him who was at the space station with him and he also asked him when he was landing back on Earth. The astronaut said his work was nearly finished and that he was landing on Earth in four days!

2 Read and learn.

Reported speech: *Wh-* questions

When you report *Wh-* questions, the word order changes.

Direct speech:	Reported speech:
"Where are you?" →	He asked him where he was.
"Why are you in space?" →	He asked him why he was in space.
"What do you do in space?" →	He asked him what he did in space.
"Who else is at the space station?" →	He asked him who else was at the space station.
"When are you landing on Earth?" →	He asked him when he was landing on Earth.

3 Read and circle.

1 "What's your name?" Sarah asked.
Sarah asked her what *was her name* / *her name was.*
2 "Where do you live?" Tess asked.
Tess asked him where *he lives* / *he lived.*
3 "What is your favorite food?" asked Josh.
Josh asked him what his favorite food *is* / *was.*
4 "Why is Sandy sad?" asked Jon.
Jon asked me why *was Sandy* / *Sandy was* sad.
5 "When are we eating lunch?" asked Dave.
Dave asked him when we *were eating lunch* / *are eating lunch.*
6 "Who is your teacher?" asked Jessica.
Jessica asked them who *was their teacher* / *their teacher was.*

4 Speaking Talk about the questions. Irregular verb list Workbook 6 page 136

110 Unit 11 Reported speech: *Wh-* questions

Complete Grammar Time Exercise 1 on page 124 of Workbook 6.

Lesson Three SB page 110

Grammar 1

Learning outcomes

To use reported speech to report *wh-* questions

Speaking: reporting questions that have been asked

Language

Core: *He asked him where he was. He asked him why he was in space. He asked him what he did in space. He asked him who was at the space station with him. He asked him when he was landing on Earth.*

Materials

CD 104

Oxford iTools Digital classroom • Unit 11 • Grammar 1

Warmer

- Discuss space and space travel with the class. Ask questions such as *Can you name any planets / famous astronauts? Why do astronauts travel to space? How can we learn about space?*

1 Listen and read. Who was interviewed on the news? 104

- Play the recording. Students listen and follow along.
- Ask the gist question *Who was interviewed on the news?*

ANSWER

An astronaut was interviewed on the news.

- Play the recording again. Ask further comprehension questions, e.g. *Where was the astronaut? What had he fixed?*

2 Read and learn.

- Read the rules and examples in the box together. Ask *What happens to the tense? What happens to the order of the words?*
- Practice examples together. Write the sentences below on the board. Ask students to help you rewrite them as reported speech: *"Where are your books?" I asked Erin. / "Who is your best friend?" I asked her. / "When are you going out?" I asked her. / "What are you doing?" I asked her. / "When are you meeting Evie?" I asked her.*

3 Read and circle.

- Look at the example and read it together. If necessary, remind students how word order changes when we use reported speech.
- Students read the sentences and circle the correct words.

ANSWERS

1. her name was 2. he lived 3. was 4. Sandy was 5. were eating lunch 6. their teacher was.

4 Talk about the questions.

- Focus on the picture. Ask *What are the children doing?*
- Ask a pair of students to read the example sentences in speech bubbles to the class.
- Ask students to work in pairs. They take turns to report what one of the children asked for their partner to say which child asked it.
- Review the activity together. Ask different students to report a question for the class to say who asked it.

Differentiation

Below level:

- Ask students to underline the question words in Exercise 4. Ask a student to read the question. Work together to make the sentence with reported speech using this model *He / She asked him / her ….* Continue and encourage students to make sentences on their own. Then put them in groups to complete the activity. Monitor and elicit as needed.

At level:

- Students complete the activity.

Above level:

- After students finish, switch pairs. Ask students to pretend the astronaut is female and change their sentences to use *she* and *her*. Monitor students' work.

Further practice

Grammar Time, Workbook page 124
Workbook page 102
Online Practice • Unit 11 • Grammar 1

Lesson Four Grammar 2

1 Listen and read. Why can't Chip hear Professor? 105

PROFESSOR & CHIP

2 Read and learn.

Reported speech: commands

Use *told* with reported commands.

Direct speech:	Reported speech:
"Turn off your cell phone!"	He told us to turn off our cell phones.
"Don't touch my computer!"	He told me not to touch his computer.

Reported speech: requests

Use *asked* with reported requests.

Direct speech:	Reported speech:
"Please leave quietly at the end of the show."	He asked them to leave quietly at the end of the show.

3 Read and write *asked* or *told*.

1 "Sit down!" said the teacher.
The teacher told the class to sit down.

2 "Please can you clean up your room," said Alan's mother.
Alan's mother ______ him to clean up his room.

3 "Don't eat the cake!" Jane said.
Jane ______ Ray not to eat the cake.

4 "Don't talk!" said the teacher.
The teacher ______ the children not to talk.

5 "Please can you buy some milk," said Jim's mom.
Jim's mom ______ him to buy some milk.

6 "Turn off your phones!" said the guide.
The guide ______ the children to turn off their phones.

4 Write the sentences in reported speech.

1 "Turn off the TV!" said Fin's mom. — Fin's mom told him to turn off the TV.
2 "Please listen carefully," said the museum guide. — ______ the children ______.
3 "Please can you sit down?" said the teacher. — ______ the class ______.
4 "Don't be late!" said Harry's mom. — ______ him ______.
5 "Clean up your room!" said Maya's dad. — ______ her ______.
6 "Can you help me with my homework?" said Mark. — ______ his dad ______.

Complete Grammar Time Exercise 2 on page 125 of Workbook 6.

Reported commands and requests Unit 11 111

Lesson Four SB page 111

Grammar 2

Learning outcomes

To use reported speech to report commands

To use reported speech to report requests

Language

Core: *He told us to turn off our cell phones. He told me not to touch his computer. He asked them to leave quietly.*

Materials

CD 105

Oxford iTools Digital classroom • Unit 11 • Grammar 2

Warmer

- Tell students that Professor and Chip are watching a show about space. Ask students how people should behave when they are watching a show or a movie in a theater. What should / shouldn't they do?

1 Listen and read. Why can't Chip hear Professor? 105

- Play the recording. Students listen and follow along. Ask the gist question *Why can't Chip hear Professor?*

ANSWER

Chip can't hear Professor because he is listening to his MP3 player.

- Play the recording again. Students re-read the text. Ask further comprehension questions, e.g. *What are the Professor and Chip watching? What should they do with their cell phones?*

2 Read and learn.

- Read the rules and examples in the boxes together. Ask *Which word do we use to report commands? Which word do we use to report requests?* Ask students to look at the language used in direct speech. Ask *How do we know when something is a command and when it is a request?*
- Ask students to re-read Exercise 1 and find a reported command and a reported request.

3 Read and write *asked* or *told*.

- Ask students to look at the example. Ask *Is this a command or a request? How do we know?*
- Ask students to read the sentences and circle the correct words.
- Review answers together.

ANSWERS

1. told 2. asked 3. told 4. told 5. asked 6. told

4 Write the sentences in reported speech.

- Before students look at the exercise, copy the direct speech from the example onto the board. Ask students to help you rewrite it as reported speech.
- Ask students to look at the exercise in their books. Read the example together. Ask students to read the requests and commands and rewrite them as reported speech.

Differentiation

Below level:

- Students practice making sentences using *told* or *asked* based on these quotes: *Open your books. / Please repeat that. / Don't worry. / Can I borrow a pen?* Monitor and elicit as needed. Then students complete the activity.

At level:

- Students complete the activity.

Above level:

- After students finish, put them into pairs. Ask them to imagine they are at the movie theater with Professor and Chip. One student should be the announcer and think of more rules. The other should repeat the sentences using reported speech. Monitor and elicit as needed.

ANSWERS

1. Fin's mom told him to turn off the TV.
2. The museum guide asked the children to listen carefully.
3. The teacher asked the class to sit down.
4. Harry's mom told him not to be late.
5. Maya's dad told her to clean up her room.
6. Mark asked his dad to help him with his homework.

Further practice

Grammar Time, Workbook page 125

Workbook page 103

Unit 11 Language practice worksheet, Assessment and Resource CD-ROM

Online Practice • Unit 11 • Grammar 2

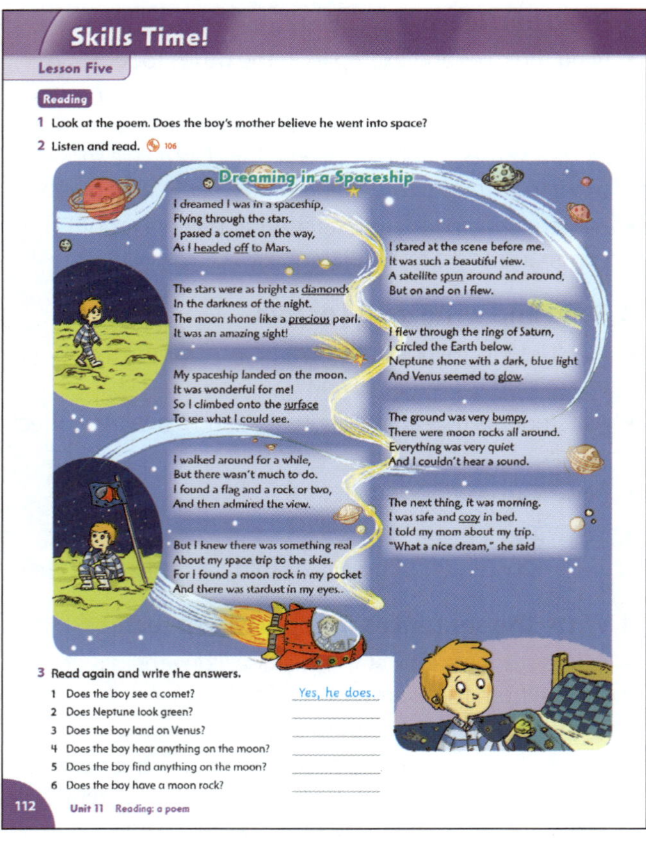

Skills Time!

Lesson Five

Reading

1 Look at the poem. Does the boy's mother believe he went into space?

2 Listen and read. 106

Dreaming in a Spaceship

I dreamed I was in a spaceship,
Flying through the stars.
I passed a comet on the way,
As I headed off to Mars.

The stars were as bright as diamonds
In the darkness of the night.
The moon shone like a precious pearl.
It was an amazing sight!

My spaceship landed on the moon.
It was wonderful for me!
So I climbed onto the surface
To see what I could see.

I walked around for a while,
But there wasn't much to do.
I found a flag and a rock or two,
And then admired the view.

But I knew there was something real
About my space trip to the skies.
For I found a moon rock in my pocket
And there was stardust in my eyes..

I stared at the scene before me.
It was such a beautiful view.
A satellite spun around and around,
But on and on I flew.

I flew through the rings of Saturn,
I circled the Earth below.
Neptune shone with a dark, blue light
And Venus seemed to glow.

The ground was very bumpy,
There were moon rocks all around.
Everything was very quiet
And I couldn't hear a sound.

The next thing, it was morning.
I was safe and cozy in bed.
I told my mom about my trip.
"What a nice dream," she said

3 Read again and write the answers.

1 Does the boy see a comet? Yes, he does.
2 Does Neptune look green?
3 Does the boy land on Venus?
4 Does the boy hear anything on the moon?
5 Does the boy find anything on the moon?
6 Does the boy have a moon rock?

112 Unit 11 Reading: a poem

Lesson Five SB page 112

Skills Time!

Skills development

Reading: read a poem

Language

Recycled: vocabulary and structures seen previously

Extra: *head off, spun, diamond, precious, Saturn, Neptune, Venus, glow, surface, view, below, loop, Milky Way, bumpy, cozy, stardust*

Materials

CD 106; a copy of the poem cut into different verses for each group of four students (optional)

Oxford iTools Digital classroom • Unit 11 • Reading

Warmer

- Tell students they are going to read a poem about a boy who went to space. Ask students to make predictions about what things the boy sees and does. Write the predictions on the board.

1 Look at the poem. Does the boy's mother believe he went into space?

- Ask students to look at the pictures. Ask *What can you see? What did the boy do in space?*
- Ask students to skim the poem, without reading in detail, to find the answer to the gist question.

ANSWER

No, the boy's mother doesn't believe he went into space.

2 Listen and read. 106

- Tell students they are going to listen to the text. Tell them to follow along, but not to worry if they don't understand every word.
- Play the whole recording.
- Ask students to look at the list of predictions on the board. Review them together. Ask which ones were correct.
- Play the recording again, pausing to ask comprehension questions, e.g. *Where did the boy head to? Where did the boy land?*
- Answer any questions students have, and elicit the meanings of any unknown words from context.

3 Read again and write the answers.

- Ask students to look at the example. Ask them to find the part of the poem that tells them that the boy saw a comet (line 3 of the first verse).
- Ask students to read the text again and write short answers to the rest of the questions.
- Ask the questions for students to say the short answers.

Differentiation

Below level:

- Play *Lip reading* (see page 8) using the new words from the poem.

At level:

- Write the following sentences on the board. Students write *True* or *False*: *The boy headed off to Mars. He saw a satellite. / He circled Venus. / It was very quiet on the moon. / There was a lot to do on the moon. / The boy had moondust in his eyes.*

Above level:

- Play *Vanishing verse* (see page 9) based on the poem. Monitor and help as needed.

ANSWERS

1. Yes, he does. 2. No, it doesn't. 3. No, he doesn't.
4. No, he doesn't. 5. Yes, he does. 6. Yes, he does.

Further Practice
Workbook page 104
Online Practice • Unit 11 • Reading

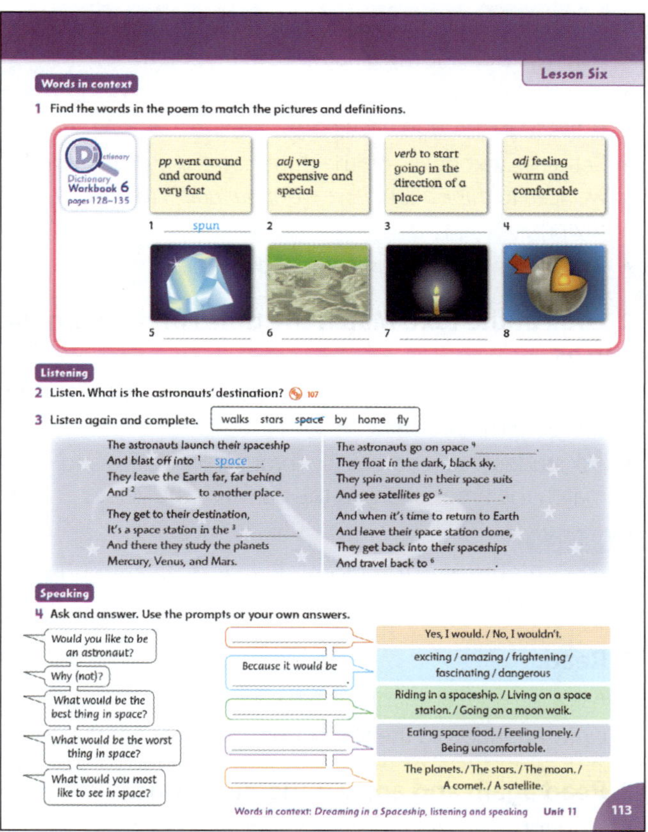

Lesson Six

Words in context

1 Find the words in the poem to match the pictures and definitions.

Dictionary Workbook 6 pages 128–135

pp went around and around very fast
adj very expensive and special
verb to start going in the direction of a place
adj feeling warm and comfortable

1 spun 2 ______ 3 ______ 4 ______

5 ______ 6 ______ 7 ______ 8 ______

Listening

2 Listen. What is the astronauts' destination? 107

3 Listen again and complete. walks stars ~~space~~ by home fly

The astronauts launch their spaceship
And blast off into [1] space .
They leave the Earth far, far behind
And [2] ______ to another place.

They get to their destination,
It's a space station in the [3] ______.
And there they study the planets
Mercury, Venus, and Mars.

The astronauts go on space [4] ______.
They float in the dark, black sky.
They spin around in their space suits
And see satellites go [5] ______.

And when it's time to return to Earth
And leave their space station dome,
They get back into their spaceships
And travel back to [6] ______.

Speaking

4 Ask and answer. Use the prompts or your own answers.

Would you like to be an astronaut?
Why (not)?
What would be the best thing in space?
What would be the worst thing in space?
What would you most like to see in space?

Because it would be ______.

Yes, I would. / No, I wouldn't.
exciting / amazing / frightening / fascinating / dangerous
Riding in a spaceship. / Living on a space station. / Going on a moon walk.
Eating space food. / Feeling lonely. / Being uncomfortable.
The planets. / The stars. / The moon. / A comet. / A satellite.

Words in context: *Dreaming in a Spaceship*, listening and speaking Unit 11 113

Lesson Six SB page 113

Skills Time!

Skills development

Dictionary: discover meaning of words in context

Listening: listen for specific detail

Speaking: ask and answer questions about space travel

Language

Words in context: *head off, spun, diamond, precious, glow, surface, bumpy, cozy* (Student Book); *beams, imagine, launch, observatory* (Workbook)

Extra: *blast off (v), far, spin around, dome, fascinating*

Materials

CD 107; Dictionary Workbook pages 128–136

Oxford iTools Digital classroom • Unit 11 • Words, Listening, Speaking

Warmer

- With books closed, ask students what they remember about the poem from the previous lesson.
- Ask questions if necessary, e.g. *Where did the boy go? What did he find the next morning?*

1 Find the words in the poem to match the pictures and definitions.

- Ask the students to look at the definitions and pictures. Explain that all the words they need are underlined in the poem on page 112.
- Ask students to look at the poem again and find the underlined words. They read the sentences containing each word and try to determine the meaning from the context.
- Students turn back to page 113 and write the correct word under each definition and picture.

ANSWERS

1. spun 2. precious 3. head off 4. cozy
5. diamond 6. bumpy 7. glow 8. surface

2 Listen. What is the astronauts' destination? 107

- Tell students they are going to hear a recording of another poem. They listen and find out what the astronauts' destination is.
- Play the whole recording. Elicit the answer.

ANSWER

The astronauts' destination is a space station in the stars.

3 Listen again and complete.

- Ask students to look at the poem. Tell them they are going to hear the recording again. This time they must fill in the blanks with the missing words.
- Ask students to read the poem before you play the recording.
- Play the recording, pausing for students to write the words. Play it again for students to complete their answers.
- Go through the answers together.

ANSWERS

1. space 2. fly 3. stars 4. walks 5. by 6. home

4 Ask and answer. Use the prompts or your own answers.

- Ask students to look at the example. Choose a strong student and ask him / her questions.
- Ask students to work in pairs. Tell them to take turns to ask their partner questions. Their partner must answer using the prompts or his / her own ideas.

Differentiation

Below level:

- Read the questions aloud to the students. Pause after each one, and ask them to circle their answer from the prompts. Then put students into pairs to complete the activity.

At level:

- Students complete the activity.

Above level:

- After students finish, switch pairs. Ask students to ask and answer *Would you like to be a deep sea diver?* Monitor and elicit as needed.

Further practice

Workbook page 105

Unit 11 Speaking skills worksheet, Assessment and Resource CD-ROM

Online Practice • Unit 11 • Words in context, Listening, and Speaking

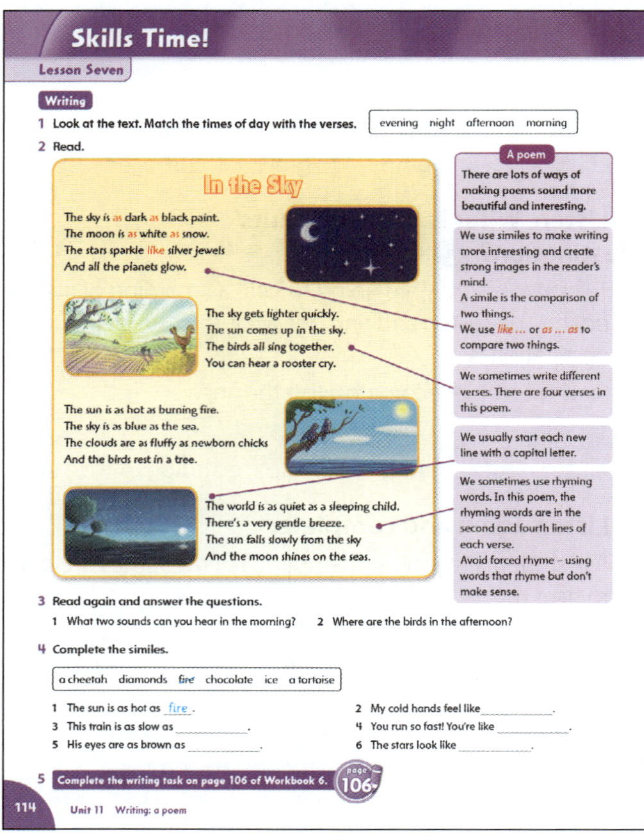

Skills Time!

Lesson Seven

Writing

1 Look at the text. Match the times of day with the verses.

evening night afternoon morning

2 Read.

In the Sky

The sky is as dark as black paint.
The moon is as white as snow.
The stars sparkle like silver jewels
And all the planets glow.

The sky gets lighter quickly.
The sun comes up in the sky.
The birds all sing together.
You can hear a rooster cry.

The sun is as hot as burning fire.
The sky is as blue as the sea.
The clouds are as fluffy as newborn chicks
And the birds rest in a tree.

The world is as quiet as a sleeping child.
There's a very gentle breeze.
The sun falls slowly from the sky
And the moon shines on the seas.

A poem

There are lots of ways of making poems sound more beautiful and interesting.

We use similes to make writing more interesting and create strong images in the reader's mind.
A simile is the comparison of two things.
We use *like* … or *as* … *as* to compare two things.

We sometimes write different verses. There are four verses in this poem.

We usually start each new line with a capital letter.

We sometimes use rhyming words. In this poem, the rhyming words are in the second and fourth lines of each verse.
Avoid forced rhyme – using words that rhyme but don't make sense.

3 Read again and answer the questions.

1 What two sounds can you hear in the morning? 2 Where are the birds in the afternoon?

4 Complete the similes.

a cheetah diamonds fire chocolate ice a tortoise

1 The sun is as hot as fire.
2 My cold hands feel like ______.
3 This train is as slow as ______.
4 You run so fast! You're like ______.
5 His eyes are as brown as ______.
6 The stars look like ______.

5 Complete the writing task on page 106 of Workbook 6. page 106

114 Unit 11 Writing: a poem

Lesson Seven SB page 114

Skills Time!

Skills development

Writing focus: understand the structure of a poem

Writing outcome: write a poem

Language

Recycled: vocabulary and structures seen previously

Extra: *simile, image, comparison, come up, rooster, fluffy*

Materials

Writing poster 11; a copy of the text from poster 11, Assessment and Resource CD-ROM, for each student

Oxford iTools Digital classroom • Unit 11 • Writing

Warmer

- Ask students what they remember about the poem from page 113. Discuss poems together. Ask *Do you like reading poems? Do you have a favorite poem? Can you remember any of the words?*

Poster 11: A poem

- Hand out a copy of the poster text to each student.
- Ask students the "Before reading" questions. Encourage them to discuss and share their ideas.
- Ask students to read the text silently. Ask comprehension questions, e.g. *How does the snow fall in winter?* Ask *Do you like the poem? Why / Why not?*
- Read the first two boxes on the left-hand side of the poem. Ask *What do we do to make poems easier to read?*
- Read the remaining two text boxes on the left and below. Ask *Where are the rhyming words in the poem?*
- Ask students to read the poem again and find examples of similes. Go through each one.
- Read the text boxes on the right-hand side. Ask *What do we need to think about if we want our poem to have a good rhythm?*
- Ask students the "After reading" questions.

1 Look at the text. Match the times of day with the verses.

- Ask students to look at the pictures. Point to each one and ask *What can you see?*
- Ask students to read quickly through the poem and match the times of day in the box with the verses.

ANSWER

Verse 1: night Verse 2: morning Verse 3: afternoon
Verse 4: evening

2 Read.

- Ask a different student to read each verse to the class.
- Draw attention to the text boxes to the right of the poem.

3 Read again and answer the questions.

- Students read the text silently and answer the questions.

ANSWERS

1. You can hear the birds singing and the rooster crying.
2. In the afternoon the birds are resting in a tree.

4 Complete the similes.

- Ask students for suggestions for other things to compare the sun to.
- Students complete the similes with words from the box.

Differentiation

Below level:

- Ask students to re-read the poem, pick their favorite verse, and draw it.

At level:

- Students complete the activity.

Above level:

- Ask students to write a poem called "In the Water", modeled on the poem from page 114.

ANSWERS

1. fire 2. ice 3. a tortoise 4. a cheetah
5. chocolate 6. diamonds

5 Complete the writing task on page 106 of Workbook 6.

- Refer students to the Workbook to complete the writing task. Go through the activity with them first.

Further practice

Workbook page 106

Unit 11 Writing skills worksheet, Assessment and Resource CD-ROM

Online Practice • Unit 11 • Writing

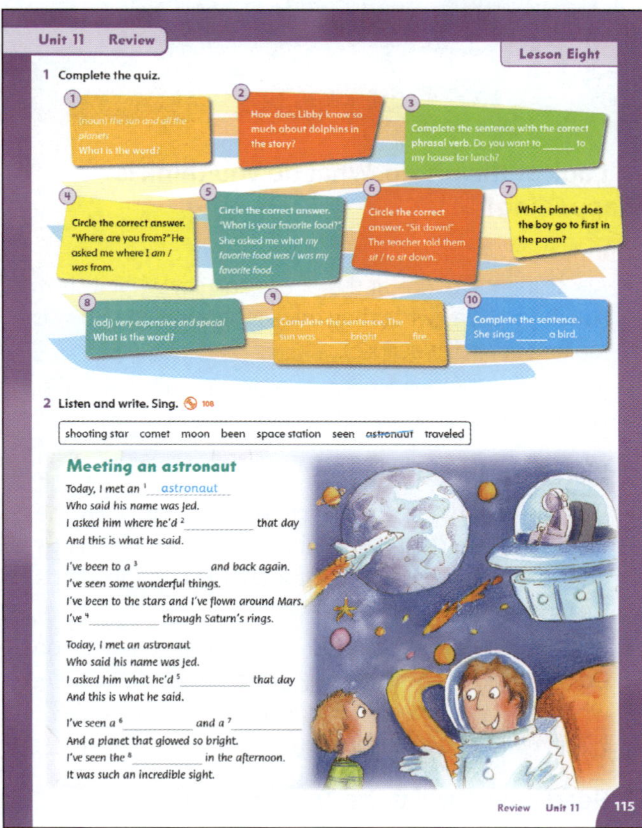

Unit 11 Review

Lesson Eight

1 Complete the quiz.

1 (noun) the sun and all the planets What is the word?

2 How does Libby know so much about dolphins in the story?

3 Complete the sentence with the correct phrasal verb. Do you want to ______ to my house for lunch?

4 Circle the correct answer. "Where are you from?" He asked me where I *am* / *was* from.

5 Circle the correct answer. "What is your favorite food?" She asked me what *my favorite food was* / *was my favorite food*.

6 Circle the correct answer. "Sit down!" The teacher told them *sit* / *to sit* down.

7 Which planet does the boy go to first in the poem?

8 (adj) *very expensive and special* What is the word?

9 Complete the sentence. The sun was ______ bright ______ fire.

10 Complete the sentence. She sings ______ a bird.

2 Listen and write. Sing. 108

shooting star comet moon been space station seen ~~astronaut~~ traveled

Meeting an astronaut

Today, I met an [1] astronaut
Who said his name was Jed.
I asked him where he'd [2] ______ that day
And this is what he said.

I've been to a [3] ______ and back again.
I've seen some wonderful things.
I've been to the stars and I've flown around Mars.
I've [4] ______ through Saturn's rings.

Today, I met an astronaut
Who said his name was Jed.
I asked him what he'd [5] ______ that day
And this is what he said.

I've seen a [6] ______ and a [7] ______
And a planet that glowed so bright.
I've seen the [8] ______ in the afternoon.
It was such an incredible sight.

Review Unit 11 115

Lesson Eight SB page 115

Unit 11 Review

Learning outcomes

To review vocabulary and structures practiced previously

To use vocabulary and structures from the unit in the context of a song

Language

Recycled: vocabulary and structures seen previously

Materials

CD 108

Oxford iTools Digital classroom • Unit 11 • Review

Warmer

- Play *Book race* (see page 8) to review words and structures from the unit.
- Read these sentences and give students 20 seconds to find each one:
  He told us to turn off our cell phones. (Lesson 4)
  The sun is as hot as burning fire. (Lesson 7)
  First, he asked him where he was. (Lesson 3)
  The ground was very bumpy. (Lesson 5)
  The stars sparkle like silver jewels. (Lesson 7)
  They float in the dark, black sky. (Lesson 6)
  The stars were as bright as diamonds. (Lesson 5)
  We need to move this dolphin back into the sea. (Lesson 1)

1 Complete the quiz.

- Tell students they are going to do a quiz based on the unit. Students can work individually, in pairs, or in teams.
- Students work with books open to page 115. They may not refer to other lessons in the unit.

ANSWERS

1. solar system 2. Because she watched an interview with a dolphin expert on TV. 3. come over 4. was 5. my favorite food was 6. to sit 7. Saturn 8. precious 9. as, as 10. like

2 Listen and write. Sing. 108

- Focus students' attention on the picture. Ask *What can you see?*
- Play the whole song as students follow along.
- Play the song again, pausing for students to write the missing words.
- Play the recording a third time if necessary.
- Review the answers. Ask students to read each line aloud, saying the missing word.
- Play the recording once more. Students sing along.

Differentiation

Below level:

- Play *Order the letters* (see page 9) using the words from the song. You may also wish to include the words from pages 109 and 113.

At level:

- Write the following things on the board. Ask students to read the song again and find them as quickly as possible. (Answers are given in brackets.): *the astronaut's name (Jed) / two reported questions (I asked him where he'd been that day; I asked him what he'd seen that day) / two planets (Mars and Saturn) / a planet which has rings (Saturn) / four things that you can sometimes see from Earth (a comet, a shooting star, stars, and the moon) / a place where people live and work in space (a space station)*

Above level:

- Play *A long sentence* with the key vocabulary from the song (see page 8).

ANSWERS

1. astronaut 2. been 3. space station 4. traveled 5. seen 6. comet 7. shooting star 8. moon

Further practice

Workbook page 107
Unit 11 test, Assessment and Resource CD-ROM
Progress certificate, Assessment and Resource CD-ROM
Online Practice • Unit 11 • Review

Science Time!

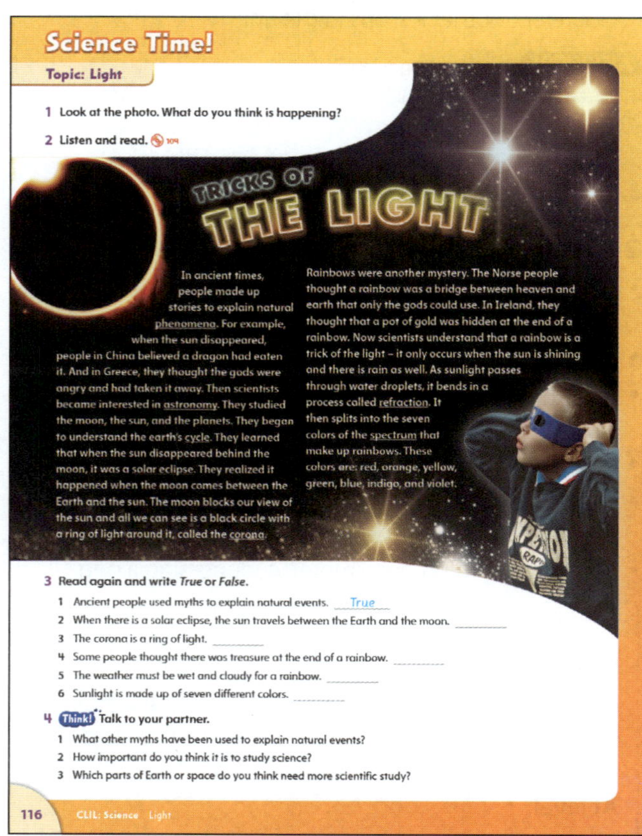

Science Time!

Topic: Light

1 Look at the photo. What do you think is happening?

2 Listen and read. 109

TRICKS OF THE LIGHT

In ancient times, people made up stories to explain natural phenomena. For example, when the sun disappeared, people in China believed a dragon had eaten it. And in Greece, they thought the gods were angry and had taken it away. Then scientists became interested in astronomy. They studied the moon, the sun, and the planets. They began to understand the earth's cycle. They learned that when the sun disappeared behind the moon, it was a solar eclipse. They realized it happened when the moon comes between the Earth and the sun. The moon blocks our view of the sun and all we can see is a black circle with a ring of light around it, called the corona.

Rainbows were another mystery. The Norse people thought a rainbow was a bridge between heaven and earth that only the gods could use. In Ireland, they thought that a pot of gold was hidden at the end of a rainbow. Now scientists understand that a rainbow is a trick of the light – it only occurs when the sun is shining and there is rain as well. As sunlight passes through water droplets, it bends in a process called refraction. It then splits into the seven colors of the spectrum that make up rainbows. These colors are: red, orange, yellow, green, blue, indigo, and violet.

3 Read again and write *True* or *False*.

1 Ancient people used myths to explain natural events. True
2 When there is a solar eclipse, the sun travels between the Earth and the moon. ______
3 The corona is a ring of light. ______
4 Some people thought there was treasure at the end of a rainbow. ______
5 The weather must be wet and cloudy for a rainbow. ______
6 Sunlight is made up of seven different colors. ______

4 Think! Talk to your partner.

1 What other myths have been used to explain natural events?
2 How important do you think it is to study science?
3 Which parts of Earth or space do you think need more scientific study?

116 CLIL: Science Light

Topic: Light SB page 116

Learning outcomes

To learn some useful content and language about light

Language

Core: *phenomena, astronomy, cycle, solar eclipse, corona, refraction, spectrum*

Extra: *dragon, blocks, droplets, splits*

Materials

CD 109

Oxford iTools Digital classroom • Science Time! • Light

Warmer

Critical Thinking

- Tell students that they are going to learn about light in this lesson. Ask them to think of all the things in the world (natural and manmade) that give off light.

Lead-in

Critical Thinking

- Ask students why we need light (*so that we can wake up and work, so that we have energy, so that plants will grow, etc*).

1 Look at the photo. What do you think is happening?

Critical Thinking

- Ask students to look at the photo and say what it shows. Ask them to say what they think is happening (a boy is looking at a solar eclipse).
- Ask students if they have ever seen an eclipse and, if so, what happened and what it looked like.

2 Listen and read. 109

- Play the recording for students to listen and follow the text in their Student Books. Elicit / Teach the meanings of any unknown words, or ask students to find the words in their dictionaries.
- Play the recording again. Ask comprehension questions, e.g. *What did people in China / Greece think had happened when the sun disappeared? What causes a solar eclipse? What makes a rainbow appear?*

3 Read again and write *True* or *False*.

- Explain that students need to find information in the text to decide whether each sentence is true or false. Read out the first sentence and allow students time to look at the text and find the correct answer.
- Students complete the rest of the activity individually.

ANSWERS

1. True 2. False 3. True 4. True 5. False 6. True

4 Think! Talk to your partner.

Critical Thinking

- Read out the questions and elicit suggestions from students around the class.

Collaboration

- Put students in pairs to discuss their answers.
- Have pairs report back to the class.

Differentiation

Below level:

- Divide the class into three groups. Assign one question to each group. Students talk together to decide on the best answer to their question.
- Invite students from each group to report their answer to the class.

At level:

- Students complete the activity.

Above level:

- When students have finished discussing the questions and have reported back to the class, ask them to choose a natural phenomenon and make a new myth about it.
- Invite students to tell the class about their myth.

Further practice

Workbook page 108

Online Practice • Science Time!

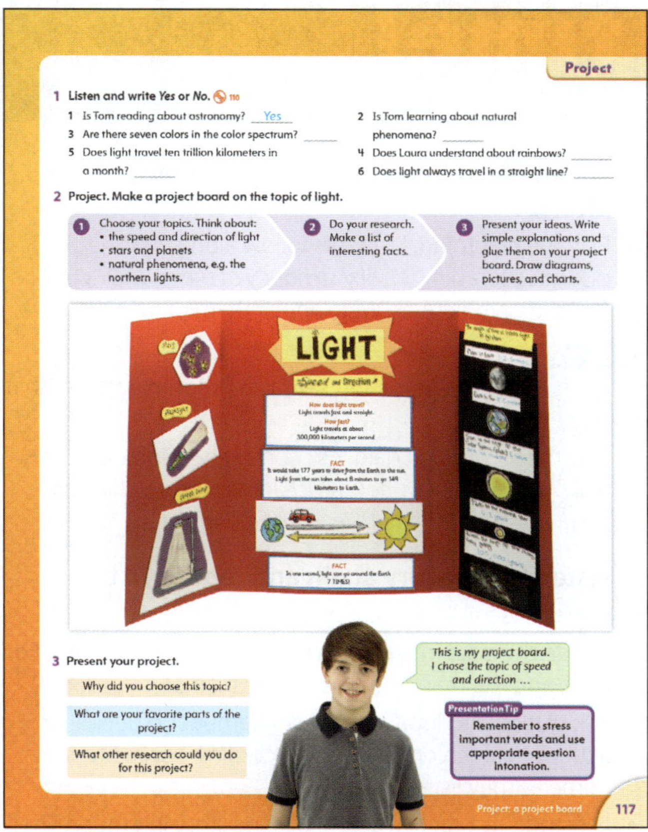

Project

1 Listen and write *Yes* or *No*. 110

1 Is Tom reading about astronomy? Yes
2 Is Tom learning about natural phenomena? ____
3 Are there seven colors in the color spectrum? ____
4 Does Laura understand about rainbows? ____
5 Does light travel ten trillion kilometers in a month? ____
6 Does light always travel in a straight line? ____

2 Project. Make a project board on the topic of light.

1 Choose your topics. Think about:
- the speed and direction of light
- stars and planets
- natural phenomena, e.g. the northern lights.

2 Do your research. Make a list of interesting facts.

3 Present your ideas. Write simple explanations and glue them on your project board. Draw diagrams, pictures, and charts.

3 Present your project.

Why did you choose this topic?

What are your favorite parts of the project?

What other research could you do for this project?

Presentation Tip
Remember to stress important words and use appropriate question intonation.

Project: a project board 117

Project SB page 117

Learning outcomes

To listen and answer questions *Yes* or *No*

To make a project board on the topic of light

Language

This is my project board. I chose the topic of speed and direction …

Materials

CD 110; card; paper; colored pens or pencils; scissors; glue

Oxford iTools Digital classroom • Science Time! • Project

Warmer

- Ask students what they can remember about the text on Student Book page 116. Ask them to say what myths / stories they know about the sun or moon.

1 Listen and write *Yes* or *No*. 110

- Play the recording. Students need to answer each question *Yes* or *No*.
- Play the recording once through. Play it again, pausing after each answer is mentioned so that students have time to think about their answers.
- Invite pairs of students to read out the questions and answers.

ANSWERS

1. Yes 2. Yes 3. Yes 4. Yes 5. No 6. Yes

2 Project. Make a project board on the topic of light.

Creativity

- Explain that students are going to make a project board on the topic of light. Ask *What do you need to make this project?* Elicit *card, paper, colored pens or pencils, scissors, glue*.
- Focus on the instructions. Ask a student to read out the instructions to the class.
- Divide the class into groups of three or four. Hand out a large sheet of card, sheets of paper, scissors, and glue to each group.
- The students decide on a topic and find information on the Internet or in science books. They then draw pictures, diagrams, or charts and write facts and explanations about their chosen topic and glue them onto the card. They write a heading on the card and label the pictures / photos.

NOTE: You can print out information about the topics in advance to save time in the lesson.
Students can use a computer to write and print out their information for the project boards.

Differentiation

Below level:

- Make a class project board about light. Divide the class into five groups and assign one of the following topics to each group: the sun; the stars and planets; rainbows; the northern lights; speed and direction of light.
- Students can use science books or the Internet to make a list of interesting facts about their topic. They write their facts on pieces of paper and draw pictures to illustrate them.
- Divide a large piece of card into five sections and have a student write a large heading (LIGHT) at the top. Students stick their facts and pictures into the correct sections on the project board.

At level:

- Students complete the activity.

Above level:

- When students have completed their project board, ask them to write three questions about their project board, then swap project boards with another group. When they have finished reading each other's project boards, they can ask and answer the questions.

3 Present your project.

Communication

- Put students into groups of three or four. Tell them that they are now going to talk about their project with each other.
- Demonstrate by either holding up a completed project board, or using the example in the Student Book. Talk about the project, as in the example. Point to any pictures you mention.
- Students talk in groups.
- Invite individual students to stand up and present their projects to the class.

Further practice
Workbook page 109
Online Practice • Science Time!

12 Vacation time!

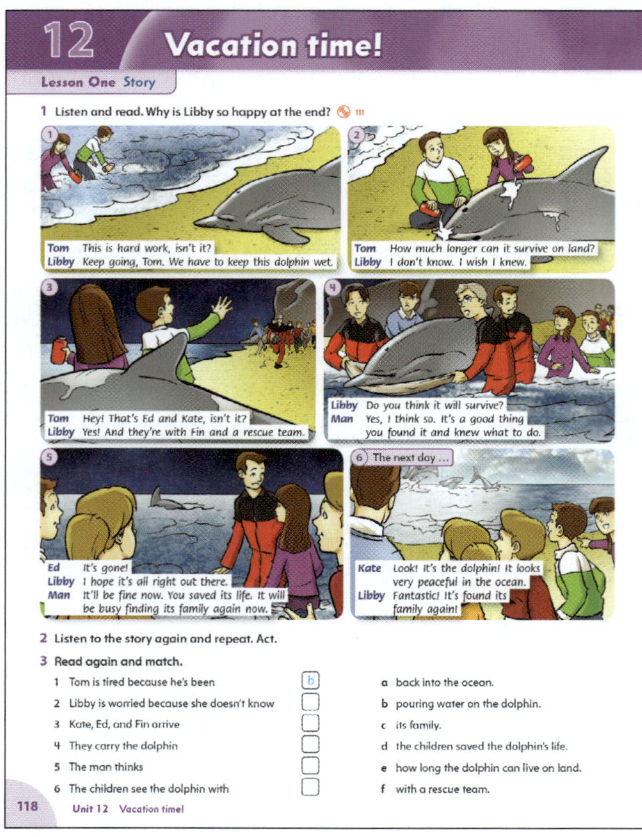
12 Vacation time!

Lesson One Story

1 Listen and read. Why is Libby so happy at the end? 111

1
Tom This is hard work, isn't it?
Libby Keep going, Tom. We have to keep this dolphin wet.

2
Tom How much longer can it survive on land?
Libby I don't know. I wish I knew.

3
Tom Hey! That's Ed and Kate, isn't it?
Libby Yes! And they're with Fin and a rescue team.

4
Libby Do you think it will survive?
Man Yes, I think so. It's a good thing you found it and knew what to do.

5
Ed It's gone!
Libby I hope it's all right out there.
Man It'll be fine now. You saved its life. It will be busy finding its family again now.

6 The next day …
Kate Look! It's the dolphin! It looks very peaceful in the ocean.
Libby Fantastic! It's found its family again!

2 Listen to the story again and repeat. Act.

3 Read again and match.

1 Tom is tired because he's been [b] — a back into the ocean.
2 Libby is worried because she doesn't know [ ] — b pouring water on the dolphin.
3 Kate, Ed, and Fin arrive [ ] — c its family.
4 They carry the dolphin [ ] — d the children saved the dolphin's life.
5 The man thinks [ ] — e how long the dolphin can live on land.
6 The children see the dolphin with [ ] — f with a rescue team.

118 Unit 12 Vacation time!

Lesson One 

Story

Learning outcomes

To read and understand a story

To act out a story

Language

Introducing vocabulary (Lesson 2) through a story

Extra: *rescue team*

Materials

CD 111

Digital classroom • Unit 12 • Story

Warmer

- Ask students to tell you what they remember about the last episode. If necessary, ask questions, e.g. *What did the children find? What did Ed and Kate do?*
- Ask students if they remember what was happening at the end. (*It was getting dark and Ed and Kate had not returned with Fin.*) Ask students to make predictions about what will happen in the final episode.

1 Listen and read. Why is Libby so happy at the end? 111

- Play the recording. Students follow along. Ask the gist question *Why is Libby so happy at the end?* Discuss students' predictions. Were any of them correct?

ANSWER

Libby is happy because she sees the dolphin again with its family.

- Play the recording again. Ask comprehension questions, e.g. *Does Libby know how much longer the dolphin can survive on land? Who arrives with Ed and Kate?*

2 Listen to the story again and repeat. Act.

- Play the recording, pausing for students to repeat.
- Divide the class into groups of five to play Tom, Libby, Ed, Kate, and the man from the rescue team.
- Ask students to look at the story frames and decide on actions for each one. Play the recording again. Students mime as they listen.
- Let students practice acting out the story in groups. Then ask one or two groups to act for the class.

Differentiation

Below level:

- Ask students to underline words in the story they don't know. Have them first guess the meaning with context clues. Then look the words up in a dictionary. Have students take out their notebooks and write the definitions in their own words.

At level:

- Put students in pairs. Everyone reads the story again and writes three true / false statements in his / her notebook without showing their partner. Students swap notebooks and write *True* or *False* without looking at the story. Students check answers by looking at the story.

Above level:

- Extend the "at level" activity to six statements.

3 Read again and match.

- Focus on the example. Ask students where the story tells us Tom is getting tired (frame 1 – Tom says that keeping the dolphin wet is hard work).
- Students read and match the sentence halves.

ANSWERS

1. b 2. e 3. f 4. a 5. d 6. c

Further practice

Workbook page 110

Online Practice • Unit 12 • Story

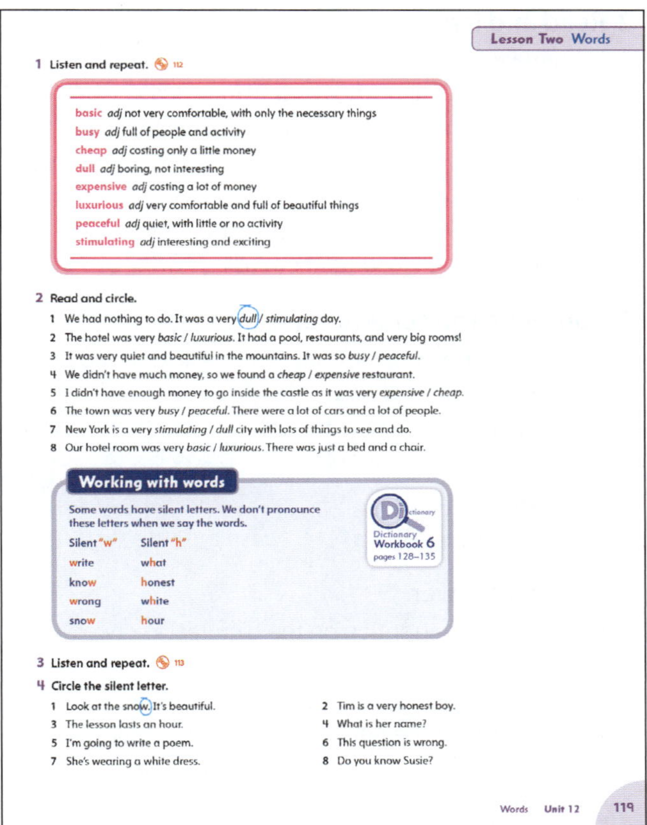
Lesson Two Words

1 Listen and repeat. 112

basic *adj* not very comfortable, with only the necessary things
busy *adj* full of people and activity
cheap *adj* costing only a little money
dull *adj* boring, not interesting
expensive *adj* costing a lot of money
luxurious *adj* very comfortable and full of beautiful things
peaceful *adj* quiet, with little or no activity
stimulating *adj* interesting and exciting

2 Read and circle.

1 We had nothing to do. It was a very *dull* / *stimulating* day.
2 The hotel was very *basic* / *luxurious*. It had a pool, restaurants, and very big rooms!
3 It was very quiet and beautiful in the mountains. It was so *busy* / *peaceful*.
4 We didn't have much money, so we found a *cheap* / *expensive* restaurant.
5 I didn't have enough money to go inside the castle as it was very *expensive* / *cheap*.
6 The town was very *busy* / *peaceful*. There were a lot of cars and a lot of people.
7 New York is a very *stimulating* / *dull* city with lots of things to see and do.
8 Our hotel room was very *basic* / *luxurious*. There was just a bed and a chair.

Working with words

Some words have silent letters. We don't pronounce these letters when we say the words.

Silent "w"	Silent "h"
write	what
know	honest
wrong	white
snow	hour

Dictionary Workbook 6 pages 128–135

3 Listen and repeat. 113

4 Circle the silent letter.

1 Look at the snow. It's beautiful.
2 Tim is a very honest boy.
3 The lesson lasts an hour.
4 What is her name?
5 I'm going to write a poem.
6 This question is wrong.
7 She's wearing a white dress.
8 Do you know Susie?

Words Unit 12 119

Lesson Two SB page 119

Words

Learning outcomes

To identify and use adjectives for describing places

To identify the silent letters "w" and "h" in certain words

Language

Words: *cheap, expensive, peaceful, busy, luxurious, basic, stimulating, dull*

Working with words: *write, know, wrong, snow, what, honest, white, hour* (Student Book); *wrap, rhino, wheel, grow* (Workbook)

Materials

CD 112–113 Dictionary Workbook pages 128–135; two small pieces of paper for each student (optional)

Oxford iTools Digital classroom • Unit 12 • Words

Warmer

- Discuss summer vacation together. Ask *Did you go on vacation last year? Where did you go? Where did you stay? What was it like?* Write the adjectives on the board.

1 Listen and repeat. 112

- Ask students to look at the words and their definitions. Ask them to read silently.
- Tell students you are going to play a recording of the words for them to listen and repeat.
- Play the recording, pausing after each word. Students repeat. Play the recording again. Students listen and repeat. Repeat as often as necessary.
- Ask students to say the words for the class.
- Focus attention on the words on the board. Did students mention any of the adjectives from Exercise 1?

NOTE: Remind students to consult the Dictionary pages in their Workbooks when completing Exercise 2.

2 Read and circle.

- Read the instructions and the example together. Ask students what to do in this exercise.
- Ask students to read the sentences and circle the correct words.
- Review answers together. Ask different students to read aloud.

ANSWERS

1. dull 2. luxurious 3. peaceful 4. cheap
5. expensive 6. busy 7. stimulating 8. basic

3 Listen and repeat. 113

- Before doing the activity, focus on the *Working with words* section. Ask *What are the silent letters?*
- Play the recording. Students listen and repeat the words.
- Play the recording again. Students listen and repeat. Repeat as often as necessary.

4 Circle the silent letter.

- Write the example on the board. Ask *Which letter is silent?* Encourage a confident student to come to the front and circle the *w* in *snow*.
- Students read the sentences and circle the silent letters.

Differentiation

Below level:

- Give students two small pieces of paper. Ask them to write *w* on one and *h* on the other. Students should listen and hold up the paper with the correct silent letter. Read the words from the box in random order. Then students complete the activity.

At level:

- Students complete the activity.

Above level:

- After students finish, ask them to go back to Exercise 1 and write sentences for each new word. Encourage them to include words with silent letters. Make this a game by giving two points for each correct sentence and a bonus point for each word with a silent letter. Tally the points to find the 1st, 2nd, and 3rd place winners.

ANSWERS

1. Look at the snow. It's beautiful.
2. Tim is a very honest boy. 3. The lesson lasts an hour.
4. What is her name? 5. I'm going to write a poem.
6. This question is wrong. 7. She's wearing a white dress.
8. Do you know Susie?

Further practice

Workbook page 111

Online Practice • Unit 12 • Words

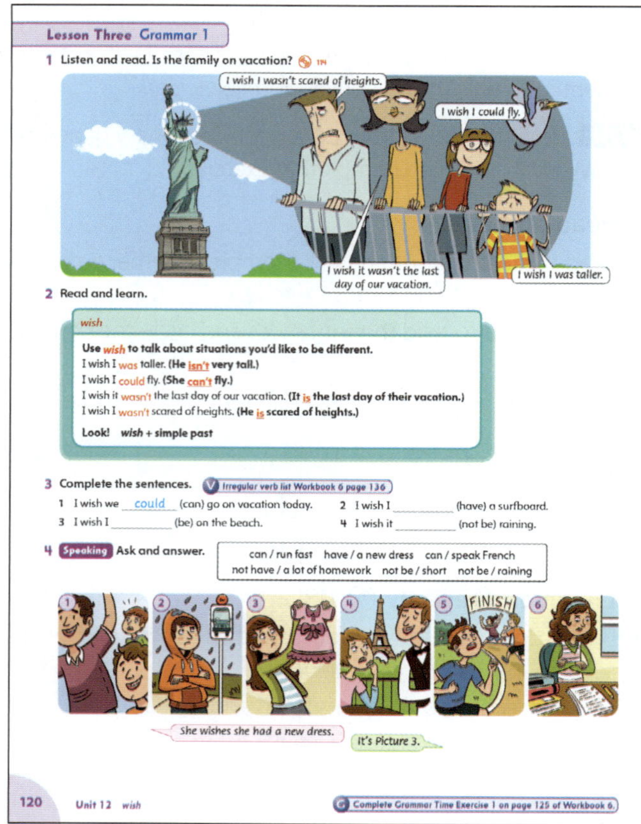

Lesson Three Grammar 1

1 Listen and read. Is the family on vacation? 114

2 Read and learn.

wish

Use *wish* to talk about situations you'd like to be different.
I wish I was taller. **(He isn't very tall.)**
I wish I could fly. **(She can't fly.)**
I wish it wasn't the last day of our vacation. **(It is the last day of their vacation.)**
I wish I wasn't scared of heights. **(He is scared of heights.)**

Look! ***wish* + simple past**

3 Complete the sentences. Irregular verb list Workbook 6 page 136

1 I wish we could (can) go on vacation today.
2 I wish I ______ (have) a surfboard.
3 I wish I ______ (be) on the beach.
4 I wish it ______ (not be) raining.

4 Speaking Ask and answer.

can / run fast have / a new dress can / speak French
not have / a lot of homework not be / short not be / raining

120 Unit 12 *wish*

Complete Grammar Time Exercise 1 on page 125 of Workbook 6.

Lesson Three SB page 120

Grammar 1

Learning outcomes

To use *wish* to talk about situations you'd like to be different

Speaking: using *wish* to talk about situations people would like to change

Language

Core: *I wish I was taller. I wish I could fly. I wish it wasn't the last day of our vacation. I wish I wasn't scared of heights.*

Extra: *surfboard*

Materials

CD 114; a strip of paper for each student (optional)

Oxford iTools Digital classroom • Unit 12 • Grammar 1

Warmer

- Discuss dream vacations together. Ask students *Where would you most like to go on vacation? What would you like to do? What would you stay in?*

1 Listen and read. Is the family on vacation? 114

- Ask students to look at the pictures. Ask *Where are the family? Which famous tower are they visiting?*
- Play the recording. Students follow along. Ask the gist question Are the family on vacation?

ANSWER

Yes, they are. (It's the last day of their vacation.)

- Play the recording again. Ask comprehension questions, e.g. *What is Dad scared of? Does Mom want to go home?*

2 Read and learn.

- Read the rule and example together. Ask *What do we use "wish" for? Which tense do we use in these sentences?*
- Practice together. Write the sentences below on the board or use your own. *I'm not on vacation. / I can't speak Spanish. / I'm scared of spiders.*
- Tell students you would like these situations to be different. Ask them rewrite them using *I wish*.

3 Complete the sentences.

- Focus attention on the example and read it together. Ask *Which tense do we use here?*
- Ask students to complete the sentences with the correct form of the verb in brackets.

ANSWERS

1. could 2. had 3. was 4. wasn't

4 Ask and answer.

- Focus students' attention on the pictures. Ask two students to read the speech bubbles.
- Put students in pairs. They take turns choosing pictures and saying what the person wishes. They should use the prompts to help them. Their partner says the number of the picture.
- Monitor the activity, checking that students are forming their sentences correctly.

Differentiation

Below level:

- Put students in pairs. Have them look at Exercise 4 again. One student makes a sentence with the words in the box, e.g. *I wish I could run fast.* The other student says whether they agree (*Me too*) or disagree (*Not me*). Monitor and help as needed.

At level:

- Ask students to write a wish on a strip of paper, without showing anyone. They put their name on the paper and fold it up. Collect the papers and redistribute them so that everyone has a different student's wish. Ask a student to say what is on his / her paper, without saying the student's name. The class guesses whose it is, e.g. Student: *He wishes he was surfing.* Class: *Carlos!* Continue until all the wishes have been read and guessed.

Above level:

- Ask students to think of a wish. Then ask them to write a short paragraph about the wish and why they chose it, e.g. *I wish I had a dog because I love animals. If I had a dog, I would…* If time permits, they can share with the class.

Further practice

Grammar Time, Workbook page 125
Workbook page 112
Online Practice • Unit 12 • Grammar 1

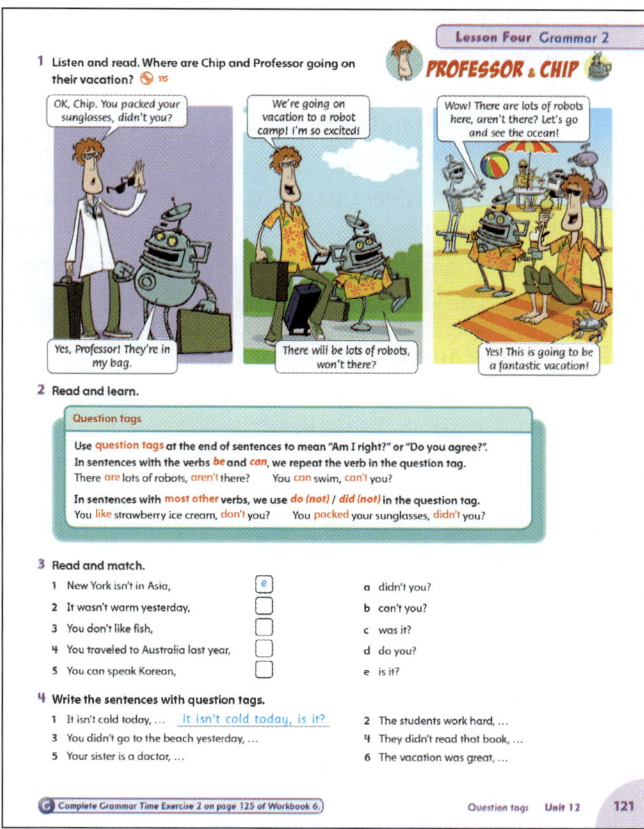

Lesson Four Grammar 2

PROFESSOR & CHIP

1 Listen and read. Where are Chip and Professor going on their vacation? 115

2 Read and learn.

Question tags

Use question tags at the end of sentences to mean "Am I right?" or "Do you agree?".
In sentences with the verbs *be* and *can*, we repeat the verb in the question tag.
There are lots of robots, aren't there? You can swim, can't you?

In sentences with most other verbs, we use *do (not)* / *did (not)* in the question tag.
You like strawberry ice cream, don't you? You packed your sunglasses, didn't you?

3 Read and match.

1 New York isn't in Asia, [e]
2 It wasn't warm yesterday, [ ]
3 You don't like fish, [ ]
4 You traveled to Australia last year, [ ]
5 You can speak Korean, [ ]

a didn't you?
b can't you?
c was it?
d do you?
e is it?

4 Write the sentences with question tags.

1 It isn't cold today, … It isn't cold today, is it?
2 The students work hard, …
3 You didn't go to the beach yesterday, …
4 They didn't read that book, …
5 Your sister is a doctor, …
6 The vacation was great, …

Complete Grammar Time Exercise 2 on page 125 of Workbook 6.

Question tags Unit 12 121

Lesson Four SB page 121

Grammar 2

Learning outcomes

To use question tags to mean "Am I right?" or "Do you agree?"

Language

Core: *There are lots of robots, aren't there? You can swim, can't you? There will be lots of robots, won't there? You like strawberry ice cream, don't you? You packed your sunglasses, didn't you?*

Materials

CD 115

Oxford iTools Digital classroom • Unit 12 • Grammar 2

Warmer

- Ask *Do you think Professor and Chip ever go on vacation? Where do you think they go? What do you think they do on vacation?*

1 Listen and read. Where are Chip and Professor going on their vacation? 115

- Play the recording. Students follow along. Ask the gist question.

ANSWER

Chip and Professor are going to a robot camp for their vacation.

- Play it again for students to re-read the text. Ask comprehension questions, e.g. *Where has Chip put his sunglasses? What is at the robot camp?*

2 Read and learn.

- Read the rules and examples together. Ask students *When do we use question tags?* Establish that we use them to check we are right or to invite people to agree with us.
- Draw attention to the verbs in the question tags. Ask *Is the verb the same as the one in the sentence? Is it positive or negative?*
- Write the sentences. Ask students to help you write the question tags:
  You're Mexican, ______? / You cleaned your room, _______? You can speak French _______? / There will be a test at the end of the semester, ______?

3 Read and match.

- Look at the example together. Ask students *Why is the question tag positive?* Establish that when the sentence is negative, the question tag is positive, and when the sentence is positive, the question tag is negative.
- Ask students to look at the exercise in their books. They match the sentences with the correct question tags.

ANSWERS

1. e 2. c 3. d 4. a 5. b

4 Write the sentences with question tags.

- Before students look at the exercise, write the example on the board and ask them for the correct question tag.
- Ask students to complete the rest of the sentences.

Differentiation

Below level:

- Write scrambled sentences from Exercises 3 and 4 on the board. Ask students to close their books and write the sentences in their notebooks. Monitor and help as needed.

At level:

- Students complete the activity.

Above level:

- Play *True or false?* (see page 9). Use sentences from the lesson or make up your own.

ANSWERS

1. It isn't cold today, is it?
2. The students work hard, don't they?
3. You didn't go to the beach yesterday, did you?
4. They didn't read that book, did they?
5. Your sister is a doctor, isn't she?
6. The vacation was great, wasn't it?

Further practice

Grammar Time, Workbook page 125
Workbook page 113
Unit 12 Language practice worksheet, Assessment and Resource CD-ROM
Online Practice • Unit 12 • Grammar 2

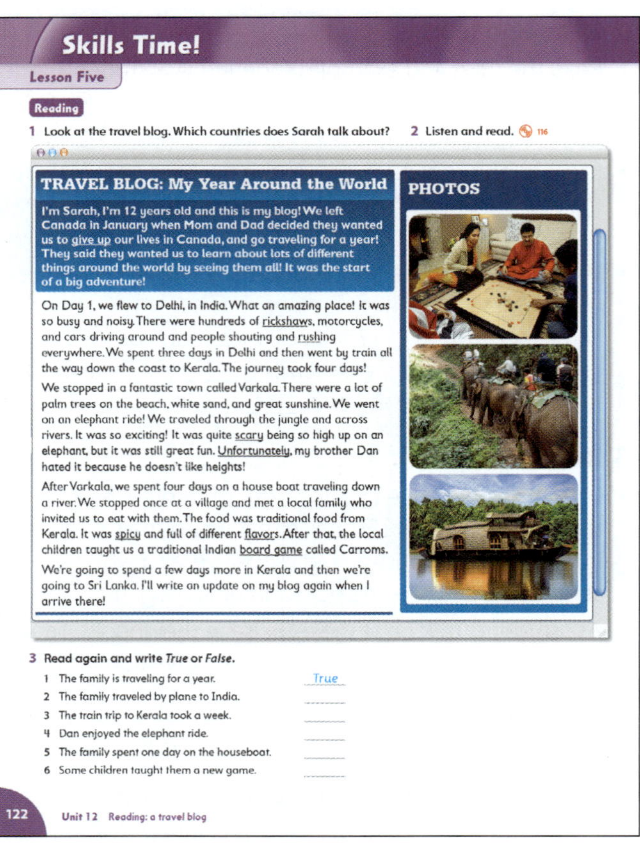

Skills Time!

Lesson Five

Reading

1 Look at the travel blog. Which countries does Sarah talk about?

2 Listen and read. 116

TRAVEL BLOG: My Year Around the World

I'm Sarah, I'm 12 years old and this is my blog! We left Canada in January when Mom and Dad decided they wanted us to give up our lives in Canada, and go traveling for a year! They said they wanted us to learn about lots of different things around the world by seeing them all! It was the start of a big adventure!

On Day 1, we flew to Delhi, in India. What an amazing place! It was so busy and noisy. There were hundreds of rickshaws, motorcycles, and cars driving around and people shouting and rushing everywhere. We spent three days in Delhi and then went by train all the way down the coast to Kerala. The journey took four days!

We stopped in a fantastic town called Varkala. There were a lot of palm trees on the beach, white sand, and great sunshine. We went on an elephant ride! We traveled through the jungle and across rivers. It was so exciting! It was quite scary being so high up on an elephant, but it was still great fun. Unfortunately, my brother Dan hated it because he doesn't like heights!

After Varkala, we spent four days on a house boat traveling down a river. We stopped once at a village and met a local family who invited us to eat with them. The food was traditional food from Kerala. It was spicy and full of different flavors. After that, the local children taught us a traditional Indian board game called Carroms.

We're going to spend a few days more in Kerala and then we're going to Sri Lanka. I'll write an update on my blog again when I arrive there!

PHOTOS

3 Read again and write *True* or *False*.

1 The family is traveling for a year. True
2 The family traveled by plane to India. ______
3 The train trip to Kerala took a week. ______
4 Dan enjoyed the elephant ride. ______
5 The family spent one day on the houseboat. ______
6 Some children taught them a new game. ______

122 Unit 12 Reading: a travel blog

Lesson Five SB page 122

Skills Time!

Skills development
Reading: read an Internet blog

Language
Recycled: vocabulary and structures seen previously

Extra: *blog, give up, India, rickshaws, rush, palm tree, scary, unfortunately, house boat, spicy, flavors, Indian, board game, update*

Materials
CD 116

Oxford iTools Digital classroom • Unit 12 • Reading

Warmer
- Elicit or teach the word *blog*. Ask students *Why do people write blogs on the Internet? What do they write about? Have you read / written any?*
- Tell students they are going to read an Internet blog about a girl who is traveling for a year with her family. Ask students to make predictions about the things she might write about.

1 Look at the travel blog. Which countries does Sarah talk about?
- Ask students to skim the text, without reading in detail, to find the answer to the gist question. Elicit the answer from the class.

ANSWER

Sarah talks about India and Sri Lanka.

2 Listen and read. 116
- Tell students they are going to listen to a recording of the travel blog. Tell them to follow along, but not to worry if they don't understand every word.
- Play the whole recording.
- Play the recording again, pausing to ask comprehension questions, e.g. *Where does Sarah go first? What is Delhi like?*
- Answer questions students have and elicit the meanings of any unknown words from context.

3 Read again and write *True* or *False*.
- Ask students to read the instructions and look at the example. Ask students to re-read the first paragraph and find the sentence that tells them Sarah's family is traveling for a year.
- Ask students to re-read the text and write *True* or *False* next to the remaining sentences.
- Review answers together.

Differentiation

Below level:
- Have a spelling bee with the words from the lesson. Children stand in a row at the front of the classroom. Say a word, and ask the first child to spell it. If correct, he / she stays at the front. If incorrect, he / she sits down, and the next student tries. Continue until there is only one student left. That student is the winner.

At level:
- Ask students to read the text again and write five questions for their partner to answer. Students swap papers with their partner and answer each other's questions.

Above level:
- Discuss Sarah's blog in groups. Ask *Do you think Sarah's trip sounds exciting? Would you like to go traveling for a year? Which countries would you like to visit?* Students can report back to the class if time allows.

ANSWERS

1. True 2. True 3. False 4. False 5. False 6. True

Further Practice

Workbook page 114

Online Practice • Unit 12 • Reading

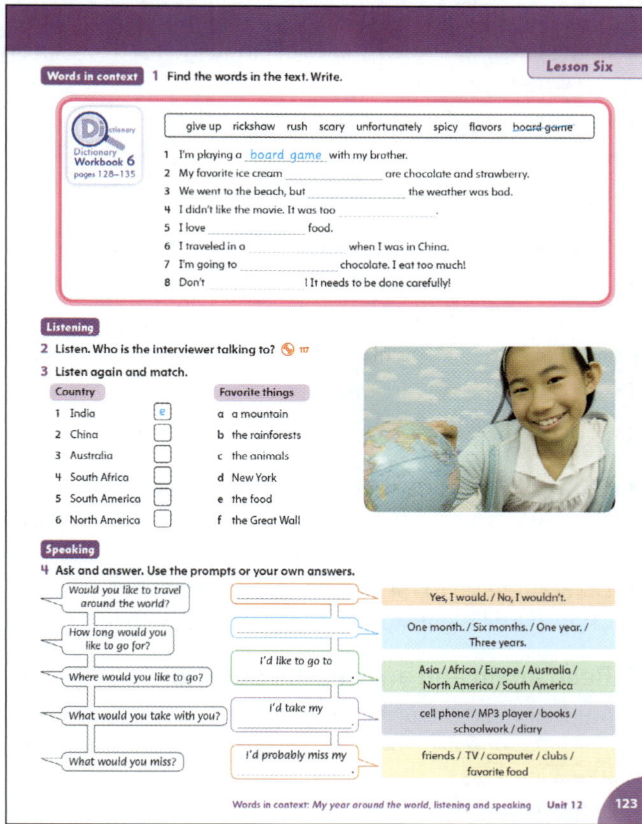

Lesson Six

Words in context **1 Find the words in the text. Write.**

Dictionary Workbook 6 pages 128–135

give up rickshaw rush scary unfortunately spicy flavors ~~board game~~

1 I'm playing a board game with my brother.
2 My favorite ice cream __________ are chocolate and strawberry.
3 We went to the beach, but __________ the weather was bad.
4 I didn't like the movie. It was too __________.
5 I love __________ food.
6 I traveled in a __________ when I was in China.
7 I'm going to __________ chocolate. I eat too much!
8 Don't __________! It needs to be done carefully!

Listening

2 Listen. Who is the interviewer talking to? 117

3 Listen again and match.

Country		Favorite things
1 India	e	a a mountain
2 China		b the rainforests
3 Australia		c the animals
4 South Africa		d New York
5 South America		e the food
6 North America		f the Great Wall

Speaking

4 Ask and answer. Use the prompts or your own answers.

Would you like to travel around the world?	__________	Yes, I would. / No, I wouldn't.
How long would you like to go for?	__________	One month. / Six months. / One year. / Three years.
Where would you like to go?	I'd like to go to __________.	Asia / Africa / Europe / Australia / North America / South America
What would you take with you?	I'd take my __________.	cell phone / MP3 player / books / schoolwork / diary
What would you miss?	I'd probably miss my __________.	friends / TV / computer / clubs / favorite food

Words in context: *My year around the world*, listening and speaking Unit 12 123

Lesson Six SB page 123

Skills Time!

Skills development

Dictionary: discover meaning of words in context

Listening: listen for specific detail

Speaking: ask and answer questions about world travel

Language

Words in context: *give up, rickshaw, rush, scary, unfortunately, spicy, flavors, board game* (Student Book); *perfect, coral reef, orangutan, market* (Workbook)

Materials

CD 117; Dictionary Workbook pages 128–135

Oxford iTools Digital classroom • Unit 12 • Words, Listening, Speaking

Warmer

- With books closed, ask students what they remember about the blog from the previous lesson.
- Ask questions if necessary, e.g. *What did Sarah and her family decide to do? Where did they go?*

1 Find the words in the text. Write.

- Ask students to look at the words in the box.
- Explain that the words are underlined in the text on page 122.
- Ask students to look at the text again and find the underlined words. They read and try to determine the meanings from context.
- Students then complete the sentences on page 123.

Differentiation

Below level:

- Ask students to close their Student Books, take out their Workbooks, and turn to page 128. Divide students into teams. Tell students you are going to say a word, and they have to find it in the dictionary. Whoever finds it first, gets a point. Say each of the vocabulary words. The team with the most points wins.

At level:

- Play *Write one thing* (see page 9) to practice the vocabulary. Use the topics below: *my favorite board game, a scary memory, something I'd like to give up, a flavor I love*

Above level:

- Ask students to write a sentence for each new word. If time permits, students share with the class.

ANSWERS

1. board game 2. flavors 3. unfortunately 4. scary 5. spicy 6. rickshaw 7. give up 8. rush

2 Listen. Who is the interviewer talking to? 117

- Tell students to listen to someone being interviewed about their travels and find out who is talking.
- Play the whole recording. Then elicit the answer.

ANSWER

The interviewer is talking to Sarah.

3 Listen again and match.

- Tell students they are going to listen to the recording again. Ask them to match each country to Sarah's favorite thing there.
- Before playing the recording, allow time for students to read the lists.
- Play the recording as many times as necessary, pausing for students to write the letters.

ANSWERS

1. e 2. f 3. b 4. c 5. a 6. d

4 Ask and answer. Use the prompts or your own answers.

- Ask students to look at the example. Choose a confident student and ask him / her questions.
- Ask students to work in pairs. Tell them to take turns to ask their partner questions. Their partner must answer using the prompts or his / her own ideas.

Further practice

Workbook page 115

Unit 12 Speaking skills worksheet, Assessment and Resource CD-ROM

Online Practice • Unit 12 • Words in context, Listening, and Speaking

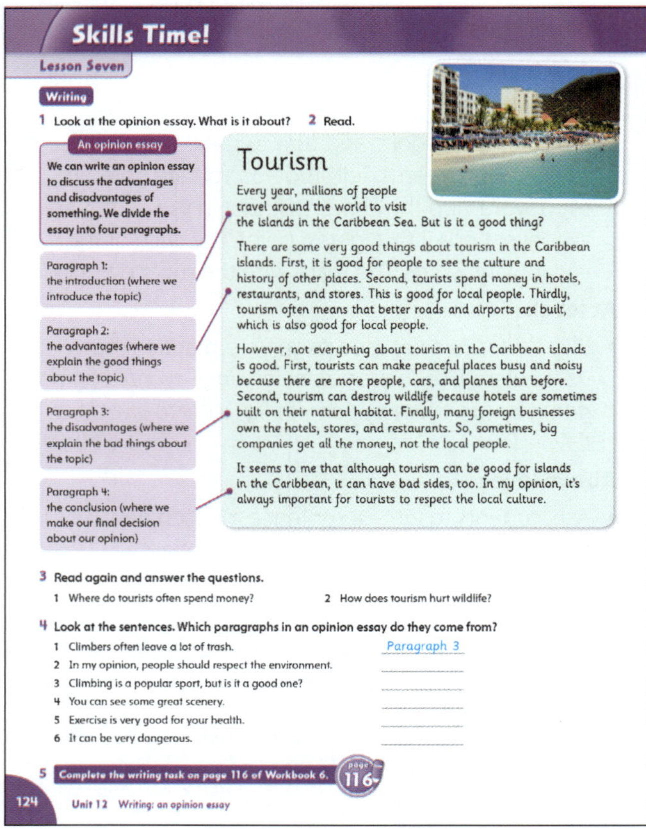

Skills Time!

Lesson Seven

Writing

1 Look at the opinion essay. What is it about? 2 Read.

An opinion essay

We can write an opinion essay to discuss the advantages and disadvantages of something. We divide the essay into four paragraphs.

Paragraph 1: the introduction (where we introduce the topic)

Paragraph 2: the advantages (where we explain the good things about the topic)

Paragraph 3: the disadvantages (where we explain the bad things about the topic)

Paragraph 4: the conclusion (where we make our final decision about our opinion)

Tourism

Every year, millions of people travel around the world to visit the islands in the Caribbean Sea. But is it a good thing?

There are some very good things about tourism in the Caribbean islands. First, it is good for people to see the culture and history of other places. Second, tourists spend money in hotels, restaurants, and stores. This is good for local people. Thirdly, tourism often means that better roads and airports are built, which is also good for local people.

However, not everything about tourism in the Caribbean islands is good. First, tourists can make peaceful places busy and noisy because there are more people, cars, and planes than before. Second, tourism can destroy wildlife because hotels are sometimes built on their natural habitat. Finally, many foreign businesses own the hotels, stores, and restaurants. So, sometimes, big companies get all the money, not the local people.

It seems to me that although tourism can be good for islands in the Caribbean, it can have bad sides, too. In my opinion, it's always important for tourists to respect the local culture.

3 Read again and answer the questions.

1 Where do tourists often spend money?
2 How does tourism hurt wildlife?

4 Look at the sentences. Which paragraphs in an opinion essay do they come from?

1 Climbers often leave a lot of trash. Paragraph 3
2 In my opinion, people should respect the environment. ______
3 Climbing is a popular sport, but is it a good one? ______
4 You can see some great scenery. ______
5 Exercise is very good for your health. ______
6 It can be very dangerous. ______

5 Complete the writing task on page 116 of Workbook 6. page 116

124 Unit 12 Writing: an opinion essay

Lesson Seven SB page 124

Skills Time!

Skills development

Writing focus: structure an opinion essay

Writing outcome: write an opinion essay

Language

Recycled: vocabulary and structures seen previously

Extra: *essay, tourism, advantage, disadvantage, paragraph, respect (v)*

Materials

Writing poster 12; a copy of the text from poster 12, Assessment and Resource CD-ROM, for each student

Oxford iTools Digital classroom • Unit 12 • Writing

Warmer

- Ask students what tourism is. Elicit types of tourism in your country. Ask students *Do you think tourism is good or bad? Why?*

Poster 12: An opinion essay

- Hand out the text from the poster to each student.
- Ask students the "Before reading" question. Encourage them to discuss and share their ideas.
- Ask students to read the text silently. Ask comprehension questions, e.g. *What are the good / bad things about tourism?*
- Read the text boxes on the left-hand side. Ask *How many paragraphs do we divide an opinion essay into? What do we write in paragraph 1 / 2 / 3 / 4?*
- Read the first text box on the right. Ask students to look at the text and find examples of language used to express the writer's opinion.
- Read the rest of the text boxes to the class.
- Put students in pairs. They ask and answer the "After reading" questions. Discuss some of their answers.

1 Look at the opinion essay. What is it about?

- Ask students to look at the picture and the title of the essay. Ask the gist question.

ANSWER

The essay is about tourism.

2 Read.

- Ask a different student to read each paragraph to the class. Ask comprehension questions, e.g. *How many people visit the Caribbean islands every year?*
- Draw attention to the text boxes to the left of the essay. Choose a different student to read aloud each text box.

3 Read again and answer the questions.

- Students read the text silently and answer the questions.

Differentiation

Below level:

- Ask students to re-read the essay and write down three good and three bad things about tourism in the Caribbean.

At level:

- Students complete the activity.

Above level:

- Put students in groups and ask them to think of a topic for an opinion essay. Ask them to outline their essay, using the format from the "at level" activity.

ANSWERS

Tourists often spend money in hotels, restaurants and shops.
Tourism can hurt wildlife because hotels are sometimes built on their natural habitat.

4 Look at the sentences. Which paragraphs in an opinion essay do they come from?

- Remind students of the essay's structure. Ask *What do we write in the first / second / third / fourth paragraphs?*
- Ask students to read the sentences and write down the paragraphs they are taken from.

ANSWERS

1. Paragraph 3 2. Paragraph 4 3. Paragraph 1
4. Paragraph 2 5. Paragraph 2 6. Paragraph 3

5 Complete the writing task on page 116 of Workbook 6.

- Refer students to the Workbook to complete the writing task. Go through the activity with them first.

Further practice

Workbook page 116

Unit 12 Writing skills worksheet, Assessment and Resource CD-ROM

Online Practice • Unit 12 • Writing

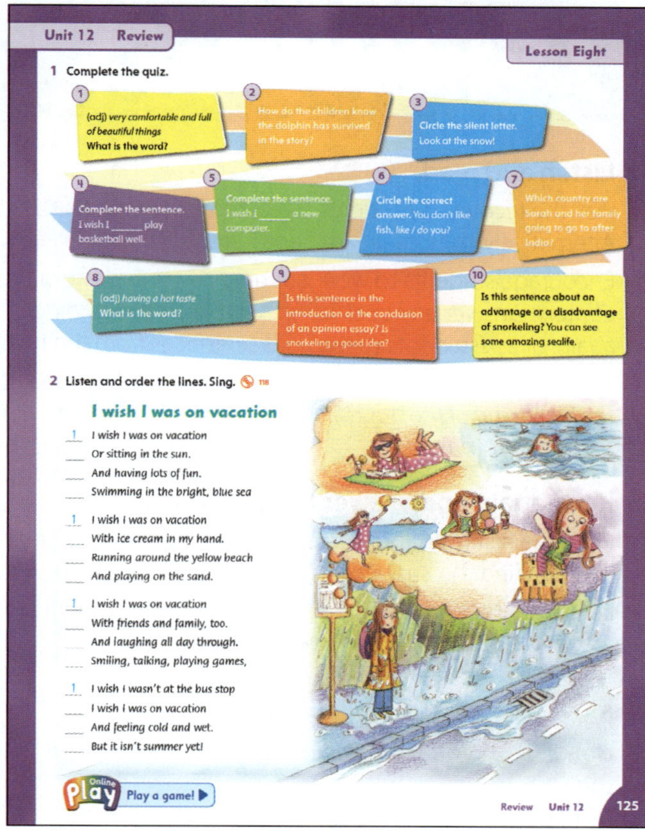
Unit 12 Review

Lesson Eight

1 Complete the quiz.

1. (adj) *very comfortable and full of beautiful things* What is the word?
2. How do the children know the dolphin has survived in the story?
3. Circle the silent letter. Look at the snow!
4. Complete the sentence. I wish I ______ play basketball well.
5. Complete the sentence. I wish I ______ a new computer.
6. Circle the correct answer. You don't like fish, *like / do* you?
7. Which country are Sarah and her family going to go to after India?
8. (adj) *having a hot taste* What is the word?
9. Is this sentence in the introduction or the conclusion of an opinion essay? Is snorkeling a good idea?
10. Is this sentence about an advantage or a disadvantage of snorkeling? You can see some amazing sealife.

2 Listen and order the lines. Sing. 118

I wish I was on vacation

1 I wish I was on vacation
___ Or sitting in the sun.
___ And having lots of fun.
___ Swimming in the bright, blue sea

1 I wish I was on vacation
___ With ice cream in my hand.
___ Running around the yellow beach
___ And playing on the sand.

1 I wish I was on vacation
___ With friends and family, too.
___ And laughing all day through.
___ Smiling, talking, playing games,

1 I wish I wasn't at the bus stop
___ I wish I was on vacation
___ And feeling cold and wet.
___ But it isn't summer yet!

Online Play Play a game!

Review Unit 12 125

Lesson Eight SB page 125

Unit 12 Review

Learning outcomes

To review vocabulary and structures practiced previously

To use vocabulary and structures from the unit in the context of a song

Language

Recycled: vocabulary and structures seen previously

Extra: *bus stop*

Materials

CD 118, pieces of paper (optional)

Oxford iTools Digital classroom • Unit 12 • Review

Warmer

- Play *Book race* (see page 8). Read these sentences and give students 20 seconds to find each one:
  This is going to be a fantastic vacation! (Lesson 4)
  You saved its life. (Lesson 1)
  What an amazing place! (Lesson 5)
  There are some very good things about tourism in the Caribbean islands. (Lesson 7)
  You packed your sunglasses, didn't you? (Lesson 4)
  How much longer can it survive on land? (Lesson 1)
  We went on an elephant ride! (Lesson 5)
  I wish I could fly. (Lesson 3)

1 Complete the quiz.

- Students work individually, in pairs, or in teams to answer the quiz, without referring to the unit.

ANSWERS

1. luxurious 2. Because they see it the next day with its family. 3. Look at the sno(w). 4. could 5. had 6. do 7. Sri Lanka 8. spicy 9. the introduction 10. an advantage

2 Listen and order the lines. Sing. 118

- Focus students' attention on the picture. Ask *What is the girl doing? What does she wish she was doing?*
- Tell students the words are in their books, but the lines are in the wrong order. Ask students to read silently.
- Play the song. Students listen and point to each line.
- Play the song again, pausing for students to number the lines in order.
- Play the recording a third time. Students complete their answers.
- Review answers. Ask a different student to read each line.
- Play the recording once more. Students sing along.

Differentiation

Below level:

- Put students into groups. Assign each group a phrase, e.g. *sitting in the sun, playing on the sand.* Students decide on actions for their phrases. Then play the song. Students stand and do their action when they hear their phrase.

At level:

- Write each verse on pieces of paper. Leave blanks for key words. Divide the class into three groups to play a memory game. Ask students to close their books. Ask students to work together to fill in the missing words. Play the song again to check answers.

Above level:

- Divide the class into four groups, one for each verse. Give each group a piece of paper. Students work together to recall the verse and write it down. Monitor and help. Students open their books to check answers.

ANSWERS

Verse 1: 1, 4, 2, 3
Verse 2: 1, 3, 2, 4
Verse 3: 1, 2, 4, 3
Verse 4: 1, 3, 2, 4

Further practice

Workbook page 117
Unit 12 test, Assessment and Resource CD-ROM
Progress test 4, Assessment and Resource CD-ROM
Skills test 4, Assessment and Resource CD-ROM
Values 4 worksheet, Units 10–12, Assessment and Resource CD-ROM
Writing portfolio 4 worksheet, Assessment and Resource CD-ROM
Progress certificate, Assessment and Resource CD-ROM
Online Practice • Unit 12 • Review

Extensive reading

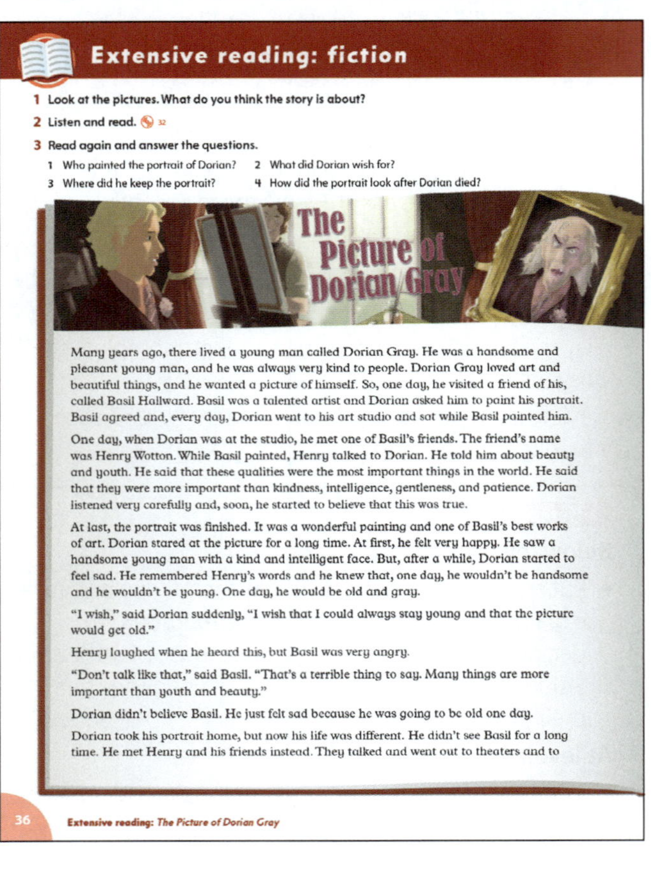

Extensive reading: fiction

1 Look at the pictures. What do you think the story is about?

2 Listen and read. 32

3 Read again and answer the questions.

1 Who painted the portrait of Dorian? 2 What did Dorian wish for?
3 Where did he keep the portrait? 4 How did the portrait look after Dorian died?

The Picture of Dorian Gray

Many years ago, there lived a young man called Dorian Gray. He was a handsome and pleasant young man, and he was always very kind to people. Dorian Gray loved art and beautiful things, and he wanted a picture of himself. So, one day, he visited a friend of his, called Basil Hallward. Basil was a talented artist and Dorian asked him to paint his portrait. Basil agreed and, every day, Dorian went to his art studio and sat while Basil painted him.

One day, when Dorian was at the studio, he met one of Basil's friends. The friend's name was Henry Wotton. While Basil painted, Henry talked to Dorian. He told him about beauty and youth. He said that these qualities were the most important things in the world. He said that they were more important than kindness, intelligence, gentleness, and patience. Dorian listened very carefully and, soon, he started to believe that this was true.

At last, the portrait was finished. It was a wonderful painting and one of Basil's best works of art. Dorian stared at the picture for a long time. At first, he felt very happy. He saw a handsome young man with a kind and intelligent face. But, after a while, Dorian started to feel sad. He remembered Henry's words and he knew that, one day, he wouldn't be handsome and he wouldn't be young. One day, he would be old and gray.

"I wish," said Dorian suddenly, "I wish that I could always stay young and that the picture would get old."

Henry laughed when he heard this, but Basil was very angry.

"Don't talk like that," said Basil. "That's a terrible thing to say. Many things are more important than youth and beauty."

Dorian didn't believe Basil. He just felt sad because he was going to be old one day.

Dorian took his portrait home, but now his life was different. He didn't see Basil for a long time. He met Henry and his friends instead. They talked and went out to theaters and to

36 Extensive reading: *The Picture of Dorian Gray*

Extensive reading: The Picture of Dorian Gray SB pages 36–37

Learning outcomes

To read a fictional text independently

To read and work out meaning through context

Language

Extra: *pleasant, studio, youth, quality (n), kindness, intelligence, gentleness, patience, hard, cruel, lend, cold, selfish, withered*

Materials

CD  32

Culture note: The Picture of Dorian Gray

The Picture of Dorian Gray was written by Oscar Wilde and first published in 1890. The Irish-born author is best known for his plays and collections of short stories.

Warmer

- Ask students to help you compile a list of adjectives describing appearance and personality. Write ideas on the board. Ask which of the adjectives are positive or negative.

1 Look at the pictures. What do you think the story is about?

- Ask students to look at the pictures and describe the portrait using some of the adjectives on the board. Ask what kind of person they think Dorian is.

2 Listen and read. 32

- Play the recording. Students listen and follow the text. Alternatively, they can read silently at this stage.
- Encourage students to work out unknown words from the context. Answer any questions, then play the recording again, or ask students to read out sentences from the text.
- Ask comprehension questions, e.g. *What was Dorian like at the beginning of the story? How did Dorian change? How did the painting change?*

3 Read again and answer the questions.

- Read the first question aloud. Ask students to look at the text and find the answer.
- Let students complete the activity, then invite students to read the questions and answers in pairs.

ANSWERS

1. Basil Hallward painted the picture of Dorian.
2. Dorian wished that he could always stay young and that the picture would get old.
3. Dorian kept the picture locked in a small room.
4. After Dorian died, the picture looked as handsome and young as it had when it was first painted.

4 Discuss.

- Discuss the questions as an open class activity or in groups.

Differentiation

Below level:

- Play *Questions for answers* (see page 9) to check students' story comprehension.

At level:

- Play *Talk!* (see page 9) using the discussion questions as topics. Monitor students' speech.

Above level:

- Extend the "at level" activity to 45 or 60 seconds. Monitor students' speech.

Extensive reading: non-fiction

1 Look at the pictures. Which country do you think this is?

2 Listen and read. 61

Diaries from Delhi

My name's Suzie. I'm eighteen years old and I'm a student from London. Three weeks ago, I was teaching English in a language school in Tokyo. The job ended, and I decided to take a holiday! I wanted to travel around the world. I put some clothes in a backpack, found my passport, bought a new pair of trainers and said goodbye to my friends. I was sad to go, but I was looking forward to my new adventure.

I've always wanted to go to India, so I bought a ticket to Delhi. I caught a taxi to the airport. I remember feeling really nervous. Was I doing the right thing? Should I stay in Tokyo? Or maybe I should go back home to London? I phoned my mum from the airport and she told me not to worry. If I wasn't happy, she said, I could give it up and come home. I sat on the aeroplane feeling a bit happier. I watched a few films and the time passed quickly. I chatted to the people around me and, by the time we arrived, I'd made some new friends. One of them was from Delhi. She gave me the address of a hotel and that's where I spent my first night.

The next day, I explored Old Delhi, which is the traditional part of the city. Chandni Chowk is the main street. It's very busy, full of cars, cycle rickshaws, hand-pulled carts, people and animals. You can find the oldest and busiest markets in India here, selling all kinds of things, including jewellery, material, perfume and, of course, street food. I love *golgappa* which is a kind of bread filled with chickpeas and spicy potatoes. Indian sweets are delicious, too.

One of the most interesting places I've visited in Delhi is Humayun's Tomb. This monument looks a bit like the famous Taj Mahal in Agra, but it's older. The tomb was built in 1570. It's a very beautiful building and is surrounded by beautiful gardens. Another great place to go is the Red Fort, which was built in 1638. You can see a sound and light show in the evening, which is really amazing.

I'm going to spend a few more days in Delhi because I love it so much. Tomorrow, I'm planning to visit the National Museum because I've heard that the art is fantastic. After that, I'll be back on the road! I'll let you know where I decide to go.

Bye for now!

Suzie

66 Extensive reading: *Diaries from Delhi*

Extensive reading: Diaries from Delhi SB pages 66–67

Learning outcomes

To read diary entries about Delhi independently

To read and work out meaning through context

Language

Extra: *cycle rickshaws, hand-pulled carts, chickpeas, tomb, cab, bazaar, candy, temple, mosque*

Materials

CD  61

Warmer

- Ask students which places they have traveled to and which places they would like to travel to.
- Tell students that they are going to read diary entries about an interesting place in this lesson. Ask if they keep diaries and what kind of things they write about in their diaries.

1 Look at the pictures. Which country do you think this is?

- Ask students to look at the photos and describe what they can see and what the people are doing in each photo.
- Ask students to guess which country the photos show.

2 Listen and read. 61

- Play the recording. Students listen and follow the text. Alternatively, students can read silently at this stage.
- Encourage students to work out unknown words from the context. Answer any questions, then play the recording again, or ask students to read out sentences from the text.
- Ask comprehension questions, e.g. *Where was Suzie three weeks ago? What transport did Suzie see in Old Delhi? Which places as Suzie visited?*

3 Read again and complete the chart. All the words are in the diaries.

- Ask students where Suzie is from (London) and where Joe is from (New York). Explain that some words are different in British English and American English, but they have the same meanings. Ask students what differences they can think of between British English and American English, e.g. *store/shop, pavement/sidewalk, mobile phone/cell phone.*
- Point to the word *holiday* in the chart. Ask students to find the word in Suzie's diary, then ask them to find the word *vacation* in Joe's diary.
- Let students complete the activity, then invite them to read the words in the chart aloud. As an extension, ask students to close their books and play a memory game in teams. A student from Team A says a word from the chart (e.g. *sweets*). A student from Team B says whether the word is British or American English, then says the matching word (e.g. *candy*). Repeat with students from each team in turn, awarding one point for each correct answer.

ANSWERS

1. trainers 2. mum 3. films 4. cab 5. airplane 6. candy

4 Discuss.

- Discuss the questions as an open class activity or in groups.

Differentiation

Below level:

- Play *Questions for answers* (see page 9) to check students' story comprehension.

At level:

- Play *Talk!* (see page 9) using the discussion questions as topics. Monitor students' speech.

Above level:

- Extend the "at level" activity to 45 or 60 seconds. Monitor students' speech.

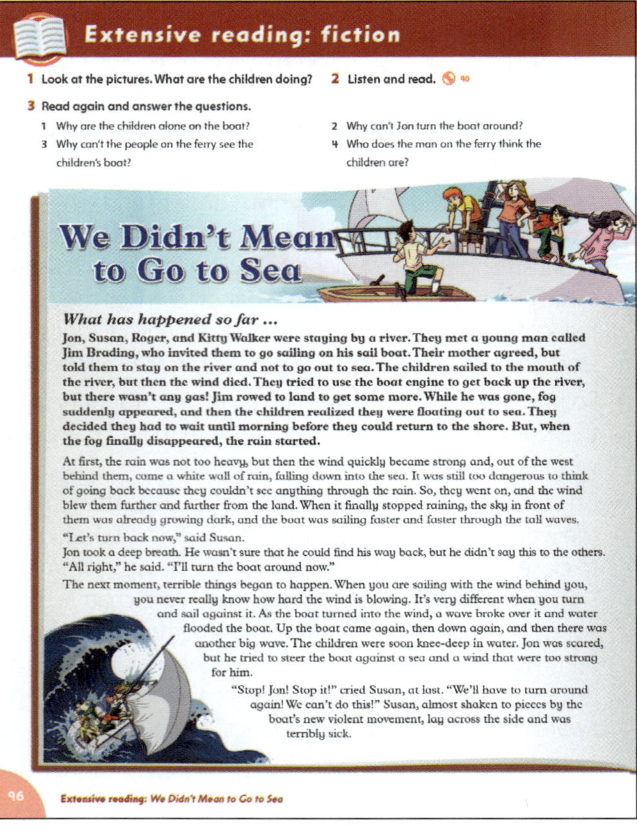

Extensive reading: fiction

1 Look at the pictures. What are the children doing?

2 Listen and read. 90

3 Read again and answer the questions.

1 Why are the children alone on the boat?

2 Why can't Jon turn the boat around?

3 Why can't the people on the ferry see the children's boat?

4 Who does the man on the ferry think the children are?

We Didn't Mean to Go to Sea

What has happened so far ...

Jon, Susan, Roger, and Kitty Walker were staying by a river. They met a young man called Jim Brading, who invited them to go sailing on his sail boat. Their mother agreed, but told them to stay on the river and not to go out to sea. The children sailed to the mouth of the river, but then the wind died. They tried to use the boat engine to get back up the river, but there wasn't any gas! Jim rowed to land to get some more. While he was gone, fog suddenly appeared, and then the children realized they were floating out to sea. They decided they had to wait until morning before they could return to the shore. But, when the fog finally disappeared, the rain started.

At first, the rain was not too heavy, but then the wind quickly became strong and, out of the west behind them, came a white wall of rain, falling down into the sea. It was still too dangerous to think of going back because they couldn't see anything through the rain. So, they went on, and the wind blew them further and further from the land. When it finally stopped raining, the sky in front of them was already growing dark, and the boat was sailing faster and faster through the tall waves.

"Let's turn back now," said Susan.

Jon took a deep breath. He wasn't sure that he could find his way back, but he didn't say this to the others. "All right," he said. "I'll turn the boat around now."

The next moment, terrible things began to happen. When you are sailing with the wind behind you, you never really know how hard the wind is blowing. It's very different when you turn and sail against it. As the boat turned into the wind, a wave broke over it and water flooded the boat. Up the boat came again, then down again, and then there was another big wave. The children were soon knee-deep in water. Jon was scared, but he tried to steer the boat against a sea and a wind that were too strong for him.

"Stop! Jon! Stop it!" cried Susan, at last. "We'll have to turn around again! We can't do this!" Susan, almost shaken to pieces by the boat's new violent movement, lay across the side and was terribly sick.

96 Extensive reading: *We Didn't Mean to Go to Sea*

Extensive reading: We Didn't Mean To Go To Sea

SB pages 96–97

Learning outcomes

To read an excerpt from a story independently

To read and work out meaning through context

Language

Extra: *invite, die, appear, wave (n), turn back, turn around, against, steer, shaken to pieces, violent, course, cabin, pump (n), rise, seasick, horn, in one piece*

Materials

CD 90

Culture notes

We Didn't Mean to Go to Sea was written in 1937 by Arthur Ransome. It is the seventh book in his *Swallows and Amazons* series of adventure books for children.

Warmer

- Ask students if they have ever been on a sailing boat. Ask them to share their experiences with the class. Was it exciting / fun / scary?
- Ask the class to think about what the dangers of sailing might be. Ask *What could go wrong?*

1 Look at the pictures. What are the children doing?

- Ask students to look at the pictures. Point to each one and ask *What are the children doing? What has happened?*
- Encourage students to predict what the story is about.

2 Listen and read. 90

- Play the recording. Students listen and follow the text. Alternatively, students can read silently at this stage.
- Encourage students to work out unknown words from the context. Answer any questions they have, then play the recording again.
- Ask comprehension questions, e.g. *What did Jim Brading invite the children to do? Why did the boat go out to sea? Why couldn't Jon turn the boat around?*

3 Read again and answer the questions.

- Look at the first question together. Ask students to look at the first paragraph again and find the sentence that tells them why the children are alone on the boat.
- Ask students to read the whole text again and answer the rest of the questions.

ANSWERS

1. The children are alone because Jim had to row to land to get more petrol.
2. Jon can't turn the boat around because the wind is too strong.
3. The people on the ferry can't see the children's boat because there aren't any lights on it.
4. The man on the ferry thinks the children are fishermen.

4 Discuss.

- Discuss the questions as an open class activity or in groups.

Differentiation

Below level:

- Play *Questions for answers* (see page 9) to check students' story comprehension.

At level:

- Play *Talk!* (see page 9) using the discussion questions as topics. Monitor students' speech.

Above level:

- Extend the "at level" activity to 45 or 60 seconds. Monitor students' speech.

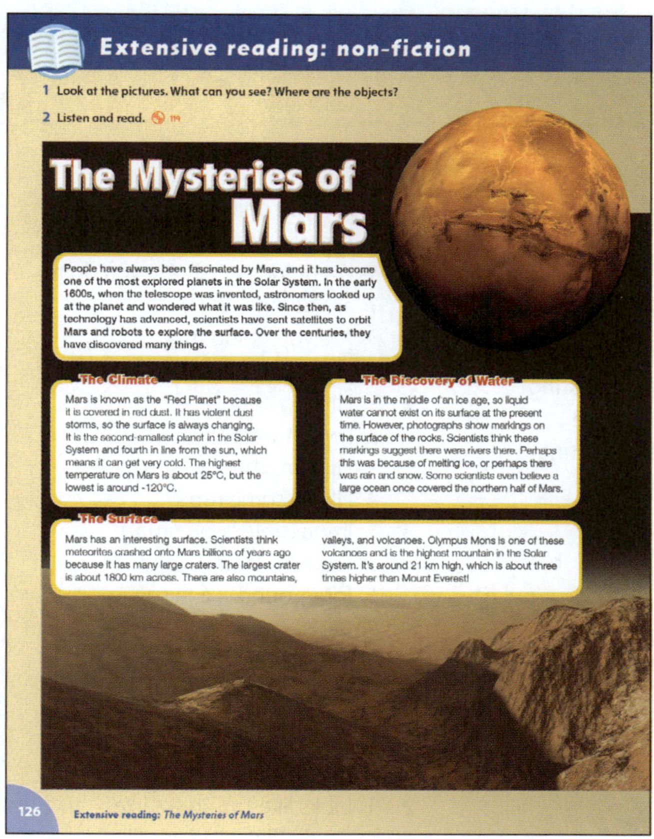

Extensive reading: non-fiction

1 Look at the pictures. What can you see? Where are the objects?

2 Listen and read. 119

The Mysteries of Mars

People have always been fascinated by Mars, and it has become one of the most explored planets in the Solar System. In the early 1600s, when the telescope was invented, astronomers looked up at the planet and wondered what it was like. Since then, as technology has advanced, scientists have sent satellites to orbit Mars and robots to explore the surface. Over the centuries, they have discovered many things.

The Climate

Mars is known as the "Red Planet" because it is covered in red dust. It has violent dust storms, so the surface is always changing. It is the second-smallest planet in the Solar System and fourth in line from the sun, which means it can get very cold. The highest temperature on Mars is about 25°C, but the lowest is around -120°C.

The Discovery of Water

Mars is in the middle of an ice age, so liquid water cannot exist on its surface at the present time. However, photographs show markings on the surface of the rocks. Scientists think these markings suggest there were rivers there. Perhaps this was because of melting ice, or perhaps there was rain and snow. Some scientists even believe a large ocean once covered the northern half of Mars.

The Surface

Mars has an interesting surface. Scientists think meteorites crashed onto Mars billions of years ago because it has many large craters. The largest crater is about 1800 km across. There are also mountains, valleys, and volcanoes. Olympus Mons is one of these volcanoes and is the highest mountain in the Solar System. It's around 21 km high, which is about three times higher than Mount Everest!

126 Extensive reading: *The Mysteries of Mars*

Extensive reading: The Mysteries of Mars

SB pages 126–127

Learning outcomes

To read a factual text about Mars

To read independently and work out meaning through context

Language

Extra: *fascinated, astronomers, orbit, surface, dust, ice age, markings, meteorites, craters, mission, unmanned, launch (v), remote-controlled, rover, trapped, computerized, geology, commercial, intention, demand (n), reality*

Materials

CD  119

Warmer

- Ask students to name the planets in the solar system. Ask if they know the names of any of the planets in English. Write their answers on the board. Ask students what they know about these planets.
- Tell students that they are going to read about a planet in this lesson.

1 Look at the pictures. What can you see? Where are the objects?

- Ask students to look at the pictures and name the items they can see. Ask where they think the objects are (on Mars).

2 Listen and read. 119

- Play the recording. Students listen and follow the text in their Class Books. Alternatively, they can read silently at this stage.
- Encourage students to work out unknown words from the context. Answer any questions they have, then play the recording again, or ask students to read out sentences from the text.
- Ask comprehension questions, e.g. *What is the climate like on Mars? Why do scientists think that there was once water on Mars? What can you see on the surface of Mars?*

3 Read again and answer the questions.

- Read out the first question. Ask students to look at the text and find the answer.
- Let students complete the activity, then invite students to read out the questions and answers in pairs. As an extension, you can ask students to think of more questions about the text for their partner, or play a quiz game in two teams.

ANSWERS

1. Mars is called the "Red Planet" because it is covered in red dust.
2. Olympus Mons is a volcano.
3. The first spacecraft to land on Mars was called Viking 1.
4. Curiosity landed on Mars in 2012.

4 Discuss.

- Discuss the questions as an open class activity or in groups.

Differentiation

Below level:

- Play *Questions for answers* (see page 9) to check students' story comprehension.

At level:

- Play *Talk!* (see page 9) using the discussion questions as topics. Monitor students' speech.

Above level:

- Extend the "at level" activity to 45 or 60 seconds. Monitor students' speech.

Workbook answer key

Starter

Page 2

1 1 Fin 2 Libby 3 Kate
4 Fin / Libby 5 Libby / Fin
6 Tom 7 Tom 8 Fin

2 a play, costumes b river, park
c first aid, helped d soccer, seats
e time, future

Page 3

3 1 vacation / play 2 Jim / Fin
3 country / town 4 clean / dirty
5 horse / bike 6 piano / soccer

4 1 They went to Florida.
2 Fin and Libby
3 Do Something Different
4 Tom 5 Canada

5 1 Club 2 cousins 3 year
4 capsule 5 cleaned 6 learned
7 joined 8 cap

Page 4

1 1 I'm watching 2 I'm not enjoying
3 isn't winning 4 is doing
5 Do you want
6 I don't like

2 1 Two boys were kicking a soccer ball.
2 The woman was reading a book.
3 Two children were riding (their) bikes.
4 The woman was drinking coffee.
5 The man was carrying a shopping bag.
6 The ducks were eating bread.

3 1 was doing 2 were playing
3 arrived 4 was driving
5 was looking 6 started
7 was studying, called
8 were traveling, stopped

Page 5

1 1 did, done 2 made, made
3 eat, eaten 4 break, broke
5 spoke, spoken 6 sell, sold
7 swim, swam 8 ride, rode

2 1 broken 2 spoke 3 swam
4 done 5 ate 6 ridden

3 1 took 2 flown 3 wore
4 ridden 5 seen 6 went

Unit 1

Page 6

1 1 paint, walls 2 impossible, draw
3 famous, world 4 know
5 meet, library

2 a 3 b 5 c 1 d 4 e 2

3 1 b 2 a 3 c 4 b

4 Students' own answers

Page 7

1 1 art gallery 2 mural
3 sculptures 4 paintings
5 portraits 6 landscape

2 1 unlucky 2 unhappy
3 immature 4 uninteresting

3 1 unpopular 2 impolite
3 unhappy 4 uninteresting
5 immature 6 unlucky

Page 8

1 1 h 2 e 3 a 4 c 5 b
6 d 7 f 8 g

2 1 'm going to call
2 are going to paint
3 is going to make
4 aren't going to play
5 's going to meet
6 'm going to buy
7 isn't going to come
8 're going to start

3 1 are going to 2 'll 3 'll
4 'll 5 is going to 6 'll
7 is going to 8 'm going to

Page 9

1 1 Are 2 meeting 3 I'm not
4 is 5 We're having 6 are you

2 1 is having 2 is meeting
3 are catching 4 starts
5 are having 6 are taking

3 1 Where is Tony visiting with his class? He's visiting an art gallery.
2 What time are they meeting? They're meeting at 9.00 a.m.
3 How are they traveling? They're traveling by train.
4 Where are they having lunch? They're having lunch in the garden.
5 What are they doing after lunch? They're taking a boat trip after lunch.

Page 10

1 b) An adventure on the river

2 a 2 b 6 c 5 d 1 e 4 f 3

Page 11

1 1 row 2 tie 3 floating 4 hit
5 staring 6 smoke

2 1 bank 2 oars 3 lightning
4 grab

3 1 bank 2 smoke 3 oars
4 floating 5 hit 6 splash

Page 12

1 a fire

3 Students' own answers

Page 13

1 1 Are you going to 2 I'll
3 Are you going to 4 I'm not
5 I'm going to 6 Are you doing
7 are going 8 I'll
9 Are you going to
10 I'm not

2 1 I'll help her.
2 I won't wear this.
3 I'll paint the sky.
4 I'll use some rope.

3 1 impossible 2 staring
3 mural 4 landscape
5 foreground 6 a sun
7 tie 8 oars

Fluency Time! 1

Page 14

1 1 b 2 d 3 a 4 c

2 1 looks like 2 looks like
3 smells like 4 feels like

3 Students' own answers

Page 15

1 1 False 2 True 3 False
4 True 5 False

2 Students' own answers

3 Students' own answers

4 Students' own answers

Unit 2

Page 16

1 a 4 b 1 c 5 d 3 e 2

2 1 False 2 True 3 False
4 True 5 False 6 False

3 1 mural 2 world 3 library
4 countries 5 pictures
6 terrible

Page 17

1 1 ice skating 2 skiing
3 baseball 4 ice hockey
5 mountain biking 6 caving
7 rock climbing 8 paragliding

2 1 disagree 2 incomplete
3 disappear 4 invisible

3 1 invisible 2 dishonest
3 incomplete 4 correct
5 disagree 6 sensitive
7 disappears 8 disobeys

Page 18

1 1 we'll 2 isn't 3 I'll
4 I won't be 5 You'll

2 1 'll make 2 see 3 won't go
4 'll finish 5 Will, wear

3 1 If it rains, we'll play in the gym.
2 If we repair my bike, I'll ride it this afternoon.
3 If the rain doesn't stop, the game won't start.
4 If she isn't careful, she'll fall down.
5 If their goalkeeper catches the ball, they'll win.
6 If it doesn't snow this year, we won't go skiing.

Page 19

1 1 d 2 c 3 e 4 a 5 b
2 1 'd buy 2 lived 3 'd travel
4 was 5 played 6 joined, 'd play
7 had, 'd buy 8 went, 'd take
3 Students' own answers

Page 20

1 c) He's working for an environmental group.
2 1 True 2 True 3 False 4 False
5 True 6 False

Page 21

1 1 freedom 2 snorkeling
3 talented 4 equipment
5 wildlife 6 pearl
2 1 skills 2 provide 3 protect
4 volunteer
3 1 volunteer 2 provide
3 equipment 4 skills 5 protect
6 snorkeling

Page 22

1 1 What is sailing? 2 How to learn
3 Safety 4 Equipment
2 Students' own answers

Page 23

1 1 rock climbing 2 equipment
3 baseball 4 ice skating
5 dislike 6 snorkeling
7 inexperienced
2 1 will, help 2 'll use 3 will, come
4 will, do 5 won't win 6 is
3 1 'd ride it in the mountains
2 'd score lots of goals
3 lived in Switzerland
4 went paragliding
5 wouldn't go with them

Health Time!

Page 24

1 c
2 1 False. It lasts for four hours.
2 True 3 True
4 False. You can pick up a spider if you want to.
5 False. Diego found that breathing slowly helped.
6 False. Diego knew that the spider wasn't dangerous.

Page 25

1 1 snakes 2 quickly
3 breathing 4 Blood, brain
5 more slowly 6 more
2 1 responses 2 concentrate
3 heart 4 muscles 5 pupil
6 digestive 7 palms
3 1 bites 2 proves 3 course
4 chest
4 Students' own answers

Unit 3

Page 26

1 1 late 2 pictures 3 sports
4 buildings 5 likes
2 a 5 b 3 c 1 d 2 e 6 f 4
3 1 difficult / easy
2 murals / drawings
3 unhappy / happy
4 month / week
5 ideas / food

Page 27

1 1 traditional 2 delicious
3 disgusting 4 original
5 deserted 6 bright
2 1 luxurious 2 mountainous
3 mysterious
3 1 dangerous 2 adventurous
3 mysterious 4 poisonous
5 furious 6 hazardous
7 mountainous 8 luxurious

Page 28

1 1 just 2 already 3 yet
4 yet 5 just
2 1 before 2 just 3 already
4 before 5 already 6 yet
3 1 've lived, since
2 've studied, for
3 haven't seen, since
4 haven't eaten, since
5 hasn't rained, for
6 has worked, since
7 has played, since
8 haven't been, for

Page 29

1 1 Have you ever been
2 went 3 We rode
4 Have you ever done
5 've had 6 did you go 7 was
2 1 Has he ever tried skiing?
2 When did he go skiing?
3 Has he ever seen the Red Sea?
4 What did he do there?
5 Has he ever visited New York?
6 When did he go to New York?
3 Students' own answers

Page 30

1 b) Celebrating the chili!
2 1 e 2 b 3 a 4 d 5 f 6 c

Page 31

1 1 dish 2 demonstration
3 garlic 4 celebrated 5 lasted
2 1 on the floor 2 music
3 eat 4 melons
3 1 celebrate 2 bricks
3 demonstrations 4 recipes
5 decorate 6 desserts
7 lasts 8 hang 9 bunches

Page 32

1 Students' own answers
2 Students' own answers
3 Students' own answers

Page 33

1 1 for, since 2 since, for
3 for, since 4 for, since
2 1 've already been
2 've never tasted
3 Have, ever tried
4 went 5 ate 6 tried
7 enjoyed 8 've met
3 1 amazing 2 awful
3 deserted 4 bright
5 original 6 traditional
7 disgusting 8 delicious

Unit 4

Page 34

1 1 b 2 c 3 e 4 a 5 d
2 1 future 2 ideas 3 drawing
4 transportation 5 date 6 club
7 best 8 visitors
3 1 True 2 False 3 True 4 False

Page 35

1 A motorcycle, truck
B yacht, barge
C hot-air balloon, helicopter
1 motorcycle 2 truck 3 yacht
4 barge 5 helicopter
6 hot-air balloon
2 1 c 2 a 3 d 4 b
3 1 look for 2 look up
3 look up to 4 look after
5 look into 6 look ahead

Page 36

1 1 since 2 all 3 for 4 for
5 all 6 all
2 1 have been sailing
2 has been driving
3 have been using
4 has been traveling
5 has been riding
6 have been flying

3 1 She's been studying for four hours.
2 He's been painting all day.
3 You've been watching TV since lunchtime.
4 Jack's been waiting at the station for 50 minutes.
5 They've been playing chess since two o'clock.
6 We've been cooking all morning.

4 a 4 b 1 c 6 d 2 e 5 f 3

Page 37

1 1 d 2 e 3 b 4 f 5 c 6 a

2 1 you've 2 been 3 repairing
4 been 5 has 6 camping

3 1 Has Mom been doing the shopping? Yes, she has.
2 Has Dad been washing the car? No, he hasn't.
3 Have Mick and Greg been playing tennis? No, they haven't.
4 Has Joanna been drawing pictures? Yes, she has.
5 Have the neighbors been working in the yard? Yes, they have.
6 Has it been raining? No, it hasn't.

Page 38

1 b) Across the desert by camel

2 1 True 2 True 3 False 4 False
5 False 6 True

Page 39

1 1 mud 2 loads 3 ideal
4 Local 5 private 6 balance

2 1 sand dunes 2 4 x 4 vehicle
3 package 4 railroad

3 1 railroad 2 connects
3 packages 4 balance 5 loads
6 mud 7 ideal 8 4 x 4

Page 40

1 a saddle b pedals c handlebar
d wheels e chain f brake

2 Students' own answers

3 Students' own answers

Page 41

1 1 a 2 c 3 a 4 b 5 c 6 b

2 1 have, been doing
2 've been working
3 Have, been studying
4 haven't
5 Have, been painting
6 has been making

3 1 We've been traveling since 9.30.
2 I've been reading my book since ten o'clock.
3 My brother has been watching a movie for 20 minutes.
4 Mom has been sleeping for an hour.
5 Dad has been doing puzzles since 10:30.
6 We've been flying over the ocean for ten minutes.

Fluency Time! 2

Page 42

1 1 c 2 f 3 a 4 d 5 b
6 g 7 e

2 1 special 2 don't 3 sure
4 wants 5 love

3 1 Are you doing anything special on Sunday?
2 Why don't you come with us?
3 I'm not sure
4 Mom wants to go shopping with me.
5 We're going to the café.
6 I'd love to.

Page 43

1 1 They're at school.
2 They're wearing their own clothes.
3 Because her mom wants her to go shopping.
4 Yes, she does.
5 Yes, he does.

2 anything special, Why don't, not sure, to go shopping, Can you, love to, See you

3 Students' own answers

4 Students' own answers

Unit 5

Page 44

1 1 Inventions 2 1970s 3 three
4 bike 5 fly

2 1 b 2 e 3 d 4 a 5 c

3 Students' own answers

Page 45

1 1 invented 2 discovered
3 devices 4 inspiration
5 designed 6 experiments

2 1 enjoyment 2 payment
3 development 4 entertainment

3 1 enjoyment 2 arrangement
3 entertainment 4 payment
5 development 6 equipment

Page 46

1 1 was 2 was 3 is 4 was
5 was 6 wasn't 7 are 8 were

2 1 are enjoyed 2 was invented
3 were brought 4 were put
5 was made 6 was opened
7 are sold

3 Students' own answers

Page 47

1 1 P 2 A 3 P 4 P 5 A

2 1 is being built
2 is being cooked
3 is being washed
4 are being painted
5 is not being used

3 1 Clothes are being washed.
2 A wall is being painted.
3 Ice cream is being sold.
4 Photos are being taken.
5 Pizzas are being made.
6 A car is being repaired.

Page 48

1 a) graphite c) clay

2 1 a 2 a 3 b 4 a 5 c 6 b

Page 49

1 1 clay 2 sharp 3 hollow
4 reservoir 5 nibs 6 rotates

2 1 string 2 underwater 3 rod
4 press

3 1 rod 2 string 3 rotates
4 hollow 5 sharp 6 underwater

Page 50

1 1 To begin with, phones were made of metal and wood.
2 In 1876, the first telephone call was made.
3 Soon after, Bell Telephone Company was started.
4 During the late 1870s, telephone systems lines were installed in most American cities.
5 In 1891, the first phone call was made to another country.

2 Students' own answers

Page 51

1 1 Glasses were invented in 1248. Today, they are worn by many people to help them see better.
2 This building was designed by a Spanish artist called Gaudí. Today, it is visited by many tourists.
3 This machine is used to cut bread. It was invented in 1928.
4 X-rays were discovered in 1895. Now they are used by doctors to look at bones.

2 a 3 b 1 c 2 d 4

3 1 Experiments 2 device
3 reservoir 4 press 5 clay
6 achievement

Science Time!

Page 52

1 C, B, D, A

2 1 non-renewable 2 Coal 3 wind
4 working out 5 panels 6 sun

Page 53

1 a walls / roof
b non-renewable / renewable
c friend / grandparents
d boring / exciting
e electricity / energy
f noisy / quiet

2 1 renewable 2 fossil fuels
3 blades 4 generator 5 panels
6 silicon 7 energy
3 1 work out 2 run out 3 engineer
4 fashion designer
3 Students' own answers

Unit 6

Page 54

1 1 e 2 c 3 a 4 b 5 d
2 1 travels 2 pedals 3 lifts
4 avoids 5 pushes 6 lands
3 1 first / second
2 balloon / computer
3 traffic / transportation
4 car / bike
5 swim / fly
6 Science / Inventions

Page 55

1 1 surfing 2 downloaded
3 attaching 4 upload
2 1 speaker 2 bug 3 mouse
4 chip
3 1 picture 2 2 picture 2
3 picture 1 4 picture 1

Page 56

1 1 take 2 be picked up
3 be provided 4 be shown
5 won't be given
2 1 I'll work 2 will be made
3 will be cleaned
4 will be washed 5 'll win
6 will be used
3 1 You will be taken to New York in a private plane.
2 You will be driven to your hotel in a luxury car.
3 You will be given tickets for plays and movies.
4 Your essays will be printed in the newspaper.
5 The essays won't be judged until March 1st.
6 The winners will be called by April 1st.

Page 57

1 1 True 2 True 3 False
4 False 5 True 6 False
2 1 have been taken out
2 has been switched on
3 has not been written
4 has not been switched on
5 has been eaten
6 have not been put away
3 1 Have the computers been used? No, they haven't.
2 Has the car been cleaned? Yes, it has.
3 Has the package been opened? No, it hasn't.
4 Have the lights in the classroom been switched off? Yes, they have.

Page 58

1 1 The first cell phone call
2 The first cell phone for the public
3 The market for cell phones
4 Cell phones today
2 1 True 2 False 3 False
4 False 5 True 6 True

Page 59

1 1 created 2 experimental
3 immediately 4 complications
5 market 6 huge
2 1 ordinary 2 public
3 available 4 expect
3 1 created 2 huge
3 immediately 4 experimental
5 cursor 6 expect
7 president 8 complications

Page 60

1 Students' own answers
3 Students' own answers

Page 61

1 1 predict, A 2 connected, P
3 surf, A 4 downloaded, P
5 bugs, A
2 1 created 2 president
3 experimental 4 complications
5 market 6 immediately
3 1 The soup has been made.
2 The bread has been cut.
3 The cake hasn't been eaten.
4 The drinks haven't been poured.
5 The clothes have been washed.
6 The mail has been opened.

Unit 7

Page 62

1 1 explorers 2 map 3 compass
4 flags 5 after 6 hours
7 win 8 luck
2 1 south / north
2 map / compass
3 lake / river
4 fire / storm
5 house / cave
6 small / dark
3 Students' own answers

Page 63

1 1 map 2 treasure 3 compass
4 north 5 east 6 binoculars
7 west 8 south
2 1 driver 2 artist 3 builder
4 guitarist
3 1 explorer 2 artist 3 builder
4 driver 5 guitarist 6 tourist

Page 64

1 1 b 2 d 3 e 4 c 5 a
2 1 which 2 which 3 which
4 who 5 which 6 which
3 1 I'd like to meet a person who has been to Antarctica.
2 I have some jeans which were made in Hong Kong.
3 A penguin is a bird which can swim underwater.
4 My friends are people who go to my school.
4 Students' own answers

Page 65

1 1 who 2 that 3 who
4 who 5 that 6 that
2 1 c 2 b 3 d 4 a
3 1 Neil Armstrong was an astronaut who / that walked on the moon.
2 Mount Everest is a mountain which / that is in Nepal.
3 The sand cat is a small, wild cat which / that lives in the desert.
4 Marco Polo was a traveler who/that went to China in the 13th century.
5 In the museum there are some maps which / that were made by early explorers.

Page 66

1 **b)** the ship was carrying gold
3 1 good 2 for shopping
3 two days later 4 fill with
5 were rescued 6 a year

Page 67

1 1 iceberg 2 voyage 3 sank
4 search 5 shipwreck 7 clues
2 1 on board 2 deck 3 harbor
4 souvenirs
3 1 voyage 2 icebergs
3 on board, sank 4 search, shipwreck 5 souvenirs 6 harbor

Page 68

1 1 such as 2 for instance 3 like
4 for example
2 Students' own answers
3 Students' own answers

Page 69

1 1 A compass is an instrument which / that shows you north, south, west and east.
2 A novelist is a person who / that writes books.
3 A voyage is a long trip which / that is made by sea.
4 Tourists are people who / that travel on vacation.
5 The *Titanic* was the ship which / that sank in the North Atlantic in 1912.

2 1 map 2 harbor 3 guitarist
4 voyage 5 shipwreck 6 treasure
3 1 artist 2 binoculars 3 sank
4 south 5 hurricane 6 voyage

Fluency Time! 3

Page 70

1 1 OK 2 Yes, OK. 3 Do
4 that's fine. 5 Could
6 Yes, of course.
2 1 Can, OK 2 Could, sorry
3 Do, fine
3 1 Can you show me 2 Can I have
3 Is it OK if 4 Do you mind

Page 71

1 1 False 2 [Need to see DVD]
3 False 4 False 5 False 6 True
2 1 Is it OK if I borrow your gloves? I can't find mine.
2 No, sorry! I'm wearing them.
3 Could I close the window, please? I'm freezing.
4 Yes, of course. It has been getting cold this week.
5 Do you mind if I wear my scarf? I'm so cold today.
6 No, that's fine, Ben. Go ahead.
3 Suggested answers:
1 Is it OK if / Can I have (some chips), Mom / Dad?
2 Could / Can I have a drink, please?
3 Could I go to the bathroom, please?
4 Students' own answers

Unit 8

Page 72

1 a 3 b 1 c 5 d 2 e 4
2 1 c 2 a 3 a 4 b 5 c
3 Students' own answers

Page 73

1 1 site 2 investigation
3 evidence 4 strange
5 mysterious 6 fascinating
2 1 enjoyable 2 breakable
3 preferable 4 understandable
3 1 breakable 2 believe
3 understandable 4 acceptable
5 prefer 6 enjoy

Page 74

1 1 c 2 e 3 b 4 d 5 a
2 1 had left 2 arrived 3 dropped
4 went 6 had forgotten
3 1 After Sara had finished her homework, she went to the movies.
2 After the girls had gone grocery shopping, they came home.
3 After Tim had travelled for five hours, he arrived at the airport.
4 After Luis and Carla had eaten (their) lunch, they visited their grandma.

Page 75

1 1 hadn't done 2 hadn't eaten
3 hadn't flown 4 hadn't given
5 hadn't caught
2 1 Had the ship hit a rock? No, it hadn't.
2 Had all the people disappeared? Yes, they had.
3 Had they left (any) money and clothes on the ship? Yes, they had.
4 Had the captain written in his book? Yes, he had.
5 Had the weather been stormy? No, it hadn't.
3 Students' own answers

Page 76

1 c) 800
2 1 South Pacific 2 three 3 100,000
4 stone 5 More 6 can't

Page 77

1 1 incredible 2 climate 3 soil
4 historians 5 cleared away
6 figures
2 1 statue 2 erupt 3 quarry
4 platform
3 1 sketches 2 erupt
3 comfortable 4 statue
5 quarry 6 platform

Page 78

1 1 b 2 e 3 g 4 h 5 f
6 d 7 a 8 c
2 Students' own answers

Page 79

1 1 site 2 ancient 3 soil
4 artifacts 5 figure 6 historian
2 1 had read 2 had left 3 told
4 hadn't finished 5 hadn't erupted
6 discovered
3 1 The movie had started before we arrived.
2 When Jack got to the store, it had closed.
3 I realized I had not turned off my cell phone.
4 Had you seen a monkey before you went to the zoo?

History Time!

Page 80

1 b) He died when he was 19.
2 1 b 2 a 3 b 4 b 5 c 6 b

Page 81

1 1 school 2 Roman ruin
3 a ceramic vase 4 how people were governed 5 France
6 paintings
2 1 prehistoric 2 features
3 ceramics 4 technology 5 dig
6 remains 7 governed
3 1 tomb 2 striped 3 container
4 coffin
4 Students' own answers

Unit 9

Page 82

1 1 door / chest 2 maps / coins
3 Tom's / Kate's 4 Kate's / Fin's
5 zoo / museum
2 1 d 2 c 3 a 4 e 5 b
3 1 discovered 2 searching
3 lost 4 wall 5 chest
6 taken 7 museum

Page 83

1 1 water bottle 2 matches
3 fishing line 4 needle and thread
5 first aid kit 6 whistle
2 1 weather 2 whether 3 brake
4 break 5 some 6 sum
7 by 8 buy
3 1 meet 2 see, seen
3 flower, buy 4 weather
5 some, here 6 brake

Page 84

1 1 hadn't 2 wouldn't 3 hadn't
4 would 5 had 6 would
2 1 would have helped
2 had left
3 hadn't seen
4 would have played
5 had sent
6 wouldn't have been
3 1 If they had taken a map, they wouldn't have gotten lost.
2 They wouldn't have taken the wrong direction if they had taken a compass.
3 If they had crossed the bridge, they would have found the right path.
4 They wouldn't have lost their water bottle if they had been more careful.
5 If they had worn good walking boots, their feet wouldn't have gotten sore.

Page 85

1 1 False 2 True 3 True 4 False
5 False 6 False
2 3 You shouldn't make a fire here.
4 You can eat at the café.
5 You should take your trash home.
6 You can sleep in a tent or an RV here.
3 1 shouldn't 2 don't have to
3 must 4 should 5 shouldn't
6 ought to 7 have to
4 Students' own answers

Page 86

1 **b)** surviving after a shipwreck
2 1 adventure / island
2 parents / aunt 3 floods / storms
4 six / five 5 dolphins / seals
6 find / build

Page 87

1 1 storm 2 survivors 3 shelter
4 cut down 5 walls 6 fence
2 1 seal 2 hunt 3 alone 4 hut
3 1 Survivors 2 storm 3 hut
4 cut down 5 hunt 6 seals

Page 88

1 Students' own answers
2 Students' own answers

Page 89

1 1 had listened, would have understood
2 had run, would have won
3 would have made, hadn't forgotten
4 had known, would have called
5 wouldn't have gotten, had had
6 hadn't eaten, wouldn't be
2 1 must 2 should 3 don't have to
4 mustn't 5 shouldn't 6 have to
7 ought not to 8 ought to
3 1 supplies 2 pocket knife
3 matches 4 shelter
5 survivor 6 whistle

Unit 10

Page 90

1 a 4 b 2 c 6 d 3 e 1 f 5
2 1 Fin 2 Kate 3 Tom 4 Libby
5 Ed
3 1 All over the world.
2 50
3 The artists.
4 On the beach.
5 The name of your favorite sculpture.

Page 91

1 1 official languages 2 bilingual
3 mother tongue
4 mother tongue 5 accents
6 dialects 7 multilingual
8 fluent
2 1 c 2 a 3 d 4 b
3 1 discovery 2 forgery
3 recovery 4 bravery
5 machinery 6 robbery

Page 92

1 1 wanted 2 was 3 had had
4 had been 5 were learning
2 1 were 2 loved 3 had visited
4 were planning 5 was looking
6 would get
3 1 liked her skirt, was nice
2 had cooked the pasta, would make some salad
3 had read that book at school
4 was going to Brazil in July

Page 93

1 1 myself 2 yourself 3 himself
4 herself 5 itself 6 ourselves
7 yourselves 8 themselves
2 1 myself 2 ourselves
3 themselves 4 himself 5 itself
3 1 yourself, myself 2 himself, herself
3 ourselves, themselves
4 itself, yourselves

Page 94

1 1 c) How many languages are spoken in Papua New Guinea?
2 a) What are the official languages?
3 d) Why do people speak English there?
4 e) Where did the languages come from?
5 b) How have so many languages survived?
2 1 True 2 False 3 False 4 True
5 False 6 False

Page 95

1 1 international 2 continent
3 disappear 4 population
5 Altogether 6 century
7 official 8 predict
2 1 tribe 2 inhabitants
3 communicate 4 isolated
3 1 tribe 2 population 3 isolated
4 inhabitants 5 communicate

Page 96

1 Students' own answers
2 Students' own answers
3 Students' own answers

Page 97

1 1 fluent 2 population
3 centuries 4 bilingual
5 disappear
2 1 was 2 had arrived
3 had studied 4 spoke
5 would disappear
3 1 ourselves 2 myself
3 yourself 4 himself 5 herself
6 themselves

Fluency Time! 4

Page 98

1 1 d 2 b 3 g 4 a 5 e
6 c 7 f
2 1 should, should 2 should, could
3 should, could
3 1 What can we do?
2 That won't work.
3 We could try calling Mom.
4 I think we should go home.
5 What do you think we should do?

Page 99

1 1 They are wearing jackets and pants.
2 They are going home.
3 There's no phone signal.
4 Because they are scared (because someone is hiding behind a tree).
5 Because the person behind the tree is Ben.
2 in the park, home, worried
Where are we?
What shall we do?
We could try calling Mom and Dad.
They look at their phones.
What can we do?
scared, they start to run
3 Students' own answers
4 Students' own answers

Unit 11

Page 100

1 a 4 b 1 c 6 d 2 e 5 f 3
2 1 b (picture b) 2 e (picture a)
3 a (picture c) 4 c (picture d)
5 d (picture e) 6 f (picture f)
3 1 No, they can't.
2 She saw an interview on TV.
3 Yes, they do.
4 Pouring water on it.

Page 101

1 1 constellations 2 shooting star
3 comet 4 telescope 5 astronaut
6 space shuttle 7 solar system
8 space station
2 1 come on 2 come off
3 come up 4 come across
3 1 on 2 back 3 across 4 over
5 off 6 up

Page 102

1 1 his 2 she 3 her 4 he
2 1 astronomers did 2 she worked
3 a person needed 4 she liked
5 she looked at
3 1 what her favorite planet was
2 when she started work
3 what she liked best about her job
4 what she was studying at the moment
5 who else worked with her

Page 103

1 1 to come in 2 asked 3 not to 4 me
2 1 asked Frank to close
2 asked Jen to send
3 asked the boys to phone
4 asked Ron to clean
5 asked Helen not to leave
3 1 told him to wash his hands
2 told her to be careful
3 told the class not to talk
4 told him not to forget his helmet

Page 104

1 a) Dreaming of space
2 1 b 2 a 3 c 4 c

Page 105

1 1 head off 2 surface 3 bumpy 4 cozy 5 glow 6 diamonds 7 spins
2 1 launch 2 observatory 3 beams 4 imagine
3 1 spin 2 diamond 3 imagine 4 bumpy 5 surface 6 beams

Page 106

1 1 kites 2 snow 3 diamonds 4 drum 5 shooting star 6 toast
2 Students' own answers

Page 107

1 1 why he was in Littlewood
2 where he was going next
3 not to forget to visit their new stadium
4 when his next competition was
5 what he did in his free time
2 1 telescope 2 comet 3 constellation 4 space shuttle 5 astronauts 6 heading
3 1 precious 2 glowed 3 spun 4 bumpy 5 shooting stars

Science Time!

Page 108

1 Students' own answers
2 1 rainbow / solar eclipse
2 going to sleep / waking up
3 colorful / gray 4 before / after
5 same /opposite
6 shadows / sunlight

Page 109

1 1 f 2 e 3 d 4 b 5 a 6 g 7 c
2 1 Astronomers 2 cycle 3 corona 4 spectrum 5 solar eclipse 6 Refraction 7 phenomena
3 1 nocturnal 2 towards 3 artificially 4 row
4 Students' own ideas

Unit 12

Page 110

1 1 The children 2 Libby 3 the rescue team 4 the ocean 5 The dolphin
2 1 shark 2 realized 3 waves 4 wet 5 a rescue team 6 carry
3 1 rescues 2 equipment 3 dolphins 4 hospital 5 volunteer 6 hours

Page 111

1 1 basic 2 luxurious 3 cheap 4 stimulating 5 expensive 6 dull
2 1 w 2 h 3 h 4 w
3 1 (W)rite 2 r(h)ino 3 (h)our 4 sno(w) 5 (w)rap 6 (h)onest 7 (w)heel 8 gro(w)

Page 112

1 1 could 2 lived 3 wasn't 4 he 5 had 6 didn't
2 1 I wish my glasses weren't broken.
2 I wish my family liked soccer.
3 I wish I was taller.
4 I wish my bedroom was bigger.
5 I wish I could play the guitar.
6 I wish I didn't have curly hair.
3 a 3 b 4 c 1 d 5 e 6 f 2
4 Students' own answers

Page 113

1 1 aren't you 2 can't he 3 do you 4 weren't they 5 does she 6 did it
2 1 isn't it 2 did you 3 can't they 4 doesn't she
3 1 You're Mr Adams, aren't you?
2 You don't like cold weather, do you?
3 We need postcards, don't we?
4 Venice is amazing, isn't it?
5 We can't swim here, can we?
6 You went to Mexico last year, didn't you?

Page 114

1 a 3 b 2 c 4 d 1
2 1 Thailand 2 China 3 Australia 4 Thailand 5 Borneo 6 Borneo

Page 115

1 1 rickshaw 2 rush 3 board game 4 Unfortunately 5 scary 6 spicy 7 flavors 8 give up
2 1 orangutan 2 perfect 3 coral reef 4 market
3 1 market 2 rush 3 rickshaw 4 perfect 5 coral reef 6 orangutan 7 scary 8 Unfortunately

Page 116

2 Students' own answers
3 Students' own answers

Page 117

1 1 could 2 could 3 had 4 wasn't
2 (left to right) 1, 3, 2, 4
3 1 basic, isn't it, luxurious, didn't we
2 expensive, aren't they, cheap, can't we
3 peaceful, don't you
4 stimulating, didn't he

Grammar Time

Unit 1

going to: plans and intentions, *will / won't*: decisions and offers as we speak

1 1 Tony is going to play tennis this afternoon.
2 I feel really tired. I won't come to the movies tonight.
3 We're not going to England. We're going to Canada!
4 You look tired. Sit down! I'll make you a cup of coffee.
2 1 Tina is meeting Mia at the shopping mall.
2 They're taking the bus at eleven o'clock.
3 They're not having lunch at the café.
4 Where are they having lunch?

Unit 2

First conditional

1 1 If Harry visits us, we'll go to the museum.
2 Will you wash the dishes if I cook the dinner?
3 If I'm hungry, I'll eat a sandwich.

Second conditional

2 1 If you called Evie, you wouldn't be bored.
2 If Fred got up ealier, he wouldn't be late for school.
3 Would you eat lots of rice if you lived in Japan?

Unit 3

Present perfect: *since / for / already / yet / before / just*

1 1 She's had her new bike since her birthday.
2 You've been ill since Tuesday.
3 My parents have worked in the same job for 15 years.
2 1 The children haven't seen the ocean before.
2 We've just come back from the movies.
3 Have you finished it yet?
4 I've already finished the cake.

Simple past and present perfect

3 1 Yesterday we went to the museum.
2 I haven't seen Ingrid for a long time.
3 We have lived in this house for 10 years.
4 Frank has been to Thailand before.

Unit 4

Present perfect progressive (1)

1 1 We have been playing baseball since three o'clock.
2 Sarah has been cooking for two hours.
3 Charlie has been traveling all day.
4 Amy has been swimming all day.

Present perfect progressive (2)

1 1 I'm wet because I've been walking in the rain.
2 We're hot because we've been playing tennis.
3 Your clothes are dirty. Have you been playing soccer?
4 They're not hungry because they've been eating lots of cookies.

Unit 5

The passive (simple present and simple past)

1 1 Pizza was invented in Italy.
2 Every day, letters and postcards are sent around the world.
3 Computers weren't used in schools 30 years ago.
4 Cakes are eaten all over the world.

The passive (present progressive)

2 1 Photos are being taken of each class.
2 Tickets are being sold outside the stadium.
3 The children haven't been sent home early today.

Unit 6

The passive (future)

1 1 You will be taken to the museum.
2 We won't be given lunch. We will have to take sandwiches.
3 Will children be taught at home in the future?
4 Will they be driven by bus?

The passive (present perfect)

2 1 I lost my watch, but it has been found now.
2 The grass is very long. It hasn't been cut for a long time.
3 Have the children been taken home?
4 Has he been taken to the station? No, he hasn't.

Unit 7

Relative pronouns: *who*, *which*

1 1 A compass is a navigational instrument which shows you where north is.
2 An architect is a person who designs buildings.
3 A saw is a tool which you use for cutting wood.

Relative pronoun: *that*

2 1 A flashlight is something which / that gives you light.
2 The *Mayflower* was the ship which / that sailed to the U.S.A. from England in 1620.
3 Can you remember the name of the explorer that / who first went to Antarctica?
4 Alexander Bell was the person that / who invented the telephone.

Unit 8

Past perfect

1 1 When I arrived at school, I realized that I had forgotten all my books.
2 The children all passed the test because they had worked hard.
3 I had eaten a big lunch, so I didn't want any cake.

Past perfect: negative sentences and questions

2 1 I was hungry because I hadn't eaten my lunch.
2 Ruby hadn't finished her homework before her friends arrived.
3 Had they eaten Chinese food before they had it on Friday?

Unit 9

Third conditional

1 1 If it hadn't rained, we would have had lunch outside.
2 If I had known about the TV show, I would have watched it.
3 If Anita hadn't lost your number, she would have called you.
4 If I hadn't been ill, I wouldn't have missed your party.

Modal verbs

2 1 You should take your camera when you go on vacation.
2 You shouldn't talk during the concert – it isn't polite.
3 If you want to get fit, you ought to do more exercise.
4 You don't have to wear a swimming cap, but it's a good idea.

Unit 10

Reported speech: statements

1 1 He said he wanted to be a pilot.
2 He said he would help her with her homework.
3 They said they had won the game.
4 She said she was enjoying this game of tennis.
5 They said they had had a great day.

Reflexive pronouns

2 1 Did the children enjoy themselves at the park?
2 I made myself a delicious sandwich.
3 Dad taught himself Portuguese when he was young.
4 We bought ourselves tickets for the game.

Unit 11

Reported questions: *Wh-* questions

1 1 Sally asked Erin where her house was.
2 Tim asked me what my favorite song was.
3 I asked the little girl why she was crying.
4 Lily asked a man when the bus arrived.

Reported commands and requests

2 1 The teacher told the class to stop that noise.
2 The teacher asked Layla to close the window.
3 Annie told Polly not to forget her book.
4 My mom asked me to turn down the TV.

Unit 12

wish

1 1 I wish I wasn't scared of spiders.
2 I wish I had a bike.
3 I wish you could stay longer.
4 I wish it wasn't so hot today.

Question tags

2 1 These pictures look great, don't they?
2 You don't eat meat, do you?
3 Mia can ski, can't she?
4 Those boys aren't from our school, are they?

Wordlist

Words in bold are core words that children will be able to use actively by the end of each unit. The remaining words are those they will have come across in songs and stories, and in reading and listening passages.

Starter Unit

eat /iːt/
bought (pp) /bɔːt/
break down (v) /breɪk 'daʊn/
Canada /'kænədə/
caught (pp) /kɔːt/
convention /kən'venʃn/
costumes /'kɒstjuːms/
cousin /'kʌzn/
eaten (pp) /'iːtn/
fly /flaɪ/
flown (pp) /fləʊn/
found (pp) /faʊnd/
France /frɑːns/
go /gəʊ/
gone (pp) /gɒn/
got (pp) /gɒt/
Great! /greɪt/
grow /grəʊ/
grown (pp) /grəʊn/
had (pp) /hæd/
hear /hɪər/
ice hockey /'aɪs hɒki/
kept (pp) /kept/
made (pp) /meɪd/
see /siː/
seen (pp) /siːn/
Spain /speɪn/
speak /spiːk/
spoken (pp) /'spəʊkən/
taken (pp) /'teɪkən/
time capsule /'taɪm kæpsjuːl/
take /teɪk/
used (pp) /juːzd/
wear /weər/
worn (pp) /wɔːn/
write /raɪt/
written (pp) /'rɪtn/

Unit 1

art gallery /'ɑːt gæləri/
background /'bækgraʊnd/
bank /bæŋk/
birthday /bɜːθdeɪ/
borrow /'bɒrəʊ/
bucket /'bʌkɪt/
chocolate /'tʃɒklət//
coast /kəʊst/
come back /kʌm 'bæk/
cotton /'kɒtən/
crab /kræb/
excitedly /ɪk'saɪtɪdli/
exciting /ɪk'saɪtɪŋ/
exhibition /ˌeksɪ'bɪʃn/
explore /ɪk'splɔːr/
fisherman /'fɪʃəmən/
fishing boat /'fɪʃɪŋ bəʊt/
fishing net /'fɪʃɪŋ net/
fix /fɪks/
flag /flæg/
float (v) /fləʊt/
foreground /'fɔːgraʊnd/
French /frentʃ/
friendly /'frendli/
grab /græb/
happy /'hæpi/
hit /hɪt/
immature /ˌɪmə'tjʊər/
impatient /ɪm'peɪʃnt/
impolite /ˌɪmpə'laɪt/
impossible /ɪm'pɒsəbl/
in the distance /ɪn ðə 'dɪstəns/
interesting /'ɪntrəstɪŋ/
in trouble /ɪn 'trʌbl/
island /'aɪlənd/
Italian /ɪ'tæljən/
landscape /'lændskeɪp/
lifeboat /'laɪfbəʊt/
lightning /'laɪtnɪŋ/
lucky /'lʌki/
matches /'mætʃɪz/
mature /mə'tʃʊər/
mend /mend/
Mexican /'meksɪkən/
missing /'mɪsɪŋ/
mural /'mjʊərəl/
ocean /'əʊʃn/
oars /ɔːz/
pack (v) /pæk/
painting /'peɪntɪŋ/
patient /'peɪʃnt/
plastic /plæstɪk//
polite /pə'laɪt/
popular /'pɒpjələr/
portrait /'pɔːtrət/
possible /'pɒsəbl/
proud /praʊd/
punctuation /ˌpʌŋktʃu'eɪʃn/
rescue /'reskjuː/
row /rəʊ/
sail (v) /seɪl/
sculpture /'skʌlptʃər/
silk /sɪlk/
smoke /sməʊk/
smoking /'sməʊkɪŋ/
speech marks /'spiːtʃ mɑːks/
splash /splæʃ/
stare /steər/
stormy /'stɔːmi/
theme /θiːm/
thunder /'θʌndər/
tie (v) /taɪ/
tropical /'trɒpɪkl/
unfriendly /ʌn'frendli/
unhappy /ʌn'hæpi/
uninteresting /ʌn'ɪntrəstɪŋ/
unlucky /ʌn'lʌki/
unpopular /ʌn'pɒpjələr/
untie /ʌn'taɪ/
unusual /ʌn'juːʒuəl/
volcano /vɒl'keɪnəʊ/
waves /weɪvz/

Unit 2

agree /ə'griː/
amazing /ə'meɪzɪŋ/
appear /ə'pɪər/
Australia /ɒ'streɪlɪə/
baseball /'beɪsbɔːl/
Brazil /brə'zɪl/
Caribbean /kærə'biːən/
caving /'keɪvɪŋ/
compete /kəm'piːt/
competition /ˌkɒmpə'tɪʃn/
complete /kəm'pliːt/
concept map /'kɒnsept mæp/
correct /kə'rekt/
deep /diːp/
disagree /dɪsə'griː/
disappear /ˌdɪsə'pɪər/

dishonest /dɪs'ɒnɪst/
dislike /dɪs'laɪk/
disobey /ˌdɪsə'beɪ/
diving /'daɪvɪŋ/
drawing /'drɔːɪŋ/
environment /ɪn'vaɪrənmənt/
equipment /ɪ'kwɪpmənt/
experienced /ɪk'spɪəriənst/
free-diver /'friː daɪvər/
free-diving /'friː daɪvɪŋ/
freedom /'friːdəm/
future /'fjuːtʃər/
gymnastics /dʒɪm'næstɪks/
helmet /'helmɪt/
hobby /'hɒbi/
honest /'ɒnɪst/
hoop /huːp/
ice skating /'aɪs skeɪtɪŋ/
incomplete /ˌɪnkəm'pliːt/
incorrect /ˌɪnkə'rekt/
inexperienced /ˌɪnɪk'spɪəriənst/
insensitive /ɪn'sensətɪv/
instructor /ɪn'strʌktər/
intonation /ˌɪntə'neɪʃn/
invisible /ɪn'vɪzəbl/
like /laɪk/
mountain biking /'maʊntən baɪkɪŋ/
obey /ə'beɪ/
paragliding /'pærəglaɪdɪŋ/
pearl /pɜːl/
popular /'pɒpjələr/
presenter /prɪ'zentər/
protect /prə'tekt/
provide /prə'vaɪd/
record /'rekɔːd/
rock climbing /'rɒk klaɪmɪŋ/
scared /skeəd/
section /'sekʃn/
sensitive /'sensətɪv/
skiing /'skiːɪŋ/
skills /skɪlz/
snorkeling /'snɔːkəlɪŋ/
spider /'spaɪdər/
springs /sprɪŋz/
talented /'tæləntɪd/
train (v) /treɪn/
underground /ʌndə'graʊnd/
visible /'vɪzəbl/
volunteer /ˌvɒlən'tɪər/

wetsuit /wetsjuːt/
wildlife /'waɪldlaɪf/
windsurfing /'wɪndsɜːfɪŋ/
world record /wɜːld 'rekɔːd/

Unit 3

adventure /əd'ventʃər/
adventurous /əd'ventʃərəs/
amazing /ə'meɪzɪŋ/
awful /'ɔːfl/
bang /bæŋ/
Best wishes /best 'wɪʃɪz/
break up /'breɪk ʌp/
brick /brɪk/
bright /braɪt/
building /'bɪldɪŋ/
bunch /bʌntʃ/
celebrate /'selɪbreɪt/
celebration /ˌselɪ'breɪʃn/
complaint /kəm'pleɪnt/
danger /'deɪndʒər/
dangerous /'deɪndʒərəs/
decorate /'dekəreɪt/
delicious /dɪ'lɪʃəs/
demonstration /ˌdemən'streɪʃn/
deserted /dɪ'zɜːtɪd/
dessert /dɪ'zɜːt/
disgusting /dɪs'gʌstɪŋ/
dish /dɪʃ/
fame /feɪm/
famous /'feɪməs/
fantastic /fæn'tæstɪk/
festival /'festɪvl/
fireworks /'faɪəwɜːks/
float (n) /fləʊt/
food stall /'fuːd stɔːl/
furious /'fjʊəriəs/
fury /'fjʊəri/
garlic /'gɑːlɪk/
hang /hæŋ/
hazard /'hæzəd/
hazardous /'hæzədəs/
healthy /'helθi/
igloo /'ɪgluː/
invitation /ˌɪnvɪ'teɪʃn/
invite /ɪn'vaɪt/
Italy /'ɪtəli/
jam /dʒæm/
last (v) /lɑːst/
luxurious /lʌg'ʒʊəriəs/

luxury /'lʌkʃəri/
mountain /'maʊntən/
mountainous /'maʊntənəs/
mysterious /mɪ'stɪəriəs/
mystery /'mɪstri/
necklace /'nekləs/
original /ə'rɪdʒənl/
pancake /'pænkeɪk/
picnic /'pɪknɪk/
poison /'pɔɪzn/
poisonous /'pɔɪzənəs/
prize /praɪz/
procession /prə'seʃn/
(the) Pyramids /'pɪrəmɪdz/
reason /'riːzn/
recipe /'resəpi/
snack /snæk/
spring /sprɪŋ/
traditional /trə'dɪʃənl/
treat (n) /triːt/
type /taɪp/

Extensive reading 1

alight /ə'laɪt/
burn (v) /bɜːn/
ceremony /'serəməni/
cold /kəʊld/
consecutive /kən'sekjətɪv/
create /kri'eɪt/
cruel /kruːəl/
disability /ˌdɪsə'bɪləti/
expression /ɪk'spreʃn/
flag /flæg/
gentleness /'dʒentlnəs/
hard /hɑːd/
heat /hiːt/
hold /həʊld/
host (v) /həʊst/
inspire /ɪn'spaɪə(r)/
intelligence /ɪn'telɪdʒəns/
introduction /ˌɪntrə'dʌkʃn/
invade /ɪn'veɪd/
kindness /'kaɪndnəs/
lend /lend/
light (v) /laɪt/
local /'ləʊkl/
medal /'medl/
motto /'mɒtəʊ/
national anthem /'næʃnəl ænθəm/
pass (v) /pɑːs/

patience /'peɪʃns/
physical /'fɪzɪkl/
pleasant /'pleznt/
procession /prə'seʃn/
quality /'kwɒləti/
raise /reɪz/
record (n) /'rekɔːd/
represent /ˌreprɪ'zent/
selfish /'selfɪʃ/
studio /'stjuːdiəʊ/
style /staɪl/
take part /teɪk pɑːt/
withered /'wɪðəd/
wonderful /'wʌndəfl/
youth /juːθ/

Unit 4

4 x 4 vehicle /'fɔːr baɪ fɔːr viːəkl/
ability /ə'bɪləti/
African /'æfrɪkən/
airport /'eəpɔːt/
Asia /'eɪʃə/
balance /'bæləns/
barge /bɑːdʒ/
burner /'bɜːnər/
bush /bʊʃ/
canal /kə'næl/
causal connective /'kɔːzl kə'nektɪv/
Chinese /tʃaɪ'niːz/
clear (v) /klɪər/
coach /kəʊtʃ/
complicated /'kɒmplɪkeɪtɪd/
connect /kə'nekt/
controls /kən'trəʊlz/
desert /'dezət/
develop /dɪ'veləp/
diagram /'daɪəgræm/
engine /'endʒɪn/
envelope /'envələʊp/
environment /ɪn'vaɪrənmənt/
Fantastic! /fæn'tæstɪk/
form /fɔːm/
gas /gæs/
go down /gəʊ 'daʊn/
gondola /'gɒndələ/
heat (v) /hiːt/
height /haɪt/
helicopter /'helɪkɒptər/
hot-air balloon /hɒt eər bə'luːn/
hurry (v) /'hʌri/
ideal /aɪ'diːəl/
invention /ɪn'venʃn/
layer /'leɪər/
loads /ləʊdz/
local /'ləʊkl/
motorized /'məʊtəraɪzd/
log /lɒg/
look after /lʊk 'ɑːftər/
look ahead /lʊk ə'hed/
look for /lʊk 'fɔːr/
look forward to /lʊk 'fɔːwəd tuː/
look into /lʊk 'ɪn tuː/
look around /lʊk a'raʊnd/
look up /lʊk 'ʌp/
look up to /lʊk 'ʌp tuː/
manager /'mænɪdʒər/
motorcycle /'məʊtəsaɪkl/
motorized /'məʊtəraɪzd/
mud /mʌd/
package /'pækɪdʒ/
parachute /'pærəʃuːt/
pilot /'paɪlət/
private /'praɪvət/
process diagram /'prəʊses daɪəgræm/
propane gas /prəʊpeɪn 'gæs/
railway /'reɪlweɪ/
release /rɪ'liːs/
rise /raɪz/
rowing boat /'rəʊɪŋ bəʊt/
rudder /'rʌdər/
runway /'rʌnweɪ/
sand dunes /'sænd djuːnz/
sink (v) /sɪŋk/
South Africa /saʊθ 'æfrɪkə/
spray (v) /spreɪ/
steer /stɪər/
submarine /'sʌbməriːn/
survive /sə'vaɪv/
technical /'teknɪkl/
transport /'trænspɔːt/
valve /vælv/
vehicle /'viːəkl/
Venetian /veniːʃn
waterbus /'wɔːtər bʌs/
wing /wɪŋ/
yacht /jɒt/

Unit 5

accident /'æksɪdənt/
achieve /ə'tʃiːv/
achievement /ə'tʃiːvmənt/
advertise /'ædvətaɪz/
agree /ə'griː/
agreement /ə'griːmənt/
ancient /'eɪnʃənt/
arrange /ə'reɪndʒ/
arrangement /ə'reɪndʒmənt/
artificial /ˌɑːtɪ'fɪʃl/
attach /ə'tætʃ/
award /ə'wɔːd/
ballpoint pen /'bɔːlpɔɪnt pen/
biography /baɪ'ɒgrəfi/
blind /blaɪnd/
bone /bəʊn/
(to be) born /tə bi 'bɔːn/
build /bɪld/
cartridge /'kɑːtrɪdʒ/
cell phone /'sel fəʊn/
chewing gum /'tʃuːɪŋ gʌm/
clay /kleɪ/
code /kəʊd/
come up with /kʌm 'ʌp wɪð/
communication /kəˌmjuːnɪ'keɪʃn/
company /'kʌmpəni/
contact (v) /'kɒntækt/
container /kən'teɪnər/
culture /'kʌltʃər/
design /dɪ'zaɪn/
develop /dɪ'veləp/
development /dɪ'veləpmənt/
device /dɪ'vaɪs/
dip /dɪp/
discover /dɪ'skʌvər/
dot /dɒt/
during /'djʊərɪŋ/
edge /edʒ/
Egyptian /'ɪdʒɪpʃn/
electricity /ɪˌlek'trɪsəti/
electric light /ɪ'lektrɪk laɪt/
enjoy /ɪn'dʒɔɪ/
enjoyment /ɪn'dʒɔɪmənt/
entertain /ˌentə'teɪn/
entertainment /ˌentə'teɪnmənt/
equip /ɪ'kwɪp/
equipment /ɪ'kwɪpmənt/
events /ɪ'vents/
excite /ɪk'saɪt/

excitement /ɪk'saɪtmənt/
experiment /ɪk'sperɪmənt/
extreme /ɪk'striːm/
factory /'fæktəri/
feather /'feðər/
fill up /fɪl 'ʌp/
fix /fɪks/
flavor /'fleɪvər/
fountain pen /'faʊntən pen/
gravity /'grævəti/
gum /gʌm/
happen /'hæpən/
hollow /'hɒləʊ/
ink /ɪŋk/
inspiration /ˌɪnspə'reɪʃn/
instead /ɪn'sted/
invent /ɪn'vent/
invention /ɪn'venʃn/
laboratory /lə'bɒrətri/
launch (v) /lɔːntʃ/
light bulb /laɪt bʌlb/
machine /mə'ʃiːn/
mark (n) /mɑːk/
mechanical /mə'kænɪkl/
mop /mɒp/
move /muːv/
movement /'muːvmənt/
need /niːd/
nib /nɪb/
object /əb'dʒekt/
pay /peɪ/
payment /'peɪmənt/
pick up /pɪk 'ʌp/
plant /plɑːnt/
point /pɔɪnt/
press /pres/
quill pen /ˌkwɪl 'pen/
raised /reɪzd/
record /rɪ'kɔːd/
research (v) /rɪ'sɜːtʃ/
reservoir /'rezəvwɑːr/
rocket /'rɒkɪt/
rod /rɒd/
rotate /rəʊ'teɪt/
ruin (v) /'ruːɪn/
sharp /ʃɑːp/
soft /sɒft/
source /sɔːs/
space /speɪs/
squeeze /skwiːz/

store (v) /stɔːr/
string /strɪŋ/
substance /'sʌbstəns/
successful /sək'sesfl/
suggest /sə'dʒest/
taste (v) /teɪst/
tiny /'taɪni/
traffic /'træfɪk/
translate /træns'leɪt/
underwater /ˌʌndə'wɔːtər/
wheel /wiːl/
zero gravity /zɪərəʊ 'grævəti/

Unit 6

access (v) /'ækses/
attach /ə'tætʃ/
available /ə'veɪləbl/
backwards /'bækwədz/
billion /'bɪljən/
booklet /'bʊklət/
bug /bʌg/
cable /'keɪbl/
chip /tʃɪp/
complication /ˌkɒmplɪ'keɪʃn/
connect /kə'nekt/
Cool! /kuːl/
create /kri'eɪt/
created /kri'eɪtɪd/
cursor /'kɜːsər/
device /dɪ'vaɪs/
disconnect /dɪskə'nekt/
download /ˌdaʊn'ləʊd/
earthquake /'ɜːθkweɪk/
environment /ɪn'vaɪrənmənt/
expect /ɪk'spekt/
experimental /ɪkˌsperɪ'mentl/
file /faɪl/
government /'gʌvənmənt/
heading /'hedɪŋ/
huge /hjuːdʒ/
immediately /ɪ'miːdiətli/
Internet /'ɪntənet/
judge (v) /dʒʌdʒ/
land (v) /lænd/
laptop /'læptɒp/
left (adv) /left/
left (pp) /left/
lift (v) /lɪft/
log off /lɒg 'ɒf
log on /lɒg 'ɒn/

male /meɪl/
market /'mɑːkɪt/
Mars /mɑːz/
match (n) /mætʃ/
modem /'məʊdem/
mouse /maʊs/
nail /neɪl/
network /'netwɜːk/
ordinary /'ɔːdnri/
packed lunch /pækt 'lʌntʃ/
president /'prezɪdənt/
public /'pʌblɪk/
quotation marks /kwəʊ'teɪʃən mɑːks/
quote /kwəʊt/
report (n) /rɪ'pɔːt/
research /'riːsɜːtʃ/
right (adj) /raɪt/
right (adv) /raɪt/
saw (n) /sɔː/
saw (pp) /sɔː/
software /'sɒftweər/
speaker /'spiːkər/
surf /sɜːf/
sweet (adj) /swiːt/
sweet (n) /swiːt/
switch off /swɪtʃ ɒf/
technology /tek'nɒlədʒi/
topic /'tɒpɪk/
upload /ˌʌp'ləʊd/
weigh (v) /weɪ/
webpage /'webpeɪdʒ/
website /'websaɪt/
wire /'waɪər/
World Wide Web /'wɜːld waɪd web/

Extensive reading 2

airplane /'eəpleɪn/
bazaar /bə'zɑː(r)/
cab /kæb/
candy /'kændi/
carriage /'kærɪdʒ/
chickpea /'tʃɪk piː/
coat /kəʊt/
crossroad /'krɒsrəʊd/
distant /'dɪstənt/
drown /draʊn/
forehead /'fɔːhed/
groom /gruːm/
hand-pulled cart /hænd pʊld kɑːt/

harness /'hɑːnɪs/
mosque /mɒsk/
mom /mɒm/
movie /'muːvi/
on business /ɒn 'bɪznəz/
silence /'saɪləns/
sneakers /'sniːkəz/
taxi /'tæksi/
temple /'templ/
tomb /'tuːm/
trainers /'treɪnəz/
vacation /və'keɪʃn/

Unit 7

art / ɑːt/
artist /'ɑːtɪst/
backpack /'bak-ˌpak/
beneath /bɪ'niːθ/
binoculars /bɪ'nɒkjələz/
borrow /'bɒrəʊ/
build /bɪld/
builder /'bɪldər/
cave /keɪv/
clue /kluː/
compass /'kʌmpəs/
destroy /dɪ'strɔɪ/
diary /'daɪəri/
drive /draɪv/
driver /'draɪvər/
drown /draʊn/
east /iːst/
entrance /ɪn'trɑːns/
environmentalist / ɪnˌvaɪrən'mentəlɪst/
examine /ɪg'zæmɪn/
explore /ɪk'splɔːr/
explorer /ɪk'splɔːrər/
flag /flæg/
for example /fɔːr ɪg'zɑːmpl/
for instance /fɔːr 'ɪnstəns/
guide /gaɪd/
guitar /gɪ'tɑːr/
guitarist /gɪ'tɑːrɪst/
harbor /'hɑːbər/
historian /hɪ'stɔːriən/
hurricane /'hʌrɪkən/
iceberg /'aɪsbɜːg/
journal /'dʒɜːnl/
journalist /'dʒɜːnəlɪst/
laptop /'læptɒp/

map /mæp/
mind (v) /maɪnd/
missing /'mɪsɪŋ/
Nepal /'nepɔːl/
north /nɔːθ/
novel /'nɒvl/
novelist /'nɒvəlɪst/
octopus /'ɒktəpəs/
orangutan /ɔːˌræŋ uː'tæn/
paint /peɪnt/
painter /'peɪntər/
passenger /'pæsɪndʒər/
personalized /'pɜːsənəlaɪzd/
pollution /pə'luːʃn/
proper /'prɒpər/
rainforest /'reɪnfɒrɪst/
safe (a) /seɪf/
scuba diver /'skuːbə daɪvər/
search /sɜːtʃ/
shelter / 'ʃeltər/
shipwreck /'ʃɪprek/
south /saʊθ/
species /'spiːʃiːz/
stripy /'straɪpi/
such as /sʌtʃ 'æz/
temple /'templ/
tour /tɔːr/
tourist /'tɔːrɪst/
treasure /'treʒər/
unsinkable /ʌn'sɪŋkəbl/
valuable /'væljuəbl/
variety /və'raɪəti/
voyage /'vɔɪɪdʒ/
west /west/
write /raɪt/
writer /'raɪtər/

Unit 8

accept /ək'sept/
acceptable /ək'septəbl/
advisable /əd'vaɪzəbl/
advise /əd'vaɪz/
ancient /'eɪnʃənt/
archeological /ˌɑːkiə'lɒdʒɪkl
archeologist /ˌɑːki'ɒlədʒɪst/
artifact /'ɑːtifækt/
astronaut /'æstrənɔːt/
attraction /ə'trækʃn/
believable /bɪ'liːvəbl/
believe /bɪ'liːv/

break /breɪk/
breakable /'breɪkəbl/
brochure /'brəʊʃə/
calendar /'kælɪndər/
chest /tʃest/
climate /'klaɪmət/
come down /kʌm 'daʊn/
comfort /'kʌmfət/
comfortable /'kʌmfətəbl/
condor /'kɒndɔːr/
connect /kə'nekt/
crew /kruː/
enjoy /ɪn'dʒɔɪ/
enjoyable /ɪn'dʒɔɪəbl/
entrance /ɪn'trɑːns/
erupt /ɪ'rʌpt/
evidence /'evɪdəns/
experience /ɪk'spɪəriəns/
fascinating /'fæsɪneɪtɪŋ/
figure /'fɪgər/
guard (v) /gɑːd/
huge /hjuːdʒ/
human /'hjuːmən/
incredible /ɪn'kredəbl/
interview /'ɪntəvjuː/
investigation /ɪnˌvestɪ'geɪʃn/
Italy /'ɪtəli/
lifeboat /'laɪfbəʊt/
mysterious /mɪ'stɪəriəs/
obviously /'ɒbviəsli/
on board /ɒn 'bɔːd/
persuade /pə'sweɪd/
Peru /pə'ruː/
platform /'plætfɔːm/
prefer /prɪ'fɜːr/
preferable /'prefrəbl/
quarry /'kwɒri/
reason /'riːzn/
reasonable /'riːznəbl/
robbery /'rɒbəri/
site /saɪt/
sketch /sketʃ/
soil /sɔɪl/
South America /saʊθ ə'merɪkə/
spider /'spaɪdər/
stadium /'steɪdiəm/
stand back /stænd 'bæk/
statue /'stætʃuː/
strange /streɪndʒ/

stretch /stretʃ/
tourist /'tɔːrɪst/
tower /'taʊər/
underneath /ˌʌndə'niːθ/
understand /ˌʌndə'stænd/
understandable /ˌʌndə'stændəbl/
usable /'juːzəbl/
use /juːz/
well-known /wel'nəʊn/

Unit 9

advice /əd'vaɪs/
afraid /ə'freɪd/
alone /ə'ləʊn/
alternative /ɔːl'tɜːnətɪv/
Arctic /ɑːktɪk/
attract /ə'trækt/
brake /breɪk/
break /breɪk/
bullet point /'bʊlɪt pɔɪnt/
buy (v) /baɪ/
by (prep) /baɪ/
calm /kɑːm/
coin /kɔɪn/
cut down /kʌt 'daʊn/
dangerous /'deɪndʒərəs/
emergency services /i'mɜːdʒənsi sɜːvɪsɪz/
fence /fens/
first aid kit /ˌfɜːst 'eɪd kɪt/
fishing line /'fɪʃɪŋ laɪn/
flour (n) /'flaʊər/
flower (n) /'flaʊər/
fresh /freʃ/
frightened /'fraɪtnd/
give off /gɪv 'ɒf/
hear (vb) /hɪər/
here (adv) /hɪər/
hunt /hʌnt/
hut /hʌt/
imperative /ɪm'perətɪv/
in order to /ɪn 'ɔːdər tuː/
layer /'leɪər/
matches /'mætʃɪz/
meat (n) /miːt/
meet (v) /miːt/
mountain /'maʊntən/
needle and thread /niːdl ən 'θred/
newspaper /'njuːzpeɪpər/
panic /'pænɪk/
pocket knife /'pɒkət ˌnaɪf/
possessions /pə'zeʃnz/
raft /rɑːft/
remind /rɪ'maɪnd/
rescue /'reskjuː/
rescuer /'reskjuːər/
rope /rəʊp/
safely /'seɪfli/
sails /seɪlz/
scene /siːn/
sea /siː/
seal /siːl/
see /siː/
seen (pp) /siːn/
shelter /'ʃeltər/
shore /ʃɔːr/
smoke /sməʊk/
so that /'səʊ ðət/
some /sʌm/
storm /stɔːm/
sum /sʌm/
supplies /sə'plaɪz/
survival /sə'vaɪvl/
survivor /sə'vaɪvər/
tent /tent/
tips /tɪps/
tools /tuːlz/
trekking /'trekɪŋ/
turn off /tɜːn 'ɒf/
wall /wɔːl/
water bottle /'wɔːtər bɒtl/
weather /'weðər/
whether /'weðər/
whistle /'wɪsl/

Extensive reading 3

against /ə'geɪnst/
appear /ə'pɪər/
architect /'ɑːkɪtekt/
argue /'ɑːgjuː/
bury /'beri/
cabin /'kæbɪn/
clever /'klevər/
colorful /'kʌləfl/
course /kɔːs/
destroy /dɪ'strɔɪ/
detail /'diːteɪl/
dies /daɪ/
engineer /ˌendʒɪ'nɪər/
eruption /ɪ'rʌpʃn/
fight /faɪt/
great /greɪt/
greedy /'griːdi/
grow /grəʊ/
harbor /'hɑːbər/
horn /hɔːn/
in one piece /ɪn wʌn 'piːs/
invite /ɪn'vaɪt/
natural disaster /nætʃrəl dɪ'zɑːstər/
plenty /'plenti/
politician /ˌpɒlə'tɪʃn/
pottery /'pɒtəri/
pump (n) /pʌmp/
rich /rɪtʃ/
ring (n) /rɪŋ/
rise /raɪz/
seasick /'siːsɪk/
selfish /'selfɪʃ/
shaken to pieces /'ʃeɪkən tə 'piːsɪz/
steer /stɪər/
successful /sək'sesfl/
surround /sə'raʊnd/
system /'sɪstəm/
tragic /'trædʒɪk/
tsunami /tsuː'nɑːmi/
turn back /tɜːn 'bæk/
turn round /tɜːn 'raʊnd/
violent /'vaɪələnt/
war /wɔːr/
water (v) /'wɔːtər/
wave (n) /weɪv/

Unit 10

accent /'æksənt/
address (v) /ə'dres/
advertisement /ædvə'taɪzmənt/
Africa /'æfrɪkə/
altogether /ˌɔːltə'geðər/
Arabic /'ærəbɪk/
Asia /'eɪʃə/
bake /beɪk/
bakery /'beɪkəri/
bilingual /ˌbaɪ'lɪŋgwəl/
brave /breɪv/
bravery /'breɪvəri/
breeze /briːz/
business /'bɪznəs/
century /'sentʃəri/
communicate /kə'mjuːnɪkeɪt/
communication /kəˌmjuːnɪ'keɪʃn/

confidence /'kɒnfɪdəns/
continent /'kɒntɪnənt/
cook /kʊk/
cycle /'saɪkl/
deliver /dɪ'lɪvər/
delivery /dɪ'lɪvəri/
dialect /'daɪəlekt/
directly /də'rektli/
disappear /ˌdɪsə'pɪər/
discover /dɪ'skʌvər/
discovery /dɪ'skʌvəri/
dominant /'dɒmɪnənt/
fluent /'fluːənt/
foreign /'fɒrən/
forge /fɔːdʒ/
forgery /'fɔːdʒəri/
French /frentʃ/
German /'dʒɜːmən/
go away /gəʊ ə'weɪ/
Greek /griːk/
Hindi /'hɪndi/
Indonesia / ɪndə'niːziə/
in total /ɪn 'təʊtl/
inhabitant /ɪn'hæbɪtənt/
international /ˌɪntə'næʃnəl/
isolated /'aɪsəleɪtɪd/
itself /ɪt'self/
Japanese /dʒæpə'niːz/
Latin /'lætɪn/
layout /'leɪaʊt/
lively /'laɪvli/
machine /mə'ʃiːn/
machinery /mə'ʃiːnəri/
Malaysia / mə'leɪziə/
Mandarin /'mændərɪn/
mother tongue /'mʌðə tʌŋ/
multilingual /ˌmʌlti'lɪŋgwəl/
myself /maɪ'self/
native speaker /ˌneɪtɪv 'spiːkər/
North America /nɔːθ ə'merɪkə/
nurse /nɜːs/
nursery /'nɜːsəri/
official language /əfɪʃl 'læŋgwɪdʒ/
ourselves /ɑː'selvz/
perform /pə'fɔːm/
personal /'pɜːsənl/
persuade /pə'sweɪd/
persuasive /pə'sweɪsɪv/
population /pɒpju'leɪʃn/

Portuguese /pɔːtʃu'giːz/
positive /'pɒzətɪv/
practical /'præktɪkl/
predict /prɪ'dɪkt/
pronounce /prə'naʊns/
recover /rɪ'kʌvər/
recovery /rɪ'kʌvəri/
rob /rɒb/
robbery /'rɒbəri/
Russia /'rʌʃə/
Russian /'rʌʃn/
sand /sænd/
shark /ʃɑːk/
sights /saɪts/
Singapore /sɪŋə'pɔːr/
South America /saʊθ ə'merɪkə/
Spanish /'spænɪʃ/
Thailand /'taɪ lænd/
themselves /ðəm'selvz/
town hall /ˌtaʊn 'hɔːl/
translation /træns'leɪʃn/
tribe /traɪb/
university /juːnɪ'vɜːsəti/
worldwide /wɜːld'waɪd/
yourself /jɔː'self/
yourselves /jɔː'selvz/

Unit 11

admire /əd'maɪər/
astronaut /'æstrənɔːt/
beams /biːmz/
below /bɪ'ləʊ/
blast off (v) /'blɑːst ɒf/
breeze /briːz/
bumpy /'bʌmpi/
come across /kʌm ə'krɒs/
come back /kʌm 'bæk/
come in /kʌm 'ɪn/
come off /kʌm 'ɒf/
come on /kʌm 'ɒn/
come out /kʌm 'aʊt/
come around /kʌm ə'raʊnd/
come up /kʌm 'ʌp/
comet /'kɒmɪt/
comparison /kəm'pærɪsn/
constellation /ˌkɒnstə'leɪʃn/
destination /ˌdestɪ'neɪʃn/
diamond /'daɪəmənd/
dome /dəʊm/
Earth /ɜːθ/

expert /'ekspɜːt/
explain /ɪk'spleɪn/
far /fɑːr/
fascinating /'fæsɪneɪtɪŋ/
float /fləʊt/
fluffy /'flʌfi/
forced /fɔːst/
glow /gləʊ/
head off /hed 'ɒf/
image /'ɪmɪdʒ /
imagine /ɪ'mædʒɪn/
launch /lɔːntʃ/
loop /luːp/
Mars /mɑːz/
Milky Way /ˌmɪlki 'weɪ/
moon /muːn/
Neptune /'neptjuːn/
observatory /əb'zɜːvətri/
pattern /'pætn/
precious /'preʃəs/
rhythm /'rɪðəm/
rhyme /raɪm/
satellite /'sætəlaɪt/
Saturn /'sætən/
shape /ʃeɪp/
sheep /ʃiːp/
shooting star /ˌʃuːtɪŋ 'stɑːr/
simile /'sɪməli/
snug /snʌg /
solar system /'səʊlə sɪstəm/
space shuttle /'speɪs ʃʌtl/
space station /'speɪs steɪʃn/
spin round /spɪn 'raʊnd/
spun /spʌn/
stardust /'stɑːrdʌst/
stressed /strest/
summer /'sʌmər/
surface /'sɜːfɪs/
syllable /'sɪləbl/
telescope /'telɪskəʊp/
Venus /'viːnəs/
verse /vɜːs/
view /vjuː/

Unit 12

advantage /əd'vɑːntɪdʒ/
basic /'beɪsɪk/
blog /blɒg/
board game /'bɔːd geɪm/
bus stop /'bʌs stɒp/

busy /'bɪzi/
cheap /tʃiːp/
coral reef /'kɒrəl riːf/
culture /'kʌltʃər/
disadvantage /ˌdɪsəd'vɑːntɪdʒ/
dull /dʌl/
Eiffel Tower /aɪfel 'taʊər/
essay /'eseɪ/
expensive /ɪk'spensɪv/
flavors /'fleɪvərz/
give up /gɪv ʌp/
Great Wall /greɪt wɔːl/
grow /grəʊ/
heights /haɪts/
honest /'ɒnɪst/
hour /'aʊər/
house boat /'haʊs bəʊt/
however /haʊ'evər/
in addition /ɪn ə'dɪʃn/
India /'ɪndiə/
Indian /'ɪndiən/
jungle /'dʒʌŋgl/
know /nəʊ/
local /'ləʊkl/
luxurious /lʌg'ʒʊəriəs/
market /'mɑːkɪt/
orangutan /ɔːˌræŋ uː'tæn/
palm tree /'pɑːm triː/
paragraph /'pærəgrɑːf/
peaceful /'piːsfl/
perfect /'pɜːfɪkt/
relaxing /rɪ'læksɪŋ/
rescue team /'reskjuː tiːm/
respect (v) /rɪ'spekt/
rhino /'raɪnəʊ/
rickshaw /'rɪkʃɔː/
rush /rʌʃ/
scary /'skeəri/
scenery /'siːnəri/
sightseeing /'saɪtsiːɪŋ/
snow /snəʊ/
spicy /'spaɪsi/
stimulating /'stɪmjuleɪtɪŋ/
sunglasses /'sʌnglɑːsɪz/
surfboard /'sɜːfbɔːd/
tourism /'tɔːrɪzəm/
unfortunately /ʌn'fɔːtʃənətli/
update /ˌʌp'deɪt/
what /wɒt/
wheel /wiːl/
white /waɪt/
wrap /ræp/
write /raɪt/
wrong /rɒŋ/

Extensive reading 4

astronomer /ə'strɒnəmə(r)/
commercial /kə'mɜːʃl/
computerized /kəm'pjuːtəraɪzd/
crater /'kreɪtə(r)/
demand (n) /dɪ'mɑːnd/
dust /dʌst/
fascinated /'fæsɪneɪtɪd/
geology /dʒi'ɒlədʒi/
ice age /aɪs eɪdʒ/
intention /ɪn'tenʃn/
launch /lɔːntʃ/
marking /'mɑːkɪŋ/
meteorite /'miːtiəraɪt/
mission /'mɪʃn/
orbit /'ɔːbɪt/
reality /ri'æləti/
remote-controlled /rɪ'məʊt kən'trəʊld/
rover /'rəʊvə(r)/
surface /'sɜːfɪs/
trapped /træpd/
unmanned /ˌʌn'mænd/

OXFORD
UNIVERSITY PRESS

Great Clarendon Street, Oxford, OX2 6DP, United Kingdom

Oxford University Press is a department of the University of Oxford. It furthers the University's objective of excellence in research, scholarship, and education by publishing worldwide. Oxford is a registered trade mark of Oxford University Press in the UK and in certain other countries

© Oxford University Press 2015

The moral rights of the author have been asserted

First published in 2015
2019 2018 2017 2016 2015
10 9 8 7 6 5 4 3 2 1

No unauthorized photocopying

All rights reserved. No part of this publication may be reproduced, stored in a retrieval system, or transmitted, in any form or by any means, without the prior permission in writing of Oxford University Press, or as expressly permitted by law, by licence or under terms agreed with the appropriate reprographics rights organization. Enquiries concerning reproduction outside the scope of the above should be sent to the ELT Rights Department, Oxford University Press, at the address above

You must not circulate this work in any other form and you must impose this same condition on any acquirer

Links to third party websites are provided by Oxford in good faith and for information only. Oxford disclaims any responsibility for the materials contained in any third party website referenced in this work

ISBN: 978 0 19 481687 8 Pack
ISBN: 978 0 19 481688 5 Teacher's Book
ISBN: 978 0 19 481689 2 Fluency DVD
ISBN: 978 0 19 481690 8 Assessment and Resource CD-ROM
ISBN: 978 0 19 481594 9 Online Practice Teacher Access Code Card

Printed in China

This book is printed on paper from certified and well-managed sources